T0305127

MACROECONOMICS AND DEVELOPMENT

Roberto Frenkel and the Economics of Latin America

EDITED BY

Mario Damill, Martín Rapetti,
and Guillermo Rozenwurcel

COLUMBIA UNIVERSITY PRESS

NEW YORK

Columbia University Press
Publishers Since 1893
New York   Chichester, West Sussex
cup.columbia.edu

Library of Congress Cataloging-in-Publication Data
Macroeconomics and development : Roberto Frenkel and the
economics of Latin America / edited by Mario Damill, Martín
Rapetti, and Guillermo Rozenwurcel.
    pages cm. — (Initiative for policy dialogue)
Includes bibliographical references and indexes.
    ISBN 978-0-231-17508-1 (cloth : alk. paper)
      1. Economic development—Latin America.
    2. Monetary policy—Latin America. 3. Fiscal policy—
Latin America. 4. Frenkel, Roberto. 5. Macroeconomics.
    I. Damill, Mario, editor. II. Rapetti, Martín, editor.
      III. Rozenwurcel, Guillermo, editor.

HC125.M2543 2015
339.5098—dc23

2015008247

Columbia University Press books are printed on permanent
and durable acid-free paper.
This book is printed on paper with recycled content.
Printed in the United States of America

c 10 9 8 7 6 5 4 3 2 1

COVER PHOTO: © Ekin Yalgin/Alamy
COVER DESIGN: Milenda Nan Ok Lee

References to websites (URLs) were accurate at the time of writing.
Neither the author nor Columbia University Press is responsible for URLs
that may have expired or changed since the manuscript was prepared.

The Initiative for Policy Dialogue (IPD) at Columbia University brings together academics, policymakers, and practitioners from developed and developing countries to address the most pressing issues in economic policy today. IPD is an important part of Columbia's broad program on development and globalization. The Initiative for Policy Dialogue at Columbia: Challenges in Development and Globalization book series presents the latest academic thinking on a wide range of development topics and lays out alternative policy options and trade-offs. Written in a language accessible to policymakers and students alike, this series is unique in that it both shapes the academic research agenda and furthers the economic policy debate, facilitating a more democratic discussion of development policies.

This book is about economic ideas regarding relevant macroeconomic problems of emerging market economies, and Latin American ones in particular. It focuses on the important contributions made by Roberto Frenkel on a variety of themes that were central in the fields of macroeconomics and development economics—from both theoretical and applied standpoints—particularly in Latin America. His contributions cover, among other issues, the analysis of financial and balance-of-payments crises; high inflation and disinflation programs; the effects of the real exchange rate on unemployment and deindustrialization; and macroeconomic policy for development.

The book is organized in six parts containing eighteen chapters that relate to some of the areas in which Frenkel made influential contributions. Part I focuses on pricing decisions, inflation, and stabilization policies. Part II is devoted to macroeconomic policy, economic development, and income distribution in Latin America. Part III deals with particular aspects of macroeconomic policy for development, paying special attention to the role of the real exchange rate in the development process. Part IV is devoted to finance and crises. Part V closes the volume, with chapters focused on general aspects of economic development.

The contributions to this volume are from distinguished scholars from Latin America and the United States who are close colleagues and collaborators of Roberto Frenkel. They have been written for a wide audience interested in the macroeconomic policy in emerging markets and economic development in Latin America, from academics and policy makers to politicians, journalists, and the civil society at large.

For more information about IPD and its upcoming books, visit www. policydialogue.org.

CONTENTS

Acknowledgments xi

Preface xiii

Mario Damill, Martín Rapetti, and Guillermo Rozenwurcel

1. An Introduction to Roberto Frenkel's Contributions to the
   Economic Ideas in Latin America I
   Mario Damill, Daniel Kampel,
   and Guillermo Rozenwurcel

   PART 1 Pricing Decisions, Inflation, and Stabilization 21

2. Markups Under Uncertainty: Variations on Price
   Decisions in High Inflation 23
   Daniel Heymann and Francisco Roldán

3. Financial Fragility, Price Indexes, and Investment Financing 47
   Julio Dreizzen

4. Uncertainty in Structural and Institutional Parameters
   and the Cost of Policy Mistakes: A Computable General
   Equilibrium Evaluation 57
   Omar Chisari, Gustavo Ferro,
   and Juan Pablo Vila Martínez

5. Monetary Policy and External Shocks in a Semidollarized
   Economy 83
   Oscar Dancourt

PART 2 Economic Development in Latin America 109

6. The Chilean Economy Since the Global Crisis 111
   Ricardo Ffrench-Davis and Rodrigo Heresi

7. Disequilibria and Risk Premia: Argentina's Experience
   During the 2000s from a Latin American Perspective 134
   Gustavo Cañonero and Carlos Winograd

8. Labor Market and Income Distribution in Latin
   America in Times of Economic Growth: Advances
   and Shortcomings 159
   Roxana Maurizio

9. Accounting for the Rise and Fall of Brazil's Growth
   After World War II 188
   Edmar Bacha and Regis Bonelli

PART 3 The Real Exchange Rate, Balance of Payments,
   and Economic Development 209

10. Balance-of-Payments Dominance: Implications for
    Macroeconomic Policy 211
    José Antonio Ocampo

11. The Real Exchange Rate, the Real Wage, and Growth:
    A Formal Analysis of the "Development Channel" 229
    Jaime Ros

12. The Real Exchange Rate and Economic Growth:
    Some Observations on the Possible Channels 250
    Martín Rapetti

PART 4 Finance and Crises 269

13. Capitalism and Financial Crises: A Long-Term Perspective 271
    Andrés Solimano

14. Financial Crises, Institutions, and the Macroeconomy 287
    José María Fanelli

15. United States Size Distribution and the Macroeconomy
    1986–2009 311
    *Lance Taylor, Armon Rezai, Rishabh Kumar,
    Nelson Barbosa, and Laura Carvalho*

16. Sovereign Credit Risk in Latin America and
    Global Common Factors   333
      Manuel Agosin and Juan Díaz-Maureira

        PART 5 Approaches to Development   355

17. Cognitive Dissonance: Postwar Economic
    Development Strategies and Bretton Woods
    International Financial Stability   357
      Jan Kregel

18. New Developmentalism as a Weberian Ideal Type   373
      Luiz Carlos Bresser-Pereira

                List of Contributors   385
                      Index   389

ACKNOWLEDGMENTS

This book could have not been published without the collaborative effort of a large group of people. We would like to start by thanking all the contributors to this volume for their terrific work. We are also grateful to Ramiro Albrieu, Eduardo Corso, Sebastián Katz, Saúl Keifman, Javier Finkman, Alfredo Schclarek Curutchet, Emiliano Libman, and Leandro Serino, who helped us review several of the chapters in this book. Adrián Ramos and Andrés López were key in the organization of the conference at the University of Buenos Aires where these chapters were first presented and discussed. Juan Sourrouille moved us with his speech at the conference. We are also indebted to Dean Alberto Barbieri for his support. The conference and this book could have not been possible without the support of our friend Leonardo Burlamaqui. Constanza Abuin, Franco Betteo, Diego Friedheim, and Gabriel Palazzo provided superb assistance during the copyediting process. We are also grateful to Joseph Stiglitz. Our editor, Bridget Flannery-McCoy from Columbia University Press, helped us live through the editorial process. We are also grateful to the Ford Foundation for financial support. Finally, we would like to express our gratitude to the staff at the Centre for the Study of State and Society. Again, thank you all!

This book is dedicated to our mentor and friend Roberto Frenkel, who has been a permanent source of intellectual stimulus, support, and affection. *Gracias Roberto*!

Mario Damill, Martín Rapetti, and Guillermo Rozenwurcel

Most economists have come across the following passage from John Maynard Keynes's obituary of Alfred Marshall, in which Keynes famously defines the characteristics of what he refers to as a "master-economist":

> The study of economics does not seem to require any specialized gifts of an unusually high order. . . . Yet good, or even competent, economists are the rarest of birds. An easy subject, at which very few excel! The paradox finds its explanation, perhaps, in that the master-economist must possess a rare combination of gifts. He must reach a high standard in several different directions and must combine talents not often found together. He must be mathematician, historian, statesman, philosopher—in some degree. He must understand symbols and speak in words. He must contemplate the particular in terms of the general, and touch abstract and concrete in the same flight of thought. He must study the present in the light of the past for the purposes of the future. No part of man's nature or his institutions must lie entirely outside his regard. He must be purposeful and disinterested in a simultaneous mood; as aloof and incorruptible as an artist, yet sometimes as near the earth as a politician.
>
> (KEYNES 1924:321–322)

Keynes certainly had high standards. The intersection of all these attributes is very likely an empty set; indeed, Keynes himself admitted that not even his mentor could fulfill these requirements: "Much, but not all, of this ideal many-sidedness Marshall possessed."

Similar to Keynes's characterization, Lance Taylor, a contributor to this volume, set the bar at a more reachable level: "Ideally one ought to be able to teach macroeconomics at the university in the morning, advise the

Minister on how to apply macroeconomics in the afternoon, and write scholarly papers on macroeconomics at night; all the while practicing the same craft" (1988:25). The sentence ends with a footnote that says, "A thought due to Roberto Frenkel."

Roberto Frenkel made important contributions on a variety of themes that were central to the study of economics in the fields of macroeconomics and development economics—both from theoretical and applied standpoints—particularly (but not only) in Latin America, as the chapters of this book testify. His contributions cover, among other issues, the analysis of financial and balance-of-payments crises; high inflation and disinflation programs; the effects of the real exchange rate on unemployment and deindustrialization; and macroeconomic policy for development.

This book contains eighteen chapters that relate to some of the areas in which Frenkel made influential contributions. The contributors are close colleagues; many are also collaborators of Frenkel—some of them former students—who appreciate and admire his work. In the next two sections we present a brief biography of Frenkel and highlight his contributions as an economist. We then summarize the overall content of the book in the last section.

CONFIESO QUE HE VIVIDO: A BRIEF BIOGRAPHY OF ROBERTO FRENKEL

The eldest of four brothers, Roberto Frenkel was born in Buenos Aires, Argentina, in 1943. His father, Vicente Frenkel, was the son of a Ukrainian Jew who had arrived in Buenos Aires in the late nineteenth century. His mother, Berta Aissin, was also born in Argentina from a Jewish family.

Frenkel received his primary and secondary education in public schools. In 1961, he entered the School of Sciences at the University of Buenos Aires to pursue a degree in mathematics. In his third year, he joined the Calculus Institute to participate in the Computational and Mathematical Modeling Research Group, where he worked on econometrics and the development of large dynamic simulation models.

After *La noche de los bastones largos* (The night of the long batons), he moved with his first wife Liliana and his elder son Diego to Caracas, where he got a position at the Central University of Venezuela.[1] Between 1967 and 1969, he taught graduate courses in mathematics and developmental economics.

Because of his affinity for leftist political groups, Frenkel and his family were invited by the authorities to leave Venezuela in 1969. As a result, the Frenkel family—including Ana, Frenkel's first daughter, who was born in Venezuela—moved to Santiago, Chile. Frenkel found a position at the Catholic University of Chile to do research and teach graduate courses in mathematics and economics at the Center for Urban and Regional Development. In 1971, he joined the socialist government of Salvador Allende, where he held several advisory positions at the Ministry of Finance until the coup d'état of General Augusto Pinochet. Not only was he fired by the military dictatorship, he also had to spend two weeks as a political refugee in the Argentine embassy before returning to Buenos Aires in September 1973.

His return to the politically unsettled climate of Buenos Aires was not easy. After spending a few years at the Federal Investment Council of Argentina coordinating a research group on regional development and later at the Bariloche Foundation as a visiting professor, he joined the Center for the Study of the State and Society (CEDES) in 1977. CEDES had been founded in 1975 by a group of young social scientists under the leadership of political scientist Guillermo O'Donnell to pursue independent and pluralistic research on democracy and development. Since his arrival, CEDES became Frenkel's second home. It was at CEDES that Frenkel met Silvina Ramos, his second wife and mother of Julia and Violeta, Frenkel's youngest daughters.

Upon the initiative of Edmar Bacha, a contributor to this volume, he was invited to spend two semesters as a visiting professor in the Department of Economics at the Pontificia Universidade Católica of Río de Janeiro (PUC-RJ), Brazil, in 1981 and 1983. These were the golden years of neostructuralism in Latin America, and the PUC-RJ was probably its mecca.

With the return of democracy in late 1983, Frenkel began to teach both graduate and undergraduate courses at the School of Economics at the University of Buenos Aires. Although he has taught at several Argentine and foreign universities during his career, the University of Buenos Aires has always remained Frenkel's sweetheart, and that affection has always been reciprocated: in 2012, the University of Buenos Aires granted him an honorary professorship, a privilege only few have.

In 1985, Frenkel joined the Alfonsín government as undersecretary advisor at the Ministry of Finance to work as the head of economic advisors of Minister Juan Sourrouille. Frenkel played a key role in designing the Austral Plan, which was an innovative stabilization program to stop high inflation that included both orthodox and heterodox elements. He remained in this position until early 1989, when Sourrouille and his team resigned. It was during these years that Frenkel taught in the morning at the university, advised the minister in the afternoon, and wrote scholarly papers on inflation and stabilization at night, as his dear friend Lance Taylor would later highlight.

During the 1990s, Frenkel focused on research and remained exclusively at CEDES while teaching at the University of Buenos Aires. He also did consultancy work for institutions such as the Inter-American Development Bank, United Nations Conference on Trade and Development, Economic Commission for Latin America and the Caribbean, Organization for Economic Cooperation and Development, United Nations Industrial Development Organization, the International Labor Organization, and the governments of Bolivia, Colombia, Uruguay, and Venezuela.

Between 1999 and 2003, he served as a member of the board of directors at the Banco de la Provincia de Buenos Aires, the second largest bank of Argentina. He had the privilege—from the point of view of a macroeconomist—of witnessing Argentina's 2001–2002 financial crisis from within. Since 2004, Frenkel has been at CEDES full time doing research and teaching at the University of Buenos Aires, remaining as active, insightful, and thought-provoking as always.

ROBERTO FRENKEL AS ECONOMIST

Roberto Frenkel's contributions have addressed a variety of issues related to economic development (or the lack thereof) of Latin American countries. Chapter 1 by Mario Damill, Daniel Kampel, and Guillermo Rozenwurcel discusses some of these issues in detail. In this section, we discuss three aspects of Frenkel as an economist that are not so common within the discipline but contributed to making him a distinguished economist.

PROBLEM-ORIENTED RESEARCH

A common way of classifying economists these days is to consider whether their research is mostly theoretical or empirical. Economists seem to be either theorists or empirical economists. It would be hard to assess Frenkel using this metric not only because he has done both but more importantly because none of these traits defines him as an economist. A better way to describe Frenkel is as a *problem-oriented economist*. The purpose of his work has always been to better understand the problems that constrained economic development in Argentina and other Latin American countries and to offer policy suggestions to overcome them. He was first puzzled by the development of a high-inflation regime in Argentina during the mid- and late 1970s. His attention rapidly shifted to the financial and external crises of Latin American countries in the early 1980s. Foreign debt over-hang and how it constrains economic growth and macroeconomic policy constituted a key area of his research during the 1980s. High inflation and disinflation strategies were also objects of his work during the 1980s. By the late 1980s and early 1990s, Frenkel discussed in several papers the flaws of the Washington Consensus approach to economic policy. He also analyzed the effects of real exchange rate appreciation on unemployment and deindustrialization, a phenomenon that affected several countries in the region during the early 1990s, after the implementation of exchange rate–based disinflation programs. It was also during the 1990s that he went back to analyzing financial and balance-of-payment crises, as the crises in Mexico, Southeast Asia, Russia, Brazil, and Argentina unfolded. Once the macroeconomy in Latin American countries stabilized during the 2000s, Frenkel shifted his interest toward pro-development policies and analyzed how macroeconomic policy should be coordinated to simul-taneously achieve low inflation, a stable and competitive real exchange rate, and balance-of-payments stability.

In a discipline in which scientific progress has become increasingly identified with being published in top journals, Frenkel's focus on real-world phenomena and how to address them is rare and inspiring.

MICROFOUNDATIONS

The issue of the microfoundations of macroeconomic theory has been a subject of intense debate since at least the 1960s. Lucas's (1976) critique on the way macroeconomics was conducted had a powerful impact on the discipline in the mid-1970s. Since then, microfoundations have been basically identified with the representation of aggregate behavior through a representative agent that optimizes an objective function intertempo-rally with rational expectations about future events. Theoretical attempts that did not adhere to this methodological approach have been largely dismissed as lacking rigorous microfoundations and have been deemed unscientific. However, Lucasian microfoundations have not been adopted by all macroeconomists, and many—including some eminent scholars such as Nobel laureates James Tobin, Robert Solow, Joseph Stiglitz, and Paul Krugman—have rejected them as the only possible game in town.[2] A shared view by critics is that the so-called ad hoc behavioral functions of many old Keynesian models are good economics because they are based on—although not necessarily derived explicitly from—sound microeconomic behavior. To put it differently, macroeconomic modeling of aggregate behavioral functions is acceptable as long as they are consistent with observed and/or plausible goal-oriented microbehavior. Moreover, critics consider causality as running in both directions: while the relevance of microfoundations in understanding macrodynamics is undeniable, so is that of *macrofoundations*—as embodied in economic, social, and political institutions, economic and productive structures, and coordination problems that arise from the interactions of heterogeneous agents at the macrolevel, among others—in understanding microeconomic behavior.

Frenkel has always been critical of Lucasian microfoundations but—like other critics—has taken microfoundations seriously. His theoretical work (and informal analysis) has always emphasized how agents behave in the environment they face. Perhaps a distinctive characteristic of his thinking was that he developed microfoundations not from axiomatic postulates—as has largely been done in Walrasian microeconomics—but from observing actual real-world behavior. The following anecdote is very telling of his approach.

The motivation to write *Decisiones de precio en alta inflación* (Price decision in high inflation [Frenkel 1979]) came after conversations with two businessmen. One of them was his own father, who had a small textile plant in Buenos Aires. After the eruption of high inflation in the mid-1970s in Argentina, Frenkel's father told his son, "I don't know exactly why but since inflation accelerated, I doubled the mark-up on the shirts I sell." The second revealing conversation came shortly thereafter and was with the owner of a large domestic appliances store, who anxiously confessed, "When I sell too many TV sets I get worried," implying that he might be underpricing his products. The conversations made Frenkel realize that the standard imperfect competition assumption of a constant markup was inadequate for environments of relative price uncertainty such as those that existed in Argentina during high-inflation years. His 1979 model shows that pricing should be based on expected costs rather than on current costs and that it may be optimal for the producer to raise the markup as a defensive mechanism to protect its working capital from the risk of relative price changes. *Decisiones* had a significant impact within the neostructuralist circles in the early 1980s and has been taught at several Argentine and Brazilian universities ever since.

THE ECONOMIST AS PUBLIC INTELLECTUAL

The word "economics" comes from the Ancient Greek *oikonomia*, which means the administration of the household. This was considered a very minor subject. For the ancient Greeks what really mattered was the *polis*—the city-state—and its study was known as *politika* (politics). Economics, as we know it today, is a European product born in the seventeenth century with the name "political economy," and its focus shifted from the study of the household to the state—hence the adjective "political."[3] Thus, economics was born as a discipline focused on public affairs and has largely remained as such ever since.

Given the nature of the subject, the layperson may think that economists—or at least macroeconomists—are always involved in the public discussion of economic issues, but this is not always the case. Professional economists often dedicate their time entirely to academic activities such as teaching, doing research, publishing articles, and attending conferences. It is no exaggeration to say that a large number of academic economists refrain from participating in public debates. Many macroeconomists have played a decisive role in shaping the way their peers think and do research but have been largely absent from public debates. Nobel laureates from very different persuasions such as John Hicks, Laurence Klein, Robert Lucas, Finn Kydland, and Edward Prescott may be considered examples of this type of economist.

This is certainly not the only type, however. Other economists have assumed the role of public intellectual, engaging in public debates and explaining to the general population what is at stake in economic policy discussions. Notable examples of this type are, among others, John Maynard Keynes, Milton Friedman, Nicholas Kaldor, Joseph Stiglitz, and Paul Krugman.

Frenkel certainly belongs to this second type of economists. Since the early 1980s, he has actively participated in public discussions about Argentina's macroeconomic policy. He has regularly written op-eds in the main newspapers of the country, especially in *La Nación*, arguably the most highly regarded newspaper of Argentina, in which he has had a monthly column since 1999. Frenkel can convey deep and thought-provoking ideas in clear Spanish and has always accepted the challenge of debates. In the early 1980s, he raised serious concerns about the financial liberalization policy of the military government and, as John Williamson remarked, his concerns "predated, if not by much, the great Argentine crisis of 1981" (1983:197). During the 1990s, he assumed a politically incorrect position by pointing out the weaknesses of the (initially) highly regarded currency board regime and the high probability that it would end up in a huge crisis, which it ultimately did. During the early 2000s, he forcefully supported President Kirchner's unorthodox policy of maintaining a stable and competitive real exchange rate. He did not hesitate to withdraw his support in 2007, when the government began to manipulate official statistics, and to denounce it publicly.

CONTRIBUTIONS TO THIS VOLUME

The introductory chapter of this volume is by Mario Damill, Daniel Kampel, and Guillermo Rozenwurcel; Damill and Rozenwurcel have been close colleagues and collaborators of Frenkel's at CEDES since the early 1980s, and Kampel is a former student who later became his collaborator. Their chapter evaluates the contributions Frenkel made to the economic analysis of Latin America since the mid-1970s on issues such as inflation and high inflation, stabilization policies, balance-of-payments and financial crises, and the role of real exchange rates in determining growth and employment in developing economies. The authors emphasize Frenkel's commitment to analytical rigor and to the social and policy relevance of the subjects upon which he focuses. They also stress the role of comparative analysis of different national cases in Frenkel's research, common to the Latin American structuralist tradition, a methodological approach that allows for a careful consideration of country-specific historical and institutional dimensions that too often gets lost in standard cross-country econometric analyses. The chapter also highlights the relevance of many of Frenkel's findings regarding the analysis of current economic problems—particularly in emerging market economies—such as economic crises, growth and employment generation, and inflation.

Part 1 focuses on pricing decisions, inflation, and stabilization policies. The first chapter of this part is by Daniel Heymann, a long-standing colleague of Frenkel's at the University of Buenos Aires and on Sourrouille's team in the Ministry of Finance during the 1980s. Along with his coauthor Francisco Roldán, Heymann develops a set of models on pricing decisions under uncertainty, extending Frenkel's classic 1979 paper in several ways. The authors explore the role of inventory management and liquidity constraints as mechanisms through which uncertainty about future unit costs may make profit-maximizing firms reluctant to sell goods in the current period, thus creating incentives to raise markups.

In the third chapter, Julio Dreizzen, a student of Frenkel's in the early 1980s, revisits two themes that were the subject of his master's thesis at PUC-RJ, which was heavily influenced by the work of Frenkel: financial fragility and inflation. In this chapter, Dreizzen considers some problems that may arise as a result of the loss of credibility of official statistical data on prices and inflation, as has been the case in Argentina since the intervention of the National Institute of Statistics and Census Bureau in early 2007. Based on the ideas of financial fragility in the tradition initiated by Hyman Minsky, Dreizzen shows that noticeable differences between actual and reported inflation may prevent the development of financial instruments that extend the maturity of financial obligations and reduce the uncertainty and cost of capital. These problems undermine productive investment and residential construction and, consequently, jeopardize economic growth.

In chapter 4, Omar Chisari, a colleague of Frenkel's at CEDES in the early 1990s, analyzes with his coauthors Gustavo Ferro and Juan Pablo Vila Martínez the role of parameter uncertainty in the design of macroeconomic policy. The authors use a computable general equilibrium model to evaluate the effects of policy intervention (changes in the tax policy) when the policy maker is uncertain about the right level of two key parameters: the degree of international capital mobility and the degree of wage indexation in the economy. To simulate different tax policy experiments, they calibrate the CGE model with Argentine data from 2006. The experiments show that the greater the degree of international capital mobility and the higher the degree of indexation in the formal labor market, the greater the damage wrong policy choices will produce.

The 2008–2009 crisis showed that the main macroeconomic challenge for a country like Peru is the management of external shocks that deteriorate the balance of payments and contracts aggregate demand. Oscar Dancourt, a collaborator of Frenkel's in several international projects, discusses the adequate monetary policy response to this kind of external shocks in chapter 5. To this end he develops an IS-LM-BP type of model to study the efficacy of different monetary policy instruments. The model is adapted to the financial conditions of Peru, where the banking system operates in both domestic and foreign currencies. With inflation targeting in operation since 2002, the short-term interest rate in domestic currency has been the most important monetary policy instrument of the last decade. Other important tools employed since 2002–2003 include reserve requirement ratios on bank deposits in domestic and foreign currencies— as well as on the banking system's short-term external debt—and sterilized interventions in the foreign exchange market. Dancourt's conclusion is that by combining a Taylor rule to target internal equilibrium, with a leaning-against-the-wind intervention in the foreign exchange market to achieve external equilibrium, monetary policy can stabilize the price level and economic activity in the face of external shocks.

Part 2 consists of four chapters on macroeconomic policy, development, and income distribution in Latin America. Starting with the 2008–2009 crisis and its contagion effects, Ricardo Ffrench-Davis, a long-standing collaborator of Frenkel's in several international projects, discusses with his coauthor Rodrigo Heresi in chapter 6 the economic policy responses and the effects of countercyclical policies in Chile until 2012. They argue that macroeconomic vulnerability to external fluctuations has made Chile's fiscal and external balances dangerously dependent on high copper prices and inflation targeting excessively dependent on a volatile and appreciated exchange rate. For the exchange rate to fulfill its allocative role efficiently—in a development strategy of the sort discussed in Part 3—it is fundamental to provide signals of medium-run stability to both investors in the real economy and producers. This requires a stable real exchange rate that responds to changes in net productivity rather than to volatility in international financial markets. The correction of macroeconomic policy needs to be conducted together with deep microeconomic reforms that are still pending. To return to the 1990s' path of sustained and more equitable growth, the authors conclude, Chile needs to move away from policies that emphasize financierism and redesign macroeconomic policies to follow a comprehensive counter-cyclical approach—one that includes regulating the capital account—and to create a development-friendly macroeconomic environment.

In chapter 7, Gustavo Cañonero and Carlos Winograd, both former students who became colleagues and collaborators of Frenkel's, elaborate on the sources of risk that arise from the interaction of the goods and financial markets by revisiting Frenkel's work on exchange rate and sovereign risk premia. The authors dispute the narrow view that states that a run on the domestic currency or a rising sovereign risk premium are always caused by an increase of the foreign debt or a decline in the stock of international reserves. They argue that market disequilibrium dynamics may not only be driven by these factors but also by declining incentives to invest. Cañonero and Winograd use this idea to analyze the rise in Argentina's risk premium observed since 2007. They suggest that the latter has not been a result of excessive absorption leading to current account imbalance and unsustainable debt accumulation. On the contrary, in light of other contemporary experiences in Latin America, it has been associated with excessive monetary and credit growth and with the lack of appropriate expected returns for capital investment opportunities.

Chapter 8 by Roxana Maurizio, a former student and close collaborator of Frenkel's, focuses on labor market performance in Latin America between 2003 and 2008. While acknowledging that the high rates of economic growth in the region had a positive impact on social and labor market indicators—as evidenced by the dynamic creation of employment, the reduction of unemployment, and the fall of income inequality and poverty—Maurizio argues that even in this positive context the region still continues to exhibit significant shortcomings in the labor market. The most evident are the high levels of unemployment, precariousness, and informality. In addition, Latin America is still one of the most unequal regions in the world. Maurizio's chapter provides an in-depth analysis of labor market and income inequality dynamics in Latin America in the new millennium.

Edmar Bacha, a friend of Frenkel's since the "golden days" of neo-structuralism at PUC-RJ in the early 1980s, examines with his coauthor Regis Bonelli in chapter 9 the long-term evolution of the Brazilian economy. They use models that emphasize the determinants of aggregate supply to help decipher the puzzle of Brazil's growth collapse after 1980. According to their analysis, the fall in capital and GDP growth between 1981 and 1992 (the lost decade) and 1993 and 1999 (the decade of reforms) was due primarily to a reduction in domestic savings and secondarily to lower capital productivity. Between that latter period and the new macroeconomic regime period (2000–2011), GDP growth showed only a shy acceleration mainly explained by increases in the use of installed capacity and higher capital productivity. Nevertheless, despite a modest increase in the output–capital ratio, domestic savings are still too low to allow for growth rates higher than the 4 percent registered in the late 2000s. The corollary is that Brazil's slow growth resulted from low rates of investment and domestic savings. If these rates do not increase, it seems that the country will be doomed to grow at the modest rates observed in recent years.

Part 3 deals with macroeconomic policy for economic development. José Antonio Ocampo, who has collaborated with Frenkel on several international projects, discusses in chapter 10 what he calls the "balance-of-payments dominance" on macroeconomic policy. Although the notion may resemble the old structuralist idea that sustained economic growth can be constrained by the lack of foreign currency, Ocampo's is a new and clarifying concept. He defines "balance-of-payments dominance" as a macroeconomic regime in which the short-term macroeconomic dynamics are largely determined by external shocks. Trade shocks play an important role—mostly via changes in the terms of trade—but in Ocampo's view international financial shocks are the main drivers of the business cycles of economies with balance-of-payments dominance. Emerging market economies typically suffer from this dominance and are prone to boom and bust cycles fueled by external financial shocks. Another problem is that macroeconomic policy in these countries tends to react procyclically to external shocks and thus contributes to a deepening of the business cycles. Ocampo argues that the policy space in these countries can be widened through a combination of managed exchange rate flexibility, a very active foreign exchange reserve management, a reduced reliance on external borrowing, and macroprudential regulations, including those directly affecting capital flows.

Jaime Ros, who has coauthored many papers with Frenkel and participated in several international projects with him, develops a model in chapter 11 to clarify a key channel—what he calls the "profitability channel," or in Frenkel's (2004) words, the "development channel"—through which the level of the real exchange rate affects the rate of economic growth in a developing country. Ros shows that a higher real exchange rate is favorable to capital accumulation and employment growth in the short term because it reduces the product wage in the tradable sector and therefore increases the sector's profitability. An important contribution of Ros's chapter is that it shows that the long-term effects on the economy (i.e., on capital stock and the level of real wages) depend on the evolution of productivity. The model shows that if productivity change is endogenous to capital accumulation, the employment gains of a transitory real exchange rate undervaluation would not be reversed and real wages would increase permanently. The latter is a result of both higher employment rates—which favor the diffusion of new technologies that reduces labor costs—and higher capital labor ratios, which raise the productivity of the economy through embodied technical progress and technological externalities.

Martín Rapetti, a former student of Frenkel's and now his colleague at CEDES, analyzes a recent body of empirical research in chapter 12 that studies the association between the level and volatility of the real exchange rate and economic growth. According to Rapetti, the empirical evidence emerging from the research surveyed in his chapter strongly suggests that real exchange rate undervaluation favors economic growth and overvaluation hurts it. These effects are observed in developing countries in the pre- and postfinancial globalization periods. These findings have passed several robustness checks, including the use of different econometric techniques and data sets. His conclusion is that the positive effect of real exchange rate undervaluation on economic growth in developing countries can be regarded as a strong empirical observation. Rapetti then analyzes which of the mechanisms proposed in the literature better fits the empirical evidence and concludes that it is what he calls the "tradable-led channel," which is essentially the same as Ros's and Frenkel's "development channel."

Part 4 is devoted to finance and crises. The first chapter of this part, chapter 13, is by Andrés Solimano, a long-standing collaborator of Frenkel's on several international projects. Solimano presents a historical overview of economic crises under capitalism and stresses the relevance of institutional and social factors in understanding these disruptive episodes. The chapter highlights the fact that the financial crisis of 2008–2009 in the United States and Europe not only challenged the view that sees the world divided between a financially stable core—the mature capitalist economies of North America and Europe—and a chronically unstable periphery—developing countries in Latin America, Africa, and Asia—but has also put under scrutiny mainstream economic theory built around the assumption of the "rational economic man." Solimano also points out the serious conceptual and operational flaws of two key institutions in charge of monetary and financial stability: the International Monetary Fund (IMF) and the central banks. He concludes that more democratic control of technocratic central banks is needed and that the power of the IMF in setting the terms of austerity programs around the world should be curbed.

In chapter 14, José María Fanelli, who has been a colleague of Frenkel's at CEDES since the early 1980s and has coauthored several articles with him, focuses on financial crises, paying particular attention to the linkages among the macroeconomy, institutions, and financial intermediation. Fanelli points out the "perverse" interactions among financial disequilibria, macroeconomic imbalances, and the (in)stability of economic institutions, all of which are typical of crisis periods. He stresses the fact that these interactions may delay the return to normality and even induce irreversible changes under certain conditions. On the financial side, permanent reversions in the process of financial development may be observed; on the real side, a crisis episode can raise the probability that the economy remains stuck in a low-growth trap or long-lasting recession, as was the case of the lost decade in Latin America in the 1980s or in Japan in the 1990s.

Lance Taylor, who has collaborated extensively and coauthored several papers with Frenkel, presents in chapter 15, together with Armon Rezai, Rishabh Kumar, Nelson Barbosa, and Laura Carvalho, an analysis of income distribution in the United States. The chapter focuses on the regressive evolution of income distribution and highlights the severe constraints that prevent the reduction of inequality in the United States. The authors develop a simulation model to illustrate how politically "reasonable" modifications in standard policy tools such as increased taxes on high-income households, higher transfers to people with low incomes, and raising wages at the bottom do not reduce economic inequality by much.

In the final chapter of part 4, Manuel Agosin, who has worked with Frenkel on several projects, and Juan Díaz-Maureira consider the importance of common global factors in the evolution of sovereign credit risk in emerging economies between 2007 and 2012. Using principal component analysis and Kalman filtering, the authors find robust evidence for the existence of a common factor in the evolution of J.P. Morgan's Emerging Markets Bond Index and credit default swaps on sovereign debt—both used as measures of sovereign risk. They also find that the co-movement between this common factor and two measures of individual–country sovereign risk rose significantly after the bankruptcy of Lehman Brothers in 2008, which has been widely regarded as the beginning of the most acute phase of the crisis. Agosin and Díaz-Maureira interpret the results as evidence to prove that changes in the availability of foreign capital to emerging economies is less dependent on internal developments of these economies than on international liquidity shocks and risk appetite, which in turn respond mostly to global factors that are exogenous to the recipient economies.

Part 5, which consists of two chapters that focus on more general aspects of economic development, closes the volume. In chapter 17, Jan Kregel, who has participated in several international projects with Frenkel, offers a demolishing critique of the way the Bretton Woods framework addressed the simultaneous objectives of pursuing international financial stability and fostering growth in developing countries. On the one hand, the framework considered that stable exchange rates were instrumental in achieving global financial stability. To maintain exchange rate stability, countries should target external account equilibrium, and in the case of running deficits, the IMF would supply financial assistance, provided the deficit country adjusted domestic absorption via fiscal contraction and devaluation. On the other hand, development policies—in the hands of UN agencies—were mainly conceived as ways of providing financial resources to developing countries to overcome their lack of domestic savings and foreign exchange. This approach to development, Kregel argues, contradicted the principles of the Bretton Woods institutions because it would require sustained balance-of-payments surpluses in developed countries that correspond to the capital outflows to developing countries—and conversely for developing countries to run balance-of-payments deficits that correspond to the acquisition of industrial imports from developed countries.

Luiz Carlos Bresser-Pereira—who has maintained a strong intellectual friendship with Frenkel since the mid-1980s, when both were fighting inflation at the governments of Brazil and Argentina, respectively—develops the concept of "new developmentalism." He explains that new developmentalism differs from old developmentalism—the theory and policy derived from the work of the pioneers of development economics—in a number of ways. Perhaps the most important difference between these two forms of developmentalism is the role of macroeconomic policy—in particular, how macroeconomic policy is coordinated to maintain fiscal sustainability, low inflation, and especially a competitive real exchange rate (or "industrial equilibrium exchange rate" in Bresser-Pereira's words). A competitive real exchange rate, Bresser-Pereira argues, is essential to avoid Dutch disease and the reliance on foreign savings, both of which are detrimental to economic development.

NOTES

1. This was a violent eviction of students and professors from the University of Buenos Aires by the federal police in July 1966. Students and professors had occupied several departments—including the mathematics department—as a way of protesting after the military government decided to intervene in the universities, which by law were autonomously governed by professors and students. In the following months hundreds of professors were fired, resigned from their positions, or abandoned the country.

2. See, for instance, Tobin (1993), Krugman (2000), Solow (2008), and Stiglitz (2011).

3. The term "political economy" first appeared in the title of a book by Antoine de Montchrestien in 1615. The discipline's name changed to "economics" after Alfred Marshall's masterpiece, published in 1890.

REFERENCES

Frenkel, R. 1979. "Decisiones de precio en alta inflación." *Desarrollo Económico* 19(75): 291–330.

Frenkel, R. 2004. "Real exchange rate and employment in Argentina, Brazil, Chile and Mexico." Paper prepared for the Group of 24. http://policydialogue.org/files /events/Frenkel_Exchange_Rate_Employment.pdf.

Keynes, J. M. 1924. "Alfred Marshall, 1842–1924." *The Economic Journal* 34(136): 311–372.

Krugman, P. 2000. "How complicated does the model have to be?" *Oxford Review of Economic Policy* 16(4): 33–42.

Lucas, R. E. 1976. "Econometric policy evaluation: A critique." In *Carnegie-Rochester Conference Series on Public Policy*, vol. 1. Elsevier: Amsterdam: 19–46.

Solow, R. 2008. "The state of macroeconomics." *Journal of Economic Perspectives* 22(1): 243–246.

Stiglitz, J. E. 2011. "Rethinking macroeconomics: what failed, and how to repair it." *Journal of the European Economic Association* 9(4): 591–645.

Taylor, L. 1988. *Varieties of stabilization experience: towards sensible macroeconomics in the third world.* Oxford: Clarendon Press.

Tobin, J. 1993. "Price flexibility and output stability: an old Keynesian view." *Journal of Economic Perspectives* 7(1): 45–65.

Williamson, J. 1983. *The open economy and the world economy: a textbook in international economics.* New York, NY: Basic Books.

MACROECONOMICS AND DEVELOPMENT

CHAPTER 1

An Introduction to Roberto Frenkel's Contributions to the Economic Ideas in Latin America

Mario Damill, Daniel Kampel, and Guillermo Rozenwurcel

Major innovations have challenged traditional economic thought in Latin America since the mid-1970s. A generation of then young economists—some of whom are now contributors to this volume—was responsible for redefining the traditional economic concepts then prevailing throughout the region. This new wave of thought was rapidly labeled "neostructuralism" because it was rooted in the Latin American structuralism associated with the intellectual production of the UN's Economic Commission for Latin America and the Caribbean since its inception. The surge of new ideas also implied the adoption of theoretical developments from several other sources. On the one hand, in relation to macroeconomics (and microfoundations of macroeconomics), these sources included a wide range of Keynesian and post-Keynesian versions (which also incorporated "disequilibrium macroeconomics") from the discipline; on the other hand, this group of young economists integrated into the analysis of financial markets the ideas of Hyman Minsky and other authors that followed the same line of research.

Roberto Frenkel has been one of the most prominent members of that innovative generation. This chapter aims to synthetically group and present some of his main ideas and contributions to date.

We can do this from a privileged point of view because we have shared many years of fruitful teamwork research with Frenkel. We have also been teaching and learning together and have had the privilege of coauthoring several articles with him.[1]

We intend to review some of his contributions from a present-day perspective. This is facilitated by the fact that major economic problems studied by Frenkel in the past are currently of great relevance, including balance-of-payments and financial crises, inflation, high inflation, and the role of competitive real exchange rates in promoting economic growth and employment. Therefore, *mutatis mutandis*, most policy lessons derived from his research on past events still remain illuminating and useful today.

Two new processes contributed to the renewal of economic thought in Latin America. First, the evolution of the macroeconomic debates in the international arena as well as its domestic repercussions must be taken into account. Neostructuralist economists were well aware of the risks of their production becoming "too idiosyncratic" (folkloric so to speak), as if a "local science" was required to understand local problems. There is no doubt that particular problems as well as local specificities often required new theoretical developments or amendments to "imported" theories, but efforts were always made to find a place for these singularities in the more general framework of the economic discipline, which thus benefited from a wider circulation of ideas and greater scope of cross-criticism.

In addition to the adoption and adaptation of analytical resources and tools provided by theoretical developments elsewhere, the other engine of change was naturally the actual evolution of the economies in Latin America itself, as well as those of developing economies around the world, which, of course, presented its own set of unique problems and challenges.

In this respect, taking into account their relevance to policy design and management, two economic processes stand out as references for Frenkel's research. First, chronic inflation, a phenomenon that for years was endemic to several Latin American economies, turned into "high inflation" in many countries in the late 1970s and early 1980s, a pathology that more recently reappeared in two Latin American countries: Argentina and Venezuela. A second phenomenon was the different paths the economies in the region took after being financially integrated into the international capital markets during the second wave of financial globalization (beginning ca. 1971), particularly in regard to the interactions and conflicts between the changing process of financial integration to international markets and the national macroeconomic and financial policies.

Beyond high inflation and stabilization (or macroeconomic stability as a whole) and financial integration, other issues gained relevance in macroeconomic analysis and policy discussions in Latin America during subsequent years. In the late 1980s and throughout the 1990s, debates arose about the economic reforms governments were applying throughout the region in the spirit of the Washington Consensus. Frenkel and others of a similar mind-set critically assessed such reform proposals, both on conceptual grounds and in terms of their practical implementation.

Afterward, Frenkel made important contributions related to the connections between the real exchange rate, economic growth and employment, and the significant changes observed in the process of financial globalization after the East Asian and Russian crises of 1997–1998 and their effects on macroeconomic policies. More recently, Frenkel has also focused on the new macroeconomic problems in emerging economies (EMEs) during the boom years of the early twenty-first century and the impacts of the global financial crisis that started in 2007.

On more methodological grounds, an important feature to highlight about Frenkel's research is the emphasis he put on comparative analysis. Although a significant part of his work focuses on Argentina, several of his contributions arose from the comparative study of different economies, oriented to establish key "stylized facts" regarding the issues under consideration. The examination of similarities and dissimilarities based on comparative case studies is a traditional component of Latin American structuralism. This approach has the advantage of making room for a careful consideration of historical processes and perspectives, which too often get lost in conventional cross-country econometric analyses.

In the next section we assess what we consider Frenkel's major contributions to be regarding the issue of financial integration and the links between this process and national macroeconomic policies. This section includes references to financial and balance-of-payments crises, because in EMEs the opening of the economy to international financial flows led in many cases to financial disruptions and balance-of-payments crises.

We then shift our discussion to high inflation, the role of exchange rates in economic growth, to finally focus on some currently relevant policy problems, strategies, and options relevant to many EMEs. While doing so, we also discuss Argentina's macroeconomic evolution and problems in the 2000s and some lessons that Frenkel's work may offer about how to approach these issues.

MACROECONOMIC AND FINANCIAL CYCLES LEADING TO CRISIS

After the recent global crisis erupted in 2007 from the subprime segment of the US financial market and quickly spilled over to the rest of the world through various channels, financial crises regained the center stage in both academic and policy debates. The international turbulence also promoted the renaissance of ideas long relegated to the background, such as Hyman Minsky's notions of the role of financial processes in modern monetary economies and the idea of an endogenous degree of financial fragility in the economy that evolves throughout the cycle.

By contrast, the absence of crises in the emerging market economies during this period also became an important issue, one which raised the need to understand the reasons for this renewed financial resilience in the developing world. This strength is particularly remarkable in the case of Latin American economies that take into account, on the one hand, the long history of frequent balance-of-payments and financial crises in the region and, on the other hand, the significant magnitude of some recent adverse shocks, especially the "sudden stop" of capital inflows, that were comparable to those that followed the crises in Southeast Asia, Russia, and Brazil in 1997–1998.

In several works, Frenkel examined some of these recent critical processes as well as those in which, facing external shocks of great magnitude, EMEs showed the ability to mitigate their impact and prevent crises. After analyzing these episodes, Frenkel obtained significant insights and drew several lessons on how to possibly prevent them (or deal with them on that basis).

As is well known, some "late" developments of the global crisis are still taking place in the periphery of the Eurozone. Several of these economies face uncertain prospects and great difficulties in recovering a fairly satisfactory macroeconomic performance. Frenkel's contributions to the analysis of crises have led some authors to make use of a set of ideas they themselves defined as "Frenkel's cycle."[2] Motivated by the analysis of the Southeast Asian crises, Lance Taylor (1998) referred to these ideas as "the Frenkel–Neftci cycle."

Frenkel's model of financial boom and bust cycles was developed in the late 1970s. It was initially conceived while he was analyzing the earliest experiences of financial openness in developing economies during the second wave of financial globalization. Indeed, such formulations first appeared in his analysis of the experiences of financial openness in the Southern Cone of Latin America, especially Argentina. Other scholars with similar approaches were developing in-depth analyses of other cases at the same time. For example, Juan Pablo Arellano and Ricardo Ffrench-Davis (1981) studied the Chilean process and its outcome.

Although every crisis is characterized by a number of idiosyncratic elements, the model of the cycle encompasses certain common features that have been present in many EME crises and more recently in the periphery of the Eurozone. The characteristics of the cycle that are common to the experiences of the Southern Cone of Latin America and many other critical processes experienced since then are briefly described next.

The starting point of the cycle has usually been an exogenous shock, such as a change in the macroeconomic policy setting. In turn, an interest rate spread appears after this change, providing an arbitrage opportunity. Typically, as in the experience of the Southern Cone, the initial shock consists of the fixation of the nominal exchange rate (or, as in those cases, the prefixation of the rate of devaluation for a certain period), whereas the economy, previously subject to various controls or restrictions, is now open to international capital movements. A precondition for the latter reform has been the liberalization of the domestic financial system in those cases in which it had been previously operating under a "financial repression" regime, so that a market-determined interest rate replaced a formerly regulated one.

Especially when starting from situations of low domestic financial development, the financial openness and fixation of the nominal exchange rate (in a manner that is initially credible, i.e., perceived as sustainable) give rise to a positive differential between domestic and external interest rates. This spread encourages changes in the composition of portfolios in favor of domestic assets, with the resulting net capital inflows. These portfolio changes increase the availability of financing (external, in a direct manner, and indirectly through the domestic banking multiplier), thus boosting aggregate demand and economic expansion.

Throughout this period, the current account of the balance-of-payments tends to deteriorate, partly because of the rise in income on the volume of imports but also because of the substitution effects (both on exports and imports) caused by the real exchange rate appreciation that results from the fixation of the nominal exchange rate. In the experience of the Southern Cone and other cases that took place later (e.g., the currency board established in 1991 in Argentina), the nominal exchange rate was employed to stabilize prices, i.e., as a nominal anchor for the economy. Because the stabilizing effect of the exchange rate policy on domestic prices generally does not operate immediately, real appreciation of the exchange rate ensues. The expansion of aggregate demand associated with net capital inflows (sometimes of great magnitude compared with domestic monetary and credit aggregates) generates upward pressure on nominal prices. The currency appreciation was very intense in some cases when the previous phase had been characterized by high or very high inflation.

Let us consider again the evolution of the current account of the balance of payments throughout Frenkel's cycle. As already mentioned, the direct income effect on imports negatively affects the trade balance in the booming phase. In addition, it counts the impact of the change in relative prices: prices of tradable goods fall in comparison to nontradable goods and services, thus contributing to a further deterioration in the current account balance. Moreover, there is also a progressive increase in the amount of payments of financial services to nonresidents that results from net capital inflows. At some point in time, the current account balance would become negative. From then on, growing net capital inflows would be required to finance an increasing current account deficit. Otherwise, international currency reserves would fall.

A crucial aspect is that, at this stage, both internal and external financial fragility increase. Regarding this issue, Frenkel extended and adapted to an open economy some notions of financial fragility and aspects of the cyclical conception of Hyman Minsky.

First, during the boom phase, optimism leads economic operators to underestimate risks and take increasingly risky financial positions. In EMEs, this essentially means assuming growing net debtor positions in foreign currency. Both the initial relative credibility of the exchange rate anchor and the improved expectations associated with economic expansion (and lower inflation in some cases) contribute to fueling optimistic expectations. Bubbles are generated in the markets for domestic assets.

Moreover, at the aggregate level, as the current account deteriorates, net foreign debt rises. With the increase in domestic banking credit fueled by capital inflows, the fragility of the domestic financial system also increases, especially in the presence of lax regulation and relatively weak bank supervision, which have been common features in the experiences of EMEs.

At some point, capital inflows fall below the rising current account deficit, and foreign reserves begin to decline. In this context, interest rates tend to rise as economic agents perceive, observing the behavior of the current account and the change in the trend of foreign currency reserves, an increasing risk.

This is the turning point of the cycle. Economic expansion slows down, and then the economic activity recedes, partly as a result of the rise in interest rates but also because of the negative effects on demand of the exchange rate appreciation that occurs throughout the boom phase, as already indicated.

Lower economic activity and higher interest rates in turn drive financial fragility, as borrowers face higher interest payments while the amount of sales tends to decline. In this scenario of financial distress, the situation may become unstable. Pessimistic expectations and negative news may lead to increases in liquidity preference (in the form of liquidity preference in foreign currency, as in the case of EMEs), capital outflows, credit crunch, deepening recession, and difficulties in the payments system. This unstable path may lead to currency and financial crises.

BACKGROUND: A CRITICISM OF THE MONETARY APPROACH TO THE BALANCE OF PAYMENTS

Frenkel's (1982) model was conceived as a portfolio model of the capital account of the balance of payments. It was designed to examine the portfolio choices of economic agents in a small and financially opened economy, with a fixed exchange rate, where arbitrage between the domestic and external financial markets operates freely. Employing this portfolio model, he examined key aspects of the price stabilization policies with the exchange rate anchor and trade and financial liberalization then being applied in Argentina, Chile, and Uruguay. In so doing, he also reviewed and criticized the monetary approach to the balance of payments (MABP), a conception that cemented the theoretical foundations of liberalization policy experience.[3]

In the MABP model, arbitrage determines the domestic interest rate, which for operations in domestic currency would equal the international rate plus the expected devaluation rate, plus a risk premium that encompasses both the "exchange rate risk" (i.e., the risk of error in the expected exchange rate variation) and the risk of default—in other words, an uncovered interest parity condition. In the MABP, the aforementioned risk premium is taken to be exogenous.[4]

In contrast to this approach, when capital movements are examined through a portfolio model of the capital account of the balance of payments, an endogenous component of risk arises that depends on the composition of the portfolios. Unlike the MABP, this means that local and international financial instruments are not considered perfect substitutes.

At this level, an important innovation in Frenkel's portfolio model of the capital account of the balance of payments was to deepen the explanation of the endogenous risk premium. In addition to the portfolio composition effect, he argued that the risk premium also depends on the behavior of certain fundamental macroeconomic variables that change along the cycle, such as the result of the current account of the balance of payments and the stock in international currency reserves, which economic agents consider to be indicators that influence the payment capacity of the residents for external financial obligations.

The endogenous behavior of the risk premium plays an important role in the "open economy–Minskyan" cyclical dynamics described in Frenkel's model. Throughout the boom phase, while the current account deteriorates, the expected devaluation may rise. The arbitrage would then increase the internal interest rate. To that effect, both greater exchange rate risk and risk of default would be added. Thus, the domestic interest rate would tend to rise over time. As mentioned previously, at some point the net capital inflows will fall short of the current account deficit and the stock of reserves will start declining, thus increasing the upward pressure on the interest rate. Given the ensuing deterioration of economic expectations, the rise in the domestic interest rate may not be enough to prevent a run against the peso, thus triggering a currency crisis.

CRISES COMPARED AND POLICY LESSONS

Frenkel and Rapetti (2009) show how such a stylized cycle has been common in several emerging market crises, including those in Latin America, Asia, and other developing countries. Frenkel (2012) goes further, making the case that the cycle was also observed in the more recent Eurozone crisis. However, he unveils several important differences between the EME crisis and the Eurozone experience. Although the mechanisms involved are quite similar during the boom phase, significant differences arise during the downturn that leads to crises.

In the EME crises, debts in foreign currency played a decisive role. When there is a period of shortage of foreign exchange and the agents' perception of risks deteriorates, investor confidence is shattered, and a crisis becomes a self-fulfilling prophecy. This is so in the absence of a lender of last resort in foreign currency whose presence and active intervention could prevent financial stress and halt the panic that may produce a run against domestic assets. Conversely, debts in foreign currency have not been decisive in the Eurozone. However, the absence of a lender of last resort to governments, because of the unwillingness or constraints faced by the European Central Bank to act in that capacity, has also played an important role.

The experiences of EMEs and the periphery of the Eurozone also present similarities regarding the role played by fiscal policy in the contracting phase. In most cases, despite intending to signal to economic actors a willingness to adjust public finances and preserve the ability to pay, fiscal policy has been blatantly procyclical in the downward phase of the cycle.

INFLATION AND REAL EXCHANGE RATES

High inflation and the relationship between the exchange rate and economic growth in developing economies were two of the main topics addressed by Frenkel's research, both theoretically and empirically. He focused not only on the causes and manifestations of high inflation but also on its implications on economic policy.

Under a high-inflation regime,[5] as past inflation is incorporated into current inflation caused by indexation, supply shocks permanently accelerate inflation. In fact, as contract lengths get shorter, the acceleration bias becomes greater. Upward changes in the international price of energy (or other irreplaceable tradable inputs), fiscal imbalances that force corrections in public utility prices, or external imbalances that require exchange rate devaluations to restore equilibrium will all increase the inflation rate as pricemakers transfer their higher costs to their products' prices. This dynamic also causes relative prices to become more inflexible, making it more difficult to absorb real shocks.[6]

Getting rid of a high-inflation regime once it is fully operative is extremely complex. In particular, disinflation policy is much more complicated than in a low inflationary context, as is typically the case in developed countries. As predicted by the theory of high inflation and as was confirmed in practice, the effectiveness of conventional disinflation policies in such a situation is extremely limited. Nominal demand contraction through monetary and fiscal measures is by itself practically ineffective in curbing inflationary inertia, but it may have strong negative effects on both the activity level and employment. It can only become effective if the increase in unemployment dismantles the indexation mechanisms. Usually, however, the political costs of unemployment tend to interrupt the disinflation effort long before such a moment is reached. In fact, one of the key lessons of Frenkel's analysis is that, under high inflation, a successful disinflation policy should include not only demand management instruments but also incomes policy measures aimed at coordinating expectations of a declining rate of inflation. Indeed, as the combination of inertia and inflationary jumps in the face of exogenous upward shocks incorporates an acceleration bias to the inflation dynamics, a credible policy shock based on the government's administered prices might help negotiate a deindexation agreement with private pricemakers and thus break inertial inflation. If complemented with appropriate monetary and fiscal measures, this can be the basis of a working disinflation strategy.

To be effective, economic policy must be able to reduce the public's expectations on inflation, thus allowing the removal of indexation of nominal prices. That is the key to ending inertia. But it will only be feasible if all relevant agents (e.g., corporations, trade unions) can coordinate their actions and simultaneously agree to leave behind adjustments based on past inflation. It is necessary that such a scheme be replaced with a forward-looking mechanism that takes into account future inflationary expectations. Logically, for those downward expectations to be formed, the government's commitment to pursuing a macroeconomic policy consistent with a declining rate of inflation is crucial. In addition, such a commitment must enjoy sufficient credibility among economic agents.

This was precisely the basis of the so-called heterodox anti-inflationary plans that were tested in different Latin American countries and beyond during the 1980s and 1990s. While discussing in detail the development of these plans and their results exceeds the scope of this chapter, let us say that in some countries, such as Israel, the high-inflation regime was successfully dismantled with programs of this sort. However, in other countries, such as Argentina, the regime remained operative and, as a result of the failure of similar programs, high inflation finally turned into hyperinflation in the late 1980s.

THE REAPPEARANCE OF INFLATIONARY
INERTIA IN ARGENTINA IN THE 2000s

As noted previously, the recent resurgence of certain features of the high-inflation regime in Argentina, although not yet fully developed, shows that the process that leads to such a regime is not such an oddity that might appear only on rare occasions. It was rather the logical consequence of certain macroeconomic features that can be observed during different times and in different countries and that can and should be theoretically analyzed.

A brief review of the current predicament in Argentina will therefore be useful because it will help illustrate the common features between what has been going on in Argentina—and in Venezuela—since the second half of the past decade and the high-inflation processes that took place in the Southern Cone and other Latin American countries from the mid-1970s to the early 1990s. It will also be important to highlight the different conditions that triggered the high-inflation dynamics both then and now.

In fact, when chronic inflation started to turn into high inflation in the mid-1970s and early 1980s, the economies affected were suffering a major exogenous shock caused by the interrupted access of their indebted public and private sectors to international financial markets. Such a shock deeply deteriorated domestic economic and social conditions and led to growing distributive conflicts that manifested themselves through a continuous acceleration of inflation.

In contrast, South America has currently been experiencing probably the greatest positive external shock in terms of trade in several decades. The bonanza has produced generalized growth in most South American countries and has helped to reduce poverty and even slightly improve equity, with the resultant softening of distributive conflicts.

Each country dealt with the bonanza in different ways, some better than others, but most managed to keep inflation under control. It was only in Argentina and Venezuela where, despite the ongoing bonanza, the political authorities decided to resort to populist myopic policies aimed merely at perpetuating power no matter the costs. That was how domestic inflation endogenously started to diverge from international rates.

What was the process like in Argentina? After the collapse of the so-called Convertibility Plan—a sort of currency board mechanism—the country underwent a deep recessionary adjustment throughout 2001 and

2002. Immediately afterward, however, a period of rapid growth and low inflation began, both of which resulted from favorable external conditions and the implementation of an appropriate policy package based on, among other instruments, "managed" floating of the exchange rate.

In this new context, Frenkel's proposal that to kick-start growth and promote development the exchange rate regime should seek a stable and competitive real exchange rate (SCRER) was explicitly adopted by authorities. As a matter of fact, the proposal proved quite useful in accelerating economic activity and employment recovery.

However, the "new" normal did not last long postcrisis. It only prevailed during the five-year period between 2003 and 2007. Indeed, the attempt to keep the policy stance based on import substitution and massive incentives to aggregate consumption unchanged proved wrong. Such a policy was quite appropriate to pull the economy away from deep recession and high unemployment, but it required significant changes once the economy began approaching full employment and potential GDP. In particular, once price competitiveness started to decline because of exchange rate appreciation that originated from the rise of international commodity prices, domestic inflationary pressures not confronted by domestic policies gradually started to resurface.[7]

Attempts to replace the exchange rate drive for a fiscal stimulus to sustain aggregate consumption instead of favoring investment and productivity growth were short-lived and, ultimately, had counterproductive results. As a result, many of the favorable outcomes achieved from previous years' policies gradually started to fade away. Since 2008, the economy halved its rate of expansion, and the previous scenario of nominal stability gave way to a quite different one that was characterized by high and rising inflation. In brief, despite a decade of unprecedented comfortable external and fiscal balances, Argentina was unable to sustain its initial growth impulse. On the contrary, the brief growth period ended up—as it has in many other instances throughout Argentina's history—trapped in a combination of financial repression, currency crisis, and high inflation. The known ghosts from the old normal were back.

The high-inflation rates of recent years are the most visible symptom of accumulated imbalances, mainly as a result of populist unsustainable policies. Moreover, the unprecedented decision to purposely distort inflation indices and other economic statistics for several years left the Argentine economy without a generally accepted and reliable inflation index. Such a "policy" began in early 2007 and was apparently adopted to reduce payments of indexed bonds issued after the default of public debt and the renegotiations with creditors, as well as to disguise true inflation and prevent the government's popular support from collapsing. Despite the alleged short-term positive effect of the measure, the decision further provoked even higher uncertainty that fueled additional rises in the rate of inflation, which at the beginning of 2014 was approximately 40 percent per year.

It is no coincidence that Argentina's economy began recording increasing and significant inflationary pressures since the wide output gap inherited from the crisis greatly narrowed around 2005. Once "full employment" was achieved, it was necessary to abandon the expansionary bias of policy to moderate the nominal expansion of aggregate demand and prevent the rapid appreciation of the real exchange rate.

However, just the opposite happened. Since mid-2005, fiscal policy had become increasingly procyclical. Public spending had grown greater than the rate of expansion of GDP and higher than tax revenue. In this context, the exchange rate and subsidized public prices remained as the only nominal anchors for the economy. Although the use of these anchors prevented domestic prices from accelerating uncontrollably, the inflation rates steadily moved upward. Currency appreciation—one of the main consequences of this policy scheme—led to a sharp deterioration in the trade balance of the industrial sector. The comfortable surplus in the energy trade balance that prevailed during the beginning of the decade was eroded as well and turned into an increasingly large deficit. The combination of these trends caused the reappearance of an external current account deficit.

It would only be a matter of time until the public reacted to the inconsistency between monetary and fiscal policies and the exchange rate anchor. The predictable outcome finally happened: as on many past occasions since 2008, capital outflows accelerated markedly, and sharp declines in international reserves began. Unwilling to admit the inflationary origin of the problem and act accordingly, the government—lacking access to external financing other than that temporarily granted by the Bank of International Settlements to the Central Bank—tolerated for a while the drop in reserves. However, when foreign reserves reached a critical level according to the agents' generalized perceptions, the administration adopted exchange rate controls, which in fact were only partially effective. In practice, a foreign exchange black market developed, and the corresponding exchange rate increasingly weighed on public expectations. Moreover, the conviction that a sizable correction in relative prices was inevitable accentuated the distributive struggle and further accelerated inflation, aggravating the prospective costs in terms of output and employment of the inevitable future adjustment.

HOW TO DEAL WITH HIGH INFLATION-CUM-RECESSION?

Today, the prevalent high and rising inflation is an acute problem, as it was in the 1970s and 1980s because of its effects both on output and on inequality and poverty. As long as adopting a robust and credible anti-inflationary strategy is delayed, the surge of a high-inflation regime becomes more likely.

As can be learned from Frenkel's research, a comprehensive anti-inflationary strategy in the face of inertial inflation cannot be merely limited to fiscal adjustment plus a reduction in monetary growth. At these high levels of inflation, the use of contractionary demand policies as the only anti-inflationary instrument would be, to use an analogy, like trying to stop a car by holding it from the radio antenna. It is necessary to complement such a policy with a broad three-party agreement (corporations, trade unions, and government) on wages and prices to coordinate expectations for a horizon of lower inflation. A primary objective of this incomes policy would be to provide a credible signal that prices will stop rising at the rate they had been growing previously. In this way, it will be possible to eliminate the inertial component of inflation, which tends to be incorporated into the wage renegotiations and determination of "fix prices" (as opposed to "flex prices" in the interpretation introduced by Hicks [1975]).

The role of these agreements is critical for coordinating the simultaneous disinflation in prices and wages required to minimize adverse effects on the level of activity and employment that arise from the reduction in monetary growth and fiscal adjustment. A second objective of this type of agreement is to contain second-round effects in inflation from corrections in the exchange rate and other regulated prices.

REAL EXCHANGE RATE AND DEVELOPMENT

Frenkel's concerns regarding the influence of the level of the real exchange rate on economic performance became widely known in Latin American policy circles during the decade-long predominance of convertibility (a currency board-like regime) that governed the Argentine economy throughout most of the 1990s. The Argentine peso was pegged to the US dollar since the launching of the disinflation program in 1991. The initial inertial inflation and the strengthening of the dollar against other currencies resulted in the strong appreciation of the peso. The unfavorable medium-term effects of the appreciated real exchange rate on employment and growth were the basis for the gradual deterioration of Argentina's economic environment in the 1990s and (along with other factors) for the development of the financial and balance-of-payments crises that led to the regime's collapse.

In a series of articles from the 2000s, Frenkel (2004, 2007, 2008) pointed out that maintaining a stable and competitive real exchange rate is one of the most important contributions macroeconomic policy can make to growth and employment. His analysis highlighted three different channels through which the level and stability of the real exchange rate may foster employment creation in developing countries: (1) its short-run effects on aggregate demand, what he called the "macroeconomic channel"; (2) its effects on the rate of economic growth (i.e., the development channel); and (3) its effect on the demand of production factors in the production process (i.e., the labor-intensity channel).

The first and second channels had received greater attention in the economic literature. Balassa (1971), Williamson (2003), and Rodrik (2008), for instance, had previously linked the real exchange rate to the development process. In their view, the expansion of the tradable sector would generate externalities that favored modernization and growth in other sectors of the economy while avoiding rent-seeking behavior by protected sectors. In addition, as has been pointed out by Ffrench-Davis (2012), exchange rate policies have become policy instruments that replaced trade restrictions in fostering development.

The need for a competitive exchange rate in the development process does not disregard the traditional arguments on the contractive short-run effects of devaluation (the macroeconomic channel), as expressed in Díaz Alejandro (1963) or Krugman and Taylor (1978). However, it does stress that the positive relation between the real exchange rate and employment in the medium term may overcome those initial impact effects.

The case of Argentina after convertibility collapsed, which happened at the turn of the twenty-first century, is again a good example of Frenkel's views on the real exchange rate development channel. Indeed, the spectacular economic recovery that took place after the collapse can be associated with a policy regime based on the preservation of a stable and competitive real exchange rate. This positive trend was initially made possible by two key achievements of the transition period: (1) the stabilization of the foreign exchange and monetary and financial markets and its favorable effects on expectations, and (2) the establishment of a managed foreign exchange regime. A stable environment was maintained throughout the following five years despite the lack of support from international financial institutions and the country's restricted access to international financial markets.

This view of the exchange rate opposes the International Monetary Fund's traditional position, which favors as little intervention as possible on the floating of the nominal exchange rate. However, under conditions of high uncertainty and weak demand for domestic currency-denominated assets, such as those that prevailed during the crisis, it seemed unwise to establish a purely floating foreign exchange regime. It was highly likely that such a move would have led to a sharp increase in the nominal exchange rate, possibly triggering a new hyperinflationary episode that could have turned Argentina into a fully dollarized economy.

As the Central Bank managed to stabilize the nominal exchange rate after the initial and unavoidable overshooting, the real rate began to follow a trend of mild appreciation caused by modest but rising domestic inflation. After stabilization, peso-denominated assets recovered their attractiveness, and their demand began to swiftly increase. Substitution of portfolio instruments in favor of these assets resulted in a steady decline in interest rates and led, as of mid-2003, to greater intervention of the Central Bank in the foreign exchange market to prevent the declining trend of the nominal parity and preserve the competitive real exchange rate that had been achieved. Indeed, 2003 can be considered the end of the transitional phase and the beginning of a five-year period of rapid growth based on the stable and competitive real exchange rate regime.

There were also other causes behind the positive output and employment results from the 2003–2007 period in Argentina: a large idle capacity and huge excess of labor supply, which provided ample room for a rapid economic expansion without significant inflationary pressures. The postdefault debt restructuring, whose first round took place in 2005, provided a very positive fiscal perspective. Thanks to growing world demand, largely pushed by China, external conditions improved. Export commodity prices soared after 2004. But it is unlikely that the economy could have taken full advantage of such a favorable environment without a relatively high and stable real exchange rate.

By 2007 conditions gradually began to change. The government insisted on expansionary monetary and fiscal policies, even when the idle capacity and excess labor supply had disappeared. Economic policy showed then a significant populist bias. Inflationary pressures became increasingly higher, but the government did not adopt any anti-inflationary policy. Instead, the nominal exchange rate, together with the prices of regulated public utilities, became the policy's nominal anchors. Consequently, the previous exchange rate policy lost its coherence, and the scheme, like the rapid growth of the immediate previous period, began to fade away.

Because of the major economic policy inconsistencies discussed previously, there is little doubt that in the recent Argentine experience that scheme was interrupted long before reaching its endogenous limits. At what point a policy scheme based on a competitive and stable exchange rate becomes useful as a tool for promoting growth and development remains, nonetheless, an open question.

Indeed, it seems clear that a scheme of this nature can only be sustained to the extent that there is policy space to continue to use sterilized intervention in the foreign exchange market and/or continue to increase the fiscal surplus. Such space, however, is not unlimited: neither domestic interest rates nor fiscal surpluses can grow indefinitely.[8] The time period for which a stable and competitive exchange rate could be sustained thus depends on the interactions of two factors: the productive structure of each economy (particularly its excess supply of labor) and the ability of financial markets to absorb Central Bank or Treasury debt.

The discussion on the time span of the stable and competitive exchange rate model is still open. To what extent and through what channels a stable and competitive exchange rate can trigger the process of systemic productivity gains, which is the key to achieving sustained growth and development, remains to be seen. What are its limits? When and how are those limits reached? On what variables do such limits depend? These are, in our opinion, fruitful questions that warrant further research.

CONCLUSIONS

Between the mid-1970s and late 1980s, Roberto Frenkel was one of the most prominent members of a group of young economists responsible for refreshing the traditional economic thought then prevailing in Latin America. That group, which was then labeled as neostructuralist, had a long-lasting influence on how to approach Latin American macroeconomic problems and related issues elsewhere in the developing world.

Throughout this chapter we have critically reviewed what we consider to be Frenkel's major contributions regarding two central issues of Latin American economics from the point of view of both short-run macroeconomics and long-term development: (1) financial integration to international capital markets and its interaction with national macroeconomic policies, which can lead to financial and balance-of-payments crises; and (2) inflation and relative prices, focusing on inertial inflation and the high-inflation regime on the one hand and the exchange rate regimes required to induce real exchange rate paths favorable to sustained growth and development on the other. We have also discussed a few of Frenkel's lessons and their implications for macroeconomic policy evaluated through some recent developments in the region, particularly in Argentina. Finally, we tried to suggest some areas for further research along the lines of his analytical contributions to development economics.

NOTES

1. See, for example, Damill and Frenkel (1987), Damill et al. (1989), Damill et al. (1991), and Fanelli et al. (1992).
2. See, for example, Bagnai (2012) and Cesaratto (2012).
3. See Johnson (1972).
4. Rodriguez (1979).
5. The concept of high-inflation regime is developed in Frenkel (1979) and Frenkel (1990).
6. On the mechanics and welfare cost of inflation see Okun et al. (1975).
7. On this point, see Frenkel and Rapetti (2012).
8. See Albrieu et al. (2012).

REFERENCES

Albrieu, R., López, A., and Rozenwurcel G. 2012. *Los recursos naturales como palanca del desarrollo en América del Sur: ¿ficción o realidad?* Buenos Aires: Red Mercosur.

Arellano, J. P. and Ffrench-Davis, R. 1981. "Apertura financiera externa: la experiencia Chilena en 1973/80." Documento de Trabajo, Santiago: CIEPLAN.

Bagnai, A. 2012. "Unhappy families are all alike: Minskyan cycles, Kaldorian growth, and the Eurozone peripheral crises." Documento Técnico, Iniciativa para la Transparencia Financiera.

Balassa, B. 1971. "Trade policies in developing countries." *American Economic Review* 61(2).

Cesaratto, S. 2012. "Controversial and novel features of the Eurozone crisis as a balance of payment crisis." Quaderni del Dipartimento di Economia Politica e Statistica, No. 640, Università de gli Studi di Siena, Italy.

Damill, M. and Frenkel, R. (1987). "De la apertura a la crisis financiera. Un análisis de la experiencia Argentina de 1977–82." *Ensayos Económicos* 37.

Damill, M., Frenkel, R., Fanelli, J. M., and Rozenwurcel, G. 1989. *Déficit fiscal, deuda externa y desequilibrio financiero*. Buenos Aires: Tesis.

Damill, M., Frenkel, R., Fanelli, J. M., and Rozenwurcel, G. 1991. "Endeudamiento forzoso y ajuste caótico." In *Respuesta a Martínez de Hoz*, O. Barsky and A. M. Bocco, eds. Ediciones Imago Mundi.

Díaz-Alejandro, C. 1963. "A note on the impact of devaluation and the redistributive effects." *Journal of Political Economy* 71.

Fanelli, J. M., Frenkel, R., and Rozenwurcel, G. 1992. "Growth and structural reform in Latin America. Where we stand." In *The market and the state in economic development in the 1990s*, Á. A. Zini, ed. North-Holland.

Frenkel, R. 1979. "Decisiones de precio en alta inflación." *Desarrollo Económico* 75(19).

Frenkel, R. 1982. "Mercado financiero, expectativas cambiarias y movimientos de capital." *Revista Desarrollo Económico* 87(22).

Frenkel, R. 1990. "El régimen de alta inflación y el nivel de actividad." In *Inflación rebelde en América Latina*, J. Arellano, ed. CIEPLAN.

Frenkel, R. 2004. "Real exchange rate and employment in Argentina, Brazil, Chile and Mexico." Paper prepared for the Group of 24, Washington, DC.

Frenkel, R. 2007. "The sustainability of monetary sterilization policies." *CEPAL Review* 93: 29–36.

Frenkel, R. 2008. "The competitive real exchange-rate regime, inflation and monetary policy." *CEPAL Review* 96.

Frenkel, R. 2012. "What have the crises in emerging markets and the Euro Zone in common and what differentiates them?" *Iniciativa para la Transparencia Financiera* 67.

Frenkel, R. and Rapetti, M. 2009. "A developing country view of the current global crisis: what should not be forgotten and what should be done." *Cambridge Journal of Economics* 33(4): 685–702.

Frenkel, R. and Rapetti, M. 2012. "External fragility or deindustrialization: what is the main threat to Latin American countries in the 2010s." *World Economic Review* 1(1): 37–56.

Hicks, J. 1975. *The crisis in Keynesian economics*. New York, NY: Basic Books.

Johnson, H. 1972. "The monetary approach to balance of payments theory." *Journal of Finance and Quantitative Analysis* 7(2).

Krugman, P. and Taylor, L. 1978. "Contractionary effects of devaluation." *Journal of International Economies* 8.

Okun, A. M., Fellner, W., and Wachter, M. 1975. "Inflation: its mechanics and welfare costs." *Brookings Papers on Economic Activity*, 2:351–401.

Rodríguez, C. 1979. "El plan argentino de estabilización del 20 de Diciembre." Documento de Trabajo, No. 5. Buenos Aires: CEMA.

Rodrik, D. 2008. "The real exchange rate and economic growth." *Brookings Papers on Economic Activity* 2: 365–412.

Taylor, L. 1998. "Lax public sector, destabilizing private sector: Origins of capital market crises." CEPA Working Paper Series III, Working Paper No. 6, New York.

Williamson, J. 2003. "Exchange rate policy and development." Paper prepared for the International Policy Dialogue, Columbia University, Barcelona, Spain.

PART 1

Pricing Decisions, Inflation, and Stabilization

Markups Under Uncertainty

VARIATIONS ON PRICE DECISIONS IN HIGH INFLATION

Daniel Heymann and Francisco Roldán

The celebrated article by Roberto Frenkel (1979) on price setting in high inflation was a pioneering contribution to the analysis of the mechanisms and effects of macroeconomic instability. It remains exemplary in several respects. First, it considered facts of daily experience (actually drawn from the concerns and behavior of participants in real market games) and searched for analytical frameworks to interpret them. The interest was at the same time practical and theoretical, micro- and macroeconomic: Frenkel wanted to understand certain patterns of the decision rules used by individual firms and relate them to the features of the inflationary regime of the time, particularly regarding the uncertainty that businesses perceived about their future costs and demands. His motivation for writing the article was "close to home," derived from concrete observations in the Argentine economy at the time and with an eye on policy implications, but the discussion was carried out on a general level and sought conclusions beyond the specificities of a narrow case. The argument used a problem-driven approach, where the analytical setup and behavioral assumptions were chosen by focusing on the issues at hand.

Frenkel also stressed the uncertainties associated with high-inflation processes, which make them quite different in nature from the representations that presume accurate forecasts on the part of agents (cf. also Ungar and Zilberfarb 1993; Heymann and Leijonhufvud 1995). The emphasis was on real (in addition to purely nominal) variability, as indicated by the association between high-inflation regimes and more volatile relative prices (see, for example, Dabús 2000). In this context, his main proposition was that inflationary turbulences that exacerbate the unpredictability of costs and demand schedules faced by firms would induce behaviors that tended to raise price markups over costs. The modeling setup featured, in particular, maximization of expected returns by firms (so that no risk-aversion effects were invoked) and coupled anticipated movements in costs and demands, implying positive perceived co-movements between these variables.

Our aim here is to revisit the theme of price setting in uncertain environments and to discuss some variants of the argument to investigate alternative mechanisms by which uncertainty could influence the level of markups. In particular, we explore the role of inventory management and liquidity constraints as channels through which imperfect knowledge of future unit costs over a wide range of potential values may make firms reluctant to sell goods in the current period, thus creating incentives to raise prices.[1]

To focus and simplify the discussion, we carry out the analysis by considering very stylized situations. The models explored in what follows contemplate two-period time horizons with two potential future states; price-setting behavior is represented as maximizing expected benefits under probabilistic risk, taking as given a known price elasticity of demand. We start by analyzing schematic versions of Frenkel's scenario and discussing the effects that induce desired increases in markups as responses to higher degrees of uncertainty faced by firms when demand and costs are correlated. We then focus on inventory management when future costs, but not demand, are volatile. By itself, cost uncertainty is insufficient to induce inventory hoarding and higher markups. We then explore the effects of liquidity restrictions combined with minimum-sales or maximum-output constraints; in these cases, inventories and markups are found to increase with the degree of cost uncertainty.

BENCHMARK MODELS: PREDETERMINED PRICES

PREDETERMINED OUTPUT

In the next two sections we consider close variants of the assumptions in Frenkel's article. Here, the firm must precommit prices and production before costs and the position of the demand schedule are revealed. The setup can be summarized as follows:

• At time t, the firm chooses prices and production levels for $t + 1$ without being informed about the level of costs and demand in that period. Real and nominal shocks for the firm are assumed uncorrelated. Real unit costs (deflated by a general price level) are denoted c_{t+1}. For simplicity, and to concentrate on the effects of real uncertainties, it is assumed that the firm posts a real ("indexed") price: $P_{t+1}^r = P_{t+1} / P_{t+1}^m$, where P_{t+1} is the nominal price of the firm and P_{t+1}^m is the aggregate price level.[2]

- The firm decides at t the volume of goods Q_{t+1} that it will bring to the market in the following period. Costs are payable and sales realized at $t+1$. Realized sales are determined by D_{t+1}, the volume demanded at the preannounced price, subject to the constraint that this does not exceed Q_{t+1}. The demand curve has constant price elasticity, and this parameter is (somehow) known by the firm $D_{t+1} = z_{t+1}\left(P_{t+1}^r\right)^{-\gamma}$, where z_{t+1} is random, as viewed from t.[3] It is assumed that unsold goods go to waste and generate no income to the firm. Thus, the value of revenues at $t+1$ is given by $z_{t+1}\left(P_{t+1}^r\right)^{1-\gamma}$.

- There are two possible states of the world j at $t+1$: a and b, characterized by the demand parameter z_{t+1}^j and real costs c_{t+1}^j; in state a, demand is comparatively high, so that $z_{t+1}^a > z_{t+1}^b$. We will consider different cases for the correlation between z_{t+1} and c_{t+1}.

- Output and prices are chosen to maximize the expectation at t of $t+1$ real profits: $E_t(B_{t+1})$. It may be noted that in this scenario, with no inventories, behavior in period t is not influenced by anticipated conditions in the future period.

With those assumptions, real benefits in state j are given by

$$B_{t+1}^j = P_{t+1}^r \min\left[Q_{t+1}, z_{t+1}^j\left(P_{t+1}^r\right)^{-\gamma}\right] - c_{t+1}^j Q_{t+1}.$$

Because production is equal in both states, expected total costs are simply volume of output multiplied by the expected value of unit costs. We can distinguish two cases: (1) the firm prefers to set output Q_{t+1} at the level that will satisfy demand at price P_{t+1}^r in state a, implying that some goods will be unsold if b is realized; and (2) the firm sets Q_{t+1} equal to the quantity demanded in the low state and thus will not supply all the volume of purchases desired by consumers if the state is a (but, by assumption, will not adjust prices).

CASE 1

Here, $Q_{t+1}(1) = z_{t+1}^a\left(P_{t+1}^r\right)^{-\gamma}$, and sales in both states are demand determined; therefore, because expected profits follow

$$E[B_{t+1}(1)] = E(z_{t+1})\left(P_{t+1}^r\right)^{1-\gamma} - z_{t+1}^a\left(P_{t+1}^r\right)^{-\gamma} E(c_{t+1}),$$

it can be seen that the chosen price in this case is

$$P_{t+1}^r(1) = \frac{\gamma}{\gamma-1} E(c_{t+1}) \frac{z_{t+1}^a}{E(z_{t+1})}.$$

The strategy of the firm is to produce a high quantity, adapted to the state of high demand, and to set a high price, larger than the one consistent with the standard markup $\frac{\gamma}{\gamma-1}$ over expected unit costs. However, this higher markup depends exclusively on demand conditions and is not influenced by uncertainty over costs.

CASE 2

Now, $Q_{t+1}(2) = z_{t+1}^b\left(P_{t+1}^r\right)^{-\gamma}$, and sales in both states are equal to the quantity demanded in state b. Thus, expected profits are

$$E[B_{t+1}(2)] = z_{t+1}^b\left(P_{t+1}^r\right)^{1-\gamma} - z_{t+1}^b\left(P_{t+1}^r\right)^{1-\gamma} E(c_{t+1}),$$

which implies the usual markup condition

$$P_{t+1}^r(2) = \frac{\gamma}{\gamma-1} E(c_{t+1}).$$

In this case, the firm sets prices and production as if it expected the low-demand case; as before, costs are taken at their expected value irrespective of their variability over states.

The firm chooses to be in case 1 if $EB_{t+1}(1) > EB_{t+1}(2)$, that is,

$$\frac{z_{t+1}^a}{z_{t+1}^b} > \left(\frac{z_{t+1}^a}{E(z_{t+1})}\right)^\gamma \quad \text{or} \quad \pi_a + \pi_b\left(\frac{z_{t+1}^b}{z_{t+1}^a}\right) > \left(\frac{z_{t+1}^b}{z_{t+1}^a}\right)^{1/\gamma},$$

where π_j indicates the probability of state j. Those inequalities establish a minimum value of the probability of the high-demand state relative to the between-states spread in the demand parameter for the high-markup case to apply. In any case, the conditions that generate the high-price behavior are unrelated to the volatility of unit costs and their correlation with the level of real demand. This feature of price setting changes if the volume of output is not precommitted but can move according to the state of demand.

PRODUCTION ON DEMAND

This scenario retains the assumption of predetermined prices but allows the firm to adjust output instantaneously in $t+1$ to match realized demand conditions.

PRICING IN REAL TERMS

As before, the firm sets at t the real price P_{t+1}^r at which it will sell at $t+1$, but now it makes output equal to demand in each state j: $Q_{t+1}^j = z_{t+1}^j \left(P_{t+1}^r \right)^{-\gamma}$. Therefore, expected profits can be expressed as $E(B_{t+1}) = \left(P_{t+1}^r \right)^{1-\gamma} E(z_{t+1}) - \left(P_{t+1}^r \right)^{-\gamma} E(z_{t+1}c_{t+1})$, which implies that the price will be

$$P_{t+1}^r = \frac{\gamma}{\gamma-1} \frac{E(z_{t+1}c_{t+1})}{E(z_{t+1})} = \frac{\gamma}{\gamma-1} \left(E(c_{t+1}) + \frac{cov(z_{t+1}, c_{t+1})}{E(z_{t+1})} \right).$$

It can be seen that the price is determined by the standard multiplier over expected costs, *plus a term* that is proportional to the *covariance* between real costs and the level of demand.

Thus, if costs and the demand for the firm's goods are positively correlated, the price is higher than the typical markup over expected unit costs; this observation also appeared in Frenkel's argument. The intuition here is that, when calculating anticipated total costs, the firm considers both unit costs and production levels: if these variables move together, the high-unit cost state gains weight in the average that determines the price. Accordingly, this effect rationalizes higher markups. However, the effect would not arise as a consequence of uncertainty about costs per se but as a result of its association with the variability of demand, in the case where high sales and high unit costs happen simultaneously. In the next sections we consider alternative scenarios to explore instances where larger markups may potentially emerge singly from cost volatility, keeping demand constant. Before that, we rapidly treat the problem just discussed in the case where the firm sets the price P_{t+1} in nominal terms and the aggregate price level is uncertain.

NOMINAL PRICING

Now, the volume of sales in each state depends on the general price level P_{t+1}^m. Real profits in state j are given by

$$B_{t+1}^j = z_{t+1}^j (P_{t+1})^{1-\gamma} \left(P_{t+1}^{m,j} \right)^{\gamma-1} - z_{t+1}^j (P_{t+1})^{-\gamma} \left(P_{t+1}^{m,j} \right)^{\gamma} c_{t+1}^j.$$

Under the assumption of no correlation between real shocks to the firm's costs and demand on the one hand and aggregate nominal shocks on the other, expected real profits are

$$E(B_{t+1}) = E(z_{t+1})(P_{t+1})^{1-\gamma} E\left[\left(P_{t+1}^m \right)^{\gamma-1} \right] - (P_{t+1})^{-\gamma} E\left[\left(P_{t+1}^m \right)^{\gamma} \right] E(z_{t+1}c_{t+1}),$$

from which the pricing rule follows thus:

$$P_{t+1} = \frac{E\left[\left(P_{t+1}^m \right)^{\gamma} \right]}{E\left[\left(P_{t+1}^m \right)^{\gamma-1} \right] E\left(P_{t+1}^m \right)} \frac{\gamma}{\gamma-1} E(z_{t+1}c_{t+1}).$$

This condition means that the firm would set its nominal price relative to the expected aggregate price $[E(P_{t+1}^m)]$, as in the case with "indexed pricing" (i.e., applying a multiplier $\frac{\gamma}{\gamma-1}$ over $E[z_{t+1}c_{t+1}]$, which, as before, depends on the covariance between real unit costs and demand), corrected by the term $\frac{E[(P_{t+1}^m)^{\gamma}]}{E[(P_{t+1}^m)^{\gamma-1}]E[P_{t+1}^m]}$, a function of the distribution of nominal prices. This term is larger than 1 because $E[(P_{t+1}^m)^{\gamma}] = E[(P_{t+1}^m)^{\gamma-1}]E(P_{t+1}^m) + cov(P_{t+1}^m)(P_{t+1}^m)^{\gamma-1}$, and the covariance is positive because the demand elasticity is $\gamma > 1$. Consequently, nominal uncertainty tends to raise the real expected price of the firm. The qualitative basis for this effect is that, under nominal pricing, there is an additional source of variability in the volume of sales and (therefore) output. Given that demand is price elastic, the impact of aggregate price volatility on expected costs is amplified (and stronger than that operating on real revenues), which would induce the firm to raise its price. Here again, it is not cost uncertainty itself but rather demand-induced shifts in the volume of output that motivate higher markups.

INVENTORY MANAGEMENT WITH COST UNCERTAINTY

In this section, we explore the incentives that a firm may have to restrict current sales to "preserve inventories" as a form of insurance against cost shocks. In what follows, unless explicitly stated, we assume that expected costs are constant over time, that is, $E_t(c_{t+1}) = c_t$. Now, the goods produced are storable, and the general setup is as follows:

• The firm starts period t with cash balances, $R_t M_{t-1}$, where M_{t-1} are financial assets accumulated at the end of $t-1$ and R_t is the real rate of return on those assets.[4] We impose the conditions that M_{t-1} and $M_t \geq 0$ so that the firm has no access to financing from one period to the other (although it may or may not be subject in each period to a "cash-in-advance" constraint in its current purchases of inputs).

• Given the values of unit costs c_t and the level of the demand curve z_t, the firm determines a volume of input purchases (inputs cannot be stored) and a production level y_t. Total costs are $c_t y_t$. The firm may be subject to liquidity constraints: in this case, $c_t y_t \geq R_t M_{t-1}$. The firm sets a real price P_t^r for that period; sales will be given by $s_t = z_t (P_t^r)^{-\gamma}$.

• Production and sales may differ in period t: unsold goods can be accumulated as inventories and costlessly carried over to the next period. Inventories at the end of t are $x_t = y_t - s_t$, with the condition $x_t \geq 0$.

• The firm realizes in t real profits $P_t^r s_t - c_t y_t$. Available financial assets can be distributed as dividends (d_t) or accumulated for use in the next period M_t, with a (possibly random) return R_{t+1}. The respective constraint is $R_t M_{t-1} + P_t^r s_t - c_t y_t = d_t + M_t$, with $M_t \geq 0$. That is, the firm is not allowed to borrow on the basis of its $t+1$ revenues. In its decisions at t, the firm maximizes an undiscounted sum of dividends in period t and expected dividends (equal to available resources) in $t+1$.

• At the beginning of $t+1$, unit costs c_{t+1} and demand z_{t+1} are realized; to focus on the role of cost uncertainty, we will assume that z_{t+1} is nonrandom.

• The firm determines a volume of production y_{t+1} and a real price P_{t+1}^r. The volume of sales is $s_{t+1} = y_{t+1} + x_t$ and, in the presence of cash constraints it is $c_{t+1} y_{t+1} \leq R_{t+1} M_t$.

• Realized profits at $t+1$ are $P_{t+1}^r s_{t+1} - c_{t+1} y_{t+1}$, and dividends are $d_{t+1} = R_{t+1} M_t + P_{t+1}^r s_{t+1} - c_{t+1} y_{t+1}$.

NO ADVANCE CASH CONSTRAINTS ON INPUT PURCHASES

Here, the demand for inputs in both periods is unrestricted. The problem of the firm at t will thus be to maximize

$$R_t M_{t-1} + z_t \left(P_t^r \right)^{1-\gamma} - c_t \left[z_t \left(P_t^r \right)^{-\gamma} + x_t \right] - M_t$$
$$+ E_t \left\{ R_{t+1} M_t + z_{t+1} \left(P_{t+1}^r \right)^{1-\gamma} - c_{t+1} \left(z_{t+1} \left[P_{t+1}^r \right]^{-\gamma} - x_t \right) \right\}$$

with the conditions

$$M_t + c_t x_t \leq R_t M_{t-1} + z_t \left[\left(P_t^r \right)^{1-\gamma} - c_t \left(P_t^r \right)^{-\gamma} \right], \; M_t \geq 0 \text{, and } x_t \geq 0.$$

The first inequality imposes nonnegative dividends in t. This means that the firm cannot issue debt that will mature in $t + 1$.

If $E_t R_{t+1} > 1$, no dividends will be distributed in t, and all the available cash of the firm will be carried over to the next period. We will assume this to be the case in what follows.

Here, cost uncertainty has no effect on the solution; the behavior of the firm will only depend on the expected values of unit costs and the returns on financial savings $E_t c_{t+1}$ and $E_t R_{t+1}$:

• If $E_t c_{t+1} < c_t E_t R_{t+1}$, the firm will not carry inventories; prices in each period (and in each state in $t + 1$) will be given by the usual markup condition.

• If $E_t c_{t+1} > c_t E_t R_{t+1}$, inventories are the best form of investment. To focus on a basic case, assume now that inventories brought from t will not be sufficient to make the firm choose zero production in any state at $t + 1$ (so that the relevant marginal costs are c_{t+1}). Then, goods available at t will be worth more if kept as inventories than if sold unless the current price is equal to the future expected price given by the expected cost plus markup $\frac{\gamma}{\gamma-1} E_t (c_{t+1})$. Consequently, the present price will be determined not by current but by anticipated costs.[5]

It may be remarked that, because demand is price elastic, the desired value of spending on inputs decreases with the level of unit costs. This simple property will be relevant in the case with cash constraints, and it implies that cost uncertainty by itself would not bias prices upward in the present setup.

CONSTRAINED INPUT PURCHASES

Now production may be limited by the availability of liquid funds to buy inputs at the beginning of the period. It is useful to distinguish between two subcases: one where the restriction may operate in the future period $t + 1$ but does not bind in t, and the other where output in t is cash constrained.

UNRESTRICTED CURRENT OUTPUT

In this case, cash balances carried over from period $t - 1$ suffice to gain command over the quantity of inputs required at the one-period profit-maximizing output given by the volume of demand at price $\frac{\gamma}{\gamma-1} c_t$. In addition, because of the more-than-unit elasticity of demand, the higher the dispersion of future costs in $t + 1$, the larger desired spending will be on inputs in state b, where costs are low (and the opposite will be the case in state a). Cost volatility will induce the firm to carry cash from t to $t + 1$ to be able to finance the large (in volume and value) input purchases it will wish to make in the low-cost state. But those cash holdings are maximized at the price-quantity pair that implements the single-period profit optimization at t. Thus, the anticipation of more variability in the future price will not induce the firm to keep more inventories and to raise its price at t.

More formally, the problem can be written as

$$\max \left\{ R_t M_{t-1} + z_t \left(P_t^r\right)^{1-\gamma} - c_t \left[z_t \left(P_t^r\right)^{-\gamma} + x_t \right] - M_t + E_t(R_{t+1}M_t) + z_{t+1} \left(P_{t+1}^r\right)^{1-\gamma} \right.$$
$$\left. - c_{t+1} (z_{t+1} \left(P_{t+1}^r\right)^{-\gamma} - x_t \right\}$$

subject to

$$c_{t+1} z_{t+1} \left(P_{t+1}^r\right)^{-\gamma} \le R_{t+1} M_t + c_{t+1} x_t$$

$$M_t + c_t x_t \le R_t M_{t-1} + z_t \left[\left(P_t^r\right)^{1-\gamma} - c_t \left(P_t^r\right)^{-\gamma} \right], \quad M_t \ge 0, \text{ and } x_t \ge 0.$$

The first inequality expresses the cash constraint in $t + 1$, namely in that the reposition value of sales in $t + 1$ cannot exceed the resources carried over from t in the form of cash balances and inventories. The next inequalities impose the same constraints as in the previous problem.

In this case, the incentive to keep inventories is influenced by the interaction between the level of costs and the intensity of the liquidity constraint, as the expected return from holding goods depends on $E_t[\frac{c_{t+1}}{c_t}(1+\mu_{t+1})]$, where μ_{t+1} indicates the multiplier of the cash restriction.[6] In the present setup, this effect goes against the accumulation of inventories when there is more uncertainty over costs. This is because, as mentioned, desired spending on inputs falls as unit costs increase. Under a mean-preserving increase in the cost spread, the firm wants to raise its spending in the low-cost state and reduce it when realized costs are high. However, inventories are less valuable when costs are low and therefore do not protect against liquidity constraints as do the holding of liquid assets obtained by selling goods in period t. Thus, the incentive is to carry financial assets forward rather than inventories.

RESTRICTED CURRENT OUTPUT

Now, the resources available at t do not allow the firm to purchase all its desired inputs; then, the volume of goods at hand to sell or keep as inventories is determined by $c_t y_t = c_t(s_t + x_t) = R_t M_{t-1}$. Still, larger unit costs in the high-cost state a in $t+1$ would induce the firm to spend less on inputs (if unrestricted), whereas cheaper inputs in state b would make it desirable to realize a higher value of input purchases. Therefore, here too, the anticipation of a larger spread between the costs in both future states does not, *ceteris paribus*, tend to increase current markups: if the firm did that to keep inventories, it would miss profitable opportunities to produce in the low-cost state.

Then, the value of sales in t will be restricted by the production limit and the desired inventories $P_t^\gamma s_t = z_t^{1/\gamma}(y_t - x_t)^{1-1/\gamma}$, and the firm will maximize

$$z_t^{1/\gamma}(y_t - x_t)^{1-1/\gamma} - M_t + E_t\left\{R_{t+1}M_t + z_{t+1}\left(P_{t+1}^r\right)^{1-\gamma} - c_{t+1}\left[z_{t+1}\left(P_{t+1}^r\right)^{-\gamma} - x_t\right]\right\}$$

subject to

$$c_{t+1}z_{t+1}\left(P_{t+1}^r\right)^{-\gamma} \le R_{t+1}M_t + c_{t+1}x_t$$

$$M_t + c_t x_t \le z_t^{1/\gamma}(y_t - x_t)^{1-1/\gamma}, \quad M_t \ge 0, \text{ and } x_t \ge 0.$$

The second inequality expresses the usual nonnegative dividend constraint for period t, where the fact that $M_{t-1}R_t = c_t y_t$ has been taken into account.

The profitability of holding inventories by restricting current sales (and thus raising current prices) depends on the value of $E_t[c_{t+1}(1+\mu_{t+1})]$, which declines rather than increases as the dispersion of c_{t+1} increases. The negative dependence of inventories with respect to future cost spreads can be verified in numerical simulations, as in figure 2.1,[7] which shows results of simulations of the case in which, holding expected future costs

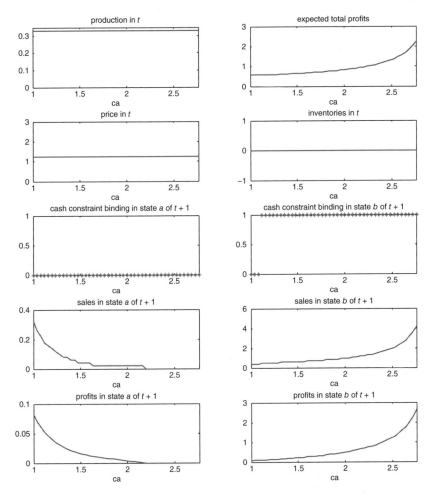

Figure 2.1 Restricted current output and cash constraint on future input purchases.

constant at $E(c_{t+1}) = c_t = 1$, the dispersion is increased. The horizontal axes show the cost in the high-cost state. Relevant parameters of the simulation are $\gamma = 5$, $\pi_a = 1/3$, and $R = 1.05$. It can be seen that the firm does not hold inventories at any point: it produces in the first period at the static optimum and uses the proceeds to buy inputs in both states at $t + 1$.

   If now future expected costs are allowed to differ from c_t and the firm decides to hold inventories in t (because of an expected increase in costs), a larger spread induces a fall in desired inventories. This is shown in figure 2.2, where $c_t = \frac{1}{2} E(c_{t+1})$. Here the result is due to the fact that,

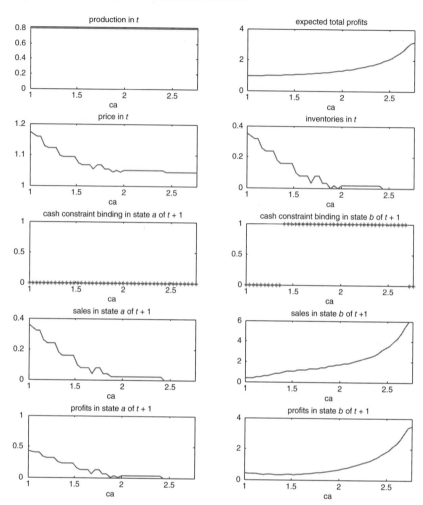

Figure 2.2 Restricted current output and cash constraint on future input purchases with expected increase in costs.

as previously stated, liquid assets constitute a better insurance than inventories because total desired spending on inputs declines with unit costs. It can be noted that carrying inventories is costly to the firm when it is cash constrained in the low-cost state in period $t + 1$. This is because the firm could produce $\frac{c_t}{c_{t+1}} > 1$ goods in state b for each unit produced at t, which would put it closer to achieving the optimal sales in that state.

It would follow that liquidity constraints by themselves do not suffice to make cost uncertainty induce lower current sales and higher prices to preserve inventories. The reason lies in the negative covariance between

unit and total costs. If this relation is clear in the model, it is also coun-
terintuitive in practice: when the price of inputs increases, the level of
activity of firms does not contract "gracefully" in a way that allows an easy
reduction in total outlays. One would rather expect a positive association between input prices and total costs. In addition, the model allows
the firm to expand without limits (subject perhaps to a cash-in-advance
limit), which, as was just seen, may induce low-price "liquidations" to
take advantage of low-cost scenarios, even if expected unit costs increase.
We now explore some variants of the model that modify those features.

CAPACITY LIMITS ON OUTPUT

Now, in addition to the potential cash constraints on input purchases in
both periods, the firm is conditioned in $t + 1$ by some physical limit on
its scale of operation, as measured by the level of production (although
sales from inventories remain unrestricted). The intuitive consequence
of this capacity restriction is that, once that limit is reached, the desired
value of input purchases in the low-cost state diminishes in the event of
a mean-preserving increase in cost spreads in $t + 1$. Then, as c_{t+1}^b falls, so
will the value spent on inputs in state b and, if the demand elasticity is
not too high, it may well become lower than the desired expenditure on
inputs in state a. Here also it is useful to distinguish between the cases
where the cash constraint binds or is not binding in t.

UNRESTRICTED CURRENT OUTPUT

The firm can finance the input purchases required to achieve profit maximization in t by setting price $p_t = \frac{\gamma}{\gamma-1} c_t$. We will focus on the case in
which the capacity limit is truly binding, that is, where the cash con-
straint is not operative at the $t + 1$ maximum level of output.

Now, in fact, the firm is not cash constrained, because the proceeds
from its profit-maximizing sales in t allow it to finance the maximum
desired spending on inputs at the capacity limit y^1. Even if the cost
spread is large enough so that the capacity constraint is reached in the
low-cost state, the firm will still maximize profits in t by setting prices
through the standard markup condition.

By assumption, the purchase of inputs in the high-cost state to sell
at price $p_{t+1}^a = \frac{\gamma}{\gamma-1} c_{t+1}^a$ will be unrestricted given the profits realized at t.
If the firm has spare capacity in t and no cash constraints, it could increase
its production of goods in t and keep the excess output as inventories to

offset the production limit in the low-cost state. However, because the firm would be choosing the same amount of sales, this policy would have no impact on prices. The incentive to carry inventories would emerge if $-c_t E(R_{t+1}) + \pi_b MI^l_{t+1} + \pi_a c^a_{t+1} > 0$, where MI^l_{t+1} is the marginal income in $t+1$ when sales are at their capacity volume. This means that the firm increases profits if it incurs in cost $c_t E(R_{t+1})$ (measured in $t+1$ values), lowers expected costs in state a (by producing one unit less while keeping sales constant), and relaxes by one unit the capacity constraint in state b. Even if this condition calls for holding inventories, however, it would still not provide an incentive for higher prices. Figure 2.3 shows this result in simulations.[8]

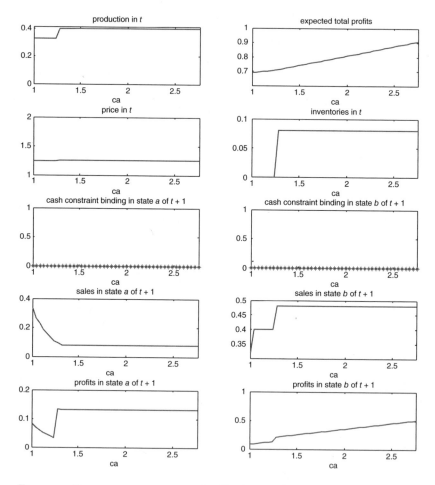

Figure 2.3 Current output unconstrained by financial restriction, cash constraint on future input purchases, and maximum limit on output.

RESTRICTED CURRENT OUTPUT

In this setting, the firm is cash constrained at t so that its current production is lower than the profit-maximizing level. Assume now that, if the firm produces and sells at the maximum possible level in t, the capacity constraint (and not the cash limit) is operative in the low-cost state b. Now, the possibility of increasing production in the current period to save costs in state b in $t + 1$ is not available. The firm may try to "save inventories" through lower sales by raising prices at t. That would be convenient if $-MI_t E(R_{t+1}) + \pi_b MI_{t+1}^l + \pi_a c_{t+1}^a > 0$, where MI_t is the marginal revenue in t; carrying inventories requires cutting sales in t.

If that condition holds, the firm does have an incentive to increase markups as the costs dispersion increases. It would derive from a combination of effects: (1) an impossibility of increasing production in the current period because of financing constraints, (2) a limit on the productive capacity that restricts the "cash requirements" for productive uses in a future low-cost state, and (3) a sufficiently high level of costs in state a (compared with the marginal revenue in the current period adjusted by the return on financial savings).

Figure 2.4 shows simulation results for this case. In the scenario analyzed previously, where the firm was not cash constrained in t, it chose to increase production and hold inventories to alleviate its restriction on sales in state b. By contrast, the firm is now unable to increase production in t because of the financing constraint. Thus, the incentive to keep inventories is translated into lower sales in the current period that, in turn, imply setting a higher price.

MINIMUM VOLUME OF OPERATION

In the scenarios discussed previously, the firm was supposedly able to reduce its volume of sales in the high-cost state by moving continuously along a given isoelastic demand curve. The assumption does not seem wholly adequate. A shop with almost empty shelves is unlikely to attract sufficient customers to sell even the small quantity of goods available. If, for example, we introduce the restriction that the firm has to operate with a minimum level of activity, it is no longer the case that the desired value of spending in inputs declines monotonically when unit costs increase. In fact, once that minimum is reached, the amount of resources necessary to be in business becomes proportional to unit costs.[9] If the firm wants

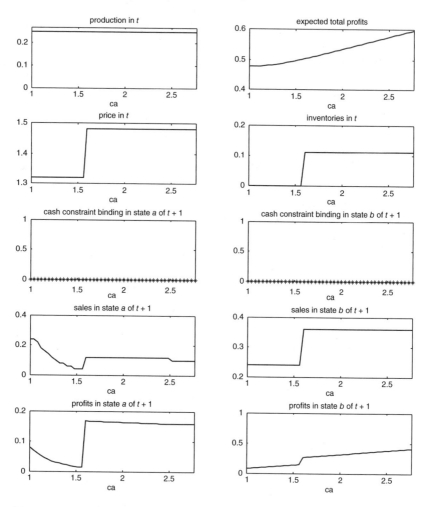

Figure 2.4 Restricted current output and cash constraint on future input purchases with a maximum output constraint.

to satisfy the constraint in the future, it may have to sacrifice sales in the current period and, in so doing, the availability of financial resources in the low-cost state. We can distinguish two cases: one in which the firm is somehow led to open the establishment in any relevant, feasible, circumstances in $t + 1$ (e.g., because of large contractually committed costs if it does otherwise or reputational effects that will affect earnings in future periods left out of the model); and the other in which, once having observed the cost shock, the firm can choose between operating at the minimum level or closing down. Another division of scenarios appears according to whether the firm is constrained or unconstrained in its production in t.

UNCONDITIONAL OPERATION IN t + 1;
UNCONSTRAINED PRODUCTION IN t

Here, the firm must make sure that its level of sales in $t+1$ does not fall below the critical value y^c, which implies being able to buy an equivalent amount of inputs at cost $c_{t+1}^j y^c$ in states $j = a, b$. In addition, we assume that its resources allow it to operate without cash restrictions in t. The relevant constraint on the minimum scale of activity is in state a, that is:[10]

$$[R_t M_{t-1} - c_t(s_t + x_t) + p_t s_t]\frac{R_{t+1}}{c_{t+1}^a} + x_t \geq y^c. \tag{2.1}$$

The purchasing power over inputs in state a of the financial assets available after purchasing inputs for production in t (destined for sale, s_t, or for inventory accumulation, x_t) and realizing sales, plus inventories carried over to $t+1$, must be at least equal to the minimum scale of operation y^c. We will suppose that this inequality can be satisfied. (Otherwise, the firm will simply close in state a in $t+1$ and pay the resulting penalties; from the point of view of its behavior in t, the high-cost state would then be irrelevant because nothing could be done to avoid closing down.)

If, as assumed in this case, the firm is unconstrained in its input purchases in t, it can buy enough inputs to generate sales equal to the volume of demand at the standard markup price $p_t = \frac{\gamma}{\gamma-1}c_t$. The firm will implement this profit-maximizing price–sales policy and choose total production to satisfy the minimum activity constraint in $t+1$. It may be noted that inventories will be accumulated only if $R_{t+1}\frac{c_t}{c_{t+1}^a} < 1$, that is, if the real (gross) rate of return of financial assets in terms of inputs at $t+1$ in state a is less than unity.[11] If this condition holds, the level of inventories may be positive to satisfy the constraint. However, this will only mean increasing production in period t beyond the level of sales, not higher markups in that period.

Figure 2.5 shows simulation results. Because it is unconstrained in its current production, the firm does not raise prices in period t but rather increases production when it demands inventories to meet the minimum activity restriction.

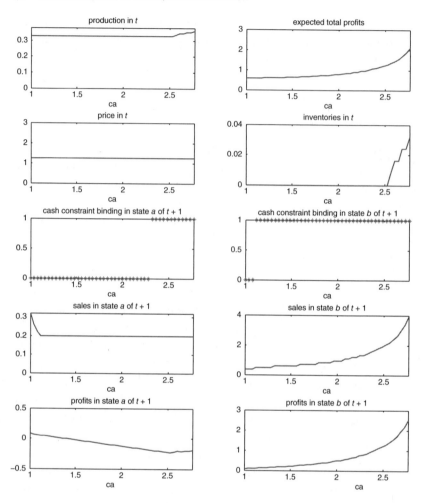

Figure 2.5 Unconstrained output at *t* and cash constraint on future input purchases with a minimum scale of operation.

UNCONDITIONAL OPERATION IN t + 1;
CONSTRAINED PRODUCTION IN t

Now, assume that equation 2.1 cannot be satisfied with sales at time *t* in their current profit-maximizing levels while meeting the condition

$$[R_t M_{t-1} - c_t(s_t + x_t) + p_t s_t] \geq 0 .$$

The firm will then be cash constrained in *t*. When $R_{t+1} \frac{c_t}{c_{t+1}^a} < 1$, inventory holding is more convenient than financial assets to transfer resources from *t* to the high-cost state in *t* + 1. The firm will then use all its cash in t to buy inputs $R_t M_{t-1} = c_t(s_t + x_t)$. The constraint on the minimum level of operation can now be written as

$$\left(\frac{R_t M_{t-1}}{c_t} - x_t \right)(p_t - c_t)\frac{R_{t+1}}{c_{t+1}^a} + x_t = y^c. \qquad (2.2)$$

The first term of the equation indicates the purchases of inputs in state a attainable with the profits earned in period t: here, holding additional inventories implies fewer sales in that period. If the firm holds an additional unit of x_t, it gains the availability of the good and the (financial) returns on the saved costs in t, while it forgoes the revenues that it does not realize in t. A tightening of the constraint (a larger y^c) will call for a change in inventories to satisfy equation 2.2. Then, an increase in x_t would cause three effects: 1) a direct increment in the amount of goods available in $t + 1$; 2) a reduction in the volume of sales in t and, therefore, a fall in the cash balances to finance input purchases in $t + 1$; and 3) a partial offsetting of 2) through higher prices in t. If $p_t[(1-\frac{1}{\gamma})-c_t]\frac{R_{t+1}}{c_{t+1}^a} < 1$, the direct effect dominates and, therefore, the firm will choose higher inventories and markups when facing a higher sales requirement.[12]

The effect of uncertainty over future costs in inducing higher prices and markups in the present would come about because of cash constraints on input purchases (both now and in the future) and because of the requirement that the firm should not deter customers by appearing to be stocked out, which makes its total operating costs higher in the "bad state" as the price of inputs in that state increases and thus induces the behavior of "saving inventories" to cover against that eventuality.

A similar argument applies for the case in which c_{t+1}^a is varied. Figure 2.6 shows simulated results for this case. As the costs in state a increase, the firm first reduces its output and sales in that state until it hits the constraint on the minimum level of operation. As the spread in costs continues to grow, higher costs imply a tighter financial constraint, which requires carrying more inventories to satisfy the restriction. Because production cannot be raised in t, sales in that period must be sacrificed, which brings about higher prices and markups.

CONDITIONAL OPERATION IN t + 1 WITH FINITE COST OF CLOSING; CONSTRAINED INPUT PURCHASES IN t

In this case, the firm must comply with the minimum activity constraint in each period if it decides to open and realize positive sales, but it can

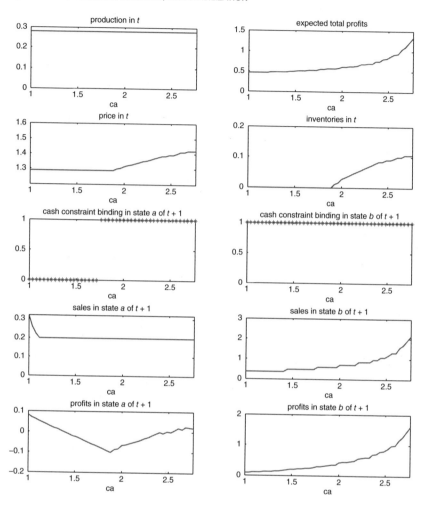

Figure 2.6 Restricted current output and cash constraint on future input purchases with a minimum scale of operation.

also choose to remain closed and have zero activity. In practice, such action can be expected to entail different types of costs, pecuniary and reputational; we represent them by a given quantity of inputs h. Now, the firm must compare its returns (as analyzed in the previous point) when it stays open in state a in $t + 1$ and satisfies the minimum scale constraint with those that it obtains when it closes in that state and takes the penalty h.

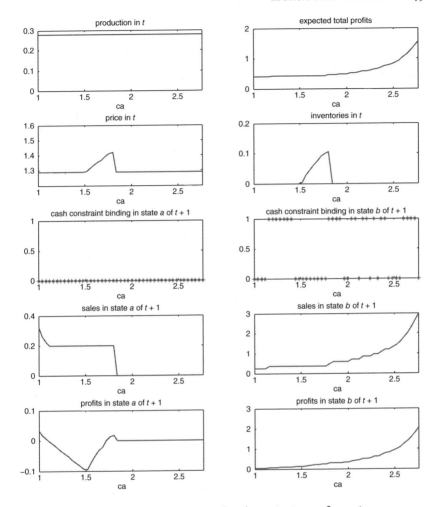

Figure 2.7 Restricted current output and cash constraint on future input purchases with a minimum capacity constraint and finite default cost.

Figure 2.7 shows the results of one such comparison. It can be seen that, when the cost range increases, at some level the firm starts carrying inventories by restricting sales and raising prices in period t; however, there is a limit beyond which the decision is to close down in state a, which implies abstaining from inventory formation and is thus associated with a lower price in t. In effect, the firm pays the price h for being able to "ignore" the (very) high-cost scenario.

CONCLUSIONS

We have analyzed several scenarios of price-setting problems for a firm subject to uncertainty about the future level of unit costs. By itself, disregarding possible correlations between costs and demand, a larger cost variability, with the risk of facing high costs in some states, would not induce behaviors that lead the firm to raise current prices to keep inventories. This results from the negative correlation between (exogenous) unit costs and (endogenous) total costs, which dilutes the cost-saving role of inventories. However, in alternative scenarios, both variables can be decoupled, and inventories may then serve as insurance against future cost variability.

Among such cases, we studied situations characterized by a combination of financial constraints on the value of inputs that the firm can purchase and difficulties in operating at very low levels of activity or very high levels of output. In these scenarios, total costs may increase with unit costs even though demand is price elastic. These circumstances, which generate incentives for inventory-saving increases in markups, do not seem far-fetched, especially in settings of high inflation such as those considered by Roberto Frenkel in his time-honored study.

NOTES

1. The literature on inventory decisions has emphasized production-smoothing incentives (cf. Blinder 1986) or the presence of menu or ordering costs (Sheshinski and Weiss 1977, 1983). Other effects that have been discussed include avoidance of stockouts under uncertainty about demand (Aguirregabiria 1999; Kryvstov and Midrigan 2013). Kashyap et al. (1994) showed empirical results that suggested that liquidity restrictions play an important role in explaining inventory behavior.

2. Given the assumed independence of the real costs and the demand schedule faced by the firm with respect to aggregate price level shocks, this unrealistic feature of the model does not substantially alter the argument. The consequences of uncertainty about aggregate prices are briefly discussed below under Nominal Pricing.

3. In his article, Frenkel discussed potential effects of high inflation in reducing price elasticities of demand, an outcome that may come about, for example, through higher costs of search (cf. Tommasi 1994). This is certainly a relevant effect, which will tend to increase markups; for the sake of simplicity, we leave it out of the picture to concentrate on the repercussions of cost uncertainty.

4. In principle, the firm may have accumulated inventories x_{t-1}. For the sake of simplicity, we will assume these to be zero.

5. If a is the high-cost state, the condition for non-zero production in both states at $t+1$, which implies that pricing policy hold would be that inventories resulting from

present sales at price $\frac{\gamma}{\gamma-1}E_t[c_{t+1}]$ and making $M_t = 0$ are smaller than the desired volume of sales in state a, or:

$$\frac{M_{t-1}R_t}{c_t} + \frac{z_t}{c_t}\left[\left(\frac{\gamma}{\gamma-1}E_t[c_{t+1}]\right)^{1-\gamma} - c_t\left(\frac{\gamma}{\gamma-1}E_t[c_{t+1}]\right)^{-\gamma}\right].$$

6. Similarly, the return on M_t can be expressed as $E_t[R_{t+1}(1+\mu_{t+1})]$.

7. It can be noted that the graphs show an increase in expected profits as the cost variability gets higher. This is simply due to the fact that, because the exercise keeps constant by assumption the expected value of unit costs, in high-variability scenarios the firm faces very favorable conditions in the low-cost state b, which more than compensate for the reduced levels of activity and profits in the high-cost state a.

8. Figure 2.3 shows an increase in profits in state a as the cost in that state increases. The calculation refers to realized benefits given by sales minus costs incurred in that state; the costs associated with the production of goods carried as inventories and sold in $t + 1$ are imputed in period t. The higher profits thus reflect cost savings in $t + 1$ against higher costs in t.

9. The question of whether the firm would want to remain open in the high-cost state under the constraint will be addressed below, in the case where the level of activity of the firm can go to zero by paying a finite cost.

10. In this setting, we will assume that the return on financial assets R_{t+1} is nonstochastic. If the minimum sales constraint must be satisfied unconditionally, randomness in that return would only strengthen the incentive to carry inventories.

11. It will be recalled that we are maintaining the assumption that $R_{t+1} > \frac{E_t c_{t+1}}{c_t}$, so that the expected return on financial assets in terms of inputs is positive. Under the constraint on the minimum level of activity, the firm, although risk-neutral, has to concern itself specifically with meeting the condition in state a.

12. This is true in the margin, when the firm is already holding positive inventories. However, the nature of the problem is that the firm would prefer to sell all of its production in t, if it were not for future liquidity constraints. Therefore, it only chooses to hold a positive level of inventories when it is unable to finance the production of y^c with the proceeds from selling at price $\frac{\gamma}{\gamma-1}c_t$ at t.

REFERENCES

Aguirregabiria, V. 1999. "The dynamics of markups and inventories in retailing firms." *Review of Economic Studies* 66(2): 275–308.

Blinder, A. S. 1986. "Can the production smoothing model of inventory behavior be saved?" *The Quarterly Journal of Economics* 101(3): 431–453.

Dabús, C. 2000. "Inflationary regimes and relative price variability: evidence from Argentina." *Journal of Development Economics* 62(2): 535–547.

Frenkel, R. 1979. "Decisiones de precio en alta inflación." *Desarrollo Económico* 19(75): 291–330.

Heymann, D. and Leijonhufvud, A. 1995. *High inflation.* Oxford, UK: Oxford University Press.

Kashyap, A. K., Lamont, O. A., and Stein, J. C. 1994. "Credit conditions and the cyclical behavior of inventories." *The Quarterly Journal of Economics* 109(3): 565–592.

Kryvstov, O. and Midrigan, V. 2013. "Inventories, markups and real rigidities in menu cost models." *Review of Economic Studies* 80(1): 249–276.

Sheshinski, E. and Weiss, Y. 1977. "Inflation and costs of price adjustment." *Review of Economic Studies* 44(2): 287–303.

Sheshinski, E. and Weiss, Y. 1983. "Optimum pricing policy under stochastic inflation." *Review of Economic Studies* 50(3): 513–529.

Tommasi, M. 1994. "The consequences of price instability on search markets: toward understanding the effects of inflation." *American Economic Review* 84(5): 1385–1396.

Ungar, M. and Zilberfarb, B. Z. 1993. "Inflation and its unpredictability—theory and empirical evidence." *Journal of Money, Credit and Banking* 25(4): 709–720.

CHAPTER 3

———

Financial Fragility, Price Indexes, and Investment Financing

Julio Dreizzen

At the beginning of the 1980s, I had the opportunity to attend the seminars that Roberto Frenkel taught at the Centro de Estudios de Estado y Sociedad. In one of these seminars, he discussed "A Theory of Financial Fragility," an article by Hyman Minsky that was published in 1977. This article, and the subsequent exploration of the rest of Minsky's work, grabbed me because of its capacity to explain with crystalline clarity the key role played by the balance sheets of economic agents in the business cycle. Some time later, I incorporated Minsky's theoretical framework into the singularities of the Argentine economy in my master's thesis at the Pontifícia Universidade Católica do Rio de Janeiro, where I discussed and formalized Minsky's financial fragility in the context of an inflationary economy with macroeconomic instability (Dreizzen 1985).

In this chapter, I use Minsky's model to demonstrate that differences between actual inflation and the one published by the institution in charge of official statistics prevent financing mechanisms that could extend the terms of payment and reduce uncertainty and the cost of capital. Therefore, these discrepancies conspire against the growth of both productive investment and home construction. This experiment is rooted in the Argentine experience since 2007, when official inflation figures began to run systematically lower than those calculated by the private sector.

Minsky's central ideas about the cycle and financial crises have been reappraised in different areas, to the point of spreading the concept of a "Minsky moment" to the international economy (Frenkel and Rapetti 2009).

Recently, Minsky's book *Stabilizing an Unstable Economy* (2008) was reedited. In the first edition (1986), he summarized his main theoretical developments. The subprime mortgage crisis in the United States and the one faced now in Europe have simultaneously unraveled a series of questions that can be analyzed from Minsky's perspective:

- Uncertainty regarding cash flows to be generated by the debtors, and hence, their payment capacity
- Weaknesses of the models and the implied assumptions for the valuation of assets that support debts
- Mistakes committed by both rating agencies and the market at the moment of assessing risks

This chapter builds a model to focus on the first issue, i.e., the uncertainty in regard to the generation of funds on the part of debtors and their capacity to face their financial obligations. This approach is particularly useful as a framework for discussing the mechanisms for the financing of productive investment, as well as home construction.

Macroeconomic instability and high inflation restrain the development of a long-term credit market that would promote investment in infrastructure and access to housing of the middle- and low-income sectors of the population and reduce the interest rate and refinancing risks. I will demonstrate that the current distortions in the official price index in Argentina generate additional difficulties in developing this market.

This chapter focuses on issues of long-term financing under the analytical framework of Minsky's model and does not intend to deal with the impact that the distortions in the official price index generate on private sector expectations, public and social policies, public finances, etc.

The risks of borrowing in foreign currency became apparent with the devaluation of 2002 in Argentina, when there was a strong imbalance between the cash flows and debt burden for both the public and private sectors. That is why I believe that foreign credit is not appropriate for most economic units and that the existence of a long-term credit market in local currency is a must. Nonetheless, countries with chronic and high inflation present serious difficulties for the emergence of this market. The absence of a "currency" that serves as a unit of account is one of the key reasons for this question. This is true for bank loans, as well as for capital markets.

Several countries in the region, such as Chile, Brazil, Mexico, and Uruguay, have adopted solutions that use units of account adjusted by either general or specific price indexes.

Loans adjusted by the general price index do not reflect the evolution of the debtor's payment capacity: in Dreizzen (1985) I proposed mechanisms of indexation that are based on the evolution of the relative price linked to each debtor to minimize this risk. To avoid mismatching assets and liabilities, each financial entity has to raise funding adjusted by the general price index and lend it to each company adjusted by the price index of its sector. The proportion lent with the price index of each sector should be the same as the weight of such sector in the general price index.

This proposal could also be made more flexible if subsets of entities, or the system as a whole, trade loans already lent in a manner to balance the portfolios, observing that—although at the moment of providing the financing this does not occur—the restriction of proportionality of the loan portfolio with the basket of each sector in the general price index is fulfilled at the level of each entity after the loan transfers in the secondary market. Systems with indexation based on sector prices have been implemented in various countries, including Argentina, France, and Israel (see Giersh et al. 1974; Gersfelt 1976; Brenner and Patinkin 1977; Organización Techint 1983).

Regarding capital markets, it would be possible to issue bonds adjusted by the general price index for the investor and the placement of funds in the same proportion of each sector weight in the general price index. There have also been experiences of issuance of indexed instruments based on the price of commodities (oil, agriculture), exchange rates, interest rates, etc., for investors that use them either as instruments of hedging or to take speculative long or short positions.

In the case of loans for housing that are lent to the wage earner, the question becomes more complex. The debtor will prefer to ensure a high correlation between the debt services and the level of earned income. Obviously, the funds providers (banks or investors in the capital market in the case of securitized mortgages) will also seek to implement a mechanism that minimizes the risk of mismatches and, therefore, the rate of defaults. Most fund providers (except for some pension funds that adjust their future payment obligations by the wage evolution) will not be interested in this kind of wage indexation for their assets.

Henceforth, in the case of housing, a system can be used in which the balance of the debt is adjusted by the general inflation index, whereas the debt service is adjusted by the wage index. In this case, the term of amortization (and the number of installments) becomes indefinite; thus, it requires that some agent in the system (most likely a governmental agency) covers possible negative liquidity gaps. This system could also be extended to corporate credit, with the advantage that it does not require that the weights of the different sectors in the total amount of credit have the same proportion as in the general price index. Argentina's largest state-owned bank and Corporacion Andina de Fomento provided project finance in this way: the installment was a fixed proportion of the annual cash flow and therefore the maturity became unknown. The same happens when the source of repayment of a loan depends on the cash flow generated by the sale of an asset.

The analysis that I will develop can be applied both to private and state-owned banks. The latter, either directly or through state funds channeled through private banks, provides loans to compensate for market failures that arise from information asymmetries and high costs to obtain it, or to finance projects with positive externalities that produce socially profitable results but are not attractive from the private point of view (Levy Yeyati et al. 2007). In this case, the adoption of the most appropriate types of loans that I discuss in this chapter diminishes fiscal costs for a given level of state promotion. In Latin America, the most relevant case is the one of the Brazilian Development Bank, which lends directly to companies and on-lends through commercial banks.

Under the theoretical framework proposed by Minsky, I will explain in the rest of this chapter the relevance of the availability of inflation indexes that reflect the actual price variation as a necessary condition before these long-term financing mechanisms can be implemented.

MINSKY AND THE FINANCING STRUCTURES

Minsky proposes a taxonomy of financing structures divided into three categories: hedge, speculative, and Ponzi. These three types of financing are defined by the ratio between the future payment obligations of debt and the expected cash flows.

The first financial structure, hedge, arises when for all the relevant future periods the expected cash flows are enough to pay the debt services—both principal and interest. This would be the case in a profitable firm that finances its investments with long-term loans or bonds. In addition, a country with a balance of payments strong enough to pay the services of principal and interests of its external debt will have a hedge financing structure.

In the second type of financing, speculative, the expected cash flows for some shorter-term periods are not sufficient for the payment of principal, although they are sufficient for the payment of interests. What is critical in this financing structure is that it forces the debtor to refinance maturities, irrespective of the financial conditions at the moment of such debt refinancing. Nevertheless, it is estimated that in the long term the cash flows will be enough to cover the payment of both principal and interest. The speculative financing structure is just the short-term financing of long positions. This is one of the characteristics of the banking system that has longer maturities in its assets than in its liabilities.

Finally, in the third structure, Ponzi, the flows are not sufficient for the payment of either principal or interest. Hence, the debt level grows in each period with the capitalization of refinanced interests. Should this situation be prolonged, the debtor will face not only a problem of liquidity but also of solvency.

As reported by Kindleberger (1978), Charles Ponzi promised in 1929 to pay a 50% interest with funds from new 45-day deposits. The scheme collapsed as soon as it was first suspected that the money would not be repaid. More recently, the international press called the Madoff affair a new case of Ponzi financing.

Irrespective of the financing structures (hedge, speculative, or Ponzi), we should notice that the units are negatively affected if the cash flows are finally lower than the expected ones. Nevertheless, the speculative and Ponzi units (but not the hedge) are also vulnerable to the behavior of the financial markets, and their continuity can be endangered if faced with a financial disruption. As long as the conditions of access to the credit markets in which they refinance their maturities deteriorate, these units can face difficulties for their operations even in positive circumstances.

The mix of hedge, speculative, and Ponzi financing structures in an economy is a determining factor of its financial fragility. Minsky asserts that in the period of the cycle when the economy is growing and the asset prices rise, there is a tendency to overestimate the future. When the cycle reverses, there is a rapid and deep change in expectations that generates a sudden "deleverage." This process, which is characterized by its endogenous component, has taken place in the recent US real estate crisis. The excessively optimistic expectations gave rise to speculative and Ponzi financing positions that were followed by a violent reversion of these expectations, a fall in the values of assets that secured debts, a sudden and disordered deleverage of the private sector, and the obvious decline of investment and GDP.

Frenkel and Rapetti (2009) differentiated Minsky's endogenous cycles in the developed economies from the exogenous components of the cycle in the developing economies, where it is triggered by financial and external policies that are usually unsustainable in the long run.

A gloomier pessimism in the expectations about the economic situation or in the financial markets can lead a hedge financing unit to become speculative or a speculative unit to become Ponzi. This is the case for many mortgage debtors in the United States and Europe, which today are considered Ponzi but were hedge at the moment the financing was approved. Another illustrative example is the case of several European economies that in a very short period of time have dramatically increased their risk according to the market perception.

Ponzi financing does not necessarily imply a bad economic situation over the long term but an extreme sensitivity in advance of changes in the conditions of the financial market, in light of which the debtor has an inelastic demand for credit to refinance his debts.

FINANCING STRUCTURES AND FINANCIAL FRAGILITY

As I have explained previously, Minsky proposed three financing structures. I will formalize these structures based on what I presented in Dreizzen (1985, 2010). Minsky's taxonomy is based on the relationship between the debt services—amortization (a) and interests (i)—and the cash flows (g). The coefficient of financial fragility (F) is defined as $F = (a + i)/g$.

The financing will be hedge if the expected F, $E(F)$ is ≤ 1, speculative if $E(F)$ is > 1 and $E(g)$ is $\geq i$, and Ponzi if $E(F)$ is > 1 and $E(g)$ is $< i$, in all future periods relevant for the analysis. Notice that in the formula of financial fragility, both F and g are stochastic variables with uncertain values, but that is not the case of the services of amortization (a) and interests (i).

Debtors under these three financing categories are affected by changes in sales volumes as well as in gross margins on sales (in $), but the focus of our analysis will be on the variations of prices to demonstrate that an official price index, with values that differ substantially from actual inflation, creates additional difficulties for the emergence of a long-term credit market in local currency and therefore increases financial fragility.

To simplify the analysis, I will assume that there is only one period of time in the future and that the only variable that determines the variation of the fund generation (g) from one period to the next is the rate of variation of the general level of prices (dp), regardless of variations of both quantities and relative prices (sales price and unit costs change at the same rate)—matters that have already been analyzed in Dreizzen (1985, 2010). Therefore, $F = D^\circ (1 + i)/g^\circ (1 + dp)$, where D° is the debt at the end of period 0 and g° is the generation of funds in the same period.

A reduction in the uncertainty about the coefficient of fragility F means reducing the probability that the situation of the debtor "ex-post" differs from the ex-ante expectations. This issue is related to the discussion regarding the uncertainty about the generation of funds and the capacity of payment of the debtor units in the economy as outlined in the first section above. To illustrate the issue in real-world terms, the lower the financial fragility, the lower the variance of the ratio F and hence the lower the probability of events as those that occurred recently in many developed countries, where this ex-post indicator radically differed from its ex-ante values both for the public and private sectors. To focus on the problems created in the credit market by the absence of a credible price index, note that my approach differs from Minsky's: I incorporate as a measure of financial fragility the *uncertainty* regarding the coefficient F, while Minsky only considers its expected value.

Given the level of $E(F)$, I will measure this uncertainty by the variance of F (Var F). I will evaluate Var F for fixed-rate loans and loans indexed by the official price index (o).

For a given expected level of F, $E(F)$, a given loan system of credits with a lower Var F will be more convenient. Depending on the scope of analysis, the lower the variance of F, the lower the uncertainty about the financial fragility of an economic unit or of the system as a whole.

WHICH LOAN SYSTEM MINIMIZES FINANCIAL FRAGILITY?

For a fixed interest rate (i) loan, under the assumptions of the previous section,

$$F(i) = D^\circ (1 + i)/g^\circ (1 + dp).$$

To simplify the algebra, I will work with linear approximations, assuming small rates of variation:

$$F(i) = (D^\circ/g^\circ) (1 + i - dp)$$

$$\text{Var } F(i) = k \text{ Var } dp, \tag{3.1}$$

where $k = (D^\circ/g^\circ)^2$. For a loan in local currency indexed by the official inflation rate (do) and with a real interest rate r,

$$F(do) = (D^\circ/g^\circ) (1 + do + r - dp)$$

$$\text{Var } F(do) = k [\text{Var } dp + \text{Var } do - 2 \text{ Cov } (dp,do)]. \tag{3.2}$$

The variance of F (i.e., financial fragility) will be smaller the smaller the variances of the actual and official inflation, and the greater the covariance between them.

If the inflation index is properly measured, dp and do are equal. Therefore, in a loan adjusted by the official inflation rate, Var F becomes null, and financial fragility is minimized:

$$F(do) = (D^\circ/g^\circ) \, (1 + r)$$

$$\text{Var } F(do) = 0.$$

The distortion in the measurement of the official price index introduces additional uncertainty regarding the financial robustness of the economic units that are indebted with loans adjusted by that index and constitutes an additional factor that hinders the development of a local currency long-term credit market.

Let us now compare the credit adjusted by the official index with the one that has a fixed interest rate. From equations 3.1 and 3.2, we conclude that credits indexed by the variation of the official price index (do) will be convenient when there is a high covariance between the actual and official inflations (i.e., the price index is well measured) and the volatility of the official inflation is small:

$$\text{Var } F(do) < \text{Var } F(i) \quad <=> \quad \text{Cov } (dp,do) > \tfrac{1}{2} \text{Var } do.$$

Conversely, the one at a fixed interest rate will be more convenient as long as there is a low covariance between the actual inflation and the official one and the volatility of the official inflation is high.

Let me reiterate that I am not analyzing the level $E(F)$ but the uncertainty Var (F) of the financial fragility. Still, it is important to clarify that as far as there is a consistent deviation between the official price index and the actual change in prices, the real interest rate r will also reflect that distortion. For instance, if the official rate always underestimates inflation, the demand and supply for indexed credit will increase the real interest rate r. But this means that the borrower will accelerate the repayment of the loan, as the higher real interest rate r (used in a loan adjusted by official inflation) will have two components: the real interest rate that reflects actual inflation and the compensation for the expected difference between actual and official inflation that represents an amortization of debt in real terms. The debt is indexed by the underestimated official index, and to compensate for that underestimation there is an additional payment of interest into r by the borrower. This underestimation does not constitute an advantage for the borrower, as the company will face a higher real interest rate r, which will include both a portion of the actual real interest rate to compensate for inflation and a portion of debt amortization in real terms. All of these factors will undermine the demand for credit, discourage investment, and constitute additional difficulties for developing a long-term credit market in an inflationary economy.

CONCLUSIONS

Economies with macroeconomic instability and high inflation present tough challenges for developing a long-term credit market in local currency. In this chapter, by formalizing some of the concepts proposed by Hyman Minsky, I have demonstrated that distortions in the measurement of the official price index introduce additional difficulties for the development of that long-term credit market; increase uncertainty, capital costs, and financial fragility; and therefore discourage investment in capital goods by corporations, housing construction, and economic growth.

The removal of these distortions in the official price index constitutes a necessary (but not sufficient) condition for developing a local currency long-term credit market. The absence of a credible official price index hinders the possibility of creating a "currency" that reduces uncertainty about the debtor's payment capacity. Therefore, it generates "short-termism" in the credit market and increases capital costs.

The objective of this chapter has been to focus on the distortions in the official price index and its impact on the credit market. I have not discussed the problem of the utilization of a general index to adjust loans when strong variations of relative prices take place. In Dreizzen (1985), I showed with a model similar to the one of this chapter why financial indexation systems based on general price indexes are difficult to implement in contexts of erratic variations of inflation and strong fluctuations in relative prices. In those situations, there is a resistance of the economic units to index their debts. To solve this problem, I have proposed the use of sector price indexes for the adjustment of loans to reduce uncertainty about the debtor's payment capacity. I have also made a proposal to avoid transferring the uncertainty regarding relative prices to the lender or to the bond investors in the credit or capital markets. For this system to work the behavior of these sector prices have to be reflected appropriately in the statistics that the official agency publishes. Should this not be the case, we will face the same difficulties for the construction of a long-term credit market as those discussed in this chapter.

REFERENCES

Brenner, R. and Patinkin, D. 1977. "Indexation in Israel." In *Inflation theory and anti-inflation policy*, E. Lundberg, ed. London: Palgrave Macmillan: 134–156.

Di Tella, G. 1979. "Price oscillation, oligopolistic behaviour and inflation: the Argentine case." *World Development* 7(11–12): 1043–1052.

Dreizzen, J. 1985. *Fragilidad financiera e inflación*. Buenos Aires: Ediciones CEDES.

Dreizzen, J. 2010. "Financiamento do investimento." In *Novos dilemas da política econômica*, E. Bacha and M. Baumgarten, eds. Rio de Janeiro: LTC: 201–224.

Frenkel, R. and Rapetti, M. 2009. "A developing country view of the current global crisis: what should not be forgotten and what should be done." *Cambridge Journal of Economics* 33(4): 685–702.

Gersfelt, T. 1976 "Financial indexation." In *Indexation of monetary assets and obligations—arguments for and against*, International Savings Bank Institute, ed. Geneva: ISBI.

Giersh, H. 1974. *Essays on inflation and indexation*. Washington, DC: American Enterprise Institute for Public Policy Research.

Kindleberger, C. P. 1978. *Manias, panics and crashes: a history of financial crises*. London: Palgrave Macmillan.

Levy Yeyati, E., Micco, A., and Panizza, U. 2007. "A reappraisal of state-owned banks." *Economia* 7(2): 209–247.

Magnus, G. 2008. "Managing Minsky." UBS Investment Research, Report No. 146.

Minsky, H. P. 1977. "A theory of systemic fragility." In *Financial crises: institutions and markets in a fragile environment*, edited by E. J. Altman and A. W. Sametz, 138–152. New York, NY: Wiley.

Minsky, H. P. 2008. *Stabilizing an unstable economy*. New Haven, CT: Yale University Press.

Organización Techint. 1983. "La política financiera en el espejo de la teoría." *Boletín Informativo* 229: 65–81.

CHAPTER 4

Uncertainty in Structural and Institutional Parameters and the Cost of Policy Mistakes

A COMPUTABLE GENERAL EQUILIBRIUM EVALUATION

Omar Chisari, Gustavo Ferro, and Juan Pablo Vila Martínez

In a small open economy, structural and institutional parameters are important in the design of policy interventions in uncertain environments. Reduced endowments and poverty do not help to compensate negative shocks and, in such a case, policy mistakes could yield not only undesired effects but also deleterious and lasting ones as well.[1] Relative price signals tend to be blurred, and policy mistakes that result from a bad diagnosis and/or wrong therapies could be particularly costly for a developing economy. Ill-designed policy decisions could trigger (or accelerate) capital flight, negatively affecting output and employment in the short run and jeopardizing physical capital accumulation and economic growth in the long run. These issues have been a permanent focus of Roberto Frenkel's work.

Although we place the analysis in a Walrasian general equilibrium setting, we depart from the traditional presentation and assume unemployment. We also assume that some proportion of capital is internationally mobile; i.e., it can be reallocated to the rest of the world at no cost. In contexts of unemployment and fiscal/external imbalances—chronic problems in Latin American economies—a general equilibrium approach cannot be used without specifying how prices are determined when market forces fail to automatically correct the disequilibria. Preserving the basic general equilibrium framework as a reference for the economy, we ensure the consistency of the model by introducing the role of structural and institutional information to widen the scope of the analysis.

Although there is a tendency to disregard their relevance by academics and policy makers, the approach we follow in this chapter is not new. Several economists have highlighted the role of structural and institutional parameters in uncertain environments. Many significant decisions are often made because of uncertainty about how wages will be modified as a consequence of changes in prices and/or how capital will be allocated between domestic and foreign assets after changes in their expected return.[2] Moreover, uncertainty or incomplete knowledge that leads to erroneous conjectures is important in economies with poor-quality data. We follow Frenkel's concerns about structural and institutional parameters and evaluate their role by conducting several experiments and analyzing how sensitive the results are to changes in the value of these parameters.

Our approach assumes that a priori policy makers are benevolent but capable of making mistakes in their diagnoses and in their appraisal of the structural and institutional parameters. We will assume that they are not well informed or uncertain about the true value of parameters. Given their limited knowledge about the effects of their policies or because they find that omniscience is expensive, policy makers might discard or disregard certain courses of action and promote others without a proper ex-ante evaluation. Ill-informed policy makers are more prone to misjudgments and therefore make bad decisions. Several episodes seem to confirm this belief. Damill and Frenkel (2010), for example, explain capital flight events in Argentina as a combined result of poor macroeconomic fundamentals and policy mistakes. We do not necessarily assume rational expectations that would imply an end to the business cycle learning process (Heymann 2008).

For evaluation purposes, we simulate some tax policy shocks using a computable general equilibrium (CGE) model with unemployment calibrated with 2006 data from Argentina. We carry out experiments assuming different values of two structural parameters: the degree of international capital mobility and the rules of wage indexation.

One of our initial hypotheses is that the greater the degree of international capital mobility and the more complete indexation in the formal labor market wages are, the greater the damage bad policies will produce. In a partial equilibrium context, all taxes impose distortions that grow with the square of tax rates. The factual impossibility of applying lump-sum taxes implies the need for suboptimal ones to raise revenue. This, in turn, is applied to provide public goods, redistribute income (motivated by some social goal), and stabilize the business cycle. The effects of taxation go beyond a partial equilibrium analysis. Because of its general equilibrium consequences, tax policy is also conditioned by structural (and institutional) parameters.

In this chapter, we follow a broad definition of capital flight: it encompasses both hoarding foreign currency cash and holding foreign financial instruments. International capital mobility has a *de jure* aspect (i.e., whether it is legal or not to carry out transactions with nonresidents and holding foreign assets and debts), as well as a *de facto* aspect (i.e., whether agents actually find ways to funnel their resources into foreign assets). We are interested in the *de facto* aspect. By definition, specific capital in the economy is immobile and a sunk cost (its recoverable value is lower than its opportunity cost). In turn, financial capital is liquid and mobile, with a higher or lower cost in each context depending on the *de jure* aspect. We only consider the positive dimension of the analysis. Under no circumstances can the results of the exercises carried out in this chapter be understood as policy prescriptions, i.e., suggestions for normative prescriptions. However, we hope to make the case that simulation models such as the ones carried out in this chapter can help policy decisions by complementing perspectives or conjectural results, especially when less evident or intuitive effects are taken into account (mostly general equilibrium effects).

Following this introduction is a summary of the literature linked to the problem under study. The third section, "The Model and the Institutional Setting," provides the institutional setting of the discussion, whereas the fourth section refers to the CGE model we use. The section on computational simulations discusses the simulations, i.e., the computational experiments. We then present the results of those experiments. "Decisions with Unknown Probabilities" discusses the choice of taxes that a policy maker will make under different behavior criteria in the face of uncertainty or decision making conducted in complete ignorance in the manner of Luce and Raiffa (1957). The chapter ends with a summary of the main conclusions.

LITERATURE

Frenkel's (1986) recommendation to take into account structural and institutional parameters for economic analysis was a highly significant contribution. First, he pointed out a dichotomy in the theoretical literature of inflation. On the one hand, some views treat real wages as the rest of the economy's relative prices based on a Walrasian mechanism of general equilibrium conditions. Consequently, they neither separate the labor market from commodity markets nor require explicit hypotheses on the nominal wage dynamics. On the other hand, some approaches state that the interaction of prices and nominal wages determines real wages. A common feature of the Latin American experience is the weight institutional factors have in determining private sector nominal wages. The literature shows a wide scope of conceptions among the explicit hypotheses on nominal wages. At one end, wages only depend on the condition of the labor market (supply and demand). Alternative theories—institutional, sociological, structural, or post-Keynesian—emphasize different aspects of the transactions in the labor market. These views assume that unemployment is not purely cyclical. The ways wages are determined are very specific in time and space. Culture, habit, conventions, and ethics fit one category of institutional wage setting. The type and degree of union organization and rules and tacit assumptions of the bargaining process make up a second set of aspects. A third group can include the nature of the political regime and the state policy orientation. These institutional and structural factors are substantially less stable in developing countries.

Frenkel and Ros (2006) present a model of the rate of unemployment determinants, the channels through which the real exchange rate influences unemployment performance, as well as empirical results in Latin American countries. They identify three channels through which the real exchange rate influences employment performance: first through its effects on output level in the short run (i.e., the macroeconomic channel); second through its effect on the technological choices in firms and sectors (i.e., the labor intensity channel); and third through its influence on economic growth and the pace of job creation (i.e., the development channel). Formal sector unemployment is affected by capital accumulation, which generates increases in the productivity of the economy's formal sector and the migration of informal workers to the formal sector because of wage differences. They highlight that most of the development literature attributes the generation of externalities that favor modernization and growth in other sectors of the economy to the expansion of the tradable sector. A depreciated real exchange rate is relatively easy to implement and is a way to subsidize all tradable sectors without incurring administrative costs and/or risking rent-seeking behavior and corruption.

Because our simulations basically test how the economy responds to changes in taxation, we examine taxation and optimal taxation in conditions of unemployment. We believe that exploring the case of taxation is not only interesting for its macroeconomic impact but also because an ad valorem tax charged on total costs is equivalent to a markup, the only difference being that the revenue is transferred to the government instead of being cashed by the owners of the firms. Our simulations, which assume markup increases in manufacturing and services, confirm this result.

One of the first papers to analyze the subject of taxation and unemployment was Marchand et al. (1989), who emphasized how relevant the presence of unemployment is to optimal tax determination. They considered modifying the Ramsey rule and found that the relative tax structure has to be modified because unemployment affects welfare. Hence, taxes charged on inelastic goods have to be lower than the Ramsey rule recommendation if the affected sectors create employment. They did not consider the case of real wage determination or the scenario of international capital mobility; instead, their model stated that capital is specific and immobile, even among sectors of the economy.

Azariadis and Pissarides (2004) studied the response of domestic unemployment rates to shocks in total factor productivity for economies with different capital mobility. Higher capital mobility affects the dynamics of unemployment. In an environment with capital mobility, unemployment responds faster and with more amplitude to total factor productivity shocks. If an economy is hit by such a negative shock, it reduces labor demand, but its capital stock cushions the fall in demand. If capital can leave the country in the pursuit of higher rates of return abroad, the cushion is not as effective, but unemployment increases more. Workers' incomes and jobs become relatively less secure than capital returns. In the absence of capital mobility, the key influence on employment is capital accumulation financed with local savings. In the absence of a perfect correlation in the shocks within countries, the variance of employment with capital mobility is always higher than the variance with immobile capital. The maximum variance is achieved when the shocks are perfectly and negatively correlated. They also show that the average unemployment rate does not necessarily increase with higher capital mobility. Instead, its variance rises.

Boehringer et al. (2004) presented an applied general equilibrium modeling approach to analyze the unemployment effects of labor tax modifications in an economy where wages are determined through firm–union bargaining at the sectorial level. The general equilibrium approach provides a comprehensive framework for studying public interventions. The simultaneous explanations of income generation and spending allow us to address both efficiency and distributional effects of policy shifts. To track the causal chain from policy intervention in labor markets, it is necessary to explicitly model the wage-setting process.

The inclusion of capital mobility in the analysis has also been discussed in the literature. Fullerton and Lyon (1986) suggested taking capital mobility into account when evaluating tax policy choices to illustrate and investigate the more general problem of uncertain parameter values. Koskela and Schöb (2000) stated that, according to conventional wisdom, internationally mobile capital should not be taxed or should be taxed at a lower rate than labor when the latter is immobile. In the presence of unemployment, the conventional wisdom is challenged. Under involuntary unemployment, the supply of labor is locally infinitely elastic. According to the Ramsey rule, labor should not be taxed at a higher rate than other factors with similar elasticity.

As Frankel (1992) pointed out, there are at least four distinct definitions of perfect capital mobility, listed here in ascending order of specificity. The first, the Feldstein–Horioka test, concludes that exogenous changes in national savings rates do not affect investment rates; in the second, real interest parity, international capital flows equalize real interest rates across countries; in the third, uncovered interest parity, capital flows equalize expected rates of return on countries' bonds, regardless of exposure to exchange risk; and in the fourth, covered interest parity, capital flows equalize interest rates across countries when contracted in a common currency.[3]

THE MODEL AND INSTITUTIONAL SETTING

In this section, we present a brief discussion of the basic elements of the model in a simplified version by focusing on the role of two parameters (or rules): (1) wage determination—specifically the indexation rule—and (2) the degree of international capital mobility.

The determination of wages can result from several factors. There can be sociological and political drivers ("insiders" and "outsiders" in the labor market), as well as other main determinants such as the influence of unions, imperfect information ("isles model"), or the need to give incentives for efficiency (wages of efficiency). In any case, the way wages vary over time can be studied econometrically.

The degree of capital mobility is related to the ability of the capital holders to limit the fall in their rate of return, even hoarding it or reallocating it to the rest of the world. In a dual vision of the model, it can be said that the capital mobility is the counterpart to the normal rate of profit.

Let us focus on the basic elements of our model by looking at a simplified version of the computable general equilibrium model. Although we have several agents in our CGE model, let us assume that there is only one representative household that maximizes utility.

Equation 4.1 gives the equalization of the rate of substitution with relative prices, corrected by ad valorem taxes, in this case only charged on good 1 (the general model includes several taxes, agents, and goods):

$$U_1/U_2 = (1 + t_1)P_1/P_2. \tag{4.1}$$

Equation 4.2 gives the budget constraint. It is assumed that there is only one kind of labor, L_0 (W is the wage rate) but two kinds of capital—fixed and mobile—between industries. There is one unit of specific capital in each industry, and its prices are indicated with π_i. (This can be alternatively interpreted as total profits of the sector with constant returns to scale.) The endowment of internationally mobile capital, owned by the domestic household, is given by K_0 and its remuneration R^*. In the benchmark scenario, the proportion of fixed capital owned by the domestic household with respect to mobile capital is therefore $2/K_0$ (in fact, this parameter can be unobservable and uncertain):

$$P_1C_1 (1 + t_1) + P_2C_2 = WL_0 + R^*K_0 + 1\,\pi_1 + 1\,\pi_2. \tag{4.2}$$

Equations 4.3 to 4.6 characterize profits in sector 1, the production function, and the first-order conditions that result from profit maximization, respectively. The price received by producers is the net of expenses in intermediate inputs, both domestic (a) and imported (α). Imported goods are used as the numeraire.

$$\pi_1 = (P_1 - P_2 a - \alpha)Q_1 - WL_1 - R^*K_1 \tag{4.3}$$

$$Q_1 = F(L_1, 1, K_1) \tag{4.4}$$

$$(P_1 - aP_2 - \alpha)F_L = W \tag{4.5}$$

$$(P_1 - aP_2 - \alpha)F_K = R^*. \tag{4.6}$$

Equations 4.7 to 4.10 are analogous for sector 2:

$$\pi_2 = (P_2 - P_1 b - \beta)Q_2 - WL_2 - R^*K_2 \tag{4.7}$$

$$Q_2 = G(L_2, 1, K_2) \tag{4.8}$$

$$(P_2 - P_1 b - \beta)G_L = W \tag{4.9}$$

$$(P_2 - P_1 b - \beta)G_K = R^*. \tag{4.10}$$

Equation 4.11 corresponds to the budget condition for the public sector; in this simplified case, it is assumed that all revenue is used to hire labor (the general model includes purchases of goods, transfers to households, investments, and net changes in the financial result):

$$WL_g = t_1 P_1 C_1. \tag{4.11}$$

Equations 4.12 to 4.15 are the equilibrium market conditions. Equation 4.12 includes exports (x), equation (4.13) gives the equilibrium condition in the market for nontradable goods and services, equation 4.14 determines unemployment (un), and equation 4.15 gives the equalization of demand and supply of mobile capital:

$$C_1 + bQ_2 + x = Q_1 \tag{4.12}$$

$$C_2 + aQ_1 = Q_2 \tag{4.13}$$

$$L_1 + L_2 + L_g + un = L_0 \tag{4.14}$$

$$K_1 + K_2 + K_m = K_0. \tag{4.15}$$

Because good 1 is tradable, equation 4.16 equals domestic and foreign prices (this is the case of a small open economy):

$$P_1 = P^*. \tag{4.16}$$

Equation 4.17 corresponds to nominal wages determination as a weighted average of prices of tradable goods, nontradable goods, and imports (it is assumed that the price of imports is 1):

$$W = \gamma_1 P_1 (1 + t_1) + \gamma_2 P_2 + \gamma_3 1. \tag{4.17}$$

Equation 4.18 describes the behavior of imports as only being demanded for industrial uses. In this simplified version, we do not include imports of final goods as we do in the CGE model:

$$\alpha Q_1 + \beta Q_2 = m. \tag{4.18}$$

The eighteen unknown variables are as follows: P_1, C_1, P_2, C_2, W, π_1, π_2, L_1, L_2, un, K_1, K_2, Q_1, Q_2, L_g, m, x, and K_m.

We explore the consequences of determining taxes without knowing the total or partial value of parameters γ_i and the relative participation of mobile capital on total capital. We approximate that proportion by $2/K_0$ (when the initial prices in the benchmark are all equal to one, a hypothesis regularly adopted in computed general equilibrium); this is an uncertain parameter, and its actual value can produce significant differences between the expected impact of policies and its real effect. Moreover, even when the general equilibrium structure of the model is not controversial, the outcome can be dramatically different.

THE COMPUTABLE GENERAL EQUILIBRIUM MODEL

The simulations are based on 2006 data from Argentina. The basic data for the model were organized in a social accounting matrix (SAM). As is customary in applied general equilibrium analysis, the model is based on economic transactions in a particular benchmark year. Benchmark quantities and prices—together with exogenously determined elasticities—are used to calibrate the functional forms. For this study, we used 2006 sectorial information. The initial matrix of intermediate transactions was based on 1997 data; it was updated in Chisari et al. (2009). The income factor distribution was based on the distribution observed in Argentina in 2006 according to household income surveys. The distribution of the consumption basket per type of goods and services is based on aggregates from the household consumption survey of 2005.

Available data of the distribution of government consumption between goods and services for both national and provincial governments are from 2006. Because of a lack of information, we assume that municipal expenditures are distributed in the same proportion as the average for the other two government levels. The model includes twenty-nine production sectors: four for agriculture, one for oil and mining, sixteen for industrial goods, and eight for services.

Regarding the demand side, domestic consumer groups are divided into ten income brackets, the government, one foreign consumer, and one foreign producer. We assume that Argentina is small, which implies that it is a price taker in the international markets. Information on the government accounts was obtained from the Ministry of the Economy (National Office of the Budget). Public sector revenue and expenditures are consolidated for the federal administration, provinces, and municipalities. Considering expenditures, government consumption represents approximately 14 percent of GDP followed by household transfers (10 percent of GDP). Data on national and local taxes are from the Federal Revenue Administration and provincial ministries, respectively.[4]

The SAM also shows the positive result of the trade balance and the current account observed in 2006. The information on the balance of payments was obtained from the Central Bank of Argentina. Aggregate demand and supply in the SAM are consistent with national accounts. The consistency of these data with national accounts and sectorial information was obtained using the cross-entropy method.

A summary of the SAM for the Argentine economy of 2006 is shown in table 4.1. This small-sized SAM has three activity sectors (primary, industrial, and services), two factors (with capital representing an aggregate of land and physical and financial capital), taxes, public and private investment, and the rest of the world (ROW). Columns show the decomposition of budget conditions for agents, whereas rows represent markets.

The input–output matrix is the submatrix of the SAM that represents transactions between activity sectors (activities, activities). Below that block is the matrix of factor demands (factors, activities) followed by the matrix of taxes paid by activity (taxes, activities). The SAM separates taxes paid by exports, intermediate uses, final consumption, and investments. Finally, the matrix of imported purchases is included (ROW, activities). The totals of rows and columns of each sector are the respective gross output values. The factors accounts show how the remuneration of factors is allocated to households (households, factors). The rest of the world owns a fraction of capital.

For the demand side, we summarize the matrix of household expenditures (activities, households), government consumption (activities, government), private and public investments (activities, investments), and the vector of exports (activities, ROW). The matrices (households, households) and (households, government) correspond to transfers between agents. From the supply side, the production function in each sector is a Leontief function between value-added and intermediate inputs: one output unit requires an x percent of an aggregate of productive factors (labor, physical capital, financial capital, and land) and a $1 - x$ percent of intermediate inputs. The intermediate inputs function is a Leontief function of all goods, which is a strict complement in production. Instead, value added is a Cobb–Douglas function of productive factors.

Table 4.1 Aggregated Social Accounting Matrix of Argentina, 2006

		Activity Sectors			Factors		Taxes	Households		Government	Investment		ROW
		S01	S02	S03	L	K		H1	H2		Private	Public	
Activity Sectors	S01	7,819	61,545	18,785				3,627	2,257		1,838	266	30,767
	S02	15,207	115,971	70,928				70,000	52,175		10,127	1,466	110,497
	S03	13,410	63,004	164,495				101,381	124,315	81,248	89,509	12,959	20,771
Factors	L	9,796	32,461	154,518									
	K	59,213	61,477	176,976									
Taxes	IM	55	2,549	105				320	350		1,640		
	VAT	2,775	17,316	18,284									
	Indi	6,332	14,261	22,649									
	IX	3,182	11,529	0									
	IL	1,768	6,865	20,251									
	IK	6,347	7,563	7,126									
	IH							4,098	25,111		3,125		
Households	H1				61,053	43,861			53,443	31,325			
	H2				135,723	245,815				30,649			
Government							183,603						
Investments	Private								136,819				1,328
	Public									14,691			
ROW	S1	1,000	51,830	16,974		7,990		10,253	13,898		31,907	0	
BNI									3,820	25,691			−29,511
Totals		126,904	446,372	671,090	196,775	297,666	183,603	189,681	412,187	183,603	138,147	14,691	133,853

Note: All values are in millions of AR$. S01, agriculture and mining; S02, manufacturing; S03, trade, construction, and services; L, labor; K, capital and land; H01, first five income deciles (poorest); H02, second five income deciles (richest); IM, import tariffs; VAT, value-added tax; Indi, rest of indirect taxes; IX, tax on exports; IL, labor taxes and contributions; IK, taxes on capital; IH, taxes paid by households; ROW, rest of the world.

Private savings, public savings, and foreign savings are totaled to finance investments. The BNI (bonds nominated to individuals) row closes the model and represents the surplus or deficit of every agent; it corresponds to 2006 financial transactions.

The demand side is modeled through ten representative households, a government, and an external sector. Households buy or sell bonds, invest, and consume in constant proportions (Cobb–Douglas) given the remuneration for the factors they own and government transfers they receive. The choice of the optimal proportion of the consumption good is obtained from a nested production function in the utility function through a cost-minimization process. Government is represented as an agent that participates in markets for investments, consumes, and makes transfers to households and has a Cobb–Douglas utility function; its main source of income is tax collection (although it also makes financial transactions through the bonds account). The external sector buys domestic exports and sells imports in addition to making transactions of bonds and collecting dividends from investments.

The rest of the goods are complementary, and the elasticity of substitution among them is zero. As mentioned previously, the version of the model presented here is recursive dynamic. Investments for year t are added to mobile capital at time $t + 1$ and are allocated among sectors until their rewards are equalized.

Our CGE model has all the basic properties of the Walrasian perspective, and it is numerically solved using GAMS/MPSGE.[5] Prices for every period are computed to clear all markets simultaneously. Although we will discuss only the results for the first period, the model used is a recursive dynamic model that simulates growth for the economy based partially on the CGE for Argentina presented in Chisari et al. (2009). It is not a model of optimal growth; agents make savings decisions in period t using only information for the same period; savings are then converted in the following period $t + 1$ into additional capital. This new capital is not specific by sector but malleable, and it is fully mobile among sectors of production. Therefore, it is allocated at the same time as prices are being determined by the model; the final allocation of "brand new" capital responds endogenously to the relative profit opportunities and is reallocated until the reward for new capital is the same across all industries. Henceforth, the final industrial scale depends on market incentives determined by the model itself.

THE COMPUTATIONAL EXPERIMENTS

We propose the following computational experiments: four different tax policies, combined with two different rules of wage determination, and three different levels of international capital mobility. The latter experiment was developed to show the concavity of the curve, which relates the GDP variation to the degree of capital mobility. That means that the costs of policies become steeper when the capital is more mobile. For the sake of simplicity, we will report the figures of only two extreme results of capital mobility, which we call "high K" and "low k." Table 4.2 lists the sixteen reported cases.

The first scenario simulates a 20 percent increase in export taxes charged to each sector. This is equivalent to an expected increase in the government's revenue of 0.39 percent of GDP. In Argentina, export taxes were established in the past and generally followed important devaluations to compensate the local consumers of export goods and to limit inflationary pressures. This propensity to use export taxes resulted from the peculiar economic structure of the economy: in the

Table 4.2 Cases Under Analysis and Their Variants

1) Exports	9) Exports	2) Exports	10) Exports
W = CPI	W = CPI	W = 1	W = 1
High K	Zero k	High K	Zero k
3) VAT	11) VAT	4) VAT	12) VAT
W = CPI	W = CPI	W = 1	W = 1
High K	Low k	High K	Low k
5) Imports	13) Imports	6) Imports	14) Imports
W = CPI	W = CPI	W = 1	W = 1
High K	Low k	High K	Low k
7) Labor	15) Labor	8) Labor	16) Labor
W = CPI	W = 1	W = CPI	W = 1
High K	Low k	High K	Low k

Note: Each tax increase yields a revenue rise equal to a 20 percent increase in export taxes of all sectors. Wage indexation rules: W = CPI or W = 1. Degree of capital mobility: high = K, zero = k. CPI, consumer price index; VAT, value-added tax.

past, exports were almost exclusively based on agricultural commodities that at the same time were wage goods. We consider the following alternative policies: a value-added tax (VAT) increase, an import tariffs increase, and a payroll tax increase. In all cases, we assume an "equal-yield replacement." However, that assumption refers to revenue in nominal terms, estimated with respect to the initial prices and public income; the net result in real terms may be different and creates substantial differences between the actual one (which the general equilibrium model computes). The government is endowed with a Cobb–Douglas utility function, and we compute its welfare level as for any other household using the equivalent variation.

For all of the following simulations, we have assumed that the elasticity of substitution is one for utility functions of households and for production functions. It is only a benchmark case because the model can easily be simulated for different substitution elasticities.

The tax increases are combined with two different rules for the adjustment of wages. The first is a complete indexation to the consumer price index (CPI). The rule is compatible with Keynesian unemployment at the departure point. The second rule is the nominal rigidity of wages. When prices rise, real wages decrease, and labor employment increases. Nominal or real rigidity of wages is used here to include unemployment in the economy.

The degree of capital mobility is approximated by a special parameter that takes three different levels: 0 percent (low k), 40 percent (presented in the figures in this chapter but not in the tables), and 73 percent (high K). We numbered the cases starting with eight cases of high capital mobility (1 to 8), starting from $W = $ CPI and then proceeding with the $W = 1$ rule.[6] Cases 9 to 16 are the low capital mobility cases. Table 4.2 presents the cases in rows ordered by tax shift.

RESULTS OF SIMULATIONS

The dynamic model was calibrated for the total GDP of the economy growing at 4 percent for 2006. It excluded exogenous shocks identified for the economy in the same year. The simulations assume that the labor force is stagnant, a neutral assumption that takes into account that what matters are the comparative dynamics of the basic scenario of growth with respect to the simulated cases.

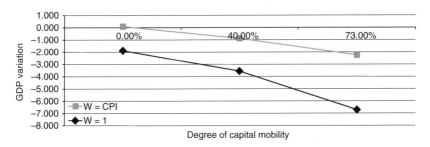

Figure 4.1 Consequences of a 20 percent export tax increase on all sectors under different degrees of capital mobility and rules of wage indexation.

The four figures in this chapter show the consequences of the decisions on GDP growth rates. The reported values are in percentage points that differ from the benchmark value. Figure 4.1 shows the results of a 20 percent export tax increase on all sectors under three different degrees of capital mobility and two different rules of wage indexation. With the constant real wage rule (i.e., the gray line) and zero capital mobility, the GDP grows at the same value as in the benchmark. When export taxes are applied, constant real wages show a reduction in real wages and an increase in real wages when they are nominally fixed (since domestic prices of tradable goods paid by consumers are falling). At the medium capital mobility level, GDP drops 1 percent as a result of the policy; finally, with high mobility, the GDP falls by more than 2 percent. The results are magnified in the nominal constant wage (black line). The losses start at almost 2 percent and reach 3.5 percent at the medium degree of capital mobility and almost 7 percent in the high capital mobility environment. Thus, the worst-case scenario is fixed nominal wages and high capital mobility. The rationale is the following: with perfect indexation, when the GDP falls below the benchmark expected growth rate, prices in the economy decelerate; because wages follow CPI, the decrease in real wages limits both the decline in GDP and the increase in the rate of unemployment. When capital mobility is low or nil, the losses for the economy are more moderate. A wrong appraisal of the true level of the parameters could give policy makers a disappointing loss in GDP if they expect low capital mobility and real wage indexation.

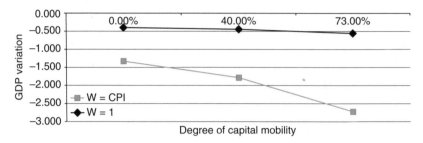

Figure 4.2 Consequences of a value-added tax increase (equal yield to a 20 percent export tax increase on all sectors) under different degrees of capital mobility and rules of wage indexation.

Figure 4.2 shows the results of a VAT increase (with equal yield for a 20 percent export tax increase in all sectors) under three different degrees of capital mobility and two rules of wage indexation. Note that the order of the black and the gray line curves is inverted with respect to the previous case. If $W = 1$ (constant nominal wages), the results are negative but modest. This is because prices are rising while real wages are falling, which stimulates the economy and reduces unemployment. The GDP declines approximately the same in the three scenarios for capital mobility, and the decline is modest (~0.5 percent). If wages are completely indexed to GDP, the concave pattern stays the same, and the drop in the GDP with respect to the benchmark is from 1.3 percent in the low capital mobility case to 2.7 percent in the high mobility case.

The third case is presented in Figure 4.3. In this case, we consider an increase in taxes on imports (equal yield rather than a 20 percent export

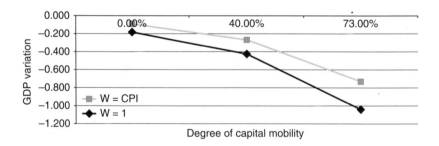

Figure 4.3 Consequences of an import tax increase (equal yield to a 20 percent export tax increase on all sectors) under different degrees of capital mobility and rules of wage indexation.

tax increase for all sectors) under both different degrees of capital mobility and rules of wage indexation. The concave pattern is the same as in the previous cases, and the gray line (real wages case) is again above the black one (nominal wages). Losses in GDP growth under both wage-setting rules are lower than in the previous cases. Again, greater losses occur when the degree of capital mobility is higher. Because most of the imports are used as intermediate inputs for manufacturing, the tax increase is absorbed by specific capital in the form of a reduction in its remuneration (a rent). Because there is also a reduction in the activity level, the general level of prices is reduced, and real wage adjustment is less damaging than constant nominal wages.

The last experiment is related to payroll taxes. Figure 4.4 presents the consequences of a labor tax increase (equal yield rather than a 20 percent export tax increase for all sectors) under the same different degrees of capital mobility and rules of wage indexation as presented previously. In this case, the difference in GDP loss between both wage rules is slight, although the decline is higher in the case of real wages. This can be attributed to the growing prices of services that result from the increase in costs; thus, nominal wages also grow when real wages are constant. However, when nominal wages are constant, the higher prices reduce real wages and in turn help to limit the decline in the level of employment.

Let us now examine the results in greater detail. To eliminate eight cases, we will not discuss the intermediate capital mobility degree and will instead concentrate on the remaining sixteen. Table 4.3 shows the case of export taxes. When capital mobility is higher (cases 1 and 2), the results in the activity level worsen. As mentioned previously, the results are the

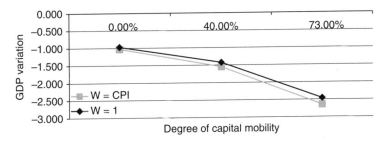

Figure 4.4 Consequences of a labor tax increase (equal yield to a 20 percent export tax increase on all sectors) under different degrees of capital mobility and rules of wage indexation.

worst when nominal wages are constant, i.e., $W = 1$. The trade balance is strongly affected in the high capital mobility cases and is moderately affected under low capital mobility.

The model offers some information about income distribution because it includes ten households corresponding to income deciles. For cases 1 and 2, the results for the lower and middle classes are negative and almost the same. Constant nominal wages reduce the employment and welfare of the poorest households, and it is not a successful instrument to defend their welfare. Instead, capital mobility would seem to be an effective instrument in protecting the welfare of the richest. The redistribution favoring the lower classes occurs in the low mobility cases. Yet, together with a decline in the welfare of the richest, the poorest and middle classes are generally worse off than in the benchmark (the exception is case 9 for the poorest). Lastly, only in one case is the fiscal balance positive (case 9).

In the high mobility scenarios, the agriculture and mining sector is the most affected because exports are concentrated in this sector. With lower capital mobility and $W = 1$, the other sectors performed worse than the primary sectors (because employment is concentrated in the

Table 4.3 20 Percent Increase in Export Taxes Under Two Different Mobility and Wage-Setting Assumptions

	Case 1[a]	Case 9[b]	Case 2[c]	Case 10[d]
GDP	−2.25	0.09	−6.72	−1.88
Fiscal result	−0.40	0.71	−3.15	−0.79
Unemployment	0.45	−0.16	4.22	1.84
Trade balance	−28.55	−0.42	−48.68	−2.94
Welfare of the poorest household	−1.41	0.39	−5.88	−1.43
Welfare of the middle-income household	−1.43	−0.04	−5.45	−1.64
Welfare of the richest household	0.75	−0.73	−0.61	−2.51
Agriculture and mining	−11.28	−1.14	−11.60	−1.90
Manufacturing	−1.15	−0.06	−7.77	−2.28
Services	−0.78	0.17	−5.38	−2.06

Note: Reported results are from the first year after the shock and show the difference between benchmark and simulation in percentage points.

[a] Export taxes (20 percent increase in all sectors): $W = $ CPI; capital mobility = 0.73.
[b] Export taxes (20 percent increase in all sectors): $W = $ CPI; capital mobility = 0.00.
[c] Export taxes (20 percent increase in all sectors): $W = 1$; capital mobility = 0.73.
[d] Export taxes (20 percent increase in all sectors): $W = 1$; capital mobility = 0.00.

manufacturing industry and especially in services). Case 9 is the most negative scenario for the economy as a whole, fiscal balance, unemployment rate, income distribution, and sectorial response.

In none of the cases does the manufacturing sector as a whole improve. This is because this sector encompasses a commodity-processing industry—which is net exporter and capital-intensive—and an import substitution subsector—which is net importer and labor-intensive.

The worst policy mistake would be, therefore, to assume that capital mobility is low when actually it is high. The mistake is even more costly if wages are not fully indexed and are downward inflexible.

Let us now examine a VAT increase that is designed to yield the same revenue as the 20 percent increase in export taxes. As mentioned previously, the results in these cases are the worst in the indexed wages context (the gray line in figure 4.2 and cases 3 and 11 in table 4.4). Under nominal wage rigidity, GDP falls moderately, the fiscal balance improves slightly, the unemployment rate falls, the trade balance worsens slightly, and the welfare of the rich and poor diminishes. The poor are generally worse off than the rich because the VAT is a tax on consumption goods and the upper income groups concentrate the savings of the economy.

Table 4.4 Increase in VATs Yields Same Revenue as 20 Percent on Export Taxes Under Two Different Capital Mobility and Wage-Setting Assumptions

	Case 3[a]	Case 11[b]	Case 4[c]	Case 12[d]
GDP	−2.72	−1.33	−0.55	−0.40
Fiscal result	−0.78	−0.10	0.58	0.62
Unemployment	1.73	0.77	−0.12	−0.18
Trade balance	−10.95	−1.40	−1.31	−0.20
Welfare of the poorest household	−2.82	−1.33	−0.63	−0.47
Welfare of the middle-income household	−2.55	−1.23	−0.61	−0.47
Welfare of the richest household	−0.84	−1.03	−0.17	−0.18
Agriculture and mining	−0.26	−0.39	−0.15	−0.03
Manufacturing	−3.35	−1.05	−0.13	0.00
Services	−2.14	−0.89	0.09	0.17

Note: Reported results are from the first year after the shock and show the difference between the benchmark and simulation in percentage points. VAT, value-added tax.

[a] VATs increase in all sectors (equal yield): W = CPI; capital mobility = 0.73.
[b] VATs increase in all sectors (equal yield): W = CPI; capital mobility = 0.00.
[c] VATs increase in all sectors (equal yield): W = 1; capital mobility = 0.73.
[d] VATs increase in all sectors (equal yield): W = 1; capital mobility = 0.00.

Table 4.5 Increase in Import Taxes Yields Same Revenue as 20 Percent on Export Taxes Under Two Different Capital Mobility and Wage-Setting Assumptions

	Case 5[a]	Case 13[b]	Case 6[c]	Case 14[d]
GDP	–0.73	–0.09	–1.04	–0.18
Fiscal result	0.28	0.63	0.08	0.56
Unemployment	0.52	–0.03	0.78	0.07
Trade balance	–2.86	0.40	–4.28	0.28
Welfare of the poorest household	–0.83	–0.04	–1.14	–0.12
Welfare of the middle-income household	–0.94	–0.24	–1.22	–0.31
Welfare of the richest household	–0.48	–0.48	–0.58	–0.56
Agriculture and mining	0.76	0.00	0.71	–0.03
Manufacturing	–2.29	–0.54	–2.73	–0.65
Services	–0.35	0.16	–0.67	0.05

Note: Reported results are from the first year after the shock and show the difference between the benchmark and simulation in percentage points.

[a] Import taxes increase in all sectors (equal yield): W = CPI; capital mobility = 0.73.
[b] Import taxes increase in all sectors (equal yield): W = CPI; capital mobility = 0.00.
[c] Import taxes increase in all sectors (equal yield): W = 1; capital mobility = 0.73.
[d] Import taxes increase in all sectors (equal yield): W = 1; capital mobility = 0.00.

The sectorial impact differs markedly from the experiments of export taxes. In only one case (3), the trade balance worsens significantly, but the damage is concentrated in the manufacturing and services sectors. Under fixed nominal wages, the effects on the sectors are negligible. The fiscal balance is positive in the two latter cases. The worst policy mistake in this case is to assume low capital mobility when—relative to perfectly indexed wages—it is actually high.

Let us now explore the import tax experiments (table 4.5). Here the results are worse under W = 1. In both wage determination scenarios, the higher the capital mobility is in the economy, the worse the results will be for GDP, unemployment, trade balance, and the welfare of the income groups.

An import tax affects the manufacturing sector more than the agriculture and mining and services sectors. This is because the manufacturing sector includes activities that import capital goods. The results would most likely be different if we allowed different tariff levels for consumption, intermediate, and capital goods. Under wage indexation, the worst policy mistake is to assume low capital mobility when it is actually high.

Table 4.6 Increase in Payroll Taxes Yields Same Revenue as 20 Percent on Export Taxes Under Two Different Capital Mobility and Wage-Setting Assumptions

	Case 7[a]	Case 15[b]	Case 8[c]	Case 16[d]
GDP	-2.64	-1.03	-2.46	-0.97
Fiscal result	-0.97	-0.12	-0.85	-0.08
Unemployment	2.40	1.18	2.23	1.12
Trade balance	-11.26	-1.04	-10.49	-0.97
Welfare of the poorest household	-2.65	-0.87	-2.46	-0.81
Welfare of the middle-income household	-2.90	-1.29	-2.73	-1.24
Welfare of the richest household	-0.85	-1.01	-0.80	-0.96
Agriculture and mining	0.50	-0.30	0.47	-0.28
Manufacturing	-4.39	-1.38	-4.11	-1.32
Services	-2.58	-1.04	-2.39	-0.97

Note: Reported results are from the first year after the shock and show the difference between the benchmark and simulation in percentage points.

[a] Labor taxes increase in all sectors (equal yield): W = CPI; capital mobility = 0.73.
[b] Labor taxes increase in all sectors (equal yield): W = CPI; capital mobility = 0.00.
[c] Labor taxes increase in all sectors (equal yield): W = 1; capital mobility = 0.73.
[d] Labor taxes increase in all sectors (equal yield): W = 1; capital mobility = 0.00.

Table 4.6 examines our last set of experiments that consider an increase in payroll taxes. High capital mobility cases are the worst for the economy, unemployment, the trade balance, and the welfare of the income classes (especially for the poor, where wages represent the greatest percentage of income). Manufacturing shows greater losses, but services—which is labor-intensive—is also strongly affected. The worst policy mistake in both wage determination cases is assuming low capital mobility when it is actually high.

DECISIONS WITH UNKNOWN PROBABILITIES

Policy makers have to make decisions very quickly and at times cannot evaluate the probability of different scenarios. The same policy may produce different outcomes depending on structural parameters, institutional environments, and historical circumstances. Let us consider now decisions with unknown probabilities—true uncertainty à la Frank Knight—and explore what a policy maker can do in such a case.[7]

We will reduce the problem to one for which there are four possible states of nature:

Nominal wage adjustment and no mobility of capital, NB
Real wage adjustment and no mobility of capital, RB
Nominal wage adjustment and capital mobility (73 percent), NA
Real wage adjustment and capital mobility (73 percent), RA

The decision maker can choose an action from the set of possible increases in taxes simulated previously (X, exports; VAT, value added; M, imports; L, labor), all of which hypothetically accrue the same revenue. This is a simplification because the policy maker could consider other possible actions or use some combination of taxes to obtain the same result. Our intention, however, is to show how the attitude toward uncertainty can modify the decision.

There is another important simplification worth mentioning. We will assume that the payoffs of every state of nature and action can be synthesized in the percentage change of GDP. This is, of course, a simplistic approach because the policy maker could be interested in other outcomes, such as income distribution and fiscal or trade balances. Table 4.7 summarizes the actions, states of nature, and payoffs.

Now, let us see which action is preferable considering the three alternative criteria:

Optimism or maximax: Assume that nature will select the most favorable state for every action.
Pessimism or maximin: Nature will play the worst state for every action.
Minimum regret or minimax: Choose the action that minimizes regret assuming that nature will play the worst state for every action.

Table 4.7 States of Nature and Payoffs (GDP Growth Rate as Percentage Point Difference from Benchmark)

	NB	RB	NA	RA
X	−1.88	0.09	−6.72	−2.25
VAT	−0.4	−1.33	−0.55	−2.72
M	−0.18	−0.09	−1.04	−0.73
L	−0.97	−1.03	−2.46	−2.64

Note: NB, nominal wage adjustment and no mobility of capital; RB, real wage adjustment and no mobility of capital; NA, nominal wage adjustment and capital mobility; RA, real wage adjustment and capital mobility; X, exports; VAT, value-added tax; M, imports; L, labor.

Table 4.8 Criteria and Payoffs

	Optimism	Pessimism	Minimum Regret
X	0.09	−6.72	6.17
VAT	−0.4	−2.72	1.99
M	−0.09	−1.04	0.89
L	−0.97	−2.64	0.79

Note: X, exports; VAT, value-added tax; M, imports; L, labor.

Undoubtedly, these criteria do not satisfy some of the axioms of behavior for a rational decision maker (such as the axiom of independence of irrelevant alternatives), but rationality can also be costly or demand additional time for the policy maker to reflect.[8] We examine which course of action will be selected given the limitations of information and knowledge.

We can see the following payoffs under the three criteria in table 4.8. The last column should be interpreted as the cost of choosing one action given the possible regret. The lower-cost action is selected under minimum regret, which in this case is that of taxes on labor even though, in principle, the action will not be chosen because it is always dominated by some other action.[9] Thus, under minimum regret, the policy maker will choose to tax nontradable goods and services, which are more labor-intensive and less capital-intensive.

However, when optimism is preferable, taxes on exports will be selected; under pessimism, taxes on imports are preferable. Thus, under optimism the policy maker prefers to tax tradable goods. Note that the cost of a mistake can be highly detrimental when taxes on exports are chosen.

CONCLUSIONS

Our simulations show that policy mistakes (or diagnostic failures) are costly and become increasingly costly with the degree of capital mobility. We can see this from the concavity of the welfare loss curve with respect to capital mobility.

The simulations also show how relevant a correct assessment of the consequences of each wage determination rule is. When prices increase, welfare losses tend to be lower in the case of nominal adjustment (i.e., $\gamma_3 = 1$) because real wages are melted away; instead, when prices fall, welfare losses drop when wages are indexed completely to CPI.

The capital intensity among sectors and the tax distribution in different activities (or its concentration in some sectors) could be important elements for computing the social cost of the tax adjustment.

Note that a markup (understood as a percentage over costs, for example) can be interpreted as an ad valorem tax privately appropriated, i.e., a full transfer from consumers. Hence, tax changes are the general cases and markup determinations the particular ones.

Our simulations should be understood as illustrations and exercises designed to augment intuition and not as policy prescriptions. They are subject to many caveats. We have not conducted sensitivity analysis for elasticities of substitution that could be relevant to the case of taxes on imports. In addition, we have not analyzed the long-term impact in a dynamic setting; capital mobility and substitution could modify the results significantly. But we do show how structural parameters are relevant to policy outcome. This, we believe, is part of Roberto Frenkel's contribution to the education of economists.

Deep uncertainty over the consequences of the decisions made by policy makers has led us to explore what course of action a policy maker will choose when faced with a Knightian environment. One action does not clearly dominate another in that case, but the approach of combining the uncertainty of structural parameters and computable general equilibrium seems to be helpful in making educated guesses. Surprisingly, from our examples, we have found that optimistic policy makers prefer to tax tradable goods, whereas the most pessimistic ones using minimum regret prefer to tax nontradable goods and services.

NOTES

1. Schumacher and Strobl (2008) summarize the evidence that shows that natural disaster shocks affect poor economies more negatively than wealthier ones.

2. See Barlevy (2009) for his discussion and summary of models, which include contributions by Sargent and Hansen.

3. The Feldstein–Horioka test consists of running a regression of the national investment rate on the national savings rate. The estimated coefficient is 1 in the case of financial autarky and 0 in the full mobility case. The test is a measure of how well the current account finances the difference between domestic savings and investment when these are subject to large and asymmetric shocks, even when it is not the ultimate test of capital mobility. The test could be biased by endogeneity (Bebczuk and Schmidt-Hebbel 2010).

4. Chisari et al. (2009) present a complete description of the sources and methods used to build the SAM for Argentina for 2006.

5. The solution of the model is obtained using the representation of general equilibrium and the mixed complementarities approach. The model is developed in the environment of GAMS/MPSGE. At present, it can interface with GAMS.

6. In fact, it is $W \geq 1$; nominal wages cannot be reduced but can be increased without considering any specific indexation rule.

7. See Barlevy (2009).

8. See, for examples, Luce and Raiffa (1957) and Binmore (2009), who discuss how these criteria perform when faced with the axiomatic basis given by Milnor.

9. In fact, one dominant action can be selected when all actions are considered simultaneously because the independence of irrelevant alternatives is not fulfilled under minimum regret. See Luce and Raiffa (1957).

REFERENCES

Azariadis, C. and Pissarides, C. 2004. "Unemployment dynamics with international capital mobility." *European Economic Review* 51(1): 27–48.

Barlevy, G. 2009. "Policymaking under uncertainty: gradualism and robustness." *Economic Perspectives* 33(2): 38–55.

Bebczuk, R. and Schmidt-Hebbel, K. 2010. "Revisiting the Feldstein–Horioka puzzle: an institutional sector view." *Económica* 4: 3–36.

Binmore, K. 2009. *Rational decisions*. Princeton, NJ: Princeton University Press.

Boehringer, C., Boeters, S., and Feil, M. 2004. "Taxation and unemployment: an applied general equilibrium approach." CESifo Working Paper Series No. 1272. Category 4: Labor markets. Presented at the Venice Summer Institute, Workshop on Policy Analysis with Numerical Models, Venice, Italy, July 2004. Munich: CESifo Group.

Chisari, O., Romero, C. A., Ferro, G., Theller, R., Cicowiez, M., Ferraro, J., González, M., Blanco, A., and Maquieyra, J. 2009. *Un modelo de equilibrio general computable para la Argentina*. Buenos Aires: PNUD.

Damill, M. and Frenkel, R. 2010. "Las políticas macroeconómicas en la evolución reciente de la economía argentina." In *Economía y crisis internacional: impacto en la República Argentina*. Buenos Aires: EDICON: 22–47.

Frankel, J. 1992. "Measuring international capital mobility: a review." *The American Economic Review* 82(2): 197–202.

Frenkel, R. 1986. "Salarios e inflación en América Latina. Resultados de investigaciones recientes en la Argentina, Brasil, Colombia, Costa Rica y Chile." *Desarrollo Económico* 25: 587–622.

Frenkel, R. and Ros, J. 2006. "Unemployment and the real exchange rate in Latin America." *World Development* 34(4): 631–646.

Fullerton, D. and Lyon, A. 1986. "Uncertain parameter values and the choice among policy options." *Journal of Public Economics* 30(1): 109–116.

Heymann, D. 2008. "Evolución y vaivenes: cincuenta años de macroeconomía." Documento de Proyecto (ARG/06003). Santiago: Economic Commission for Latin America and the Caribbean.

Koskela, E. and Schöb, R. 2000. "Optimal factor income taxation in the presence of unemployment." CESifo Working Paper Series No. 279. Munich: CESifo Group.

Luce, R. D. and Raiffa, H. 1957. *Games and decisions*. New York, NY: Wiley.

Marchand, M., Pestieau, P., and Wibaut, S. 1989. "Optimal commodity taxation and tax reform under unemployment." *The Scandinavian Journal of Economics* 91(3): 547–563.

Schumacher, I. and Strobl, E. 2008. "Economic development and losses due to natural disasters: the role of risk." Working Paper, Department of Economics, Ecole Polytechnique, Paris, France.

Van de Gaer, D., Schokkaert, E., and De Bruyne, G. 1994. "Involuntary unemployment and the marginal welfare cost of taxation in Belgium." *Tijdschrift voor Economie en Management* 39(3): 261–286.

CHAPTER 5

Monetary Policy and External Shocks in a Semidollarized Economy

Oscar Dancourt

The 2008–2009 crisis demonstrated that the main macroeconomic challenge facing an economy such as Peru's is the management of external shocks that deteriorate the balance of payments and reduce aggregate demand. The aim of this chapter is to discuss what the monetary policy should be in response to these external shocks.

The arsenal of Peruvian monetary policy has several instruments linked to the credit channel and managed floating exchange rate regime.[1] Since inflation targeting was implemented in 2002, the most important instrument of monetary policy has been a short-term interest rate (reference or policy rate) in domestic currency (DC). Another important tool during the last decade has been the reserve requirement ratios levied on bank deposits in both domestic and foreign currency (FC) and on the banking system's short-term external debt. A third key instrument of monetary policy since 2002–2003 has been sterilized intervention in the foreign exchange (FX) market.[2]

To compare the different responses of monetary policy to external shocks, these central bank's instruments are incorporated into an IS-LM-BP textbook model.[3] This Mundell–Fleming model is adapted to the financial conditions of an economy such as Peru's, which has a banking system that operates in both domestic and foreign currency.

The conclusion of this chapter is that a monetary policy, as suggested by Blanchard et al. (2010), which combines a Taylor rule for setting the interest rate, aimed at internal equilibrium, with a foreign exchange intervention policy of leaning against the wind, aimed at external equilibrium, can stabilize the price level and economic activity in the face of external shocks. These two rules imply that the central bank increases (decreases) the interest rate and buys (sells) foreign currency when favorable (adverse) external shocks occur. The foreign exchange reserves of the monetary authority play an important role in the management of external shocks. This chapter also suggests a way to implement the proposal of Damill and Frenkel (2011) regarding a target for a real competitive exchange rate in an economy such as Peru's.

THE BANKING SYSTEM'S INTEREST RATES

In this model, commercial banks make loans and take deposits in both DC and FC.[4] There is also a second source of loanable funds in both currencies: domestic banks have credit lines with the central bank in DC and foreign banks in FC. A local bond market does not exist. Thus, there are two lending interest rates, two deposit interest rates, and two basic interest rates: the central bank policy rate and the external interest rate, which are the cost of the banks' credit lines in both currencies.

The first step consists of determining the lending and deposit interest rates in both currencies as a function of the interest rates of the credit lines, the reserve requirements, and the delinquency rate. These are nominal interest rates, and a zero expected inflation rate is assumed.

If commercial banks match assets and liabilities by currency and do not speculate with the future path of the exchange rate, it is as if there were two banking systems, one operating in domestic currency and the other in foreign currency. The balance sheets of both systems without equity would be as follows:

$$L = (1 - \theta)\, D + U \tag{5.1}$$

$$L^* = (1 - \theta^*)\, (D^* + U^*), \tag{5.2}$$

where L and L^* are loans in DC and FC; θ and θ^* are reserve requirement ratios in DC and FC; D and D^* are deposits in DC and FC; and U and U^* are outstanding debt in DC with the central bank and outstanding debt in FC with foreign banks, respectively. It is assumed that credit lines in DC are exempt from reserve requirements and that the same reserve requirement ratio is applied to credit lines and deposits in FC.

If competition in the deposits market leads banks to set deposit interest rates that equal the cost of the two sources of funds (deposits and credit lines), we have that

$$\frac{i_p D}{(1 - \theta)D} = \frac{iU}{U} \tag{5.3}$$

$$\frac{i^*_{\mathrm{p}} D^*}{(1 - \theta^*) D^*} = \frac{i^* U^*}{(1 - \theta^*) D^*}, \tag{5.4}$$

where the deposit interest rates in DC and FC are i_{p} and i^*_{p}; the central bank policy rate is i; and the external interest rate of credit lines in FC is i^*. From equations 5.3 and 5.4, we get that the deposit interest rate in DC depends directly on the central bank's reference rate and negatively on the reserve requirement ratio in DC and that the deposit interest rate in FC is equal to the foreign interest rate, i.e.,

$$i_{\mathrm{p}} = (1 - \theta)i \tag{5.5}$$

$$i^*_{\mathrm{p}} = i^*. \tag{5.6}$$

If competition in the loan market leads banks to set lending interest rates that generate zero profits, the interest income from the loan portfolio will be equal to the interest expense of deposits and credit lines; expected delinquency rates are taken into account (denominated as m and m^* for loans in DC and FC, respectively), whereas operating costs are not, i.e.,

$$RL\,(1 - m) = i_{\mathrm{p}} D + iU \tag{5.7}$$

$$R^* L^*\,(1 - m^*) = i^*_{\mathrm{p}} D + i^* U^*, \tag{5.8}$$

where R and R^* are the lending interest rates in DC and FC, respectively. Substituting equations 5.1 and 5.5 into equation 5.7 and equations 5.2 and 5.6 into equation 5.8 yields the result that the lending interest rate in DC depends directly on the reference rate and that the lending interest rate in FC depends directly on the external interest rate and the reserve requirement ratios in FC. Both lending rates also depend directly on the expected rate of delinquency,[5] i.e.,

$$R = \frac{i}{1 - m} \tag{5.9}$$

$$R^* = \frac{i^*}{(1 - \theta^*)(1 - m^*)}. \tag{5.10}$$

If the maturity of loans were longer than that of deposits and credit lines, then the expected future reference and foreign interest rates would be additional factors that influence loan interest rates in domestic and foreign currency.[6]

THE IS CURVE

The next step is to introduce both lending interest rates in the IS curve. Production (Y) is determined by aggregate demand, which has two components: domestic demand (A), consumption plus investment, and the trade balance or net exports (X_n). That is,

$$Y = A + X_n = A(R, R^*, E, P, Y) + X_n(E, P, Y, Y^*). \qquad (5.11)$$

As in Krugman (1999), domestic demand (A) is an inverse function of the debt of the private sector in local and foreign currency.[7] The debt burden increases if both lending interest rates (R, R^*) rise or if the exchange rate (E) rises; the debt burden is reduced if the price level (P) or economic activity (Y) rises.[8] Net exports depend directly on the exchange rate (E) and external GDP (Y^*) and inversely on domestic GDP (Y) and the local price level (P); the price in foreign currency of foreign goods is assumed to be 1.[9]

In this way, domestic demand depends negatively on the factors that determine both lending interest rates: the central bank's reference rate, the external interest rate, the reserve requirement ratio in FC, and the delinquency rates.

As in Krugman (1999), the nominal exchange rate (and the local price level) have two opposite effects on aggregate demand. On the one hand, an increase in the exchange rate generates a higher debt burden that reduces domestic demand because banks lend in dollars to firms that sell in pesos or families who earn their income in pesos. On the other hand, an increase in the exchange rate makes domestic goods cheaper relative to foreign ones, which increases net exports. Thus, an increase in the exchange rate can be recessionary (the balance sheet effect prevails) or expansionary (the competitiveness effect prevails); we will assume that in the short run the balance sheet effect dominates over the competitiveness effect.[10]

In such a case, a linear IS curve could be defined as

$$Y = -\alpha_1 i - \alpha_2 (i^* + \theta^*) - \alpha_3 E + \alpha_4 Y^* + \alpha_5 P.$$

In the IS equation, an increase in the price level rises economic activity because the balance sheet effect is bigger than the competitiveness effect. On the one hand, the debt burden decreases with a higher price level, which raises domestic demand. On the other hand, a higher price level reduces net exports because domestic goods become more expensive relative to foreign goods. If the competitiveness effect were dominant, an increase in the price level would have the usual negative impact on economic activity.[11] In the IS equation, the expected delinquency rates are assumed to be zero.

THE LM CURVE

The third step is to introduce both deposit interest rates into the LM curve. In this model, deposits (and loans) in domestic and foreign currency are imperfect substitutes. Deposits in domestic currency are a medium of exchange and a store of value. Deposits in foreign currency are only a store of value.

The monetary base (H) is equal to banking reserves in DC if the currency in circulation is assumed to be zero. Demand for reserve requirements in DC is equal to the reserve requirement ratio (θ) multiplied by deposit demand in DC, i.e., $H = \theta D$. Demand for deposits in DC depends directly on economic activity (Y), the price level (P), and the deposit interest rate in DC, given by $i_p = (1 - \theta)i$. It is a negative function of the deposit interest rate in FC $(i_p^* = i^*)$ adjusted by expected devaluation (E^*/E). Thus, the equilibrium in the monetary base market is given by

$$H = \theta D(P, Y, i, \theta, i^*, E^*/E). \qquad (5.12)$$

As such, a lineal LM curve could be defined as

$$H = P + Y + \alpha_5 i - \alpha_7 \left(i^* + E^* - E\right) + \alpha_8 \theta,$$

where the net effect of the reserve requirement ratio in DC on monetary base demand is assumed to be positive.

Domestic currency monetary base and deposits are created when the central bank purchases dollars from the public and increases its foreign exchange position $(PosCam)$ or when commercial banks increase their loans to firms and households taking more debt (U) with the central bank, i.e.,

$$EPosCam + U = H. \qquad (5.13)$$

The central bank's net international reserves (RIN) consist of the foreign exchange position (net external assets held by the central bank) and total bank reserves in foreign currency, $\theta^*(D^* + U^*)$, which are assumed to be deposited in the central bank, i.e.,

$$RIN = PosCam + \theta^*(D^* + U^*). \qquad (5.14)$$

Finally, the financial wealth (RF) of companies and households is the sum of deposits minus loans in both currencies. This financial wealth is equal to net external assets (RIN minus commercial banks' external debt). Using equations 5.1, 5.2, 5.13, and 5.14, we obtain

$$RF = (D-L)+(D^*-L^*)E = (RIN-U^*)E \cdot \qquad (5.15)$$

THE BP CURVE

To complete the Mundell–Fleming model, we utilize the balance-of-payments equation with imperfect capital mobility, as in Ball (2012) or Mankiw (2010), instead of the uncovered interest rate parity equation with perfect capital mobility as in Krugman (1999) or Blanchard (2006).[12]

The fourth step is to introduce the lending and deposit interest rates in local and foreign currency as determinants of the capital flows in the BP curve. In this model, according to the identity of the balance of payments, the change in the central bank's international net reserves (ΔRIN) equals the dollar value of net exports ($\frac{P}{E}X_n$) plus the short-term capital flow, which is defined as the change in external debt of the domestic banking system ($U^*-U^*_{t-1}$) minus the interest payments on foreign debt ($i^*_{t-1}U^*_{t-1}$), i.e.,

$$\Delta RIN = \frac{P}{E}X_n + (U^* - \alpha U^*_{t-1}), \qquad (5.16)$$

where α is one plus the interest rate. These foreign exchange reserves have two components: the foreign exchange position of the central bank and foreign currency banking reserves, which can vary independently of one another, i.e., $\Delta RIN = \Delta PosCam + \theta^*(\Delta D^* + \Delta U^*)$, according to equation 5.14. For example, if the commercial banks take debt abroad to finance a local credit boom, loans and deposits in foreign currency will expand; thus, banking reserves in foreign currency and RIN will increase even if the central bank does not intervene in the foreign exchange market and the exchange rate is completely flexible.

Using equations 5.14 and 5.16, we can equal the result of the balance of payments with the variation in the foreign exchange position. That is,

$$\Delta PosCam = PosCam - PosCam_{t-1} = \frac{P}{E}X_n + (1-\theta^*)(U^* - \alpha U^*_{t-1})$$
$$-\theta^*(D^* - D^*_{t-1}). \qquad (5.17)$$

If the central bank does not intervene in the foreign exchange market, the foreign exchange position is constant ($\Delta PosCam = 0$).[13] External equilibrium is defined as a balance of payments that keeps the central bank's net asset position constant. Equation 5.17 implies a redefinition of capital flows, which now depend on the change in external debt of the banking system and in foreign currency deposits. In what follows, we discuss the factors that determine these capital flows (FK).

$$FK = (1-\theta)(U^* - \alpha U_{t-1}^*) - \theta^*(D^* - D_{t-1}^*).$$

The local banks' foreign debt (U^*), more volatile than deposits (D^*), is the factor that determines capital flows in practice. According to equation 5.2, the bank's foreign debt depends directly on loans and inversely on deposits. That is,

$$U^* = \frac{L^*}{1-\theta^*} - D^*.$$

Demand for loans in foreign currency depends directly on the price level (P) and economic activity (Y), as well as the lending interest rate (R) of substitute loans in local currency; it also depends inversely on the lending interest rate (R^*) in foreign currency adjusted by expected depreciation (E^*/E). Setting this demand for loans in foreign currency equal to the effectively loaned amount, we obtain[14]

$$L^* = L^*(R, R^*, E^*/E, P, Y). \tag{5.18}$$

Demand for FC deposits depends directly on the foreign interest rate (equal to the deposit rate in FC) adjusted by expected depreciation (E^*/E); it also depends inversely on the deposit interest rate in domestic currency, which in turn depends on the policy rate and the reserve requirement ratio in domestic currency. It also depends inversely on the economic activity and price level because it is assumed that this is a reserve asset. Equating this demand with the amount actually deposited, we get

$$D^* = D^*(i, i^*, E^*/E, P, Y, \theta). \tag{5.19}$$

From equations 5.2, 5.18, and 5.19, we obtain first that demand for foreign debt (U^*) depends directly on the loan and deposit interest rates in domestic currency and inversely on loan and deposit interest rates in foreign currency adjusted by expected depreciation. We then obtain that the demand for foreign debt (U^*) depends directly on the price level and economic activity, i.e.,

$$U^* = U^*(i, i^*, E^*/E, P, Y, \theta, \theta^*). \tag{5.20}$$

In equation 5.20, it is assumed that local banks are not subject to credit rationing in foreign markets.[15]

In what follows we discuss this demand for foreign debt (U^*). In equation 5.20, a rise in the policy interest rate (i) causes an increase in the foreign debt of banks because it increases both lending and deposit interest rates in domestic currency, which implies that demand for loans in foreign currency is higher (becomes more attractive) and that the demand for deposits in foreign currency is lower (becomes less attractive). The external funding (U^*) of local banks must increase if they want to lend more with less internal funding (D^*).

In equation 5.20, a rise in the foreign interest rate (i^*) causes a decrease in the foreign debt of banks because it increases both lending and deposit interest rates in foreign currency, which implies that demand for loans in foreign currency is lower (becomes less attractive) and that demand for deposits in foreign currency is higher (becomes more attractive). The external funding (U^*) of local banks must decrease if they wish to lend less with more internal funding (D^*).

In equation 5.20, a rise in the reserve requirement ratio in domestic currency (θ) causes a decrease in the foreign debt of banks because it reduces the deposit interest rate in domestic currency, which implies that demand for deposits in foreign currency is higher (becomes more attractive). The external funding of local banks (U^*) must decrease if they want to lend the same with more internal funding (D^*).

An increase in the reserve requirement ratio in foreign currency (θ^*) has two opposite effects on external debt. First, an increase of θ^* raises the lending interest rate in foreign currency, which reduces demand for loans; thus, external funding (U^*) of the local banks has to diminish if they wish to lend less while their internal funding (D^*) remains constant. But there is an opposite effect: to lend the same with constant deposits, more foreign debt is necessary if the reserve requirement ratio increases. In equation 5.20, it is assumed that the first effect dominates.

Last, in equation 5.20, an increase in economic activity or the price level increases the demand for foreign debt. The external funding (U^*) of the local banks has to increase if they lend more with less internal funding (D^*).

If we plug equations 5.19 and 5.20 into FK, we obtain an equation for the capital flows similar to the one traditionally used in IS-LM-BP models, with the exception of the presence of both reserve requirement ratios with a negative sign and of economic activity and the price level with a positive sign. Obviating the terms U^*_{t-1}, D^*_{t-1}, we have that

$$FK = FK(i, i^*, E^*/E, P, Y, \theta, \theta^*). \tag{5.21}$$

From equations 5.17 and 5.21, we finally obtain the equation of the BP curve:

$$\Delta PosCam = \frac{P}{E} X_n(E, P, Y, Y^*) + FK(i, i^*, E^*/E, P, Y, \theta, \theta^*). \tag{5.22}$$

A linear BP curve could thus be defined as

$$PosCam - PosCam_{t-1} = \alpha_9 E - \alpha_{10}Y - \alpha_{11}P + \alpha_{12}Y^* + \alpha_{13}i$$
$$-\alpha_{14}(i^* + E^*) - \alpha_{15}\theta - \alpha_{16}\theta^*,$$

where it is assumed that 1) an increase in the exchange rate improves the balance of payments and 2) an increase in economic activity or in the price level deteriorates the balance of payments through the trade balance, although it induces capital inflows as well.[16]

THE AS CURVE

Finally, we incorporate an aggregate supply (AS) curve to the IS-LM-BP model. The price of the domestic good (P) depends on a constant markup (z) and the unit labor cost $\left(\frac{W}{a}\right)$, with W being the nominal wage and a the product per worker. If we set $a = 1$, we have that $P = (1 + z)W$, which implies that the real wage in terms of the domestic good is constant. If the nominal wage depends negatively on unemployment and directly on the exchange rate, because the consumer basket includes the foreign good, a linear aggregate supply curve could be

$$P = \alpha_{17}E + \alpha_{18}(Y - Y^P),$$

where it is assumed that unemployment depends negatively on the gap between effective and potential output $(Y - Y^P)$ and that $\alpha_{17} < 1$, such that the real exchange rate $(E - P)$ changes in the same direction as the nominal exchange rate (E).

EXTERNAL SHOCKS AND MONETARY POLICY

There are two basic monetary regimes in this IS-LM-BP-AS model: one with constant rates and another with constant aggregates.[17] In the first case, the central bank sets the reference interest rate (i) in local currency and the exchange rate (E), as well as both reserve requirement ratios (θ, θ^*), and the four basic equations of the model determine economic activity (Y), the monetary base (H), the foreign exchange reserves (*PosCam*), and the price level (P). In the second regime, these four basic equations determine economic activity, the reference interest rate in local currency, the exchange rate, and the price level, whereas the central bank sets, in addition to both reserve requirement ratios, the monetary aggregates, i.e., the credit extended to local banks (U) *and* the foreign exchange position (*PosCam*), which implies that the central bank determines the monetary base (*H*).

Because it can set two of the four financial variables (*PosCam, H, i, E*) the central bank has two monetary policy tools. In addition, the central bank sets the reserve requirements in both currencies.[18] Only if the central bank chooses not to intervene in the foreign exchange market such that $\Delta PosCam = 0$, i.e., only if it opts for a freely floating exchange rate regime, will it have a unique instrument that can be the reference interest rate or the monetary base.

The basic features of this version of the Mundell–Fleming model can be presented in the framework of a conventional aggregate supply and demand model that describes a short-term equilibrium.[19] If the central bank sets the interest rate and the exchange rate, aggregate demand (AD) is obtained directly from the IS equation, and aggregate supply (AS) is the same that we saw in the previous section. That is,

$$\text{AD: } P = \frac{\alpha_1 i + \alpha_2 (i^* + \theta^*) + \alpha_3 E - \alpha_4 Y^*}{\alpha_5} + \frac{1}{\alpha_5} Y$$

$$\text{AS: } P = \alpha_{17} E + \alpha_{18} (Y - Y^P).$$

The aggregate demand curve has a positive slope because the Fisher or balance sheet effect dominates the competitiveness effect. Stability in this AS-AD model requires that the slope of aggregate demand be higher than the slope of aggregate supply, i.e., that $1 > \alpha_5 \alpha_{18}$, where all α coefficients are positive.

The increase in the nominal exchange rate ($dE > 0$) is a negative demand shock (the balance sheet effect dominates the competitiveness effect), whose strength is given by α_3. It is also a supply shock that raises the price level for any given output gap, whose strength is given by α_{17}. Here, an increase in the price level stimulates aggregate demand because it reduces the debt burden of firms and families. Hence, the indirect effect on economic activity of a devaluation through the increase in the price level is positive, whereas the direct effect is negative. If $\alpha_3 > \alpha_5\alpha_{17}$, a devaluation leads to a recession, given the stability condition of $1 > \alpha_5\alpha_{18}$. And the less steep the aggregate supply curve, the more likely it is that this devaluation leads to an increase in the price level; for example, if $\alpha_{18} = 0$, the price level increases. This is what we have assumed in figure 5.1; an increase in the exchange rate shifts the DA curve to the left and the AS curve upward from point A to B; the price level rises and economic activity falls.

A sufficient condition for a devaluation to improve the balance of payments, according to the BP equation, is that the indirect negative effect through the increase in the price level is smaller than the direct positive effect of the exchange rate, i.e., that $\alpha_9 > \alpha_{11}\alpha_{17}$.

Table 5.1 summarizes the positive or negative effects of different external adverse shocks of a transitory nature on the price level, economic activity, and the foreign reserves (foreign exchange position of the central bank) under a fixed or flexible exchange rate, given the interest rate and the rest of the exogenous variables.[20]

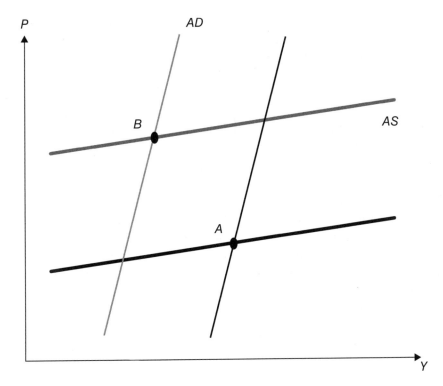

Figure 5.1 A negative external shock.

Table 5.1 Effect of External Shocks with Fixed Interest Rate

	Domestic Prices	Economic Activity	Foreign Exchange Reserves	Exchange Rate
Fixed exchange rate				
International recession	–	–	–	0
Increase in foreign interest rate	–	–	–	0
Increase in expected exchange rate	0	0	–	0
Flexible exchange rate				
International recession	±	–	0	+
Increase in foreign interest rate	±	–	0	+
Increase in expected exchange rate	±	–	0	+

If the central bank sets the interest rate and the exchange rate, an international recession $(dY^* < 0)$ or a capital outflow $(di^* > 0)$ are negative demand shocks that reduce economic activity $(dY < 0)$ and the price level $(dP < 0)$. Both shocks lead to a deterioration in the balance of payments and cause a reserve loss if the balance of payments was equilibrated in the initial situation.[21] An increase in the central bank reference rate $(di > 0)$ or in the reserve requirement ratio in foreign currency $(d\theta^* > 0)$ are also negative demand shocks.

If the central bank wishes to stabilize both economic activity $(dY = 0)$ and the price level $(dP = 0)$ in the face of a transitory external shock $(dY^* < 0)$, then it must keep the exchange rate constant $(dE = 0)$ and reduce the cost of credit in domestic currency by reducing the reference rate $(di = \frac{\alpha_4}{\alpha_1} dY^* < 0)$ to outweigh the negative effect that a drop in exports has on production and employment.[22] As shown in figure 5.1, an international recession shifts the AD curve to the left; a proper cut of the interest rate shifts the AD curve to the right, returning it to its original position; and the fixed exchange rate prevents the aggregate supply curve from moving upward when the balance of payments deteriorates. Thus, we stay at point A despite the international recession. To apply this Keynesian policy, the central bank must have enough foreign currency reserves because the drop in exports and the cut in the reference rate will generate a balance-of-payments deficit $(dPosCam = \alpha_{12} dY^* + \alpha_{13} di < 0)$ if the balance of payments was equilibrated in the initial situation.[23]

The monetary base is reduced (the deposit interest rate in local currency falls) less than the foreign exchange reserves because domestic

currency loans of commercial banks increase (due to the cut in the reference rate). These higher local currency loans are financed by an increase
in bank debt owed to the central bank.

An alternative path, keeping the exchange rate constant $(dE = 0)$, is to
make credit in foreign currency cheaper by reducing the reserve requirement ratio applied to credit lines and dollar-denominated deposits
$(d\theta^* = \frac{\alpha_4}{\alpha_2} dY^* < 0)$.[24] This option assumes that the domestic banking
system debt owed to foreign banks can increase at the same time there
is an adverse external shock.[25] This capital inflow could counteract the effect of a drop in exports on the balance of payments
$(dPosCam = \alpha_{12}dY^* - \alpha_{16}d\theta^* > 0)$.

If the central bank does not have enough foreign exchange reserves
$(dPosCam = 0)$, it has to let the exchange rate float in the face of a transitory adverse external shock. The model with a flexible exchange rate consists of three equations: the aggregate supply and demand curves already
seen and the BP = 0 curve that allows us to determine the exchange rate.
In the same fashion as before, the LM curve determines the monetary base.

If the central bank keeps the interest rate constant while the exchange
rate floats cleanly, the effects of an international recession $(dY^* < 0)$ or
capital outflow $(di^* < 0, dE^* > 0)$ are similar, as shown in table 5.1.

Under this monetary policy, these external shocks constitute, just as
before, a negative demand shock that tends to reduce economic activity
and the price level; now, however, they also constitute a supply shock that
tends to increase the price level because the exchange rate rises as the balance of payments deteriorates.

In the flexible exchange rate case, it is preferable to use a graph in
the economic activity–exchange rate quadrant instead of the activity–
price level quadrant and to directly observe the effect any change in the
external context has on these two variables. To plot figure 5.2, the AS is
inserted into both the IS and BP = 0 curves.[26] The equations of the IS
and BP = 0 curves are given by the following:

$$\text{IS: } E = \frac{\alpha_4 Y^* - \alpha_5\alpha_{18}Y^P - \alpha_1 i - \alpha_2(i^* + \theta^*)}{\alpha_3 - \alpha_5\alpha_{17}} - \frac{1 - \alpha_5\alpha_{18}}{\alpha_3 - \alpha_5\alpha_{17}}Y$$

$$\text{BP} = 0\text{: } E = \frac{-\alpha_{13}i + \alpha_{14}(i^* + E^*) + \alpha_{15}\theta + \alpha_{16}\theta^* - \alpha_{11}\alpha_{18}Y^P - \alpha_{12}Y^*}{\alpha_9 - \alpha_{11}\alpha_{17}}$$

$$+ \frac{\alpha_{10} + \alpha_{11}\alpha_{18}}{\alpha_9 - \alpha_{11}\alpha_{17}}Y.$$

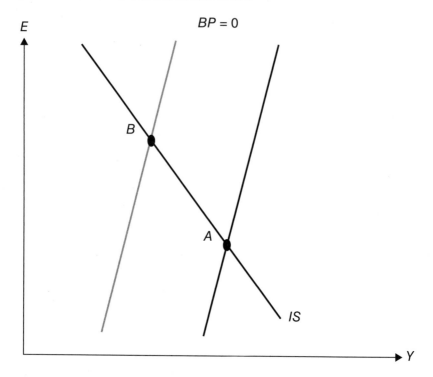

Figure 5.2. The case of capital outflows.

The IS curve has a negative slope because the depreciation of the domestic currency is contractive, i.e., $\frac{dE}{dY} = -\frac{1-\alpha_5\alpha_{18}}{\alpha_3-\alpha_5\alpha_{17}} < 0$. The BP = 0 curve has a positive slope because an increase in the exchange rate generates a surplus in the balance of payments $(\alpha_9 > \alpha_{11}\alpha_{17})$ that has to be eliminated through higher economic activity, i.e., $\frac{dE}{dY} = -\frac{\alpha_9-\alpha_{11}\alpha_{17}}{\alpha_{10}+\alpha_{11}\alpha_{18}} > 0$.

In figure 5.2, a capital outflow generated by an increase in the expected exchange rate $(dE^* > 0)$ occurs, while the central bank keeps the interest rate constant and the exchange rate floats freely. This external shock shifts the BP = 0 curve to the left from point A to B; the IS curve does not move. The exchange rate increases and economic activity falls. This result requires three conditions that were previously discussed and that define the slopes of the IS and BP curves: $1 > \alpha_5\alpha_{18}$, $\alpha_3 > \alpha_5\alpha_{17}$, and $\alpha_9 > \alpha_{11}\alpha_{17}$. For an increase in the exchange rate to push the price level up even in a recession, aggregate supply must be relatively flat; e.g., if $\alpha_{18} = 0$, the price level increases.

It is worth mentioning that if the exchange rate and the interest rate remain constant, this capital outflow does not affect economic activity or the price level and only reduces the foreign exchange reserves.

As registered in table 5.1, under a clean floating regime, a capital outflow (induced by an increase in the foreign interest rate or the expected exchange rate) or a global recession has the same effects on economic activity and the price level. In terms of figure 5.2, an increase in the expected exchange rate only shifts the BP = 0 curve to the left, deteriorating the balance of payments, whereas the other two adverse external effects shift both the BP = 0 and IS curves to the left; i.e., they deteriorate the balance of payments and reduce aggregate demand. In all cases, the exchange rate increases, and the recession is more severe than with a fixed exchange rate because devaluation is contractionary.[27]

Under a clean floating regime, monetary policy cannot stabilize both economic activity and the price level if an external adverse shock occurs. If the interest rate is reduced to fight the recession, both the exchange rate and price level rise.[28] And if the interest rate is raised to fight the increases in the exchange rate and price level, economic activity decreases.[29] In theory, if the interest rate rises, this dilemma could be solved with an expansive fiscal policy.[30] In practice, with a small government and no fiscal automatic stabilizers as in Peru, it is unlikely that the overall recessive effect of an adverse external shock and a tight monetary policy could be counterbalanced by expansionary fiscal policy or that a higher local interest rate would be able to avoid an increase in the exchange rate.[31]

FX INTERVENTION AND TAYLOR RULES

In a semidollarized economy, as we have seen, reducing the interest rate and keeping the exchange rate fixed are the adequate policy responses for stabilizing the price level and economic activity when facing external shocks that deteriorate the balance of payments and reduce aggregate demand. If the external shock only deteriorates the balance of payments, the adequate policy response for stabilizing the price level and economic activity is to keep the exchange and interest rates fixed.

However, a fixed exchange rate regime is exposed to speculative attacks. Frenkel and Rapetti (2010: 43) emphasize that, under conditions of low inflation as in Latin America since the 1990s, a limited flexibility in the exchange rate has been shown to be highly valuable. The lack of commitment to the level of the NER (nominal exchange rate) provides the economy flexibility to adjust to external shocks without resulting in reputational costs for the monetary authorities. The lack of commitment also eliminates the incentives of one-way bets in the FX market by speculators. In their portfolio choices between domestic and foreign assets (and liabilities), private agents have to assume the exchange rate risk. Therefore, a lower exposure to NER variations and lower financial fragility to external shocks is likely to be observed.[32]

If the central bank combines a Taylor rule (interest rate rises in booms and decreases in recessions) with a sterilized FX market intervention policy of leaning against the wind (buying dollars when their price falls below some target level and selling them when their price rises above this target level), it can come close to approximating this adequate policy response to external adverse shocks without being subject to the vulnerabilities inherent in a fixed exchange rate system.

According to Williamson (2010), a hybrid system such as Brazil's, where there is limited flexibility because the central bank intervenes in the FX market, with some notion of what the "adequate" exchange rate is, works better in the real world than the two exchange policies discussed in this chapter and in textbooks (either a completely fixed or a flexible exchange rate).

This hybrid exchange policy has been used in Peru since 2002–2003. The central bank purchases dollars when its target exchange rate (E^M), which is not announced, lies above the market exchange rate (E) and sells dollars when the opposite occurs. A simple intervention rule (RI) could be as follows:[33]

$$PosCam - PosCam_{t-1} = \alpha_{19}(E^M - E).$$

Plugging this equation into the BP equation, we obtain the equation of the curve BP_{RI}, which is very similar to the BP = 0 curve except that it contains the central bank's target exchange rate (E^M) in the intercept and has a smaller slope due to the effect of the α_{19} term. In the BP_{RI} curve, the balance-of-payments result is not equal to zero unless $E^M = E$.[34]

$$E = \frac{\alpha_{19}E^M - \alpha_{13}i + \alpha_{14}(i^* + E^*) + \alpha_{15}\theta + \alpha_{16}\theta^* - \alpha_{11}\alpha_{18}Y^P - \alpha_{12}Y^*}{\alpha_9 + \alpha_{19} - \alpha_{11}\alpha_{17}}$$

$$+ \frac{\alpha_{10} + \alpha_{11}\alpha_{18}}{\alpha_9 + \alpha_{19} - \alpha_{11}\alpha_{17}}Y.$$

If $E^M = E$ in the initial situation, this FX intervention rule implies that foreign exchange reserves decrease with adverse external shocks and increase with favorable external shocks. The higher α_{19} is in the RI equation, the less steep the BP_{RI} curve will be, the higher the changes in currency reserves will be, and the more similar this managed floating regime will be to a fixed exchange rate regime; conversely, the lower α_{19} is in this equation, the steeper the BP_{RI} curve will be and the more similar this regime will be to a clean floating regime.[35]

If this FX intervention rule is combined with a Taylor rule, where the policy interest rate depends directly on the output gap, it seems possible to reconcile the theory and practice of monetary policy in some emerging market economies, as proposed by Blanchard et al. (2010).[36]

If we incorporate the IS and BP_{RI} curves in a Taylor rule (RT), where the interest rate is a direct function of the output gap, as in $i = i_0 + h(Y - Y^P)$, we get

$$IS_{RT}: E = \frac{\alpha_4 Y^* - (\alpha_5\alpha_{18} - \alpha_1 h)Y^P - \alpha_1 i_0 - \alpha_2(i^* + \theta^*)}{\alpha_3 - \alpha_5\alpha_{17}}$$
$$+ \frac{1 + \alpha_1 h - \alpha_5\alpha_{18}}{\alpha_3 - \alpha_5\alpha_{17}} Y$$

$$BP_{RT}: E =$$
$$\frac{\alpha_{19}E^M - \alpha_{13}i_0 + \alpha_{14}(i^* + E^*) + \alpha_{15}\theta + \alpha_{16}\theta^* - (\alpha_{11}\alpha_{18} - \alpha_1 h)Y^P - \alpha_{12}Y^*}{\alpha_9 + \alpha_{19} - \alpha_{11}\alpha_{17}}$$
$$+ \frac{\alpha_{10} + \alpha_{11}\alpha_{18} - \alpha_{13}h}{\alpha_9 + \alpha_{19} - \alpha_{11}\alpha_{17}} Y.$$

The new system of figure 5.2 comprises the IS_{RT} and BP_{RT} curves. The Taylor rule makes the IS curve steeper and the BP curve flatter; for the BP_{RT} curve to have a positive slope in figure 5.2, α_{13} must be small. These two monetary policy rules, one that aims at internal equilibrium and the other at external equilibrium, reduce both fluctuations in the price level and in economic activity in the face of external shocks compared with a clean floating and fixed interest rate regime. As long as the α_{19} term of the FX intervention rule is large enough, no additional condition is required other than those already mentioned.

These two rules imply that the central bank increases the interest rate and buys foreign currency when favorable external shocks occur, which increase aggregate demand that leads to a boom and improves the balance of payments, thereby pushing the exchange rate downward. Conversely, the central bank lowers the interest rate and sells foreign currency when adverse external shocks take place, which diminishes aggregate demand and deteriorates the balance of payments, thus pushing the exchange rate upward.[37]

Ostry et al. (2012) proposed, on the contrary, that the central bank must lower the local interest rate in the event of a capital inflow generated by a reduction in the foreign interest rate in addition to buying dollars and, symmetrically, that it must increase the domestic interest rate if there is a capital outflow in addition to selling dollars. This policy recommendation is derived from two features that do not seem to apply to an economy such as Peru's: 1) that a decrease (increase) in the external interest rate does not affect the IS_{RT} curve but only the BP_{RT} curve to the left (right) of figure 5.1, and 2) that the IS_{RT} curve has a positive slope (must be higher than the BP_{RT} curve) in figure 5.1 because a depreciation of the national currency raises aggregate demand in the short term. These two features imply that a capital inflow causes a recession and that a capital outflow causes a boom in a flexible exchange rate regime, as in the original Mundell–Fleming model; the opposite occurs in this chapter.

With this FX intervention rule, the central bank avoids excessive appreciations and depreciations of the domestic currency relative to its target value. According to Blanchard et al. (2010: 13),

> a large appreciation may squeeze the tradable sector and make it difficult for it to grow back if and when the exchange rate decreases. Also, when a significant portion of domestic contracts is denominated in foreign currency (or is somehow linked to its movements), sharp fluctuations in the exchange rate (especially depreciations) can cause severe balance sheet effects with negative consequences for financial stability, and thus, output.

In addition, an excessive increase of the exchange rate typically raises the price level and inflation rate in an economy such as Peru's. Presumably, these considerations should be taken into account when determining the central bank's target exchange rate. This could be a way of implementing, in an economy such as Peru's, the proposal of Damill and Frenkel (2011) regarding a competitive real exchange rate target.

With respect to the price level, this monetary policy has several consequences. First, if the price level depends directly on the exchange rate and the output gap, to stabilize economic activity and the exchange rate in response to external shocks is tantamount to stabilizing the price level; in particular, this monetary policy eliminates abrupt price increases related to balance-of-payments crises generated by adverse external shocks and the lack of sufficient foreign currency reserves in the central bank.[38] Second, if there is both external $(E^M = E)$ and internal equilibrium $(Y = Y^P)$, the aggregate supply curve implies that the price level depends only on the target exchange rate of the FX intervention rule, i.e., $P = \alpha_{19} E^M$. This should be the desired price level or central bank target (the equivalent to an "inflation target" in this model) for the monetary policy, comprising both a Taylor and FX intervention rule, to be consistent.[39]

Third, there are two types of possible anti-inflationary policies. If the price level is above the target or desired level, the central bank can raise the interest rate or sell foreign currency (i.e., reduce the intervention rule's target exchange rate). If it increases the interest rate, both the exchange rate and economic activity decrease, and both reduce the price level. The situation changes if the central bank lowers the intervention rule's target exchange rate. A reduction in the target exchange rate (E^M) shifts the BP_{RI} curve to the right (figure 5.2) without moving the IS curve. We move from point B to point A. The exchange rate diminishes and economic activity increases. The price level can drop if the aggregate supply curve is relatively flat. Foreign exchange reserves decrease if the balance of payments was equilibrated in the initial situation.

CONCLUDING REMARKS

The central bank's holdings of foreign exchange reserves play a key role in the design of a monetary policy that combines a sterilized intervention FX policy of leaning against the wind with a Taylor rule for the short-term interest rate.

Keynes (1971) says in the *Treatise on Money*, volume VI, that "national systems develop devices and maintain large liquid reserves with the express object of having the power to maintain internal equilibrium over the short period, without too sensitive a regard for external events" (320). What is an adequate level of international reserves? It depends on the magnitude of adverse external shocks. According to Keynes (1971), to determine this level requires "a reasoned estimate of the magnitude of the drain which India might have to meet through the sudden withdrawal of foreign funds, or through a sudden drop in the value of Indian exports" (247). He adds that "this is the sort of calculation which every central bank ought to make. The bank of a country the exports of which are highly variable in price and quantity needs a larger free reserve. The bank of a country doing a large international financial and banking business needs a larger free reserve."

To address adverse external shock with expansionary monetary and fiscal policies, it is essential to have sufficient foreign exchange reserves. Peru's experience with the global financial crisis of 2008–2009 suggests that it is possible to avoid major recessions and substantial increases in inflation if this necessary condition is satisfied.[40]

NOTES

I am grateful to Gustavo Ganiko for his impeccable assistance.

1. The credit channel in this chapter refers to the effect that monetary policy instruments have on loan volume and the interest rates charged by banks. See Bernanke and Gertler (1995).

2. For a description of the use of these diverse instruments in Peru, see Rossini et al. (2011).

3. Regarding the motives that justify this option, see Ball (2009).

4. See Dancourt and Mendoza (2002).

5. If short-term external debt is exempt from reserve requirements, as was the case in the Peruvian economy between 1992 and 2004, the lending interest rate in FC would not depend on the FC reserve requirement ratio. The remuneration on FC banking reserves can also be included as a determinant of the lending interest rate in FC. See Dancourt and Mendoza (2002).

6. The pass-through coefficients that link changes in the reference interest rate and changes in the banking system's interest rates in DC have been increasing over the last decade, as documented by BCRP (2009); these coefficients are higher for the bank interest rates of shorter maturities.

7. To simplify, we have not considered fiscal policy and public debt. If there is no local bond market, the fiscal deficit would be equal to the increase in external public debt.

8. The exchange rate is defined as the peso value of a dollar.

9. It is assumed that the Marshall–Lerner condition holds.

10. See Rossini and Vega (2007).

11. This IS curve implies that the aggregate demand curve has a positive slope on the economic activity–price level quadrant given the interest rate; if the competitiveness effect dominates, the aggregate demand curve has the usual negative slope given the interest rate. See Tobin (1980).

12. The uncovered interest rate parity equation implies that the exchange rate is only a function of the domestic and foreign interest rates and of the exchange rate expected by the bondholders. If the home and foreign central banks set the domestic and foreign interest rates, and if the expected exchange rate is also an exogenous variable, it is clear that a sterilized purchase or sale of foreign currency by the central bank cannot

change the exchange rate. Alternatively, this interest rate parity equation implies that the central bank can only fix either the interest rate or the exchange rate. For a sterilized intervention to change the price of the foreign currency in the Mundell–Fleming model given these three exogenous variables, it is necessary to use a balance-of-payments equation as in Ball (2012) or a modified uncovered interest rate parity with a risk premium as in Krugman and Obstfeld (2001). Both versions of the Mundell–Fleming model suppose that the domestic and foreign assets are imperfect substitutes and thus introduce an additional factor, the relative supply of domestic and foreign assets, that also influences the exchange rate and that the central bank can manipulate with sterilized intervention; in both cases, the central bank can fix both the interest and exchange rates. See Dornbusch and Krugman (1976) and Dornbusch (1984).

13. It is assumed that the foreign exchange position neither earns interest income nor suffers changes in valuation.

14. A similar equation exists for the market of loans in DC. For the demands of loans and deposits in both currencies to be consistent with one other given financial wealth, it is assumed that 1) the reserve requirement ratio in DC influences only both types of deposits, and 2) the reserve requirement ratio in FC does not directly influence deposits or loans but rather only through the lending rate in FC. The loan market in DC remains in the shadow in the same way that the bond market does in the original IS-LM-BP model.

15. Banks cannot always obtain all the external debt they want at the current interest rate. During the crises of 2008–2009 and 1998–2000, Peruvian banks suffered an abrupt cut in their short-term external credit lines, a similar phenomenon to a depositor's run. These circumstances can be represented imperfectly in this framework as an increase in the foreign interest rate.

16. An increase in the exchange rate improves the trade balance in dollars if the Marshall–Lerner condition holds and if the coefficient of the exchange rate on aggregate supply is less than unity, assuming that the balance of payments was equilibrated in the initial situation. The increase in the exchange also has a positive effect on the capital account.

17. See Henderson (1984).

18. The central bank has two monetary policy tools in the models of Henderson (1984), Dornbusch (1984), Krugman and Obstfeld (2001), Tobin and Braga de Macedo (1980), and Ball (2012).

19. With a fixed exchange rate, these equilibria are not necessarily lasting because they do not exclude, for example, a balance-of-payments deficit and a sustained loss of reserves by the central bank. With a completely flexible exchange rate, they are lasting. See Tobin (1980).

20. The classic external shock in the Peruvian economy is a drop in the international prices of export commodities, which deteriorates the balance of payments and reduces aggregate demand; it is equivalent to a global recession or an increase in external interest rates, two of the adverse shocks shown in table 5.1. See Ball (2009) and Dancourt (2009).

21. It is assumed that the direct effect of both adverse external shocks that deteriorates the balance of payments dominates the indirect effect that improves the balance of payments through a decline in economic activity and the price level.

22. This result is obtained by totally differentiating the AS-AD system; it does not change if the devaluation is expansionary.

23. The Peruvian authorities responded to the external shock of 2008–2009 with a similar Keynesian policy. It was the first adverse external shock in the last half-century that was dealt with monetary and fiscal expansionary policies. From 1998 to 2000, after a similar external shock, both the interest and exchange rates were raised; the recession was much worse than the one that occurred in 2008–2009, and a banking crisis ensued. In the first case, there were enough foreign exchange reserves available; in the second, there were not. See Dancourt and Jiménez (2010).

24. These two types of expansionary monetary policies have differentiated effects on credit in DC and FC. A cut in the reference rate increases loans in DC, but it can lead to a contraction in loans in FC. The reduction in the reserve requirement ratios in FC increase loans in FC but can lead to a reduction in loans in DC.

25. During the external shocks of 1998–2000 and 2008–2009, the banking system's short-term foreign debt and domestic loans in foreign currency dropped in the Peruvian economy despite the reductions in the FC reserve requirement ratio. See Dancourt and Jiménez (2010). A capital inflow generated by a reduction in the foreign interest rate can certainly be neutralized with an increase in the reserve requirement ratio in FC. Economic activity and the price level will not change if everything else remains constant.

26. This is similar to Krugman and Obstfeld (2001) and Mankiw (2010).

27. As stated in endnote 20, it is assumed that the direct effect of these adverse external effects, which leads to a deterioration of the balance of payments, is larger than its indirect effect. If the expected exchange rate changes, there is no indirect effect.

28. A sufficient condition for a higher (lower) interest rate to cause a decrease (increase) in economic activity is that the impact of the interest rate on aggregate demand is larger than the impact on capital flows ($\alpha_1 > \alpha_{13}$) and that the impact of the exchange rate on the balance of payments is larger than its impact on aggregate demand ($\alpha_9 - \alpha_{11}\alpha_{17} > \alpha_3 - \alpha_5\alpha_{17}$).

29. The aggregate supply curve should be relatively flat. If $\alpha_{18} = 0$, the exchange rate must remain constant so that the price level does not change. The interest rate must increase to counteract the upward pressure on the exchange rate from the adverse external effect; this leads to a recession of the economy.

30. A reduction of the reserve requirement ratio in FC is ineffective when facing a capital outflow. See endnote 23.

31. Both the interest and exchange rates rose significantly during the 1998–2000 crisis in the Peruvian economy. See Dancourt and Jiménez (2010). The argumentation supposes that the α_{13} coefficient of the local interest rate in the BP curve would be a lot smaller than the α_{14} term of the external interest rate or the expected exchange rate.

32. A limited flexibility in the exchange rate can also contribute to the de-dollarization of the banking system. See Armas and Grippa (2006) and Krugman (2000).

33. In Peru, these FX interventions are sterilized so that the short-term interest rate does not vary; the central bank operates with a target zone but does not announce the limits of the exchange rate band, which Williamson (2010) criticizes. It is clear,

however, that the strength and frequency of the interventions indicate the market operators for the approximate location of this exchange rate band.

34. Dornbusch (1980) and Black (1987) combine an FX intervention rule and a balance-of-payments equation.

35. The Peruvian central bank's foreign exchange position, which represented 19 percent of GDP in early 2008, was reduced by 27 percent between April 2008 and April 2009, while the exchange rate increased 20 percent between the minimum and peak of this period.

36. Blanchard et al. (2010) ask: "Isn't it time to reconcile practice with theory, and to think of monetary policy more broadly, as the joint use of the interest rate and sterilized intervention, to protect inflation targets while reducing the costs associated with excessive exchange rate volatility?" According to Blanchard et al. (2010), "imperfect capital mobility endows central banks with a second instrument in the form of reserve accumulation and sterilized intervention. This tool can help control the external target while domestic objectives are left to the policy rate."

37. During the boom, the central bank can also raise the reserve requirement ratios on FC deposits and external credit lines or reduce the remuneration on reserve requirements in FC to raise the lending interest rate in FC. During a recession the central bank can do the opposite. Another option is to keep the reserve requirement ratio in FC at a high level and the remuneration at a low level during both booms and recessions to gradually de-dollarize the banking system and thus reduce the risk of a financial crisis. The extreme volatility of external funding, which led to the banking crisis of 1998–2000, could have precipitated another crisis in 2008–2009 had it not been for the intervention of the Peruvian central bank. See Dancourt and Jiménez (2010).

38. From 1950 to 2010, there were seven large recessions in the Peruvian economy, one in each decade with the exception of the 1980s, when there were two. In five of these recessions, inflation rose. In the last two recessions, 1998–2000 and 2008–2009, inflation declined.

39. In this chapter, the central bank's price target would not be the consumer price index, which depends on the exchange rate (E) and the domestic price level (P), according to the weights that the imported and domestic goods have on the consumer basket. Instead, the target of the central bank would be the domestic price level (P). In both cases, however, the central bank must stabilize the exchange rate and the output gap to stabilize the price level.

40. Damill and Frenkel (2011) and IMF (2010) found that emerging economies with larger foreign exchange reserves suffered milder recessions during the external crisis of 2008–2009, taking into account other factors such as the change in exports, short-term foreign debt, or the growth rate before the crisis. Dominguez et al. (2011) found that emerging economies with larger foreign currency reserves experienced higher growth after the 2008–2009 crisis, taking into account other factors such as the change in terms of trade or the growth rate before the crisis. See also Feldstein (1999).

REFERENCES

Armas, A. and Grippa, F. 2006. "Metas de inflación en una economía dolarizada: la experiencia del Perú." In *Dolarización financiera: la agenda de política*, edited by A. Armas, E. Levy Yeyati, and A. Ize, 135–162. Lima: BCRP and FMI.

Ball, L. 2009. "Policy responses to exchange rate movements." National Bureau of Economic Research Working Paper 15173. http://www.nber.org/papers/w15173.

Ball, L. 2012. *Money, banking, and financial markets*, 2nd ed. Duffield, UK: Worth Publishers.

Banco Central de Reserva del Perú (BCRP). 2009 (June). "Reporte de inflación: Panorama actual y proyecciones macroeconómicas 2009–2011." http://www.bcrp .gob.pe/docs/Publicaciones/Reporte-Inflacion/Reporte-Inflacion-22-Junio-2009 /Reporte.pdf.

Bernanke, B. S. and Gertler, M. 1995. "Inside the Black Box: The Credit Channel of Monetary Policy Transmission." *Journal of Economic Perspectives* 9(4): 27–48.

Black, S. 1987. "The effect of alternative intervention policies on the variability of exchange rates: the Harrod effect." In *Exchange rate management under uncertainty*, J. Bhandari, ed. Cambridge, MA: MIT Press: 73–82.

Blanchard, O. 2006. *Macroeconomics*, 4th ed. Upper Saddle River, NJ: Prentice Hall.

Blanchard, O., Dell'Ariccia, G., and Mauro, P. 2010. "Rethinking macroeconomic policy." IMF Staff Position Note. http://jeromevillion.free.fr/Chronique Subprimes_Documents/ChroniqueSubprimes_Blanchard2010.pdf.

Clift, J. 2010 (February 12). "IMF explores contours of future macroeconomic policy. Interview with Olivier Blanchard." *IMF Survey Magazine*.

Damill, M. and Frenkel, R. 2011. "Macroeconomic policies and performance in Latin America 1990–2010." Buenos Aires: CEDES.

Dancourt, O. 2009. "Choques externos y política monetaria." *Revista Economia PUCP* 32(64): 127–173

Dancourt, O. and Jiménez, R. 2010. "Perú: lecciones de la recesión de 2008–2009." Documentos Técnicos, Iniciativa para la Transparencia Internacional. http://www.itf.org.ar/pdf/documentos/73-2010.pdf.

Dancourt, O. and Mendoza, W. 2002. *Modelos macroeconómicos para una economía dolarizada*. Lima: PUCP Fondo Editorial.

Dominguez, K., Hashimoto, Y., and Takatoshi, I. 2011. "International reserves and the global financial crisis." National Bureau of Economic Research Working Paper 17362. http://www.nber.org/papers/w17362.pdf.

Dornbusch, R. and Krugman, P. 1976. "Flexible exchange rates in the short run." *Brookings Papers on Economic Activity* (3): 537–584.

Dornbusch, R. 1980. *Open economy macroeconomics*. New York, NY: Basic Books.

Dornbusch, R. 1984. "Comments." In *Exchange rate theory and practice*, edited by J. Bilson and R. Marston, 398–402. Cambridge, MA: National Bureau of Economic Research.

Feldstein, M. 1999. "Self-protection for emerging market economies." National Bureau of Economic Research Working Paper 6907. http://www.nber.org/papers /w6907.pdf.

Frenkel, R. and Rapetti, M. 2010. "A concise history of exchange rate regimes in Latin America." Working Paper 2010-01. University of Massachusetts, Amherst.

Henderson, D. 1984. "Exchange market intervention operations: their role in financial policy and their effects." In *Exchange rate theory and practice*, edited by J. Bilson and R. Marston, 359–406. Cambridge, MA: National Bureau of Economic Research.

International Monetary Fund (IMF) 2010. "How did emerging markets cope in the crisis?" https://www.imf.org/external/np/pp/eng/2010/061510.pdf.

Keynes, J. M. 1971. *A treatise on money: collected writings*, vols. V and VI. London: The Royal Economic Society.

Krugman, P. 1999. "Analytical afterthoughts on the Asian crisis." web.mit.edu/krugman/www/MINICRIS.htm.

Krugman, P. 2000. "Crises: the price of globalization?" Paper for the Jackson Hole Conference Global Economic Integration: Opportunities and Challenges. Federal Reserve of Kansas City, MO.

Krugman, P. and Obstfeld, M. 2001. *Economía internacional: teoría y política*, 5th ed. Madrid: Addison-Wesley.

Mankiw, N. G. 2010. *Macroeconomics*, 7th ed. Duffield, UK: Worth Publishers.

Ostry, J., Ghosh, A., and Chamon, M. 2012. "Two targets, two instruments: monetary policy and exchange rate policies in emerging market economies." IMF Staff Discussion Note. https://www.imf.org/external/pubs/ft/sdn/2012/sdn1201.pdf.

Rossini, R. and Vega, M. 2007. "El mecanismo de transmisión de la política monetaria en un entorno de dolarización financiera: el caso del Perú entre 1996 y 2006." Documento de Trabajo 2007-017. http://www.bcrp.gob.pe/docs/Publicaciones /Revista-Estudios-Economicos/14/Estudios-Economicos-14-1.pdf.

Rossini, R., Quispe, Z., and Rodríguez, D. 2011. "Capital flows, monetary policy and forex intervention in Peru." Banco Central de Reserva del Perú, Documento de Trabajo 2011-08. http://www.bis.org/publ/bppdf/bispap57r.pdf.

Taylor, J. B. 1993. "Discretion versus policy rules in practice. Carnegie-Rochester Conference Series on Public Policy 39: 195–214.

Tobin, J. 1980. *Asset accumulation and economic activity*. Chicago, IL: University of Chicago Press.

Tobin, J. and Braga de Macedo, J. 1980. "The short-run macroeconomics of floating exchange rates: an exposition." In *Flexible exchange rates and balance of payments: essays in honor of Egon Sohmen*, edited by J. Chipman and C. Kindleberger, 5–28. Amsterdam: North-Holland.

Williamson, J. 2010. "Exchange rate policy in Brazil." Peterson Institute for International Economics, Working Paper 10-16. http://www.iie.com/publications/wp /wp10-16.pdf.

PART 2

Economic Development in Latin America

CHAPTER 6

The Chilean Economy Since the Global Crisis

Ricardo Ffrench-Davis and Rodrigo Heresi

Despite evident economic and social progress since the 1990s and its return to democracy, Chile is far from being a developed economy, and its trajectory in recent decades has shown considerable volatility. For example, in 1973, Chile had reached 29 percent of the GDP per capita of the G-7 countries; in 1989, however, at the end of the Pinochet dictatorship, the share of Chile fell to scarcely 25 percent, with significant declines during the deep crisis of 1982–1983. Later, principally because of progressive reforms instituted during the 1990s, it rose to 43 percent in 2012. Particularly relevant is the fact that average annual GDP growth climbed to 7.1 percent for the years 1990 through 1998, dropped to 3.7 percent from 1999 to 2008, and to 4.0 percent for the period from 2009 to 2012.

The economy has exhibited low inflation and fiscal responsibility, but highly fluctuating aggregate demand, external imbalances, and the real exchange rate (RER) indicate that real macroeconomics, with the exception of the early 1990s (1990–1995), has been failing. With respect to income distribution, it had improved in the 1990s following a profound deterioration associated with the dictatorship's extreme neoliberal reforms during the years 1973 to 1989, although it was subject yet again to considerable swings associated with sharp changes in economic growth and its composition during the 2000s. Chile remains a highly unequal economy even today.

As a result of contagion from the international global financial crisis, economic activity experienced a sharp external shock in 2009 that gave way to a recessive adjustment. A broad spectrum of public policies was applied to counter the emergency, including a substantial increase in public expenditure, with proemployment and investment measures and monetary transfers to those with the least resources. The global crisis found Chile well prepared with a regulated and capitalized banking system, a treasury that was a net creditor to the rest of the world, and (prior to the crisis) a significant current account surplus. Additionally, Chile benefited from a sharp recovery of the terms of trade after the deep but short-termed downfall in 2008 and early 2009. By the last quarter of 2009, with the combined effects of the positive terms of trade shock and the domestic countercyclical drive, the economy was in sustained recovery.

Resolving one challenge implied by the recovery, following a recession such as the one in 2009, is relatively easy. In March 2010, when a new political alliance came to power, Chile had sufficient available capacity to allow GDP to grow, for various quarters, much faster than the productive capacity that had been created. As a result, the recessive gap between actual and potential GDP has been shrinking during the recovery process, which implies moving toward macroeconomic balance: the use of potential GDP. There is, however, a need for action on two other fronts. One is to continue correcting the workings of the economy so that middle- and low-income people become increasingly incorporated into the productive economy (implying structural reforms).[1] The other is to eliminate macroeconomic imbalances or to avoid their build-up (implying real macroeconomic reforms, including exchange rate sustainability). The first continues to be missing, and the second is failing.

Following this introduction is a brief overview of the evolution of the Chilean economy during the sixteen years of the dictatorship (1973–1989) and the four democratic governments (1990–2010). The second section examines the contagion effects of the 2008–2009 crisis, while the third looks at economic policy responses and the effects of countercyclical policies up to the end of the Bachelet presidency in March 2010. The fourth section discusses policies and outcomes up to 2012. The chapter concludes with some final remarks.

A BRIEF ACCOUNT OF DEVELOPMENT SINCE 1973

Chile is often mentioned as a paradigmatic case of successful economic reforms under authorities of very different persuasions. There is an erroneous perception that there is only "one" Chilean model that accounts for a supposedly sustained economic success since 1973. In fact, starting with the deep neoliberal economic reforms imposed by the Pinochet dictatorship, there have been various subperiods with considerably different policy approaches, changing international economic environments and leading to very different economic and social outcomes. It is a mistake to talk about one model or only one sustained outcome.[2]

The first wave of reforms (1973–1981), launched after the 1973 military coup, was marked by the implementation of an extreme neoliberal model. Drastic trade and financial liberalization were implemented without prudential regulations. Up until 1981, there was progress in containing inflation and eliminating a large public deficit—at the cost, however, of a huge external imbalance with the accumulation of a large private foreign debt. In contrast, a significantly low productive investment ratio prevailed. These disequilibria in the real economy, combined with the external shocks that the region had suffered, led to a collapse in 1982, with a 14 percent decrease in GDP, an increase in unemployment to 30 percent, and a substantial increase in poverty and inequality.

During the second phase (1982–1989), the dictatorship itself moved toward more pragmatic policies to overcome the deep crisis of 1982. These policies involved a series of public interventions that had been sharply criticized during the first phase, among which were increasing tariffs on imports, a "selective" subsidy to exports, the creation of strict regulations for financial markets, and the rescuing of bankrupt private banks. Public subsidies provided to banks and debtors climbed to an amount equivalent to 35 percent of GDP (Sanhueza 2001). A crawling peg policy for the exchange rate, under the pressure of sharp foreign currency shortages, provided a 130 percent real devaluation between the extreme appreciation recorded before the crisis that exploded in 1982 and a depreciated peak in 1988.

During the recovery, between 1986 and 1989, GDP grew robustly, but if one takes into account the recession of 1982, then annual average growth was a mediocre 2.9 percent, while income distribution suffered an additional deterioration. Overall, GDP per capita took until 1988 to return to the level achieved in 1981.

With the return of democracy in 1990, a third variation of the economic model began. The focus of the *Concertación Democrática* (Democratic Coalition), the center-left coalition of socialists and Christian democrats, was to promote "change with stability, seeking growth with equity." The crucial reforms to the inherited model included the restoration of labor rights, a tax reform to finance an increase in social expenditure, and a deep countercyclical reform to macroeconomic policies.

Box 6.1 Countercyclical Reserve Requirements on Financial Inflows During the 1990s

After returning to democratic rule in 1990, Chile—because of its economic recovery, smaller economic size, and the smooth political transition it went through—faced a greater supply of external finance (in relation to GDP) than any other Latin American country. This supply threatened to destabilize its macroeconomy and export strategy (particularly its goal of keeping a level of aggregate demand consistent with potential GDP and maintaining an exchange rate consistent with a sustainable external balance). In response, it established an unremunerated reserve requirement on financial inflows. The reserve rate, the duration for its retention at the central bank, and its coverage were adjustable according to the strength of the supply of external funds. The purpose was to make net flows consistent with the volumes that could be absorbed in productive investment while maintaining macroeconomic equilibrium. The flexibility with which the rate could be managed and its coverage allowed it to possess the virtues of a control mechanism that combined the use of relative prices and quantitative restrictions, although adjustments were performed with delays and insufficiency.

From 1990 to 1995, exchange rate appreciation and the current account deficit (as a share of GDP) were less than the average for the region. The disincentives of destabilizing short-term capital inflows provided room for instituting countercyclical exchange rate and monetary policies. Thus, Chile was able to gain control of the composition of inflows, which significantly reduced liquid short-term inflows. Together with interventions to sterilize the monetary and foreign

The macroeconomic reforms covered exchange rate policies, monetary and domestic financial regulations, and the countercyclical regulation of the capital account. These reforms were conducted from the perspective that the economic equilibrium of the "real" economy was one crucial ingredient for the achievement of growth with equity. This was the context in which Chile, during the 1990s, broadened and sustained its productive capacity, recording an average 7.1 percent annual GDP growth between 1990 and 1998, with improvements to income distribution, a sizable decline in poverty, and a diversified growth of exports.

exchange markets, this kept Chile from a destabilizing appreciation of the exchange rate and helped it maintain an aggregate demand consistent with potential GDP and the deficit in the current account within sustainable limits during the 1990s.

There is a further dynamic dimension that links the present to the future: an economy with a high rate of productive capacity utilization and long-term stable flows tends to exhibit higher productive investment ratios (Aizenman and Sushko 2011). This contributed to an increasing rate of productive investment in Chile between 1990 and 1995. Thus, it created a functional macroeconomic environment conducive to development. This countercyclical policy was increasingly weakened between 1996 and 1998 and rejected between 1999 and 2001, when it was replaced by the fashionable neoliberal belief in free exchange rates and open capital accounts.

Altogether, the evidence overwhelmingly shows that capital controls applied between 1990 and 1995 (1) modified the maturity structure of capital inflows, which reduced the speculative component; (2) allowed for the maintenance of a differential between the domestic and international interest rates, which provided room for an active monetary policy that ensured that the economy would be close to the production frontier; (3) avoided a destabilizing exchange rate appreciation (Magud and Reinhart 2006; Edwards and Rigobon 2009); and, above all, (4) contributed to a comprehensive and sustained real macroeconomic equilibrium.

Sources: Ffrench-Davis (2010b); Le Fort and Lehmann (2003); Williamson (2003).

A particular feature of this period were the capital account regulations that were instituted when there was a huge supply of financial flows into emerging economies. These vigorous countercyclical regulations were based on a flexible reserve requirement (*encaje*) or tax on financial inflows (see box 6.1) and contributed to keeping the volume of capital inflows under control, modifying their composition in favor of long-term capital and channeling financing toward productive investment, successfully avoiding an appreciation of the exchange rate and excessive domestic demand pressures. Macroeconomic stability had clear benefits for the real economy that translated into the previously mentioned growth and improvements in

capital formation, employment, and income distribution. It is worth pointing out that even though the private sector was carrying a somewhat higher
tax burden and was now obliged to respect more progressive labor rights
with increasing wages, the investment ratio increased from 13 percent of
GDP for the period 1982 to 1989 to 20 percent between 1990 and 1998.
Real macroeconomic stability was a key determinant of this improvement
and led to a level of domestic demand consistent with potential GDP and a
"stable and competitive" real exchange rate, a crucial macroprice.[3]

In the following years (1999–2008), GDP growth declined to 3.7 percent annually, and exports fell slightly to 6.1 percent, with most of the
contraction resulting from other GDP components (i.e., nonexported
GDP or output for the domestic market), which fell from an annual 6.5
percent average growth in the period 1990 to 1998 to 3.0 percent (see
table 6.1). A reduced quality of macroeconomic policies played a key role
during these years, with recurrent output gaps and large swings in the real

Table 6.1 Exports and Economic Growth, 1974–2012

	GDP	Exports	Nonexported GDP
1974–1989	2.9	10.7	1.6
		(1.8)	(1.1)
1990–1998	7.1	9.9	6.5
		(2.0)	(5.1)
1999–2008	3.7	6.1	3.0
		(1.6)	(2.2)
2009	−1.0	−4.5	0.1
		(−1.1)	(0.1)
2010	5.8	2.3	6.9
		(0.6)	(5.2)
2011	5.9	5.2	6.1
		(1.2)	(4.7)
2012	5.6	1.0	6.9
		(0.2)	(5.3)
2009–2012	4.0	0.9	4.9
		(0.2)	(3.8)
1990–2012	5.1	6.6	4.7
		(1.5)	(3.6)

Sources: Ffrench-Davis (2010b) and updates based on Central Bank data; since 2009, growth rates of
the new chained 2008 series were used.

Note: Data shown are annual average rates of growth by percentage; figures in parentheses represent the
contribution of exports and the rest of GDP (i.e., nonexports) to the percentage change in GDP.

exchange rate. The conventional recipe of low inflation and fiscal balance did not guarantee real macroeconomic balance because the consistency of effective demand with potential GDP and the sustainability of the RER were missing (see Ffrench-Davis 2006, chapters 2 and 3).

Paradoxically, during the last part of the 1990s, the independent central bank, reversing the highly successful policies of the first half of the decade, gradually adopted the neoliberal approach then in fashion: liberalization of the capital account, a freely floating exchange rate, and a monetary policy focused on inflation targeting. As a result, domestic demand and the exchange rate began to depend on financial flows, thus becoming "victims" of the globalization of financial volatility. Low inflation coexisted with aggregate demand and real exchange rate volatility. Policies increasingly moved away from a macroeconomics for development, and the economy began to cater to short-termism finance at the expense of a sustained and more equitable growth.

In contrast, in a positive move toward a countercyclical approach to macroeconomic policy, the economic authorities formalized a fiscal policy based on a structural balance rule that isolates the cyclical effects on fiscal revenue of the level of economic activity and of copper prices, thus defining an expenditure level consistent with structural or trend revenue (Tapia 2003; Velasco et al. 2010). Evidently, instability of the real economy responded to swings in private demand that were led by the midterm volatility of capital flows and terms of trade.[4]

Taken together, the performances of the four coalition governments was far superior to that of the dictatorship; annual per capita GDP growth was 3.7 percent during the period from 1990 to 2009 (counting a 2 percent drop in 2009) compared with 1.3 percent between 1974 and 1989. In addition, social policy had been strengthened and inequality somewhat reduced, although the latter continued to be shamefully high, mainly because of the regressive features of labor and financial markets, the low tax burden and the continued weakness of public education, and the reversals in macroeconomic policies during the second half of the democratic period.

After progressing under democracy, the economic agenda demanded deeper additional reforms to "guarantee" a sustained development with an emphasis on small and medium-sized enterprises (SMEs), labor training, and technological innovation. It was necessary to retake a macroeconomic path for development, which would grant greater priority to the regulation of speculative capital flows and the evolution of the RER.

THE IMPACT OF THE CRISIS: FOURTH QUARTER OF 2008 AND 2009[5]

By 2007, before the contagion of the global crisis, Chile was enjoying a notable positive shock from rising international commodity prices. As a result, it experienced an external surplus (despite a huge increase in imports), low public debt, a fiscal surplus, and significant sovereign funds and central bank international reserves. At the same time, the peak of international prices for fuel and food resulted in a persistent increase in the domestic price level, far higher than the target set by the central bank. The bank continued its policy bias in favor of the inflation target at the expense of growth; in fact, the economy moved closer to the production frontier between 2004 and 2008 but seems never to have reached it. So, toward the end of 2008, a recessive gap that started to increase with the contagion of the global crisis still prevailed. Then, when there were already clear signs of recession, with negative monthly inflation rates, the interest rate of monetary policy was still maintained at 7 percentage points above that of the US Federal Reserve.

The first shock of the global crisis contagion was on the stock market, followed by falling exports, highly depressed export prices, and capital "flight." As a result of the trade and financial external shocks, there has been a contraction in aggregate demand followed by a drop in output, employment, and capital formation since September 2008.

EXTERNAL BALANCES

It is revealing that already by late 2007 the quantum of exports was performing weakly with drops in noncopper exports, items that were more sensitive to the level and instability of the exchange rate; it implied a destabilizing appreciation. It was only several quarters later that the price of copper plunged at the same time world trade was slowing (from a growth rate of 8 percent in 2007 to 3 percent in 2008) and rushing to a sharp 12 percent drop in 2009. By the second half of 2008, the current account was experiencing a deficit of 6 percent of GDP as a result of the fall in prices and volumes exported, together with high imports led by an excessively appreciated exchange rate. A freely floating exchange rate responded excessively to fluctuations in the price of exports and concomitant financial inflows (in their typical procyclical behavior; see Ffrench-Davis 2006: 163–168).

Global financial volatility had contaminated the market for commodities, which were increasingly exposed to speculation in international financial markets. After reaching a historic peak of US$4 per pound in early 2008, the price of copper (representing approximately one-half of exports) fell abruptly to US$1.40 later that year. Additionally, the export quantum rose a mere 3.2 percent in 2008 and fell by 4.5 percent in 2009, in contrast to an annual increase of 8 percent between 1990 and 2007.

The strong domestic impact can be seen on import volumes and on the local financial market. Domestic banks increased their liquidity preference, producing a strong rise in lending interest rates and a contraction in the supply of loans. The fall in disposable income, coupled with peso depreciation and an increased uncertainty, depressed output. A recessive gap was opened that as usual reduced the investment ratio after a short lag. Depreciation and falling aggregate demand led to a 16 percent drop in the import quantum coupled with a 1 percent GDP decrease in 2009.

During the most recessive months (November 2008 to August 2009), the government repatriated a considerable amount of money from the sovereign funds to finance a fiscal deficit that had resulted from reduced revenue and increased expenditure. This bold countercyclical behavior coexisted with spectacular outflows from residents, principally associated with private pension funds, whose outflows climbed to the equivalent of 10 percent of GDP. These institutional investors, operating with forced savings from workers, had—as in 1998 and 1999—a strong procyclical behavior, which reveals a macroeconomic policy failure: they should have faced a countercyclical regulation instead (Zahler 2006). In 2009, there were total net capital outflows worth 2 percent of GDP (see table 6.2).

Table 6.2 Net Capital Flows by Institutional Sector as Percentages of GDP, 2003–2012

	2003–2007	2008	2009	2010–2011	2012
FDI net inflows	6.2	8.6	7.5	8.1	11.3
Greenfield FDI	4.9	6.3	5.6	n/a	n/a
Mergers and acquisitions	1.3	2.4	1.9	n/a	n/a
FDI net outflows	−2.1	−5.1	−4.2	−6.2	−7.9
General government	−2.2	−2.6	4.4	−1.0	−0.7
Central Bank	0.0	−3.6	−0.3	−3.5	0.1
Pension funds	−2.5	−1.6	−9.7	−0.2	−2.5
Financial and other	−1.7	7.5	0.3	1.3	3.1
Total net capital flows	−2.4	3.2	−2.0	−1.5	3.5

Sources: Based on the new series of balance-of-payments figures from the Central Bank (2003–2012); UNCTAD for mergers and acquisitions.

Note: "Financial and other" and "Total net capital flows" include errors and omissions. Negative figures imply capital outflows. FDI, foreign direct investment.

ECONOMIC ACTIVITY AND AGGREGATE DEMAND

After growing at rates above 8 percent per year between 2004 and 2008, domestic demand collapsed by the same percentage in the first three quarters of 2009 compared to the same period in 2008; in parallel, responding to the drop in domestic demand, GDP contracted 3 percent by mid-2009 compared to a 5 percent growth in the previous period and a similar figure projected for the 2009 rise in potential GDP (see table 6.3).

As tends to happen in recessions, the impact of the large recessive gap on capital formation was strong. Gross capital formation had been growing at approximately 14 percent annually (in a recovery from the recessive 1999–2003 period) but declined 12 percent in 2009, largely

Table 6.3 Fiscal Indicators, 2001–2012

	2001–2003	2004–2007	2008	2009	2010–2011	2012
GDP growth (%)	3.2	5.6	3.3	–1.0	5.8	5.6
Trend GDP growth (%)	4.0	4.9	5.0	4.9	4.6	4.9
Current copper price (US$/lb.)	0.74	2.31	3.16	2.34	3.71	3.61
Trend copper price (US$/lb.)	0.90	1.00	1.37	1.99	2.36	3.02
Fiscal income growth (%): in constant CH$2011	4.1	18.2	–9.5	–20.4	19.9	0.9
Fiscal expenditure growth (%): in constant CH$2011	3.8	7.2	9.3	16.5	5.2	4.2
Fiscal balance (% of GDP): current	–0.7	5.6	4.1	–4.4	0.4	0.6
Structural fiscal balance (% of GDP): current	1.0	1.0	0.0	–1.2	–1.6	–0.6
Fiscal income (% of GDP): current	21.2	24.6	24.2	19.0	22.1	21.9
Fiscal expenditure (% of GDP): current	21.9	19.0	20.1	23.2	21.7	21.4

Sources: Ffrench-Davis (2010b) and updates based on Public Budget Office (DIPRES) figures.
Note: Data shown represent annual averages.

because of the 21 percent contraction in machinery and equipment (mainly imported and sources of incorporation of innovation and total factor productivity).

The official unemployment rate increased from 8.3 percent in 2008 to 10.7 percent in 2009, with a regressive impact, whereas labor participation decreased in typical procyclical behavior (Ffrench-Davis 2012). According to the 2009 National Poverty Survey (CASEN), poverty, which had followed a sustained downward trend from 45 percent of the population in 1987 to 13.7 percent in 2006, halted its decline and grew to 15.1 percent.

The step back can be explained by two situational factors, the first of which is the increase in the relative cost of the food basket as a result of the jump in international food prices. If the 2006 relative prices of food had prevailed in 2009, poverty would have decreased to 11.5 percent instead of worsening to 15.1 percent and would have been below the 13.7 percent reached in 2006.[6] Second, the CASEN survey was applied in November 2009, when the labor market was still strongly depressed because of the international crisis. In the absence of effective countervailing policies, the natural outcome would have been an increase in poverty and a worsening of income distribution. It is because of the strengthened progressive social policies implemented in 2009 that the negative effects on the most vulnerable population were mitigated.

ECONOMIC POLICY RESPONSES: 2008–2009

Monetary authorities implemented measures to increase liquidity in both foreign currency and pesos. Nonetheless, for several months the cost of credit increased substantially. The central bank maintained its monetary policy rate (TPM) at 8.25 percent until the end of 2008, partly because it feared a sharp depreciation of the peso during the months of greatest uncertainty and short-term deterioration in the inflation outlook.[7] It was evident by November 2008 that inflation had reached its inflection point. It was not until January 2009 that the central bank began to reduce the TPM, which culminated in July 2009 with a rate of 0.25 percent. In the meantime, because of a perceived risk by financial institutions, there was a slow transfer of rate reductions to the users of credit, thus supporting high bank profits.

Fiscal policy was the principal force that counterbalanced the negative external shock. In fact, fiscal policy advanced from a neutral position during the cycle, which required expenditure trends to be maintained during downturns, to one with a decidedly countercyclical focus (Ffrench-Davis 2010a; Tapia 2003). In 2009, public expenditure expanded by 17 percent even though revenue had fallen by 10 percent in 2008 and an additional 20 percent in 2009, with an actual fiscal deficit of 4.4 percent of GDP in the latter year (see table 6.3).

In fact, the government shifted policies dramatically. Whereas from 2004 to 2008 it had oversaved the revenue from the positive terms of trade shock, thereby losing the opportunity to rapidly reach the potential GDP early in the process of recovery, in 2009 it made broad use of the large funding that it had accumulated in previous years by implementing strong countercyclical, proemployment, and lending policies. As table 6.3 shows, the structural surplus rule implied that the treasury had accumulated fiscal surpluses equivalent to 27 percent of GDP over the course of the previous five years, while the public sector moved from debtor to net creditor. Thus, the government had financing of its own for adopting an active fiscal policy.

Among stimulus measures, there was an emphasis on the construction of social housing and massive road investment. A number of taxes on key sectors, including fuel, credit, and SMEs, was temporarily reduced. A key mitigation policy was the delivery of two vouchers, worth approximately US$80 each for nonworking members of families within the lowest 40 percent of the income bracket. In addition, efforts were renewed to improve and extend the pension system with a reform launched in 2008 before the onset of the crisis. The reform added a solidarity pillar to the capitalization pillar; individual capitalization accounts naturally reflected the inequality that prevailed in the Chilean labor market, while the reform included a public subsidy that compensated for part of the regressive bias. Actually, the privatization of the pension system, implemented by the dictatorship in 1981, worked rather satisfactorily for only about one-third of the population; the remaining two-thirds accumulated minor or negligible pension funds or were not contributors (Arenas 2010). From July 2008, basic solidarity pensions were delivered (a monthly cash benefit provided by the state) to those over 65 years of age and who belonged to the poorest 40 percent of the population (expanded to 50 percent in 2009); it also included complements to those pensions that did not exceed approximately 1.5 times the minimum wage. Although this is a structural distributive measure, it also contributed to economic recovery.

With respect to labor markets, a subsidy was provided for the hiring of low-income youth. The beneficiaries received a subsidy that was equivalent to 20 percent of their wages and the employer one of 10 percent.

This measure encouraged the hiring of a highly vulnerable group who lacked employment experience during times of crisis. In addition, the National Copper Corporation (CODELCO), the principal public company, was capitalized with a government contribution of US$1 billion to finance its investment projects, and the capital of the *Banco Estado,* the main state bank, was increased by 50 percent, which allowed for the issuance of additional loans to small and medium-sized firms. It is clear that without the countercyclical and mitigation policies implemented by the Bachelet government during the crisis, the step back in the struggle against poverty would have been far greater.

As table 6.1 shows, the decline in GDP in 2009 centered mostly around the drop of exports, with a smaller multiplier effect on the domestic economy; the opposite was seen in previous recessions, where external shocks had larger negative multiplier effects on domestic absorption and output. This implies a return (at least transitorily) to a more effective real macroeconomic policy.

THE RECOVERY FROM LATE 2009 AND UNSUSTAINABLE IMBALANCES

USING OUTPUT CAPACITY

In 2009, the strong external negative shock from the international crisis was progressively compensated by the increasingly positive stimulus of the government's countercyclical policies that were implemented well before the rebound of the terms of trade in the latter part of the year. In the last months of the Bachelet administration (November 2009–February 2010), GDP was recovering at a solid 4 percent under the stimulus of the countercyclical policies and high export prices. Fiscal policy contributed strongly to the recovery of output, which, given a large recessive gap, was able to respond to the domestic demand–pull factors.

Chile regained a current account surplus in 2009, first as a result of the strong and fast downward adjustment of the demand for imports since late 2008 and later due to the recovery of copper prices (from US$1.4 to more than US$3 throughout the year). It was a very short negative external shock that was followed by a large positive shock in the price of copper that still prevailed by 2012. This external factor made a significant difference in subsequent macroeconomic balances.

The output gap that still remained in 2008 rose to approximately six additional points of GDP during the 2009 recession (given a 1 percent drop of GDP and an estimated 5 percent increase in potential GDP). Despite the damage caused by a severe earthquake in February 2010 that destroyed approximately 1 to 1.5 percent of capacity and 3 percent of the capital stock (see IPOM 2010), there was still significant room for actual GDP increases over the generation of new potential capacity. That was the situation in March 2010, when new authorities took power.

In 2010, as exports began to slowly grow again, it was still production geared to the domestic market that sustained the vigorous recovery. As estimated in table 6.1, exports contributed only 0.6 percent to the 5.8 percent increase in actual GDP, whereas output for the domestic market, led by a sharp recovery of effective demand, contributed 5.2 percent.

The recovery of output and employment by the last four months of the Bachelet regime was temporarily but significantly interrupted by the 2010 earthquake (in March 2010, economic activity fell 4.1 percent with respect to February).[8] In the five quarters that followed, domestic demand expanded by two digits, and the recovery of actual GDP reached a 7 percent annual rate of growth. In the process, the gap between potential and actual GDP became smaller. By 2012, actual growth was more in line with the rise in potential GDP, which authorities and market expectations estimated to be approaching an annual 5 percent, but domestic demand continued to grow faster than GDP, and, consequently, the external balance continued to worsen.

Economic recovery, in conjunction with the elapsing of the recessive gap, encouraged an increase in capital formation, particularly in equipment and machinery imports, which had been the most depressed during the contagion of the crisis. The gross investment ratio, which had fallen from a 25 percent peak in 2008 to a 22 percent plateau in 2009, hovered around 27 percent during the last four quarters. However, in response to the expansion of aggregate demand and a strong (but, we believe, unsustainable) appreciation of the exchange rate (as discussed in the next section), most imports rapidly increased.

AN OUTLIER EXCHANGE RATE: A MAIN MACROECONOMIC DISEQUILIBRIUM

As in the early 1990s, macroeconomic policy had fulfilled its duty of using productive capacity; this was a move toward one aspect of real macroeconomic equilibrium. However, in contrast with the 1990s, an external disequilibrium associated with the exchange rate policy increasingly reappeared. The weakness of the international demand for nontraditional exports was reinforced by an intense appreciation, which also discouraged nontraditional exports as well as their value added and the output of domestic producers of importables.[9]

RER appreciation has been recurrent from the beginning of the boom in commodity prices in late 2003, in an economy showing increasing signs of Dutch disease, led by a notably high price of the main Chilean export. As figure 6.1 shows, climbing imports coexisted with a volume of exports that was growing much more slowly. In fact, in the eight years from 2005 to 2012, the volume of imports rose 10.5 percent annually (including the 16 percent drop in 2009), whereas the volume of exports averaged a weak 3.0 percent (see figure 6.1). In 2012, Chile experienced a current account deficit of 3.4 percent of GDP despite a high US$3.61 price per pound of fine copper (see IPOM, March 2013); recall that its nominal level averaged US$0.74 in 2001–2003 (see table 6.3).

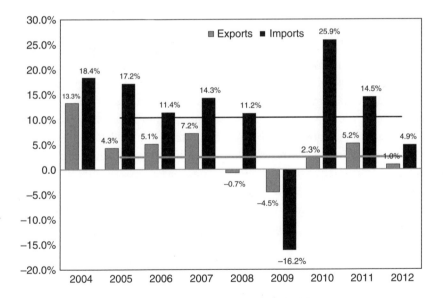

Figure 6.1. Evolution of exports and imports of goods and services, 2004–2012 (annual real growth rates). Exports and imports cover volume (quantum) of goods and services. The horizontal lines correspond to the simple average of the growth rates from 2005 to 2012; imports and exports show annual averages of 10.5 percent and 3.0 percent, respectively. *Sources:* Based on Central Bank of Chile figures in 2003 prices. Since 2009, growth rates of the 2008 chained series were used.

Between 2004 and 2012, the dynamism of export volumes fell persistently. Despite the proliferation of tariffs and other preferences embedded in the numerous free trade agreements signed by Chile, export diversification has been rather stagnant. Stagnation is associated with both the lack of productive development policies in Chile (something that has persisted since the imposition of neoliberal policies after the military coup), and with the step back on the exchange rate policy (gradually since 1996 and sharply in 1999).[10]

The failures of a freely floating exchange rate policy have been crucial in determining this outcome, as well as in wasting valuable opportunities for productive development offered by the trade agreements. The RER is currently the most significant variable that affects the allocation of resources between tradables and nontradables, the value added to gross exports, and the competitiveness of import substitutes.[11] An important part of the misleading appreciation experienced in Chile has resulted from a policy that refrains from managing exchange rate flexibility and leaves it to short-minded agents trained in managing financial flows as well as to transitory terms of trade fluctuations. The usual significant depreciations that follow significant appreciations imply that several producers of tradables are victims of a false belief of policy makers, who confuse transitory ups and downs as a permanent basis for a Dutch disease. It is quite doubtful that Chile should be adjusting toward a permanent "mineralization" of the economy. Even if the rise in the terms of trade is permanent, the adjustment should be gradual and assisted by economic policy rather than abrupt and under a "neutral" approach.

The neoliberal belief in fashion is that the monetary authority has no capacity to influence the exchange rate, as this approach implies "working against the market." The key counterargument is that there are different market segments with contradictory effects on the sources of economic growth. Consequently, policy should attempt to operate in favor of whatever segment is most relevant for productive development—i.e., the production of tradables in the case of this policy area—and avoid the misallocating effects of short-term agents or transitory terms of trade shocks that divert the exchange rate from a sustainable medium-term path. Therefore, this sort of counter cyclical intervention decidedly favors (instead of opposing) the market segments most important for economic growth.

Faced with the persistence of positive terms of trade shocks along with procyclical financial inflows that are additionally encouraged by interest rate differentials, the economy has increasingly accommodated to a real exchange rate consistent only with a high copper price.[12] The copper price in 2012 is notably greater than the historical average and (we believe) its long-run sustainable level.[13] The outcome has been the previously mentioned deficit on the current account, notwithstanding the very high copper price.

Actually, in 2012, the central bank carried out an exercise with US$2.80 as the working assumption for the trend price of copper.[14] Naturally, a trend price is an average of higher and lower prices; Chile has "benefited" from a long period of notably high prices, which is usually followed by periods of rather low prices, much below the trend (recall the several years from 1998 to 2003 in which the price hovered around a level scarcely one-fifth of the 2012 average).

In short, the continuation of a freely floating exchange rate and an open capital account is the abdication of sustainable macroeconomic balances, i.e., with aggregate demand close to the level of the productive frontier and "right" or well-aligned sustainable macroprices (e.g., the RER). In an environment of massive and volatile capital flows, with highly variable export prices, a totally freely floating exchange rate will tend to fluctuate widely, without positioning itself near the trend level consistent with sustainability.

Actually, the exchange rate has shown large mid-term volatility.[15] This volatility discourages (1) the generation of value added for natural resources; (2) the direct or indirect participation of SMEs as exporters; (3) the survival of the domestic industry that competes with imports and thus the jobs it generates; (4) productive investment in tradables; (5) taking advantage of the export opportunities offered by trade agreements; and can be (6) a major source of macroeconomic crises.

To renew sustained growth with equity, it is essential that Chile recovers its capacity to maintain real macroeconomic equilibrium. As a part of this process, the central bank should return to an exchange rate policy of managed flexibility—what Williamson (2003) called "intermediate regimes"—and reintroduce a countercyclical regulation of the capital account. The RER has been a clear outlier, as shown by the persistent gap between the rise of the quantum of imports and of exports over several years (see figure 6.1).

A NOVEL FISCAL MACROECONOMIC IMBALANCE

Chilean fiscal policy since the mid-1970s has been characterized by fairly "responsible" behavior. It was reflected in the accumulation of a large sovereign fund and its net creditor position by 2008—at the beginning of the contagion from the global crisis. As discussed previously, according to my interpretation, this policy was too conservative between 2004 and 2008; it sterilized too much of the positive external shock during those years. As table 6.3 shows, it kept a structural surplus that averaged 1 percent of GDP in 2004–2007 without seizing the opportunity to get effective demand close to potential GDP, which even by 2008 had not been reached. Moreover, a countercyclical increase in fiscal expenditure could have allowed for the financing of additional investment in human capital and in the productivity of SMEs.

Nonetheless, we also praised above the policy shift in 2009 that moved from the rather neutral structural approach to a strong counter cyclical policy, so determinant of the recovery of effective demand in that year. That policy switch implied an increase in fiscal expenditure as a share of GDP of approximately 4 percent.[16] Naturally, as a countercyclical policy, it was financed with withdrawals from the stabilization fund and not by new taxes. Because in 2010 a significant recessive gap continued to prevail, an expansionary fiscal policy was needed; in fact, 2010 expenditure was raised much faster than structural revenue (7.2 vs. 4.2 percent). Again in 2011, however, even though the rate of increase was cut by half, the level of expenditure remained high, partly with expenses related to reconstructions after the 2010 earthquake as well as with a new permanent social expenditure.[17] In 2012, when there was a consensus that the recessive gap had been closed, a structural fiscal balance (SFB) with a deficit remained, notwithstanding the very high estimate of the trend price of copper for that year (US$3.02; see table 6.3).[18] This implied that the higher permanent social expenditure was being financed with temporary revenue provided by a transitorily high price of copper.

The story is more complicated. The SFB is estimated with a trend price of copper that is provided by a copper price committee (see table 6.3). The figure provided for 2012 (US$3.02 per pound, as mentioned previously), is very high. Its high level has been explicitly internalized in the structural fiscal accounts by assuming high long-term copper prices and thus increasing the level of "structural" expenditure.[19] Year after year, the dependency of both fiscal and external balances on a boom of the copper price has deepened. In 2003, at the beginning of the boom of commodity prices, it implied a move toward equilibrium, departing from what seemed to be an excessively depressed price. It was moving toward the other extreme during the early 2010s. Fiscal policy was adding permanent expenditures without the corresponding new taxes, resting on the sustainability of a notably high copper price.[20]

The fiscal dependency on an unsustainable high price of copper (providing revenue in foreign currency) is directly associated with the destabilizing appreciation of the RER. This means that there were two deepening macroeconomic disequilibria in the Chilean economy by 2012.

CONCLUDING REMARKS

During most of the 1990s, Chile could manage its economy without being diverted by external shocks, but as that decade advanced it adopted a passive attitude when faced with the globalization of financial volatility. Since then, the exchange rate and aggregate demand—two essential components for real macroeconomic equilibrium—were dominated by the external fluctuations of the terms of trade and financial markets. By early 2013, the economy was working around full employment, which is good, but with domestic demand rising faster than GDP, a rising current account deficit, an excessively appreciated exchange rate, and a fiscal structural deficit—in a nutshell, an economy dangerously dependent on a notably high price of its main export.

A sustained drive toward convergent development implies an active macroeconomic policy that is focused on the real economy. For the economy to function well from a macroeconomic point of view, it requires (1) working close to potential GDP with an aggregate demand consistent with potential GDP, and (2) coordinating the countercyclical regulation/management of the capital account, exchange rate, and fiscal policy. The fact is that fiscal and external balances have become too dependent on a very high price of copper and inflation too much dependent on an unstable and appreciated exchange rate.

For the exchange rate to fulfill its allocative role efficiently in a development strategy, it is crucial to provide signals of more stability to (real) investors and producers in the medium term. This requires a RER that responds to changes in net productivity (à la Balassa–Samuelson) rather than to financial volatility in international markets.

The correction of macroeconomic policy should be carried out jointly with still-pending deep microeconomic reforms. These include structural reforms on the capital market that favor decision makers with long- rather than short-term horizons and the development of channels for funding opportunities to SMEs and new entrepreneurs.[21] The vacuum in research and development policy seemed to be filled somewhat when the Bachelet government announced it would launch productive development policies with a selection of "clusters"; they would be linked to exports of natural resources, seeking to increase their value added and linkages to the rest of the domestic economy.[22]

In summary, Chile has been slipping toward policies that emphasize financierism and moving away from the path that led to sustained and more equitable growth in the 1990s. The global crisis, because of its obvious link to financial volatility, should induce corrections to the international financial architecture (still pending), while emerging economies such as Chile should redesign their macroeconomic policies by adopting a comprehensive countercyclical approach—including regulation of the capital account—and promoting inclusive growth by introducing corrections to the economic development agenda.

NOTES

We appreciate the comments of Martin Rapetti, the research support of Diego Vivanco, and the translation of Anthony Tillett.

1. Reducing productivity gaps in the domestic economy—among small, large, and medium-sized firms (SMEs) and between well-trained and low-trained workers—is essential for economic development and social inclusion (Bourguignon and Walton 2007; Ffrench-Davis 2010b, chapter 7).

2. Empirical support, a description of reforms and policies, and our interpretation of outcomes can be found in Ffrench-Davis (2010b).

3. Frequently, what is taken as a "market equilibrium ER" is suddenly replaced by a quite different rate under the pressure of changes in capital flows or in the terms of trade; the new actual rate again tends to equilibrate the balance of payments but usually produces a disequilibrium in the current account. To be sustainable, the real exchange rate must reflect the relative productivity of domestic tradables vis-à-vis that of trade partners, which in conventional literature is called the Balassa–Samuelson theorem.

4. Relevant policy implications are not the short-term random walks of these variables but the mid-term fluctuations, which generate recessive gaps, deter capital formation, and induce misallocation of resources.

5. The second and third sections of this chapter make use of material developed in Ffrench-Davis and Heresi (2013).

6. For the figure of 11.5 percent, see ECLAC (2011: 74). The food basket is used to measure extreme poverty, which is then multiplied by 2 to fix the poverty line. The coefficient 2 is derived from the origin of the survey (1987), when households in quintile 3 spent half on food and the other half on the rest of goods and services. There is a measurement bias in keeping the coefficient 2 constant. In fact, given the structure of real expenditures, if food prices increase faster than the consumer price index (CPI), the coefficient should be reduced accordingly and vice versa (see Ffrench-Davis 2010b: 185).

7. The US Federal Reserve had reduced its rate to 2 percent in April 2008.

8. This figure is seasonally adjusted by the central bank and is obviously subject to large estimation errors. The drop in twelve months was originally estimated at 2 percent (of pesos in 2003); the newly chained national accounts of the bank yield a 0.1 percent decrease.

9. A domestic counterpart of appreciation and the worsening of the current account is the significant rise in the ratio of changes in the CPI of nontradables to tradables, as measured by the central bank (IPOM, September 2012, table 4.1).

10. There were several efforts to introduce productive development policies; the most promising one came from the Bachelet administration, which identified "clusters" on which to focus policy incentives (see National Council for Innovation, 2007). See a relevant discussion on the issue of structural heterogeneity and inclusive development in Infante and Sunkel (2009). I briefly return to this issue at the end of the chapter.

11. See Rodrik (2008), Frenkel and Rapetti (2010), and Ffrench-Davis (2010b, chapter 9).

12. There was a TPM gap of 5 percent.

13. Naturally, trend estimates must take care of structural changes such as the ones that occur in the quality of minerals and the cost of energy (both of which have worsened in average) and innovations (which have improved), with a net effect that has raised production costs in recent years. Additionally, there are increases in general price levels; e.g., the US CPI rose 21.4 percent between 2004 and 2012.

14. IPOM (June 2012). The September 2011 IPOM used US$2.60 as the trend price in an exercise. Heresi (2011), using a battery of econometric methods and a long-run copper price time series, estimated a trend price between US$1.80 and US$1.90 in 2010 and 2011. The Mining Council, an organization of large mining producers in Chile, estimated a trend level of US$2.70 in 2013.

15. The usual argument, that with a freely floating exchange rate the costs of foreign currency crises disappear, assumes away the allocative and regressive effects of the rate instability during the cycle.

16. The actual fiscal balance shifted from a 4 percent surplus to a 4 percent deficit between 2008 and 2009. As previously reported, fiscal revenue dropped because of the fall in copper prices, the decrease in aggregate demand, and a temporary countercyclical reduction in some tax rates.

17. An example is the elimination of a 7 percent tax on most pensions and a motherhood subsidy for working mothers.

18. See, for example, Central Bank, IPOM (September 2012).

19. The increase was 201 percent in current US dollars between the 2006 and 2012 budgets.

20. A minor tax reform was implemented in 2012 that included a permanent increase in profit taxes that had been established transitorily to finance reconstruction in areas and households damaged by the 2010 earthquake; the tax adjustments reduced the progressive personal income tax (that is paid by less than 20 percent of the highest-income earners) and created a tax reimbursement for private education. Both were regressive changes.

21. There have been a number of reforms to the capital market. However, the market continues to concentrate on the short term, and access for SMEs continues to be restrictive and expensive. A recent discussion on the maximum interest rate that the

financial system can charge for *small* loans revealed that most SMEs with access to the formal market were subject to annual rates that exceeded 40 percent (approximately a 37 percent real interest rate).

22. The government decided in 2007 that part of the revenue from a royalty, recently levied on mining companies, would be allocated to the selection of clusters made by the National Council for Innovation. This step represented a welcome change from prior criteria that emphasized neutrality in resource allocation. Unfortunately, the newly elected conservative government in 2010 reversed this decision and returned to "neutrality."

REFERENCES

Aizenman, J. and Sushko, V. 2011. "Capital flow types, external financing needs, and industrial growth: 99 countries, 1991–2007." National Bureau of Economic Research Working Paper 17228. http://www.nber.org/papers/w17228.pdf.

Arenas, A. 2010. *Historia de la reforma previsional: una experiencia exitosa en democracia.* Santiago: Organización Internacional del Trabajo (ILO).

Bourguignon, F. and Walton, M. 2007. "Is greater equity necessary for higher long-term growth in Latin America?" In *Economic growth with equity: challenges for Latin America*, edited by R. Ffrench-Davis and J. L. Machinea, 95–125. Basingstoke, UK: Palgrave Macmillan.

ECLAC 2011. "Panorama social de América Latina 2011." Santiago: CEPAL.

Edwards, S. and Rigobon, R. 2009. "Capital controls on inflows, exchange rate volatility and external vulnerability." *Journal of International Economics* 78: 256–267.

Ffrench-Davis, R. 2006. *Reforming Latin America's economies after market fundamentalism.* New York, NY: Palgrave Macmillan.

Ffrench-Davis, R. 2010a. "The structural fiscal balance in Chile." *Journal of Globalization and Development* 1(1): 1–19.

Ffrench-Davis, R. 2010b. *Economic reforms in Chile: from dictatorship to democracy,* 2nd ed. New York, NY: Palgrave Macmillan.

Ffrench-Davis, R. 2012. "Employment and real macroeconomic stability: the regressive role of financial inflows in Latin America." *International Labor Review* 151(1): 23–46.

Ffrench-Davis, R. and Heresi, R. 2013. "La economía Chilena frente a la crisis financiera: respuestas contracíclicas y desafíos pendientes." In *La gran recesión: respuestas en las Américas y Asia del Pacífico*, J. L. León, ed. Montevideo: Observatorio América Latina Asia Pacífico, in process.

Frenkel, R. and Rapetti, M. 2010. "A concise history of exchange rate regimes in Latin America." Department of Economics Working Paper 2010-01, University of Massachusetts, Amherst.

Heresi, R. 2011. "Regla fiscal y ciclos de cobre: análisis para Chile." Master's thesis, Department of Economics, University of Chile, Santiago.

Infante, R. and Sunkel, O. 2009. "Chile: hacia un desarrollo inclusivo." *CEPAL Review* 97: 135–154.

IPOM, *Informe de Política Monetaria*, quarterly, Central Bank, Santiago, several issues.

Le Fort, G. and Lehmann, S. 2003. "El encaje y la entrada neta de capitales: Chile en el decenio de 1990." *CEPAL Review* 81: 33–64.

Magud, R. and Reinhart, C. 2007. "Capital controls: an evaluation." In *Capital controls and capital flows in emerging economies: policies, practices and consequences*, S. Edwards, ed. Chicago: University of Chicago Press: 645–674.

National Council for Innovation 2007. "Hacia una estrategia nacional de innovación." Santiago: Gobierno de Chile.

National Poverty Survey, *CASEN*, government of Chile, Santiago, several issues.

Rodrik, D. 2008. "The real exchange rate and economic growth: theory and evidence." *Brookings Papers on Economic Activity*. http://www.brookings.edu/~/media/projects /bpea/fall-2008/2008b_bpea_rodrik.pdf.

Sanhueza, G. 2001. "Chilean banking crisis of the 1980s: solutions and estimation of costs." *Working Papers* 104 (August): 1–79. Santiago: Central Bank of Chile.

Tapia, H. 2003. "Balance estructural del gobierno central de Chile: análisis y propuestas." In *Serie macroeconomía del desarrollo*, No. 25. Santiago: CEPAL.

Velasco, A., Arenas, A., Rodríguez, J., Jorrat, M., and Gamboni, C. 2010. "El enfoque de balance estructural en la política fiscal en Chile." In *Estudios de finanzas públicas*. Santiago: Ministry of Finance: 5–46.

Williamson, J. 2003. "Overview: an agenda for restarting growth and reform." In *After the Washington consensus: restarting growth and reform in Latin America*, edited by P. P. Kuczynski and J. Williamson, 1–19. Washington, DC: Institute for International Economics.

Zahler, R. 2006. "Macroeconomic stability and investment allocation by domestic pension funds in emerging economies: the case of Chile." In *Seeking growth under financial volatility*, R. Ffrench-Davis, ed. New York, NY: Palgrave Macmillan: 60–95.

CHAPTER 7

Disequilibria and Risk Premia

ARGENTINA'S EXPERIENCE DURING THE 2000s FROM A LATIN AMERICAN PERSPECTIVE

Gustavo Cañonero and Carlos Winograd

This chapter draws on Roberto Frenkel's contributions to economic policy analysis and his ongoing interest in Latin American economics. This is probably a fair way to honor an economist who has mainly been motivated by the policy implications of his work.

In the current policy debate in Argentina on the sources of macroeconomic risks as reflected by financial markets, a revision of Frenkel's work on exchange rate and sovereign risk premia seems tempting. In particular, Frenkel (1983) discussed (dis)equilibria in capital markets within the framework of small open economies. He introduced exchange rate expectations nourished by evidence of imbalances in the form of external debt accumulation (current account disequilibrium), where a speculative attack on the currency could occur even without growth in domestic monetary aggregates (credit), a necessary condition under a more mainstream analysis. Likewise, Frenkel (2005) noted the endogeneity of the sovereign credit spread that results from increasing external indebtedness (as indicated by a growing external debt/export ratio) and highlighted the emergence of multiple equilibria.[1]

Following Frenkel's tradition of challenging established convictions, we use his generalized construction of dynamic risk premia to dispute a new apparent belief that a run away from domestic currency or rising sovereign risk premia should not happen without increasing external debt or declining international reserves. In this chapter, we focus on Argentina during the 2000s. Interestingly, a simplistic reading of Frenkel's analysis of the episodes of currency crises in early 1980s and debt default in the late 1990s might explain the confusion. His modeling of expectations dynamics was fed by increasing external liabilities: rising external debt led to growing currency risk premium between 1981 and 1982 under the *tablita*, the predetermined exchange rate regime implemented in Argentina in December 1978. Yet again, in Argentina's rich experience of monetary and balance-of-payments disorders, rising external debt/export ratio fueled the widening of sovereign debt spread before the 2001 debt crisis and default. However, we would like to strongly highlight in this chapter that this narrow view on speculative attacks and the balance-of-payments crisis neglects Frenkel's more generalized understanding of the expectations that were being fostered by destabilizing forces. The fundamental dynamics of market disequilibrium may be driven by unsustainable debt accumulation as well as by inconsistent monetary creation (without debt unsustainability) and/or declining incentives to invest as a new source of liability.

Within the framework of Latin American macroeconomics, we will discuss the two dimensions of risk premium (currency risk and sovereign risk) embedded in the analysis of financial markets in small open economies. On the one hand, we focus on the source of exchange rate expectations and speculative attacks—the very topic that had been discussed by Frenkel—that was portrayed in the analysis of predetermined exchange rate rules, also called active crawling peg policies within the framework and controversies of the monetary approach of the balance of payments (Frenkel and Johnson 1976). These policies were a popular disinflation strategy in the Southern Cone of Latin America in the late 1970s and early 1980s.[2] Furthermore, they were then the expression of the theoretical discussions on the proper nominal anchor in a small open economy integrated to goods and financial world markets. The monetary approach to the balance of payments (within the framework of a small open economy) provided the theoretical foundations for this policy compact.

On the other hand, our interest will extend to the discussion of sovereign country risk, or default risk. Both components of risk, the exchange risk (expectation of devaluation) and sovereign risk (in the current jargon, the premium over US Treasury rates) will contribute to financial market disequilibria. In Frenkel's economics, both components of risk may have a common source based on the level of external debt: the higher the level of debt, the higher the expected devaluation (currency risk) to service the growing debt, as well as the higher the incentives or probability to default (sovereign risk).

In this chapter, we will thus try to do justice to Frenkel's contribution by extending its application from an overly narrow interpretation. With this aim, we will also explore the real economic implications of his work on expectations that were naturally overshadowed by the study of the role of financial links, which were more vivid in the Latin American experiences of the 1980s and 90s. Indeed, and almost abusive from Frenkel's critical mind-set, we could call our revision of his "mantra," "The Real Economy, Exchange Rate Expectations, and Domestic Flows," emphasizing the goods markets (consumption and investment) instead of the financial markets.

This chapter contains five sections. The first section analyzes the relationship between external debt and risk premia, considering both exchange rate as well as sovereign risk premia. We show a relatively stable empirical correlation, over time and across Latin America; that relationship, however, begins to rupture in Argentina in 2007 (and in Venezuela around the same time) when the country's currency and sovereign risk premia started widening despite debt contraction. The second section discusses the sources of exchange rate risk; in this section we evaluate the role of external debt accumulation in Frenkel's manner, as well as money and credit growth in the mainstream tradition of monetary economics. We highlight the minor contribution of external debt growth to account for expected devaluation in Argentina during the 2000s and the more telling role of the growth of monetary aggregates. We find an important factor behind credit growth since the beginning of 2007 that shows the accommodation of a higher inflationary regime in Argentina than in the rest of the countries in the region. This trend of events starts with the campaign that led to the election of a second Kirchner administration, under Cristina Fernández de Kirchner, following her husband Néstor Kirchner, who had been elected president in 2003.

An interesting feature from a regional perspective is highlighted in this second section: credit has grown faster in Brazil than in Argentina without resulting in capital outflows or currency depreciation. However, ex-ante and ex-post returns on local currency assets in Brazil have been consistently higher than those on foreign currency assets, fueling capital inflows and currency appreciation. The evidence in Argentina shows an opposite trend, where peso returns do not seem to be covering the expected currency depreciation and credit risk, suggesting that this time around money overhang does have a more meaningful say in the economic events of the country than it had in the 1980s.

The third and fourth sections focus on the sovereign risk premium, where we note Argentina's rising default risk with falling debt ratios, thus decoupling from other Latin American economies such as Brazil, Chile, Paraguay, and Uruguay, as well as Peru and Colombia. These economies all show declining and historically low sovereign risk levels. Thus, the third section discusses the empirical evidence for exploring potential candidates for the "outlier" behavior of Argentina regarding the trend in sovereign debt risks. At first glance, there is no clear indication of relative weakness in the country's macroeconomic fundamentals other than high inflation. This section searches for some clues regarding instability or a potential unsustainable path, focusing on other dimensions of economic behavior beyond monetary and debt aggregate levels. In the fourth section we turn our attention specifically to the behavior of savings and investment trends and their composition and explore whether this could be a source of disequilibria despite the strong performance of investment in Argentina up until recently. Indeed, based on the pace of economic growth and the regional trend regarding the funding of the savings–investment gap, we argue that behind strong growth during the last decade, investment has been underperforming in the country.

The fifth section introduces a simple extension to Frenkel's model to represent the new destabilizing forces in Argentina related more to the lack of incentives to invest than to the excess capital inflows and growing external debt. In turn, the resulting capital flight seems to be the common feature of two different sources of macroeconomic disequilibria.

The chapter concludes by noting that declining capital investment opportunities are the new liabilities in Argentina's disequilibrium. We stress that the unstable economic path of Argentina since 2007 (from a credit premium perspective) is not driven by excessive absorption that leads to current account disequilibrium and unsustainable debt accumulation. On the contrary, in light of comparative Latin American economics, we find that monetary and credit growth has been fueling exchange rate risk and is coupled with the lack of an appropriate expected return for existing capital investment opportunities. These two forces have been fostering a significantly higher level of sovereign risk than in most neighboring economies across the region. Market expectations may also anticipate that, in due course, a deterioration of the external account will be inevitable as well if the current trend of events persists; however, this time it will be moderated by a low level of external debt.

In a world of high liquidity in international capital markets, but this time coupled with a long phase of very favorable terms of trade and low levels of domestic indebtedness, very high sovereign risk in Argentina results from low rates of expected return on investment. If total investment is not low, the composition of investment shows this particular feature of Argentina in the midst of recent Latin American economics. This scene of surprising lack of investment opportunities under a uniquely favorable international environment presumably results from inconsistent and uncertain domestic policies, the instability of property rights, and thus, very high discount rates for business projects. In a Keynesian fashion we could appeal to "spoiled animal spirits" or in more recent rhetoric to a negative business climate.

DEBT AND RISK PREMIA OVER TIME

As noted in Frenkel's original work on exchange rate expectations and debt sustainability, the destabilizing force in Argentina in the early 1980s and late 1990s was the unstable dynamics of foreign currency liabilities, i.e., external debt that was becoming increasingly hard to sustain. On the one hand, this trend of events was reflected in rising expectations of devaluation that ultimately led to an increasing risk premium coupled with mounting capital flight, which was the main focus of Frenkel's research in the late 1970s and early 1980s. On the other hand, disequilibria also resulted in increasing default risk, which in turn led to a widening of sovereign rate spreads. This was the main focus of Frenkel's contributions on sovereign debt premium in the late 1990s and early 2000s. Interestingly, Frenkel's approach was to consider both sources of risk premia (currency and sovereign risks) separately, not only from a perspective of time but also analytically. In Frenkel (1980), he assumes a constant credit risk premium; in the debt-related papers on sovereign risk (e.g., Frenkel 2001, 2003), he assumes the opposite.

Needless to say, it would be simple to relate the two, reinforcing their signaling of potential disequilibria that originates from a rising debt path. For example, at some point before the break of the active crawling peg exchange regime in 1982, expected depreciation rates had reached annual levels close to 200 or even 300 percent by the end of December 1981, while sovereign spreads had widened to almost 11 percent of their yearly values, or similar to the levels observed presently.[3] Exchange risk and sovereign risk may have a contagious relationship in which, quite often, explosive devaluation expectations may lead to an increasing probability of default. In turn, the latter feeds the former, and the conditions for a balance-of-payments crisis are set.

Formally, this could be presented simply by the following ex-ante uncovered interest rate parity: $i_t = i^*_t + FX^e_t + CS^e_t + CT_t$, where the local rate ($i_t$) equals the foreign currency rate (i^*_t) plus (1) the expected variation of the exchange rate (FX^e_t), (2) the expected net credit spread (CS^e_t), and (3) other transaction costs (CT_t). In Frenkel's original work the distribution of both FX^e_t and CS^e_t was a function of external debt, reflecting the dynamic aspect of risk premia, although analyzed separately.

In Argentina, starting in 2007 and even more so since 2011, growing expectations of a large correction in the exchange rate and a widening in sovereign spreads occurred despite declining external liabilities. Figure 7.1 shows the relationship between the level of public external debt and (1) the sovereign risk premium as measured by the country component of the Emerging Market Bond Index (EMBI) calculated by J.P. Morgan Chase, and (2) the spread between the official exchange rate and the rate implied by the so-called "blue chip swap," which usually involves the peso/US dollar transaction of any blue chip stock or government bond. Although total external debt might represent a more comprehensive indicator of this risk, there is not a measure available that is comparable to the public debt spread used here. In any case, total external debt default risk is correlated to the public sector external debt spread. Nonetheless, total external debt (relative to GDP) in Argentina has followed the same path as public debt, falling steadily since 2005 to almost half the level reached prior to 2001.

Figure 7.1 suggests that the strong correlation between debt size and credit spread started to weaken around early 2007, at the same time as the manipulation of official statistics of Consumer Price Index (CPI) statistics and its negative contagion effect on CPI-linked public bonds payments and pricing began. In addition, the spread between the official exchange rate and the implied exchange rate in asset transactions was insignificant until the global crisis, but after declining again by the end of 2009, it started to show a steady increase in early 2011. The mounting real appreciation of the exchange rate, which showed in a falling current account surplus, could only reinforce this path despite the low levels of national debt. Inconsistent monetary creation and persistent public policy uncertainties were the main drivers of market disequilibria, adjusted by the appropriate time lags in motion. The introduction of much tighter controls of capital flows in late 2011 simply helped to reinforce the sense of an existing disequilibrium. With a longer time span and deeper historical perspective, a rigorous econometric analysis on regime breaks and transmission lags would be of great interest in this line of research.

Thus, the very first question is whether this changing correlation between risk premia and debt ratios does not simply reflect an external factor. Unfortunately, for the purpose of comparison (or indeed fortunately for the sake of sound macroeconomic management), in most

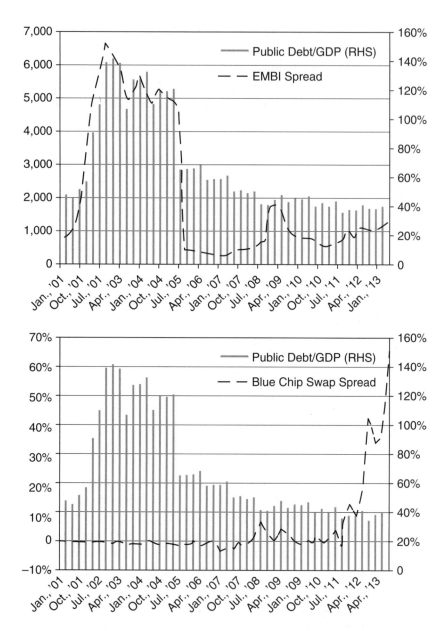

Figure 7.1 Argentina's debt ratios and risk premia over time. EMBI, Emerging
Market Bond Index. *Sources*: Argentina's Ministry of Finance and Bloomberg.

countries in the region an unofficial exchange rate market does not exist. The regional currencies mostly float with active intervention of the central banks in some cases, with the two known exceptions being Argentina and Venezuela. Obviously, one could suggest that active use of international reserves could replicate the conditions of diverging markets within floating regimes, where reserves sales are used instead of capital controls. However, this latter possibility is rejected by the fact that Latin American central banks have been accumulating more reserves per unit of current account balance than Argentina has, while the region showed real currency appreciation as a result of the commodity boom and massive capital inflows (foreign direct investment [FDI] and portfolio flows). Between 2007 and 2012, Argentina accumulated US$9 billon of international reserves while enjoying a cumulative current account surplus of US$24 billon during the same period. This compares with a US$450 billon increase of international reserves for Latin America while accumulating a current account deficit of US$150 billon. We provide a more detailed analysis of "fundamentals" candidates behind risk premia behavior later in the chapter.

For the purpose of comparison, using the sovereign spread as a proxy of a risk factor or disequilibrium measure is helpful because of its availability for all countries in the region. The relationship appears in figure 7.2, showing neatly that a declining public debt ratio in Argentina relative to the rest of the region (excluding Argentina and Venezuela) did help to achieve lower sovereign spreads until March 2007. The sovereign spread we use here is, again, the country component of the J.P. Morgan EMBI.[4] The 2008–2009 global crises exacerbated such a perception of a break in trends in 2007 for Argentina, where after a short period of stability the spread began to widen once again despite steadily declining debt ratio differentials.

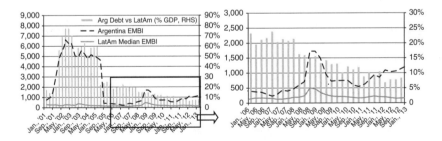

Figure 7.2 Public debt ratios and sovereign risk premium in Latin America. EMBI, Emerging Market Bond Index. *Sources*: Argentina's Ministry of Finance, Bloomberg, and Haver Analytics.

It should be highlighted that not only the stock of debt (to GDP) was rather low in 2007, but also public finance flows showed a robust position with a budget surplus.

THE ROLE OF CREDIT GROWTH REVISITED

Over the last few years, credit expansion has been rather strong in Argentina. Indeed, after hovering in the 11 to 12 percent range of GDP after the 2001 financial crisis and default, showing a very low level of financial intermediation, banking credit to the private sector moved up steadily to more than 17 percent of GDP in 2013. In the same period, the blue chip swap spread increased from an average of 1 percent to almost 80 percent. Meanwhile, local nominal interest rates have remained in the 10 to 15 percent range between 2008 and 2013, while inflation has been constantly above 20 percent according to private estimates or the few remaining credible provincial statistical agencies. As a result, with the central bank tightly controlling the exchange rate parity in the official market, the real exchange rate appreciated by more than 50 percent between 2008 and early 2013 (shown as an increase in real effective exchange rate [REER] in figure 7.3) but did not quite reach the level registered before the default cum mega-devaluation of the 2001–2002 crisis.

In other Latin American countries such as Brazil, Chile, Colombia, Peru, and Uruguay, which have been facing a boom of commodity prices similar to Argentina's, we have also observed strong currency appreciation. Given the low inflation rates of 2 and 7 percent, the common regional

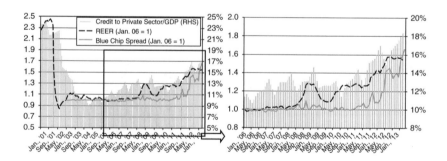

Figure 7.3   Credit growth, inflation, and real exchange rates in Argentina.
Sources: **Central Bank of Argentina, Bloomberg, and India Investment Fund.**

phenomena of real exchange appreciation in these countries have been reflected in nominal exchange appreciation cum low inflation, whereas in Argentina it was the result of high inflation coupled with slow nominal exchange depreciation.

We should highlight that these comparative trends were observed during a time of strong financial deepening in all countries in the region, whereas the degree of financial intermediation in Argentina has remained low relative to its neighbors. We observe that despite a low level of financial intermediation in Argentina, the demand for domestic assets does not accommodate a substantial increase in supply, and disequilibria appears in spreads (foreign currency), capital flight, and inflation (pressure in the goods markets) (see figure 7.4).

Since 2007, we have observed in Argentina an increasing excess demand for goods and foreign currencies, a classic situation of excessive creation of money despite a reasonable control of fiscal imbalances, at least until 2012; conversely, we have also witnessed a steady deterioration of public accounts since 2005. In view of extremely favorable terms of trade, low levels of external indebtedness and low international interest rates, the increase in absorption has not translated into significant imbalances in the current balance-of-payments account. The excess demand for foreign currency, with growing controls in the access to foreign exchange for imports and financial transactions, has therefore reflected a rising spread of the unofficial market for international currencies that reached 60 to 80 percent by the end of 2012.

Increasing credit penetration of the Argentine economy—or to some extent the degree of financial intermediation—seems to have followed a regional trend, as figure 7.5 suggests. However, since the 2001 crisis

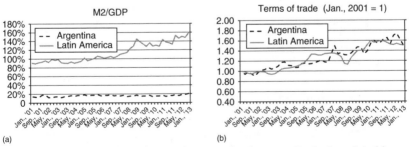

Figure 7.4 Financial deepening and commodity boom in Latin America: (a) M2/GDP; (b) terms of trade (Jan. 2001 = 1). *Sources*: Central Bank of Argentina, Bloomberg, and Haver Analytics.

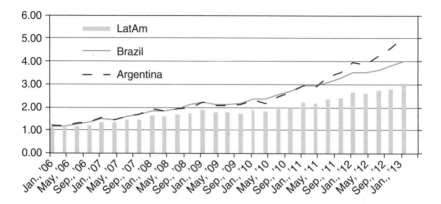

Figure 7.5   Nominal credit to private sector/GDP at constant prices (1Q2005 = 1).
Sources: **Central Bank of Argentina and Haver Analytics.**

Argentina's degree of monetization, as a percentage of GDP, has not only been below the median of Latin American countries (excluding Argentina and Venezuela) but has also increased at a much slower pace.

The degree of monetization and financial intermediation at large is lower in Argentina than in the rest of the region as a result of a number of factors: first, decades of monetary disorder, chronic high inflation and hyperinflation until the convertibility exchange regime was implemented, and price stability during the 1990s. However, we note a long-lasting hysteresis effect and slow reintermediation until the financial crisis and default of 2001 that led to a new collapse of the financial system. Thereafter, departing from the doldrums of extreme financial disorder, the gradual return to a more balanced macroeconomic path was rapidly disturbed by higher and more volatile levels of inflation than the other countries in the region. A new turn of financial disequilibrium was again fueled in Argentina by excessive money creation, persistent negative real interest rates, and the absence of a diversified menu of domestic financial assets.

Without attempting to analyze the direction of causality between money and inflation, in the absence of a rigorous econometric analysis we could state that the monetary authorities have accommodated policy to a "higher" inflationary regime. The policy compact since 2007 has been based on inconsistent regulatory policies (energy and transport)[5] and exchange rate (cum energy and transport pricing) implicit anchoring aimed at containing inflation. This policy failed, and the new inflationary path accelerated to the 20 to 25 percent range by 2010, but in the frame of a loose and inconsistent monetary policy.

That trend in prices seems to be the main source of severe and increasing relative price misalignment. Adverse exogenous shocks, or corrective devaluations (cum energy prices), may accelerate inflation, and the incentives for deeper indexation of contracts may not be far in the actual path of the Argentine economy, rendering future disinflation and relative price realignment a complex and costly affair. The country has a long memory of persistent inflation, failed disinflation, and recurrent economic crisis. If low debt levels and favorable terms of trade signal the breakers relative to past experiences, the political economy of price stabilization will still be a challenge in the future. Given the growing price misalignments and rising inflation, reasonable policy-making skills will be required for managing stabilization and averting past crises.

Returning again to the dynamics of monetary and currency management, a nonexplicit peg of the currency—moving at a much slower pace than inflation from 2007 until mid-2013—could clearly be the main suspect of generating some ground for future instability. It is worth noting, however, that Argentina's nominal credit growth since 2007 has not surpassed the growth in Brazil once adjusted by some indicator of production. (Figure 7.5 shows the stock of nominal credit as a ratio of the volume of production in the economy.) As Argentina's expected currency depreciation was increasing, Brazil was accumulating international reserves. In the case of the latter, decreasing and lower levels of inflation have had a positive impact on the demand for domestic financial assets and has led to increasing financial intermediation, whereas in Argentina we observe rising credit penetration cum strongly increasing inflation.

Nonetheless, a critical difference between Argentina and Brazil in the last few years is the fact that expected return on Brazilian real assets has constantly exceeded the expected return of foreign currency assets. Covered interest parity conditions may be the anchor of this trend of events. This explains why the Brazilian central bank has been accumulating international reserves despite a widening current account deficit. Indeed, capital inflows have led to aggressive credit growth and currency appreciation. In Argentina, domestic rates of returns have remained highly negative in real domestic terms (adjusted by inflation) and have not compensated for an expected exchange rate risk premium, thus fostering a continued capital outflow.

Table 7.1 Average Ex-Post Returns on Local Currency Assets in Argentina and Brazil

Year	Argentina			Brazil		
	Return in Goods (% Annual Avg.)[a]	Return in US$ (% Annual Avg.)[b]	International Reserve Accumulation (% GDP)	Return in Goods (% Annual Avg.)[c]	Return in US$ (% Annual Avg.)	International Reserve Accumulation (% GDP)[d]
2006	−4.0	1.2	6.6	10.6	29.0	2.8
2007	−8.1	6.8	4.4	8.0	25.1	6.4
2008	−12.5	9.2	−1.0	6.3	19.3	0.2
2009	−4.8	−5.5	−0.2	4.9	0.9	2.9
2010	−10.5	3.9	2.9	4.5	24.8	2.3
2011	−8.9	5.5	−2.6	4.7	17.4	2.4
2012	−9.8	1.1	−0.6	3.0	−7.1	1.2

Sources: Central Bank of Argentina, Central Bank of Brazil, and Haver Analytics.

[a] Badlar—CPI.
[b] Badlar—depreciation—US inflation.
[c] SELIC—CPI.
[d] SELIC—depreciation—US inflation.

Despite observing positive domestic rates in current US dollar terms, expected devaluation in Argentina did not equilibrate interest parity conditions. The latter is the mirror image of the widening currency risk premium while we observe a decline in the external debt until mid-2011 and a stable level of international reserves until at least 2012 (see table 7.1). We should also highlight that if the real exchange rate in terms of multilateral trade is strongly affected by the appreciation of the regional partners and Europe, the parity condition relative to the dollar, relevant for financial and real assets portfolio optimization, takes similar values to the levels of the late 1990s. Given the commodity boom and the levels of external debt, as well as external balance, there is no disequilibria equivalence with the past.

LOOKING AT FUNDAMENTAL REASONS BEHIND DIVERGENCE

Monetization on its own could help explain a widening currency risk premium as well as increasing sovereign risk. However, the fact that external debt has been falling and international reserves have remained stable for an extended period requires a stronger contributing factor to explain raising sovereign spreads in foreign currency.

Table 7.2 Disequilibrium Candidates

	Year	Argentina	Latin America
Real effective exchange rate	2000	100.0	100.0
(2000 = 100)	2007	44.0	108.8
	2012	58.1	114.5
Terms of trade (2000 = 100)	2000	103.1	100.5
	2007	128.4	131.0
	2012	173.1	154.6
Unit labor costs	2000	100.0	100.0
(2000 = 100)	2007	63.3	133.9
	2012	103.0	177.0
Current account (% GDP)	2000	–3.2	–2.3
	2007	2.9	0.3
	2012	0.0	–2.5
Investment (% GDP)	2000	16.6	20.2
	2007	24.6	21.8
	2012	21.8	21.6
External debt (% GDP)	2000	50.9	47.5
	2007	45.7	27.9
	2012	29.7	24.6

Sources: World Bank and Haver Analytics.

One potential explanation of rising sovereign spreads (and to some extent of the exchange rate premium as well) is that current disequilibria are simply worsening the ability to accumulate foreign currency in the future to an extent that it overshadows the declining external debt. The trade or current account balance per unit of income could provide some guideline of that. The cost of doing business in foreign currency could be another indicator of destabilizing forces, particularly in the absence of productivity gains. Related to the latter, investment growth is another key indicator. Table 7.2 provides some comparative data in this regard.

After a quick look at the data to identify candidates for disequilibria, one could see Argentina's worsening trend in trade (current) balance or unit labor cost (in US$), but the country data are not worse than the path observed in the rest of the region (as before, table 7.2 excludes Venezuela and Argentina from the regional median). Similarly, the multilateral REER in Argentina has notably appreciated since 2002 but by early 2013 was still below the level reached prior to the default.

As noted, most Latin American economies have seen their currencies appreciating in real terms during the last decade, but in Argentina the channel has occurred via higher inflation. Likewise, Argentina seems to have enjoyed a similar positive terms-of-trade shock compared with the rest of the region. More importantly, the debt deleveraging process of Argentina does not seem to be exceptional; it actually has the same pattern and even magnitude as the one observed in the rest of the region. The investment performance, however, seems relatively strong in Argentina relative to the rest of the region, at least initially, although investment ratios had converged by 2012. On the contrary, high inflation shines yet again as a strong idiosyncratic factor in Argentina's macroeconomic performance and is absent in most other Latin American economies.

Except for the decline in 2009, investment growth has been strong in Argentina since the 2002 default. Moreover, investment ratios have continuously increased until peaking prior to the international financial crisis and the Lehman collapse in 2008 and have since recovered, although they have shown a downward trend since late 2011. This sturdy performance of investment in Argentina is somewhat surprising, particularly given the deteriorating outlook for returns on investment (ex-ante and even ex-post) because of increasingly unpredictable distortionary economic policies or direct appropriation of corporate rights. Nonetheless, as we discuss later, Argentina's strong growth from 2002 to 2012 mostly explained the investment performance through the accelerator factor, overshadowing the negative business climate until economic growth decelerated enough to make this evident by the end of 2011. Looking through the composition of investment in the midst of a consumption boom may also help to clarify the apparent paradox. The analysis of this topic is attempted in the next section.

A simple examination of equity valuation and its performance from a comparative basis provides some idea of the relative unfavorable outlook for capital valuation in Argentina since 2007. An alternative indicator of Argentina's relative (un)attractiveness for investment could be observed in the behavior of foreign direct investment flows. Figure 7.6 shows the reference equity indexes in Argentina and Latin America and FDI flows as a share of GDP. As before, Latin American numbers represent the median of major countries (excluding Argentina and Venezuela). It is worth noting that reinvestment of benefits has explained more than 60 percent of FDI in Argentina in recent years. A significant share of the latter could actually reflect forced decisions that result from policy regulation, thus probably making the actual FDI numbers in Argentina overstate the desired flows, in view of voluntary decisions of the firms.

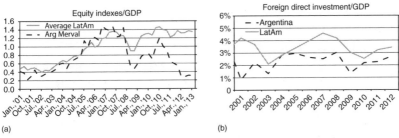

Figure 7.6 Stock exchange and foreign direct investment (FDI) relative performance: (a) equity index/GDP; (b) FDI/GDP. *Sources:* **Bloomberg and Haver Analytics.**

As highlighted before, high inflation is clearly a fundamental idiosyncratic feature of the macroeconomic scene of Argentina, somehow also suggesting unbalanced growth with persistent excess demand in a large array of markets. The sources of disequilibria in the goods markets are further discussed in what follows.

FROM DEBT OVERHANG TO UNDERINVESTMENT

The apparent contradiction between actual investment performance in Argentina and business perceptions as well as asset valuation requires some elaboration. We believe that a comprehensive analysis of the investment performance could also help us understand the phenomenon we are trying to explain: the increasing sovereign and currency risk premia despite declining external debt.

In theory and practice, starting from the market value of investment versus reposition (Tobin's q theory), fixed investment is also driven by expectations and the accelerator principle by the increasing cost of other factors of production, relative employment of existing resources, tax levels and their structures, etc. In the case of Argentina, on the one hand, we observe a strong consumption-based growth, growing real wages, full employment of capacity, and imperfect treatment of high inflation in the tax code that could well explain the good investment performance from 2003 to 2011. On the other hand, such a path for investment takes place despite growing uncertainties about property, rental rights, and regulation in a wide array of markets.

Therefore, to have a better understanding of the investment phenomenon of the last few years, we try to decompose the fundamental factors behind investment dynamics as well as the quality of the same investment behavior. We first analyze how much of a boom the recent investment performance was given by all related factors. Likewise, we look at the impact of the aggregate investment path in terms of productive factors or potential output growth capacity. We will thus investigate the composition and quality of investment to deepen the analysis of the future dynamics of economic growth.

Frenkel et al. (1997) estimated the relationship between investment and income to reject the perception that investment behavior had changed ("improved") during the structural reform period of the 1990s. They showed that this relationship had been relatively stable despite promarket reforms. We recognize the difficulties of adjusting an accurate and robust estimation but subordinate any critical discussion of the estimated investment equation to the fact that the estimation provides an out-of-sample representation of the investment function. Specifically, we use the equation estimated in that paper to "filter" the accelerator component of investment in recent years. This accelerator component is by construction the result of the firms' decisions to expand business as a result of the higher income observed, but not to the expected path of future growth.

The results are shown in figure 7.7, where actual numbers are compared with fitted investment figures based exclusively on income levels. Interestingly, this out-of-sample projection seems to suggest that actual

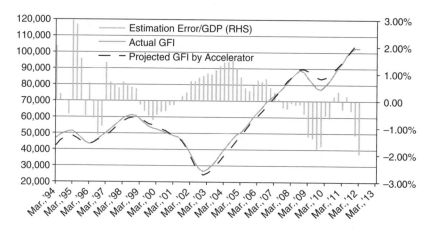

Figure 7.7 The accelerator factor has overshadowed the negative policy effect on investment. Sources: Argentina's Ministry of Finance, FIEL, and Deutsche Bank Research.

investment was underestimated by income levels from 2002 to 2006 but overstated even by the accelerator component on its own since early 2007. In other words, this exercise would suggest that GDP growth has overshadowed the post-2007 investment performance, which essentially was a reaction to the current growth performance, albeit subdued.

One could argue that Argentina's strong investment behavior in recent years is simply explained by the growing GDP, implying that there had not been a structural shift that favored neither investment in the country nor even a stable accommodation of investment to growth: investment since 2007 seems to have been lower than normal levels *ceteris paribus*.

Beyond the general view on the dynamics of aggregate investment, the relevant and difficult question about the composition and quality of investment and its impact on potential output growth remains open. Thus, looking deeper into the investment performance, we evaluate the change in the structure of investment in recent years. A motivation for this exploration hinges on the well-known fact that construction is a large proportion of investment in Argentina, which may not lead to growing production capacity in the country. Figure 7.8 reports the composition of investment by destination in the last twenty years.

One first hint as to what has happened in Argentina regarding the "puzzling" strong domestic investment behavior is the fact that

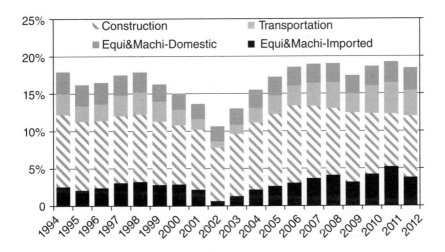

Figure 7.8 Investment by components (percentage of GDP, current prices).
Sources: Argentina's Ministry of Finance, FIEL, and Deutsche Bank Research.

construction has been always a significant component of fixed investment in the country vis-à-vis the rest of the economies of the region. Such relative importance has not changed, and it has actually increased compared with other countries where similar data are available.

Figure 7.9 shows the relative importance of construction and machinery investment for Argentina, Chile, and Mexico in the last fifteen years. It also includes the behavior of imported capital goods to complement the argument: Argentina has been historically using less imported capital goods than the rest of the region, without strong evidence of enjoying better resources or the ability to produce them locally. Therefore, even at similar levels of investment, Argentina's concentration in construction investment instead of productive investment should be taken into consideration when judging current and expected performance.

Interestingly, updating official data of the stock of capital with estimations for investment and income from FIEL—a private think tank that has produced its own statistics for decades—suggests that the stock of investment per unit of income has been declining since 2002. This could further indicate that investment has been lower than needed to maintain at least a given stock of capital per unit of output. This is shown in Figure 7.10.

A rapid examination of recent execution of investment projects in Argentina, absent major infrastructure projects, suggests that capital investment in the recent period has been of a shorter life span than in the past, introducing a faster erosion of the capital stock. Unfortunately, there are not comprehensive studies regarding investment behavior in Argentina, but a careful report by Coremberg et al. (2007) partly supports the characterization discussed previously.

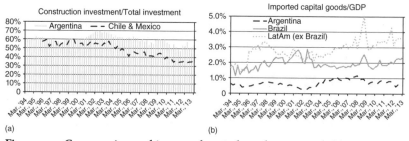

(a)   (b)

Figure 7.9 Construction and imported capital goods compared: (a) construction investment/total investment; (b) imported capital goods/GDP. *Sources*: Argentina's Ministry of Finance, FIEL, and Deutsche Bank Research.

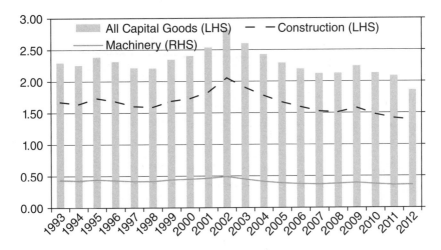

Figure 7.10 Stock of capital goods per unit of output. *Sources:* Argentina's Ministry of Finance, FIEL, and Deutsche Bank Research.

ANIMAL SPIRITS, REGULATION, PROPERTY RIGHTS, AND BUSINESS CLIMATE

The previous sections do not attempt to provide a definitive answer to the sources of increasing currency risk premia or sovereign spread. However, they should help to indicate that this time debt accumulation has no explanatory role in such phenomena. Similarly, the analysis implies that at first glance Argentina has not suffered from any idiosyncratic destabilizing force compared to the rest of the region. However, the perceived risks in Argentina's assets have worsened while they have stabilized or even declined for the rest of Latin America. We argue that the fundamentals behind such diverging behavior have not been associated with excessive external debt accumulation but the lack of attractive opportunities for investment. The latter would likely create uncertain expectations for a country's future economic performance.

From accounting identities, we know that the higher the excess of savings compared to investment, the lower the need for external debt. Similarly, the higher other sources of funding—such as FDI—the lower the need for external debt financing. Table 7.3 shows these aggregate numbers for Argentina and the rest of the region since 1980.

We can draw initial conclusions after looking at table 7.3, particularly when comparing Argentina's performance with the Latin American

Table 7.3 Savings: Investment Performance Compared (% GDNY)

	Argentina			Latin America[a]		
	1980–1982	2005–2006	2007–2012	1980–1982	2005–2006	2007–2012
Savings	19.2	26.3	25.2	18.0	22.4	24.0
Investment	24.5	23.0	23.7	23.5	21.0	24.8
CAB	–5.3	3.3	1.4	–5.1	1.9	–1.2
Net FDI	0.9	1.9	1.7	0.8	3.6	2.1
Net external debt	10.0	–12.7	0.9	4.4	–0.1	2.6
Other net external flows	–8.8	10.8	–3.2	–0.4	–3.2	–1.4
Change in internation-al reserves	–3.2	3.3	0.9	–0.4	1.3	1.9

Sources: Argentina's Ministry of Finance, FIEL, Haver Analytics, and Deutsche Bank Research.

Note: FDI, foreign direct investment.
[a] Without Venezuela.

region, excluding Venezuela. Argentina seems to reproduce the self-inflicted problems of Venezuela regarding ex-ante uncertainty on capital return. First, the increase of savings in Argentina compared to the period of high indebtedness in the 1980s is in line with the rise observed in the region. Second, the increase in savings does not show up in a similar push in investment, at least not as noticeable as the increase in savings. In this metric, Argentina's investment performance has not significantly differed from the regional pattern.

The combination of these factors (rising savings and stable investment) has allowed Argentina to finance "growth" without a destabilizing path of the current account deficit or the need to have FDI or debt as funding sources. Indeed, Argentina has underperformed in terms of receiving FDI and did not show increasing debt. Initially, starting in 2004, Argentina accumulated significant international reserves, but this trend of events has been weakening since 2007 and showed a strong reversion in 2011 and 2012 that led to persistent and rapid losses. Indeed, Argentina's exceptional turnaround in "other net external flows" from a surplus of almost 11 percent of GDP to a negative level of 3.8 percent of GDP simply reflects the steady capital outflow experienced since 2007.

When we focus on the private sector decisions to save and invest, the analysis becomes even more revealing. In Argentina, while total savings

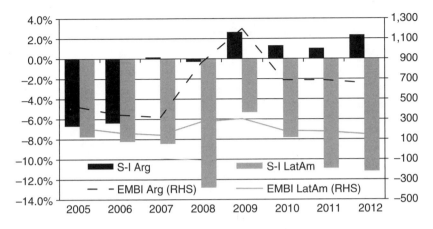

Figure 7.11 **The potential excess of net private savings.** *Sources:* **Argentina's Ministry of Finance, FIEL, Haver Analytics, and Deutsche Bank Research.**

rates have been oscillating between 24 and 25 percent of GDP since 2005, private sector savings moved from 17.2 percent of GDP in 2005 to 22.3 percent in 2012. Such an increase in the private sector savings mirrors the steady deterioration of the fiscal accounts. Meanwhile, total investment during this period only increased from 23 percent of GDP to 23.7 percent. In the rest of the countries both savings and investment ratios increased at a similar pace (see figure 7.11).

Going back to Frenkel's original framework aimed at analyzing the source of a country's risk and currency premia, we could simply add to his proposed drivers (essentially external debt) a scale factor in the supply of domestic funds that is explained by a shift in the savings behavior as a reaction to increased macroeconomic uncertainty. In addition, investment opportunities are at the same time negatively affected by the rising local cost of production (real appreciation not compensated by productivity growth). Such a push to net savings is related to the uncertainty component that affects exchange rate expectations and external credit. This increased excess of domestic savings together with limited investment opportunities could therefore foster demand for foreign currency at any given level of external debt.

Financial and trade repression in Argentina since 2011 have limited to a certain extent the usual behavioral principles that drive demand and supply functions, but they have not altered them fundamentally.

Therefore, declining investment demand could well have been playing the role that debt accumulation did in the 1980s and 1990s, as analyzed by Frenkel. In the past, it was excess external funding substituting for local savings that eventually turned out to be an unsustainable path under a fixed exchange rate regime or an appreciating real rate. In this more recent experience, it has been the excess savings that have not found an outlet for investment other than capital flight.

CONCLUSIONS

This chapter was inspired by Roberto Frenkel's research on the analysis of macroeconomic instability and crisis. His interest on financial market disequilibria in a small open economy and the lessons for economic policy led him to investigate the origin and role of currency or sovereign risk premia. One of his fundamental propositions hinged on the forces that drive unstable financial paths and speculative attacks on the currency. His innovative contribution was to highlight the role of external debt accumulation as the source of a speculative attack, even in the absence of inconsistent monetary policy. The conventional view, on the contrary, considered the latter as a necessary condition for a speculative run on the domestic currency.

A currently established conviction, at least in certain circles, suggests that a speculative attack on the currency cannot emerge without growing external indebtedness. We contest this view. We argue that in the case of Argentina since 2007, the self-inflicted negative effect of inconsistent monetary policy cum distortive (nonincentive-compatible) state interventions on private sector matters has been at the core of raising risk premia, despite the low level of external debt. Thus, severe policy-making (macroeconomic and market regulation) malpractice and significant uncertainty about the rule of law have seriously reduced the incentives to invest (particularly in equipment) and increased precautionary savings. As a result, economic agents have increasingly demanded foreign currencies, pushing risk premia upward.

We have played the devil's advocate on a number of different topics, but a certain degree of dissatisfaction remains to motivate further research on issues such as the exploration with a rigorous econometric analysis of the suggested break in trends of 2007. Another issue for further research is certainly the role of investment—its path, composition, and quality—for a better understanding of past growth performance as well as future policy recommendations.

Honoring a key lesson learned from Frenkel, we challenge established convictions that could have even been based on Frenkel's previous work but had failed to fully understand his ultimate goal: to identify the existence of destabilizing forces in the economy, free of any dogmatism or fundamentalism.

NOTES

We thank the participants at the conference in honor of Roberto Frenkel in Buenos Aires, November 2012. In particular, the thorough reading and comments of Eduardo Corso and Martin Rapetti were extremely useful. The comments of Edmar Bacha, Gaston Besanson, Omar Chisari, Mario Damill, José Fanelli, Javier Finkman, Roberto Frenkel, Daniel Heymann, Sebastián Katz, Guillermo Rozenwurcel, Lance Taylor, and Ivan Torre helped us improve the chapter.

1. The model was first published in Frenkel (2003), extending an initial analysis published in Frenkel (2001).

2. For a model of the macrodynamics of an open economy under these predetermined exchange rate rules, see Rodriguez (1982), Winograd (1983, 1988), Calvo (1986), and Végh (1991).

3. See, e.g., Damill and Kampel (1999).

4. As noted before, the use of public debt simply reflects the best matching with the measure of credit risk premium as represented by the EMBI spread. The trend in Argentina's total debt has followed a steady path, similar to the other economies of the region, implying a decline in debt levels in terms of GDP during the last decade.

5. For a detailed analysis of energy policies and pricing, as well as subsidies and the sizeable impact on the growing budget deficits, see Navajas (2015).

REFERENCES

Calvo, G. A. 1986. "Temporary stabilization: predetermined exchange rates." *Journal of Political Economy* 1319–1329.

Coremberg, A., Goldszier, P., Heymann, D., and Ramos, A. 2007. *Patrones de la inversión y el ahorro en la Argentina.* Santiago: CEPAL.

Damill, M. and Kampel, D. 1999. *Acerca de la evolución de la prima de riesgo de la deuda soberana de la Argentina.* Buenos Aires: CEDES.

Frenkel, J. A. and Johnson, H. G. 1976. *The monetary approach to the balance of payments: a collection of research papers by members of the staff of the International Monetary Fund.* Crows Nest, Australia: Allen & Unwin.

Frenkel, R. 1980. "El desarrollo reciente del mercado de capitales en la Argentina." *Desarrollo Económico* 20(78): 215–248.

Frenkel, R. 1983. "Mercado financiero, expectativas cambiarias y movimientos de capital." *El Trimestre Económico* 4(200): 2041–2076.

Frenkel, R. 2001. "Reflections on development financing." *CEPAL Review* 74: 103–117.

Frenkel, R. 2003. "Deuda externa, crecimiento y sostenibilidad." *Desarrollo Económico* 43(170): 545–562.

Frenkel, R. 2005. "External debt, growth, and sustainability." In *Beyond reforms: structural dynamics and macroeconomic vulnerability*, J. A. Ocampo, ed. Palo Alto, CA: Stanford University Press.

Frenkel, R., Bonvecchi, C., and Fanelli, J. M. 1997. "Movimientos de capitales y comportamiento de la inversión en Argentina." In *Flujos de capital e inversión productiva: lecciones para América Latina*. Santiago: McGraw-Hill.

Navajas, F. 2015. *Subsidios a la energía, devaluación y precio*, Working Paper, FIEL No. 122.

Rodriguez, C. A. 1982. "The Argentine stabilization plan of December 20th." *World Development* 10(9): 801–811.

Végh, C. 1991. "Exchange-rate-based stabilization under imperfect credibility." International Monetary Fund Working Paper 91/77.

Winograd, C. 1983. *Economía abierta y tipo de cambio prefijado. ¿Qué aprendemos del caso Argentino?* Buenos Aires: CEDES.

Winograd, C. 1988. "Exchange rate anchored stabilization, wealth effects and business cycles." Nuffield College, University of Oxford.

CHAPTER 8

Labor Market and Income Distribution in Latin America in Times of Economic Growth

ADVANCES AND SHORTCOMINGS

Roxana Maurizio

The sustained economic growth experienced by Latin America between 2003 and 2008 has had a positive impact on labor market and social indicators.[1] This has become evident through the dynamic creation of employment and the reduction of unemployment, inequality, and poverty.

However, the region continues to exhibit important deficits in the labor market. In 2009, approximately 8 percent of the active population was unemployed, and 50 percent of workers belonged to the informal sector. At the same time, nonwage earners represented a significant share of total employment (approximately 30 percent), much higher than that observed in developed countries. Most were nonprofessional own-account and informal workers.

This chapter aims to provide an in-depth analysis of labor market dynamics as well as labor income inequality in Latin America in the new millennium. In particular, the analysis will address one of the most outstanding aspects of labor markets in the region, labor informality, by studying its characteristics and distributive impacts.

The importance of this study is based, on the one hand, on the fact that both informality and inequality declined in several Latin American countries, which in many cases is in stark contrast to the dynamics observed in the 1990s. On the other hand, as already mentioned, the region as a whole continues to exhibit extremely high levels of labor precariousness and inequality, which imposes serious limits to the improvement of welfare among the population.[2]

Last, although a significant number of studies focus on the role played by returns to education in the dynamics of income distribution during the 1990s and the 2000s, fewer studies focus on the interrelations between labor informality and inequality. Hence, the comparative analysis of these dimensions between countries with heterogeneous characteristics in the region seems quite relevant

The chapter follows with a description of the current employment structure in the region, focusing on the importance of informality and own-account occupations. It then presents an analysis of labor income inequality among each group of workers and the wage gaps associated with informality and moves on to discuss the evolution of both informality and wage inequality to evaluate to what extent these two factors have been interrelated. The chapter concludes with some summary remarks.

EMPLOYMENT COMPOSITION, INFORMALITY, AND WAGE GAPS IN LATIN AMERICA: AN OVERVIEW[3]

INFORMALITY IN THE LATIN AMERICAN LABOR MARKETS

Labor informality is one of the categories of analysis that most contributes to the characterization of labor conditions in Latin America. There are at least two different approaches with different associated concepts of labor informality:

1. The *productive* approach, with its related concepts of informal sector (IS) and formal sector (FS) and employment in the IS and FS
2. The *legal* approach, with its related concepts of informal employment (informal workers; IE) and formal employment (formal workers; IF)

The concept of the IS emerged in the early 1970s in the International Labor Organization's documents for African countries (ILO 1972). It was then developed in Latin America by the Regional Employment Program for Latin America and the Caribbean to explain the growth of wide sectors of the population that were not able to participate in the processes of productive modernization through a formal labor market. Under this productive approach, informality reflects the inability of these economies to generate sufficient employment in the formal sector compared to the growth of the labor force. The IS is usually associated with small productive units with low levels of productivity, where the aim is survival rather than accumulation. Jobs generated in this sector constitute employment in the informal sector (EIS).

Along with this productive approach–based concept, IE is another concept that has been proposed in recent years. Based on a legal approach, IE refers to a different dimension of informality because it focuses directly on job conditions. In particular, this approach associates informality with the evasion of labor regulations, defining IE as the employment of workers not covered by labor legislation.

Following the ILO's suggestions, the IS is made up of employers and wage earners in establishments of fewer than five employees and nonprofessional own-account workers. The public sector is excluded from the IS. Additionally, the empirical identification of the wage earners' registration condition in each of these countries is based on the availability of information derived from these databases. In Argentina, a wage earner is considered as registered in the social security system if his or her employer pays social security contributions. In Chile and Brazil, a wage earner is considered as registered if he or she has signed a labor contract. In Bolivia, Costa Rica, El Salvador, Mexico, Paraguay, Peru, and Uruguay, registered workers are those affiliated with a pension system. Finally, in Ecuador, a registered wage earner is considered as registered if he or she receives social insurance.

As can be observed in figure 8.1, two sets of countries with different employment structures can be identified. The first group comprises Argentina, Brazil, Chile, Costa Rica, and Uruguay; the second group is made up of Bolivia, Ecuador, El Salvador, Mexico, Paraguay, and Peru. In the first group, formal wage earners in the formal sector constitute the largest group, representing 50 percent of total urban employment; informal nonwage earners, who represent approximately 20%, are the next largest group.

Informal nonwage earners constitute the largest group in the second set of countries, representing more than one-third of total employment. They are mostly nonprofessional own-account workers. Conversely, formal wage earners in the formal sector represent only 20 percent of total employment, which is 30 percent less than the first group of countries. Last, informal wage earners (in both formal and informal sectors) constitute another group of significant magnitude in the second group of countries, representing 40 percent of total employment, two times more than in the first group.

This overview shows a significant degree of heterogeneity among the employment structures of the countries in the region. It also shows that despite these important differences, employment in the informal sector and informal employment represent more than a third of total workers in all countries under study (table 8.1). Bolivia and Paraguay are placed in one extreme, where EIS (including domestic service workers) represents approximately 65 percent of the employed workforce, whereas IE (including informal domestic service workers) reaches 80 percent

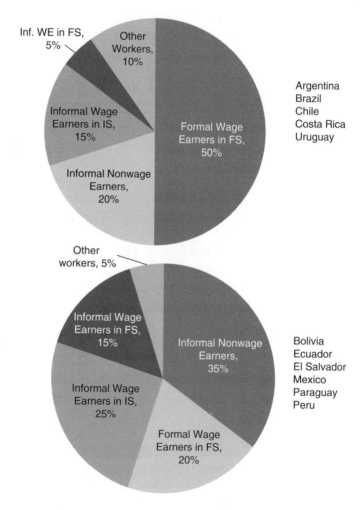

Figure 8.1 Employment composition in Latin America. Around 2010. *Source:* Author's elaboration based on household surveys.

Table 8.1 Employment Composition: Share (%) of Informality in Latin American Countries

Categories	Argentina	Bolivia	Brazil	Chile	Costa Rica	Ecuador	El Salvador	Mexico	Paraguay	Peru	Uruguay
Formal nonwage earners	5	3	2	5	4	3	2	4	3	6	4
Informal nonwage earners	18	36	23	21	21	30	29	16	31	31	21
Formal wage earners in FS	45	15	43	51	51	26	34	30	19	27	52
Informal wage earners in FS	9	16	9	9	7	14	8	20	15	12	4
Formal wage earners in IS	5	0	5	4	5	2	2	3	2	2	4
Informal wage earners in IS	10	16	8	4	7	14	13	19	16	10	5
Formal domestic service	1	0	2	2	1	1	0	0	0	0	4
Informal domestic service	6	3	6	3	4	3	4	5	9	4	5
Unpaid family workers	1	10	2	0	1	6	7	4	5	6	1
Total employment	100	100	100	100	100	100	100	100	100	100	100
Employment in the informal sector (includes domestic services)	41	65	46	34	39	57	56	46	63	55	40
Informal employment (includes informal domestic services)	44	81	47	38	40	68	62	63	76	64	36
Percentage of informal wage earners in the total wage earners	33	69	31	22	24	52	41	57	65	48	19

Source: Author's elaboration based on household surveys.

Note: FS, formal sector; IS, informal sector.

of total workers. On the other extreme, in Chile, Uruguay, and Costa Rica, these figures fall to 34 and 40 percent. In all cases except Uruguay, IE is higher than EIS.

Different categories that arise from the double classification of informality also indicate important discrepancies among countries. For example, the larger participation of informal nonwage earners stands out in Peru, Bolivia, Ecuador, El Salvador, and Paraguay, where they represent approximately one-third of total employment. In all cases except El Salvador, informal nonwage earners constitute the largest group of workers. On the contrary, in Argentina, Brazil, Chile, Costa Rica, and Uruguay, approximately half of total workers are formal wage earners in the formal sector. Finally, the percentage of nonregistered wage earners in total wage earners is very high in all countries, ranging from a minimum of 19 percent in Uruguay to a maximum of 69 percent in Bolivia (figure 8.2).

This general overview emphasizes the importance of the informal sector, informal employment, and nonregistered wage earners in the occupational structure in all countries analyzed. In addition, independent workers make up between 25 and 40 percent of the labor force in the region. Informality and independent work clearly narrow the scope of labor institutions and labor market policies.

At the same time, there is a close correlation between being a nonregistered wage earner and a worker in the informal sector (table 8.2).

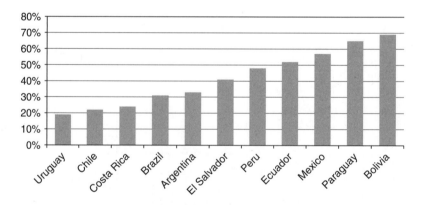

Figure 8.2 Proportion of nonregistered wage earners in total wage earners.
Source: **Author's elaboration based on household surveys.**

Table 8.2 Registered and Nonregistered Wage Earners in the Formal and Informal Sectors

	Registered Wage Earners		Nonregistered Wage Earners	
	Formal Sector	Informal Sector	Formal Sector	Informal Sector
Argentina	88.0	12.0	37.6	62.4
Bolivia	96.9	3.1	46.2	53.8
Brazil	84.6	15.4	38.4	61.6
Chile	89.1	10.9	57.7	42.3
Costa Rica	90.1	9.9	39.1	60.9
Ecuador	91.9	8.1	43.4	56.6
El Salvador	94.9	5.1	32.2	67.8
Mexico	91.7	8.3	45.7	54.3
Paraguay	90.7	9.3	37.3	62.7
Peru	91.5	8.5	45.4	54.6
Uruguay	86.5	13.5	29.0	71.0

Source: Author's elaboration based on household surveys.

This suggests the precarious nature of the jobs generated in the informal sector, where the combination of low productivity and nonfulfillment of labor regulation probably derives from low wages. However, it is important to point out that between 30 and 60 percent of nonregistered wage earners work in the formal sector, i.e., in establishments with more than five employees, a fact that suggests there may be opportunities for significantly reducing the levels of labor precariousness in the region.

As for the composition of informality in terms of different attributes, some common patterns arise (table 8.3). The less educated, the young, and women are overrepresented in the group of informal workers.[4] This differential structure suggests a priori that informal workers will have lower average incomes than formal workers because they have a vector of personal characteristics that are usually less remunerated; i.e., there is a "composition effect" against the informal. In the next three sections that follow we analyze to what extent this panorama is also accompanied by differences in the returns obtained by formal and informal workers for each of the characteristics considered.

INFORMALITY AND WITHIN INEQUALITY

One significant aspect to consider when assessing the interrelations between employment structures and the distribution of labor income is the degree of inequality among each group of workers. The Lorenz curves

Table 8.3 Characteristics of Formal and Informal Workers

Characteristics	Argentina			Bolivia			Brazil		
	Formal	Informal	Total	Formal	Informal	Total	Formal	Informal	Total
Men	58%	60%	59%	61%	54%	55%	57%	56%	56%
Years of education (avg.)	13.9	11.1	12.6	14.3	9.1	10.1	11.2	8.4	9.9
Age (avg.)	39.7	39.7	39.7	39.9	35.8	36.5	36.2	38.0	37.0

Characteristics	Chile			Costa Rica			Ecuador		
Men	61%	56%	59%	59%	57%	58%	60%	58%	58%
Years of education (avg.)	13.4	11.0	12.6	11.2	8.2	10.0	13.5	9.0	10.4
Age (avg.)	39.7	43.0	40.9	36.3	39.7	37.7	40.0	39.7	39.8

Characteristics	El Salvador			Mexico			Paraguay		
Men	58%	51%	54%	60%	60%	60%	64%	56%	58%
Years of education (avg.)	11.8	6.5	8.5	11.8	8.2	9.5	13.1	8.9	9.9
Age (avg.)	36.1	38.3	37.5	37.3	37.4	37.4	37.0	36.3	36.5

Characteristics	Peru			Uruguay		
Men	63%	50%	55%	54%	54%	54%
Years of education (avg.)	15.1	10.6	12.2	12.0	9.3	11.0
Age (avg.)	39.8	37.5	38.3	39.9	42.7	40.9

Source: Author's elaboration based on household surveys.

in figure 8.3 illustrate this point. In all countries, nonwage earners—both own-account workers and employers—show a higher level of labor income gap than wage earners as a whole.

Furthermore, according to these figures, registered wage earners are the most homogeneous group in Argentina, Uruguay, and Paraguay. In Brazil, Chile, Costa Rica, and Peru, although the Lorenz curves of registered wage earners show no dominance compared with nonregistered wage earners, the Gini coefficients confirm that in these countries they too are more homogeneous than all other employed people. The exceptions are Bolivia, Mexico (where both groups of salaried workers have the same intragroup inequality), Ecuador, and El Salvador (where the wage gap among nonregistered workers is smaller than it is among formal workers).

Therefore, formality seems to be associated with a lower spread in labor incomes in many countries under study, which implies that it is crucial to take into account the advances in formalization processes made in recent years in the analysis of distributive changes.

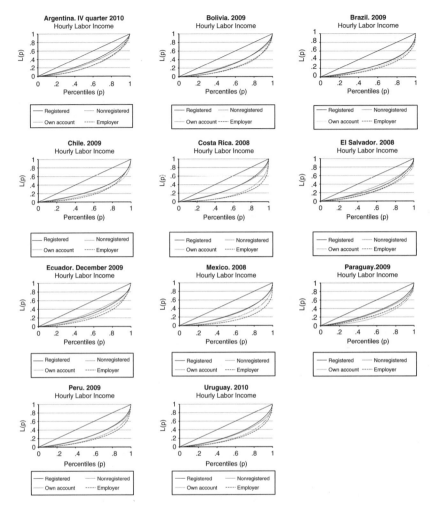

Figure 8.3 Lorenz curves of hourly labor income. *Source:* **Author's elaboration based on household surveys.**

WHERE ARE FORMAL/INFORMAL WORKERS LOCATED WITHIN THE LABOR INCOME DISTRIBUTION?

A second dimension that links informality to income inequality is the relative position of each group of workers within the labor income distribution. Figure 8.4 shows the nonparametric kernel density functions of the log of hourly wages.

Four clear facts arise from this figure. First, with the exception of Mexico and Costa Rica, nonregistered wage earners (informal workers)

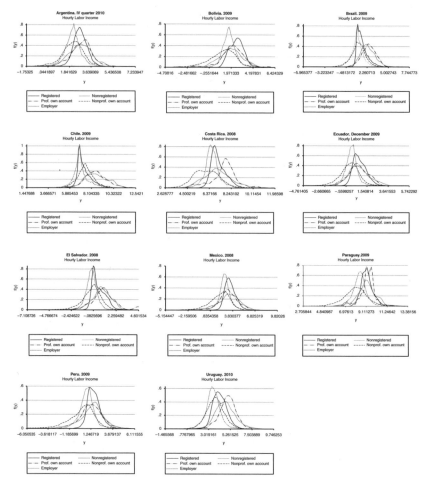

Figure 8.4 Kernel density functions of hourly labor income. *Source:* Author's elaboration based on household surveys.

have the lowest average hourly wages. However, it is important to point out that in most cases, nonprofessional own-account workers have the highest left tail in the income distribution; however, because they exhibit at the same time a wider range of values (higher intragroup inequality), the average income ends up being higher than that of informal wage earn-ers. In Mexico and Costa Rica, nonprofessional own-account workers constitute, as a whole, the poorest group. Second, employers are placed in the other extreme of the income distribution. The only exceptions to this pattern are Argentina and El Salvador, where professional own-account workers are the group with the highest average labor income. Third, the leftward position of the distribution of nonregistered wage earners compared to registered wage earners is verified in all countries considered. Finally, in all countries but Chile, registered wage earners are located in the middle of the labor income distribution, with higher wages than nonregistered and nonprofessional own-account workers but with lower wages than professional own-account workers and employers.

Therefore, the significant wage gap among salaried workers (who represent most employment, even in those countries with a high proportion of nonwage earners) is an important stylized fact in the region, as is the prevalence of very high labor informality. However, so far we cannot claim that these differentials necessarily reflect a labor segmentation phenomenon associated with informality, because they might be fully explained by the workers' personal attributes and the characteristics of the job. This topic is addressed in the section that follows.

TO WHAT EXTENT DO WAGE GAPS ASSOCIATED WITH INFORMALITY REFLECT INCOME SEGMENTATION?

The concept of income segmentation is used here to refer to labor income differentials that are not explained by the workers' individual attributes, i.e., income gaps associated with certain characteristics of the job. In particular, this section evaluates whether two salaried workers with equal personal attributes obtain different remunerations because one is a formal worker and the other an informal worker.

Informality defined according to any of the two approaches—productive and legal—is consistent with both situations with and without income segmentation. For example, under the productive approach, it could be argued that if there were no restrictions the excess of labor that cannot enter the formal sector and thus goes to the informal sector with its lower levels of productivity would result in a global fall in wages—both in the formal and informal sectors. In the legal approach, informality without segmentation could take place if formal and informal wage earners ended up receiving equal net remunerations, even when in the second case employers face additional costs related to labor regulations.

There are other arguments that account for the existence of income segmentation associated with informality, even when there are no restrictions on labor mobility or other restrictions generated by labor institutions. One of these arguments states that small firms, which are typical in the informal sector, usually operate with lower productivity levels and therefore pay lower average remunerations. Likewise, the nonfulfillment of tax obligations could make the firms work with lower levels of efficiency and productivity, which would once again result in lower wages for informal workers than those obtained by formal workers (Beccaria and Maurizio 2011). However, the mere existence of productivity differentials is not sufficient to produce wage segmentation. Therefore, it is necessary to explain why the equalizing forces of the market do not operate and why some companies—those with higher productivity—pay higher wages than the rest.

One hypothesis is based on the efficiency wages theory, which states that employers may decide to pay wages above the market reference to reduce labor turnover or to encourage greater productivity (Shapiro and Stiglitz 1984). Income segmentation could arise if firms in the formal sector use this mechanism more often than firms in the informal sector. At the same time, the existence of internal labor markets within the firms of the formal sector can isolate workers from external competition, especially the more educated workers, thus creating a wage gap between formal and informal workers.

In addition, under the legal approach, it could be said that the fulfillment of labor norms not only affects total labor costs but also the net wages paid to workers. The impact of minimum wages, collective bargaining, and unions on wage structure are examples of the latter. Therefore, an additional source of wage segmentation may be the fact that certain workers are protected by labor legislation or unions, whereas others with equal attributes are not.

Last, if the two approaches overlap and the nonfulfillment of labor legislation is greater in informal firms, the mentioned factors will complement one another to explain the presence of segmentation. For example, one worker with certain personal attributes working in a small firm could receive a lower wage than another worker with equal characteristics working in a larger firm, both because of the lower productivity levels and because the small firm faces, in general, less union pressure or does not abide by labor institutions, such as the minimum wage.

However, an important condition in obtaining these results is the presence of a deficit in the creation of formal jobs that makes workers accept lower remunerations or more precarious working conditions. This behavior is, in turn, encouraged by the lack or weakness of social protection mechanisms. To a greater or lesser extent, this is the case of Latin American countries.

To estimate income gaps associated with informality, several parametric and nonparametric methods were performed to bolster the results. Each of these methods is described in detail in the appendix at the end of this chapter. Because of space constraints, this section will only present and discuss wage gaps associated with informality according to the legal approach, computed for the group of wage earners exclusively.

Table 8.4 shows the results of selectivity corrected wage equations estimated by Heckman's two-step procedure. These figures correspond to the coefficients of the dummy variables that identify informality in the income equations. The dependent variable is the log of hourly wages. A statistically significant and important "penalty" as a result of informality is verified in all countries, suggesting the presence of income segmentation. The magnitude varies, however. Specifically, the gap of the hourly log wage between informal and formal workers is greater than 40 percent in Argentina and Ecuador, greater than 30 percent in Uruguay, and greater than 20 percent in the other countries.

Ordinary least squares (OLS) estimates the effects of the covariates only in the center of the conditional distribution. For this reason it is also of interest to know the impact of the covariates along the whole conditional income distribution. Therefore, the quantile regression method is applied to hourly labor incomes. The estimated coefficients of informality are shown in table 8.5 and reveal that the gap associated with informality is not constant across the income distribution and is larger at the lower extreme. This pattern could suggest the impact of certain labor institutions, such as the minimum wage.

The implementation of the Oaxaca–Blinder decomposition to hourly wage equations estimates (corrected by bias selection) of formal and informal workers yields very interesting findings (see table 8.6). First, in all cases, the total difference of mean incomes is significantly larger than that found using OLS. Second, when this difference is decomposed into three components—the endowment effect (which arises from the differences in the vector of characteristics among each group), the coefficient effect (which comes from the differences in the returns to those attributes), and the interaction effect—the coefficient effect is statistically significant and negative in all cases. Therefore, the segmentation hypothesis is verified again, thus indicating that, given equal attributes, an informal worker (a nonregistered wage earner) gets a lower wage than a similar formal worker (a registered wage earner).

Table 8.4 Heckman's Two-Step Estimator

Argentina 2010	Bolivia 2009	Brazil 2009	Chile 2009	Costa Rica 2008	Ecuador 2009	El Salvador 2008	Mexico 2008	Paraguay 2009	Peru 2009	Uruguay 2010
-0.423 [0.0100]	-0.267 [0.0318]	-0.280 [0.00392]	-0.257 [0.00519]	-0.206 [0.0134]	-0.412 [0.0124]	-0.210 [0.0114]	-0.260 [0.00801]	-0.275 [0.0276]	-0.246 [0.0135]	-0.325 [0.00873]

Source: Author's elaboration based on household surveys.

Note: $p < 0.01$ for all values presented. Standard errors shown in brackets.

Table 8.5 Quantile Regressions

Country	q10	q25	q50	q75	q90
Argentina	-0.582 [0.0511]	-0.489 [0.0268]	-0.395 [0.0198]	-0.319 [0.00187]	-0.267 [0.00432]
Bolivia	-0.280 [0.0286]	-0.291 [0.00213]	-0.243 [0.0562]	-0.226 [0.0272]	-0.265 [0.0220]
Brazil	-0.651 [0.00117]	-0.348 [0.00357]	-0.231 [0.00149]	-0.181 [0.000627]	-0.136 [0.00724]
Chile	-0.477 [0.0173]	-0.261 [0.00607]	-0.134 [0.00440]	-0.121 [0.00848]	-0.126 [0.00654]
Costa Rica	-0.313 [0.0152]	-0.235 [0.0108]	-0.182 [0.00886]	-0.146 [0.00706]	-0.108 [0.0266]
Ecuador	-0.547 [0.0251]	-0.432 [0.0107]	-0.356 [0.00275]	-0.323 [0.00658]	-0.317 [0.0174]
El Salvador	-0.356 [0.0209]	-0.256 [0.00676]	-0.176 [0.0106]	-0.157 [0.0191]	-0.140 [0.0612]
Mexico	-0.361 [0.0132]	-0.263 [0.00336]	-0.223 [0.00172]	-0.219 [0.000227]	-0.191 [0.00656]
Paraguay	-0.379 [0.0534]	-0.308 [0.0625]	-0.230 [0.0302]	-0.224 [0.00854]	-0.199 [0.0589]
Peru	-0.276 [0.0127]	-0.224 [0.00248]	-0.231 [0.00745]	-0.234 [0.0117]	-0.256 [0.00316]
Uruguay	-0.564 [0.0134]	-0.380 [0.000716]	-0.285 [0.000109]	-0.215 [0.00819]	-0.169 [0.0111]

Source: Author's elaboration based on household surveys.

Note: $p < 0.01$ for all values presented except for the q90 value as reported for El Salvador, which is $p < 0.05$. Standard errors shown in brackets.

Table 8.6 Oaxaca–Blinder Decomposition

	Argentina 2010	Bolivia 2009	Brazil 2009	Chile 2009	Costa Rica 2008	Ecuador 2009	El Salvador 2008	Mexico 2008	Paraguay 2009	Peru 2009	Uruguay 2010
Difference	-0.75 [0.0106]	-0.773 [0.0300]	-0.606 [0.00459]	-0.388 [0.00623]	-0.528 [0.0115]	-0.89 [0.0106]	-0.670 [0.0104]	-0.58 [0.00805]	-0.7 [0.0247]	-0.818 [0.0118]	-0.712 [0.00982]
Endowment	-0.28 [0.0151]	-0.488 [0.0324]	-0.391 [0.00494]	-0.174 [0.00568]	-0.30 [0.0189]	-0.41 [0.0165]	-0.44 [0.0176]	-0.33 [0.00774]	-0.52 [0.0311]	-0.610 [0.0148]	-0.36 [0.0559]
Coefficient	-0.37 [0.0122]	-0.218 [0.0658]	-0.343 [0.00455]	-0.247 [0.00556]	-0.23 [0.0126]	-0.38 [0.0178]	-0.28 [0.0184]	-0.3 [0.0146]	-0.45 [0.0961]	-0.35 [0.0182]	-0.321 [0.0100]
Interaction	-0.094 [0.0163]	-0.0669 [0.0679]	0.128 [0.00491]	0.0332 [0.00498]	0.00665 [0.0197]	-0.099 [0.0222]	**0.0601** [0.0235]	0.090 [0.0145]	**0.221** [0.0982]	0.150 [0.0203]	-0.0218 [0.0560]

Source: Author's elaboration based on household surveys.

Note: $p < 0.01$ for all values presented except for those in bold, which are $p < 0.05$. Standard errors shown in brackets.

In addition, the endowment effect is also significant and negative. In most cases (with the exception of Argentina and Chile), this effect is the factor that explains the largest proportion of the income gap. This reflects the fact that formal workers have a vector of characteristics that is more favorable than that of informal workers, as described previously. Specifically, it has been shown that formal workers have more human capital and a lower proportion of women, who are usually discriminated against in the labor market and thus receive lower wages than men with similar attributes. Therefore, total labor income gaps between the formal and informal are explained not only because the former has a more favorable endowment vector but also because the returns to its attributes are higher than those of the informal.

Finally, nonparametric estimates based on the matching estimator method (table 8.7) are consistent with previous results and confirm again the existence of a penalty for informality. In particular, the parameter of interest—the average treatment effect on the treated (ATT)—is significant and negative in all cases.

Therefore, the different estimates (parametric and nonparametric) point to the existence of significant income gaps in favor of formality that is not explained by differences in the observed attributes of workers. This leads to the conclusion that there is income segmentation associated with informality in all countries analyzed.

Table 8.7 Matching Estimator Method

Argentina 2010	−0.349 [0.0479]
Bolivia 2009	−0.231 [0.0909]
Brazil 2009	−0.392 [0.000888]
Chile 2009	−0.266 [0.00639]
Costa Rica 2008	−0.211 [0.00361]
Ecuador 2009	−0.414 [0.0327]
El Salvador 2008	−0.268 [0.000785]
Mexico 2008	−0.316 [0.00913]
Paraguay 2009	−0.465 [0.0400]
Peru 2009	−0.279 [0.0454]
Uruguay 2010	−0.370 [0.0196]

Source: Author's elaboration of household surveys.

Note: $p < 0.01$ for all values presented except for Bolivia 2009, which is $p < 0.05$. Standard errors shown in brackets.

The question thus arises: Which factors explain the differences in magnitude of the income gaps across countries? One hypothesis might relate these results to the role of labor institutions such as the minimum wage, collective bargaining, or unions. Additionally, these results might be affected by variables that are not observable and, thus, not included in the estimates. For example, there might be nonmonetary advantages that compensate for the lower wages of informality, making these jobs more attractive to certain individuals.[5] But given the close link between informality and poverty found in Latin American countries, the arguments that suggest that informality is a voluntary choice is not likely to apply to all workers.[6] On the contrary, the high levels of unemployment and labor precariousness experienced by these countries suggest that the insertion in informality could be the only choice for a large group of people, especially considering the previously mentioned very low coverage levels of noncontributory social protection systems in the region.

LABOR MARKET DYNAMICS: INFORMALITY AND WAGE INEQUALITY REDUCTION

Although labor informality continues to be one of the region's distinctive characteristics, its incidence has fallen in a significant number of countries, especially during the last decade. In what follows we seek to assess the effects this improvement might have had on the distribution of labor incomes. It should be pointed out that this is not intended to be an exhaustive analysis of all the dimensions that might have played a role in the evolution of labor incomes and their distribution; rather, the analysis focuses on one of the factors that might have contributed to the distributive dynamics among other possible variables such as educational inequality and returns to education, gender wage discrimination, or the effects of certain labor institutions.[7] However, the impacts of the recent evolution of informality on labor income distribution in the region have not yet been thoroughly studied.

With this aim, the dynamics of wage inequality and informality are presented next. After that follows an analysis of the evolution of informality-related wage gaps, both average wage gaps and wage differentials along the labor income distribution. Finally, the Theil index decomposition is presented, which allows us to assess whether—and to what extent—the process of formalization has contributed to the reduction of inequality in the countries under study.

DYNAMICS OF WAGE INEQUALITY AND LABOR INFORMALITY

As can be observed in figure 8.5, eight of the eleven countries under study have experienced a reduction in the proportion of nonregistered wage earners in total wage earners between the beginning and end of the first decade of the 2000s. The exceptions are Chile, where this proportion remained constant, and El Salvador and Mexico, where informality continued to grow. This general reduction of informality differs significantly from the experiences of most of these countries during the 1990s. Such reductions were more intense in the cases of Argentina and Brazil, where the proportion of informal workers fell approximately 11 percent. In Brazil, the process of wage employment formalization had already started in the mid-1990s, whereas in Argentina it began after the change in the macroeconomic regime that took place in 2002.

To provide a comprehensive discussion of the factors that enabled the process of employment formalization is beyond the scope of this chapter. However, there are at least three factors that should be mentioned: (1) fast economic growth; (2) simplification and reduction of taxes for micro-enterprises (e.g., Simples Nacional in Brazil); and (3) improvements in labor inspection (e.g., National Plan for Labor Regulation in Argentina). Nevertheless, given that some of these processes had already been present in some countries during the 1990s (although in isolation) and had no positive effects on labor formalization, it is possible to consider that all of

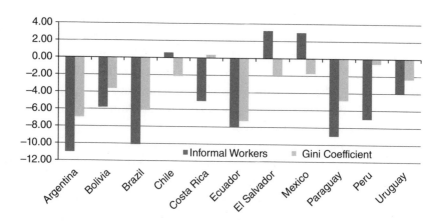

Figure 8.5   Evolution of proportion of informal workers and Gini coefficient.
Source: **Author's elaboration based on household surveys.**

these factors need to act jointly in a context of steady growth and employment creation to produce positive results in regard to informality.

At the same time, the region has also experienced a generalized reduction in labor income concentration. As can be seen in figure 8.5, the Gini index fell in all countries except Costa Rica. Again, Argentina and Brazil (and to some extent Ecuador) stand out in terms of these positive dynamics. As before, in the case of Brazil, this decreasing trend had already started in the mid-1990s, although it intensified beginning in 2002. In the case of Argentina, the turning point came in 2003. In what follows, we present some exercises that attempt to relate the processes that evolved in the region during the last decade.

EVOLUTION OF INFORMALITY-RELATED WAGE GAPS

Table 8.8 presents average wage gaps (calculated exclusively for the group of wage earners) for a group of six countries at the beginning of 2000 and end of 2010, respectively. It also shows the evolution of wage gaps along the unconditional income distribution based on the methodology proposed by Firpo et al. (2009), which allows the identification of the differential impacts of informality on different parts of the distribution. In particular, the method employed by Firpo et al. (2009) allows the estimation of the effect of different explanatory variables such as the formal/informal condition of the worker on the different percentiles of the unconditional income distribution.[8] The method is based on regressions in which the dependent variable is a transformation—the so-called recentered influence function—of the outcome variable under study, and the covariates are those usually included in these types of studies.

As can be observed in table 8.8, the average gap related to informality decreased in Brazil, Uruguay, Chile, and Paraguay. The opposite happened in Argentina and Mexico. However, the average wage gaps do not necessarily represent the behavior of gaps along different parts of the wage distribution. For instance, in the cases of Argentina, Brazil, and Uruguay, the hourly income gaps between formal and informal workers at the lower part of the distribution widened, whereas the opposite took place in the upper tail. Conversely, no changes were observed in the lowest 10th percentile of the distribution in Paraguay. In Chile, the informality-related wage gaps narrowed along the whole distribution. In Mexico, a nonmonotonic behavior was observed.

The increase of informality wage penalties is a source of wage dispersion; therefore, it is a fundamental aspect to be considered in the distributive

Table 8.8 Informality-Related Average Wage Gaps and Wage Gaps in Different Percentiles of the Unconditional Labor Income Distribution

Country	OLS	q10	q20	q30	q40	q50	q60	q70	q80	q90
Argentina										
2010	-0.438	-0.633	-0.754	-0.716	-0.626	-0.512	-0.374	-0.278	-0.159	-0.0711
	[0.0131]	[0.0164]	[0.0161]	[0.0161]	[0.0142]	[0.0230]	[0.0140]	[0.0102]	[0.0116]	[0.0197]
2003	-0.428	-0.390	-0.403	-0.282	-0.661	-0.799	-0.640	-0.504	-0.336	-0.197
	[0.0111]	[0.0241]	[0.0226]	[0.0240]	[0.0399]	[0.0243]	[0.0257]	[0.00297]	[0.0309]	[0.0222]
Brazil										
2009	-0.281	-0.932	-0.296	-0.227	-0.239	-0.180	-0.145	-0.117	-0.128	-0.122
	[0.00412]	[0.00856]	[0.00466]	[0.00508]	[0.00426]	[0.00570]	[0.00423]	[0.00559]	[0.0160]	[0.0107]
2001	-0.319	-0.698	-0.345	-0.370	-0.319	-0.273	-0.221	-0.202	-0.176	-0.147
	[0.00470]	[0.0185]	[0.00929]	[0.00739]	[0.00479]	[0.00920]	[0.00525]	[0.0118]	[0.0113]	[0.0165]
Chile										
2009	-0.216	-0.500	-0.216	-0.137	-0.106	-0.125	-0.136	-0.124	-0.124	-0.0551
	[0.00644]	[0.0372]	[0.0179]	[0.00718]	[0.00345]	[0.00474]	[0.00855]	[0.00671]	[0.0168]	[0.0101]
2000	-0.270	-0.626	-0.375	-0.249	-0.212	-0.218	-0.202	-0.168	-0.121	-0.0673
	[0.00702]	[0.00197]	[0.00172]	[0.00602]	[0.0101]	[0.00155]	[0.000508]	[0.00503]	[0.00737]	[0.0162]
Mexico										
2008	-0.197	-0.265	-0.270	-0.274	-0.258	-0.261	-0.276	-0.221	-0.194	-0.115
	[0.00872]	[0.0167]	[0.0124]	[0.0144]	[0.0111]	[0.00481]	[0.0165]	[0.00996]	[0.00138]	[0.0265]
2000	-0.161	-0.195	-0.262	-0.318	-0.311	-0.283	-0.245	-0.197	-0.0986	**0.0618**
	[0.0163]	[0.0237]	[0.0243]	[0.0152]	[0.0272]	[0.0204]	[0.0197]	[0.0272]	[0.0346]	[0.0359]
Paraguay										
2009	-0.163	0.00137	-0.165	-0.197	-0.257	-0.314	-0.291	-0.367	-0.284	-0.121
	[0.0286]	[0.0336]	[0.0301]	[0.0525]	[0.0307]	[0.0417]	[0.0412]	[0.0678]	[0.0424]	[0.0955]
2004	-0.212	0.0284	-0.121	-0.227	-0.303	-0.417	-0.461	-0.532	-0.357	-0.0542
	[0.0257]	[0.0337]	[0.0186]	[0.0180]	[0.0356]	[0.0392]	[0.0540]	[0.0690]	[0.0670]	[0.143]
Uruguay										
2010	-0.248	-0.690	-0.524	-0.420	-0.317	-0.207	-0.106	-0.0191	0.0546	0.144
	[0.0111]	[0.0178]	[0.0189]	[0.00931]	[0.0101]	[0.0109]	[0.0180]	[0.0219]	[0.0112]	[0.0191]
2006	-0.349	-0.674	-0.600	-0.541	-0.447	-0.351	-0.269	-0.211	-0.130	-0.0288
	[0.00751]	[0.0115]	[0.00648]	[0.0131]	[0.0158]	[0.0109]	[0.0102]	[0.0123]	[0.0153]	[0.00326]

Source: Author's elaboration based on household surveys.

Note: $p < 0.01$ for all values presented except for value presented in bold, which is $p < 0.05$. Standard errors shown in brackets. OLS, ordinary least squares.

analyses. Moreover, it is also relevant to try to identify the factors behind the behavior of wage gaps in the lower part of the distribution. Even though a detailed study of this matter is beyond the scope of this chapter, we mention one factor (among others) that could be related to such dynamics, which is the evolution of the real minimum wage during recent years.

In particular, as can be observed in figure 8.6, the three countries in which the informality gap widened for the lowest percentiles—Argentina, Brazil, and Uruguay—are those in which the real minimum wage recovered more intensely during the last decade.[9] On the contrary, the real minimum wage in Paraguay remained fairly constant during this period. Hence, it could be argued that as the minimum wage becomes exclusively binding for formal workers at the lower part of the distribution, it could generate a wider wage gap between the workers that are subject to such labor institutions and those who are not (informal workers).

Keifman and Maurizio (2012) found that the recovery of the minimum wage in Argentina, Brazil, and Uruguay during the 2000s had a positive and significant impact on income distribution, explained by a reduction of inequality at the lower tail of the distribution. However, this does not seem to be the case for Chile and Mexico, where other factors might have also played a role. In Chile, the recovery of the minimum wage (although with less intensity than in Argentina, Brazil, and Uruguay) was verified together with a reduction in wage gaps across the entire distribution, including the first 10th percentile; in Mexico, the stability in the

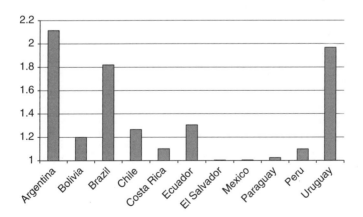

Figure 8.6 Evolution of real minimum wage between the beginning and the end of 2000s. *Source:* **Author's elaboration based on International Labor Organization data (Base Única de Salarios Mínimos de América Latina y el Caribe).**

real minimum wage was accompanied by a widening of the penalty at the lower tail of the wage distribution. Therefore, further studies need to be conducted to bolster this hypothesis and to find other factors associated with informality-related wage gaps along the wage distribution.

ASSESSING THE DISTRIBUTIONAL IMPACT OF LABOR FORMALIZATION: A DECOMPOSITION EXERCISE

Table 8.9 presents the results of the Theil index dynamic decomposition for this group of six countries. In each of the four cases in which informality decreased (Argentina, Brazil, Uruguay, and Paraguay), this contributed to the reduction of inequality, which is manifested as a positive sign in the composition effect. Conversely, both in Chile, where the proportion of nonregistered wage earners remained constant, and in Mexico, where informality actually increased during the period under analysis, the composition effect negatively contributed to the reduction of inequality.

The "between effect" is negative in Argentina, reflecting the widening of the informality-related wage gap. The contrary is observed in Brazil, Chile, and Uruguay, all countries in which the average gap decreased.

Table 8.9 Theil Index Dynamic Decomposition

Country and Years	Effects (%)				
	Variation of Theil Index	Between	Within	Composition	Total
Argentina (2003–2010)	−0.092	−19.4	89.8	29.6	100
Brazil (2001–2009)	−0.087	10.2	85.0	4.8	100
Chile (2000–2009)	−0.013	63.7	42.8	−6.5	100
Mexico (2000–2008)	−0.019	14.5	104.3	−18.8	100
Paraguay (2004–2009)	−0.010	−13.4	90.2	23.2	100
Uruguay (2006–2009)	−0.030	4.4	70.7	24.9	100

Source: Author's elaboration based on household surveys.

Mexico and Paraguay do not follow this regularity. It is important to take into account that contrary to the parametric and nonparametric analyses of wage gaps, in the Theil decomposition the between effect measures the average wage differential between formal and informal workers without controlling for other covariates. In all cases, however, the most important contribution came from the reduction of inequality within each of the two groups of workers ("within effect").

It is therefore possible to conclude that the increase in the participation of registered wage earners in total employment has been a very positive phenomenon, not only because it has extended the social security system coverage but also because it has had an equalizing effect on the distribution of labor incomes. In addition, the greater income homogeneity within this group of workers could also be a result of the relatively higher dynamism shown by both minimum wages and collective bargaining in some of these countries during the last decade.

CONCLUDING REMARKS

From 2003 to 2008, before the impacts of the international crisis, the region as a whole experienced six years of high and stable economic growth that improved labor and social indicators: higher levels of employment and lower levels of unemployment, labor informality, inequality, and poverty. Nevertheless, these improvements were insufficient to substantially modify two distinctive characteristics of the region: high levels of labor precariousness (which is strongly related to informality) and income concentration.

This chapter focused on labor informality and its characteristics and distributive impacts. In this regard, it complements other papers that analyze other dimensions associated with wage inequality such as educational inequality and returns to education, gender wage discrimination, or the distributive impacts of labor institutions.

The reduction in both the incidence of labor informality and inequality has been quite widespread throughout the region, although with different intensities in each country. These dynamics are in stark contrast to those of the 1990s. Moreover, the results confirm a positive effect of employment formalization on labor income distribution, even when in some countries such as Argentina and Brazil this came along with a widening of wage gaps between formal and informal workers in the lower tail of the distribution. One hypothesis, which should be further investigated, relates these findings to the performance of certain labor institutions, such as minimum wage and collective bargaining, which have recovered significantly in these countries.

However, despite this important progress, the huge differences that still persist in the region's working conditions require permanent action in the field of primary income distribution as a means of reducing inequality. In this context, progress in employment formalization and the strengthening of labor institutions are essential for allowing jobs to become an effective mechanism for overcoming inequality and poverty and achieving social protection. At the same time, complementing these policies by developing a comprehensive social protection system grounded in universal rights is also needed, based not only on traditional social insurance pillars but also on noncontributory components.

Finally, all of these policies should be framed within a long-term economic development strategy built on the basis of an integrated productive structure that leads to high efficiency, systemic competitiveness, and increasing labor demand. Productive convergence within a framework of high productivity standards is a necessary condition for sustained growth, employment promotion, and wage increase over time.

Data and Methodology

Microdata used in this chapter come from the regular household surveys of each country under study:

Argentina: Encuesta Permanente de Hogares
Bolivia: Encuesta de Hogares
Brazil: Pesquisa Nacional por Amostra de Domicilios
Chile: Encuesta de Caracterización Socioeconómica Nacional
Costa Rica: Encuesta de Hogares de Propósitos Múltiples
Ecuador: Encuesta Nacional de Empleo, Desempleo y Subempleo
El Salvador: Encuesta de Hogares de Propósitos Múltiples
Mexico: Encuesta de Ingresos y Gastos de los Hogares
Paraguay: Encuesta Permanente de Hogares
Peru: Encuesta Nacional de Hogares sobre Condiciones de Vida y Pobreza
Uruguay: Encuesta Continua de Hogares

METHODOLOGY
MEASUREMENT OF WAGE GAPS ASSOCIATED WITH INFORMALITY

1. First, average wage gaps between formal and informal workers are estimated using Mincer equations by OLS regression. This is the most common approach when analyzing the effect of one independent variable on labor income while controlling for the rest of the covariates. In the case that matters in this chapter, the coefficient of the variable that identifies

informality quantifies its independent impact on wage determination. The estimates are corrected for the sample selection bias using Heckman's two-step estimator.

2. OLS estimates the effects of the covariates only at the central part of the conditional distribution. However, it is relevant to identify the impact of the covariates along the entire conditional distribution of income. To do that, the quantile regression model is applied, from which it is possible to evaluate whether wage gaps remain constant, grow, or decrease along the conditional distribution. These estimates are also corrected by the sample selection bias.

3. From the estimate of wage equations, the Oaxaca–Blinder decomposition method allows the decomposition of average income gaps between formal and informal workers to be broken up into three separate effects: the endowment effect, which is the part of the differential derived from the differences in the vector of characteristics of each group; the coefficient effect, which corresponds to the differences in the returns to those attributes; and the interaction effect. The segmentation hypothesis is verified if the second effect is statistically significant and positive, thus indicating that, given equal attributes, a formal worker gets a higher wage than an informal worker. These estimates are also corrected by the sample selection bias.

4. Finally, the matching estimator method is used nonparametrically to estimate the impact of informality on labor income. The parameter of interest is the average treatment effect on the treated (ATT), which is defined as

$$\theta_{\text{ATT}} = E(\tau|D=1) = E[Y(1)|D=1] - E[Y(0)\,|\,D=1],$$

where $E[Y(1)|D=1]$ is the expected value for the treated group given that it was under treatment, and $E[Y(0)\,|\,D=1]$ is the expected value for the treated group had it not been treated.

Given that this counterfactual situation is not observed, it is necessary to resort to an alternative method to estimate the ATT. The most accurate way of identifying what would have happened to the group under treatment had it not been treated is to consider the situation of the nontreated individuals with equal (or similar) characteristics (control group).

One of the methods used to build the control group is the propensity score matching estimator, in which the propensity score of participation for the whole sample is estimated and the individuals of the treated group and the control group with similar scores are matched. In the case we are analyzing, informal workers constitute the treated group, whereas formal workers constitute the control group. There are different ways to determine which individuals in the control group will be the counterpart of the group under treatment. One way, used here, is the kernel estimator, in which the outcome of the treated individual is associated with a matched outcome given by a kernel-weighted average of the outcome of all nontreated individuals. The ATT is estimated as follows:

$$ATT = \frac{1}{N_n} \sum_{i \in n} \left(w_i - \sum_{j \in f} k_i w_j \right),$$

where w_i and w_j indicate the wage of each formal and informal worker, respectively, k_{ij} is the kernel, and N_n is the quantity of informal workers.

THEIL INDEX DYNAMIC DECOMPOSITION BY GROUPS

An important characteristic of the Theil index is that it can be decomposed in an additive way into three effects. The first, the between effect, captures the changes in differences between the average labor incomes of the groups considered. The second, the within effect, captures the changes in wage variability within each group. Finally, the third effect reflects the composition effect, which measures the distributive impacts of the changes in the relative participation of each worker category.[10] In this chapter, this decomposition helped to determine whether, and to what extent, the process of formalization has contributed to the reduction of labor income inequality in the two countries under study.

NOTES

I thank Alfredo Schclarek Curutchet for his comments.

　1. For further details about the macroeconomic performance during the 2000s in Latin America, see Damill and Frenkel (2012).

　2. For further details about the quality of employment in Latin America, see Weller and Roethlisberger (2011).

　3. The appendix presents the information sources employed in this and the following sections. Given the available information, the analysis will be focused on urban labor markets exclusively.

　4. The exceptions are Argentina, Brazil, Mexico, and Uruguay, where informality is quite balanced between genders.

5. This hypothesis is proposed by Maloney (2004) and Arias and Khamis (2008), among others.

6. See, for example, Beccaria and Groisman (2008), Beccaria et al. (2012), Deviciente et al. (2009), and Maurizio (2012).

7. A recent analysis on this topic for Latin America is presented in Cruces et al. (2011). See also Lustig and Gasparini (2011), López-Calva and Lustig (2010), and Cornia (2012).

8. This is substantially different from the quantile regression method, which estimates the impact of a covariate on the quantiles of the conditional income distribution.

9. In the case of Argentina, the minimum wage was deflated by the consumer price index of seven provinces.

10. For further details, see Mookherjee and Shorrocks (1982).

REFERENCES

Arias, O. and Khamis, M. 2008. "Comparative advantage, segmentation and informal earnings: a marginal treatment effects approach." IZA Discussion Paper 3916. http://ftp.iza.org/dp3916.pdf.

Beccaria, L. and Groisman, F. 2008. "Informalidad y pobreza: una relación compleja." In *Argentina Desigual*, edited by L. Beccaria and F. Groisman, 93–156. Buenos Aires: Universidad Nacional de General Sarmiento.

Beccaria, L. and Maurizio, R. 2011. "Mercado de trabajo, regulaciones laborales y sistemas de protección social. Enfoques relevantes para América Latina." *Revista de Economía Política de Buenos Aires* 7/8(4): 103–144.

Beccaria, L., Maurizio, R., Fernández, A., Monsalvo, P., and Alvarez, M. 2012. "Urban poverty and labor market dynamics in five Latin American countries: 2003–2008." *Journal of Economic Inequality* 11(4): 555–580.

Cornia, A. 2012. "Inequality trends and their determinants: Latin America over 1990–2011." WIDER Working Paper 2012/09. http://www.wider.unu.edu/publications/working-papers/2012/en_GB/wp2012-009.

Cruces, G., Domench, C., and Gasparini, L. 2011. "Inequality in education: evidence for Latin America." WIDER Working Paper 2011/93. http://www1.wider.unu.edu/fallinginequality/article/inequality-education-evidence-latin-america.

Damill, M. and Frenkel, R. 2012 "Macroeconomic policies, growth, employment, and inequality in Latin America." WIDER Working Paper 2012/23. http://www.wider.unu.edu/publications/working-papers/2012/en_GB/wp2012-023.

Deviciente, F., Groisman, F., and Poggi, A. 2009. "Informality and poverty: are these processes dynamically interrelated? Evidence from Argentina." ECINEQ Working Paper 146. http://www.ecineq.org/milano/WP/ECINEQ2009-146.pdf.

Firpo, S., Fortin, N., and Lemieux, T. 2009. "Unconditional quantile regressions." *Econometrica* 77(3): 953–973.

ILO 1972. "Employment, income and equality: a strategy for increasing productive employment in Kenya." Geneva: Author.

Keifman, S. and Maurizio, R. 2012. "Changes in labor market conditions and policies: their impact on wage inequality during the last decade." WIDER Working

Paper 2012/14. http://www.cpahq.org/cpahq/cpadocs/Changes%20in%20the%20 Labour%20Market.pdf.

López-Calva, F. and Lustig, N. 2010. *Declining inequality in Latin America: a decade of progress?* Washington, DC: Brookings Institution.

Lustig, N. and Gasparini, L. 2011. "The rise and fall of income inequality in Latin America." CEDLAS Working Paper 118. http://www.cedlas.econo.unlp.edu.ar /download.php?file=archivos...cedlas118.pdf.

Maloney, W. 2004. "Informality revisited." *World Development* 32(7): 1159–1178.

Maurizio, R. 2012. "Labor informality in Latin America: the case of Argentina, Chile, Brazil and Argentina." BWPI Working Paper 165/2012. http://www.bwpi .manchester.ac.uk/medialibrary/publications/working_papers/bwpi-wp-16512.pdf.

Mookherjee, D. and Shorrocks, A. 1982. "A decomposition analysis of the trend in UK income inequality." *Economic Journal* 92(368): 886–902.

Shapiro, C. and Stiglitz, J. 1984. "Equilibrium unemployment as a worker discipline device." *American Economic Review* 74(3): 433–444.

Weller, J. and Roethlisberger, C. 2011. "La calidad del empleo en América Latina." Macroeconomics of Development Series 110. http://unpan1.un.org/intradoc /groups/public/documents/uneclac/unpan045745.pdf.

CHAPTER 9

Accounting for the Rise and Fall of Brazil's Growth After World War II

Edmar Bacha and Regis Bonelli

Brazil's economic growth after World War II (WWII) can be divided into two major periods: before 1980 and after 1980. This division is clearly observed in figure 9.1, where the bars indicate yearly GDP growth rates from 1948 to 2011. Overlapping the bars, a solid line indicates the ten-year average of the yearly rates, starting in 1957 and ending in 2011. The ten-year average line leaves no doubt: there was a collapse in GDP growth after 1980 from which the country did not fully recover, even after inflation was tamed in 1994.

This chapter examines the long-term evolution of the Brazilian economy with models that emphasize the determinants of aggregate supply.[1] It updates previous work in which we used the same methodology to help decipher the puzzle of Brazil's growth collapse after 1980.[2]

The chapter is organized into five sections. The first of these sections provides a historical sketch of the period from 1947 to 2011, including the main findings of our empirical analysis. The second derives an expression to decompose the capital stock growth rate, which involves savings as well other variables that are relevant to the growth of capital, such as capacity utilization, capital output ratio, and the relative price of investment. The third section displays the numerical results of the decomposition of capital growth, seeking to explain in particular the reasons for the collapse occurring after 1980, whereas the fourth section investigates the roles of total factor productivity and capital deepening in the evolution of the GDP per worker growth rate since 1947. The final section presents a summary of the findings.

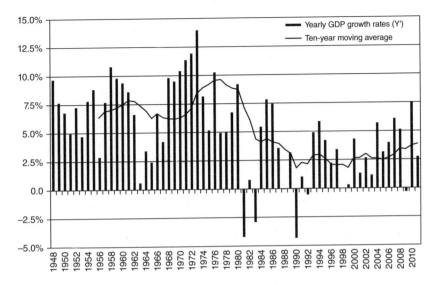

Figure 9.1   GDP growth rates (Y') and their ten-year moving average, 1948–2011. *Sources:* Ipeatada; authors' elaboration.

HISTORICAL SKETCH

To unravel the puzzle of Brazil's growth collapse after 1980, we need to go back to the 1970s, perhaps even to the 1950s.[3] On both occasions, the country suffered long-term adverse terms-of-trade shocks—a major oil shock in the 1970s and a depression in the prices of coffee in the 1950s. The policy responses in regard to the scarcity of foreign exchange could have mimicked those adopted in Southeast Asia that were aimed at increasing the "exportability" of the economy. This would have reduced the country's dependence on coffee exports in the 1950s and strengthened its capacity to pay for higher oil prices in the 1970s. The policy responses, however, were of a different nature.

Pessimism about the country's export potential, associated with the influence of coffee farmers and industrialists in the government, favored a strategy of coffee valorization and import substitution in the 1950s. The years from 1952 to 1955 were critical in setting the industrialization pattern that Brazil has followed ever since. In 1952, President Getúlio Vargas (1951–1954), under the influence of Finance Minister Horacio Lafer (1951–1953), reinstated the pre-WWII coffee valorization policy as a way of defending an exchange rate that had become overvalued at the end of the Korean War boom. In 1953, Finance Minister Oswaldo Aranha

(1953–1954) instituted a system of multiple exchange rates that punished traditional noncoffee exports, protected import substitutes, and facilitated the importation of "essential" goods, which were defined as those without a national equivalent. To support the movement toward industrialization, a national development bank (the Brazilian Development Bank) was created in 1952, and a state monopoly of crude oil (through Petrobras) was established in 1953.

The conservative vice president Café Filho (1954–1955) took over the presidency after Vargas's suicide in August 1954. His finance minister, Eugenio Gudin (1954–1955), attempted to undo the coffee valorization scheme but was forced to resign. His successor, José Maria Whitaker (April–October 1955), attempted to dismantle the system of multiple exchange rates only to be dismissed as well. Café Filho himself was impeached in the so-called democratic anticoup of November 1955.

With the election of President Juscelino Kubitschek (1956–1960), the game was over, and Brazil embarked on an import substitution industrialization path that would last until the 1980s. In the process, the relative price of capital substantially increased while the productivity of capital decreased.

Industrial protectionism under Kubitschek was associated with the promotion of foreign direct investment. This increased the rate of absorption of technical progress and sustained the GDP's growth rate. The political upheaval associated with inflation acceleration in the beginning of the 1960s temporarily interrupted this process. The technocrats who rose to power with the 1964 military coup stabilized the economy, introduced economic reforms, and raised taxation. The resulting savings and investment boom between 1965 and 1974, which was associated with a high rate of technical progress, became known as the "Brazilian economic miracle."

In the early 1970s, an overheated economy was hit by the first oil shock. The obsession with the legitimation of an authoritarian regime through short-term economic success determined a *fuite en avant* economic strategy that favored economic growth and inflation accommodation through indexation. The critical determinant of Brazil's economic future was General Ernesto Geisel's (1974–1979) decision to deal with the 1973 oil shock by promoting a capital-intensive import substitution strategy. This could only be put into practice through a deep dependence on the international recycling of the petrodollars. With the benefit of hindsight, this was an unfortunate choice, because the international scenario deteriorated continuously in the years that followed. In the domestic economy, a perfected wage indexing formula was adopted as a gradual opening of the military regime started under Geisel and continued under General João Figueiredo (1979–1985). Excessive domestic demand and wage indexation strongly increased domestic inflation and the trade deficit. The relative price of investment continued to increase, and capital productivity fell substantially between 1974 and 1984. This period was also characterized by technical regression rather than by progress. A continuously adverse international environment finally forced the country to suspend external debt payments at the end of 1982.

The financial crisis of the early 1980s put an end both to the military regime and to the country's forced growth strategy. The return to democracy in 1985 took place under accelerating inflation. The political euphoria with democratization, accelerated by the short-term success of a price and wage freeze in 1986, temporarily hid the economic inefficiencies that had been inherited from the military regime. A sequence of failed heterodox stabilization attempts and debt moratoria followed, while a new populist constitution was promulgated in 1988, thus making the country virtually ungovernable.

The debt defaults began in the last stages of the military regime, when Planning Minister Delfim Netto (1979–1984) strongly underestimated the inflation adjustment index for domestic debt in 1980 (mimicking a strategy that had been adopted by the military regime with the aim of reducing the minimum wage between 1965 and 1967). Netto followed up with a foreign debt default in December 1982. After redemocratization, President José Sarney (1985–1989) deployed three successive heterodox shocks that temporarily suspended the inflation correction of domestic debt. In early 1987, Sarney declared a unilateral moratorium on foreign debt. The largest internal debt moratorium of all was the one-year freeze on virtually all domestic financial assets at the beginning of President Fernando Collor de Mello's government (1990–1992).

Hyperinflation manifested itself but was ultimately eradicated by the Real Plan in 1994. This paved the way under President Fernando Henrique Cardoso (1995–2002) for a radical deviation from the state-led import substitution model that prevailed in the military regime. But a loose fiscal policy and excessive reliance on an exchange rate anchor (which required the support of very high real interest rates) undermined exports and private investment, thus preventing a growth resumption from taking place. After a currency crisis that culminated in January 1999, a more sensible macroeconomic policy tripod was adopted: a primary fiscal surplus sufficiently large to keep public debt under control, inflation targeting, and a floating exchange rate. Structural reforms halted the long-term increase in the relative price of investment and declining productivity of capital. Capacity utilization increased without accelerating inflation. Technical progress again manifested itself but was not enough to generate sustained growth, even after 1999, because capital accumulation was contained by a succession of adverse shocks: the bursting of the NASDAQ bubble, the internal energy crisis in 2001, the 9/11 terrorist attacks, Argentina's moratorium, and the specter of a left-wing presidency in 2002.

Rather than attempting a return to the populist state-led closed economy model of the past, as many had feared, President Luiz Inácio Lula da Silva and his successor Dilma Rousseff kept the 1999 macroeconomic policy tripod intact. With the help of a major commodity boom and large capital inflows, the economy recovered after 2004 but proved unable to recover the per capita GDP growth rates of the pre-1980 period.

With this as backdrop, the next sections develop accounting schemes for capital accumulation and GDP growth, thus providing empirical content to the historical narrative previously presented.

CAPITAL GROWTH DECOMPOSITION

This section first discusses the association between the growth rates of GDP and capital. The purpose is to motivate interest in a decomposition formula for the capital stock growth rate, involving the savings rate, the relative price of investment, the degree of capacity utilization, and the output–capital in-use ratio. An empirical analysis of the behavior of these parameters is the subject of the rest of this section.

RELATIONSHIP BETWEEN GDP AND CAPITAL GROWTH

A notable aspect of Brazil's GDP growth is that it is closely associated with the evolution of the capital stock, as evidenced in figure 9.2.

Figure 9.2 makes it clear that the collapse in GDP growth occurred along with that of the capital stock. The correlation coefficient between the two series is 0.63. But the existence of a correlation tells us nothing about causation between the variables. We used the Granger test to verify the existence and direction of causality between the series. The results suggest that capital growth Granger-causes GDP growth with a p value of

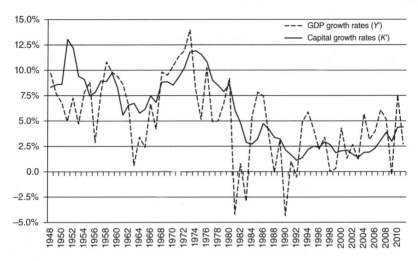

Figure 9.2   GDP (Y') and capital (K') growth rates, 1948–2011 (percentage per year). *Sources:* **Ipeatada; authors' elaboration.**

4 percent. Conversely, GDP growth also Granger-causes capital growth—but only with a *p* value of 9.1 percent. This indicates that capital growth Granger-causes GDP growth more strongly than the other way around. These results are consistent with the Solow model outside the steady state.

The next step is to identify the factors that explain capital stock growth. The starting point is the definition of the capital stock growth rate as the ratio of gross fixed investment to the capital stock less the depreciation rate:

$$K' = I/K - \delta, \tag{9.1}$$

where K' is the growth rate of the capital stock, I is real gross investment, K is the existing capital stock, and δ is the depreciation rate.

In this equation, the ratio of gross investment to capital stock (I/K) can be written as the product of the investment rate (I/Y) by the output–capital ratio (Y/K):

$$I/K = (I/Y)(Y/K). \tag{9.2}$$

On the right-hand side of equation 9.2, the investment rate (I/Y) is identically equal to the product of the savings rate by the inverse of the relative price of investment:

$$I/Y = (P_iI/P_yY)(P_y/P_i) = (S/P_yY)(P_y/P_i) = s(1/p), \tag{9.3}$$

where the first equality is only an expedient to introduce the nominal investment rate (P_iI/P_yY) and thus be able to make use of the identity between nominal investment and savings in the second equality. The third equality is merely a consequence of the definitions of $s = S/P_yY$ and $p = P_i/P_y$, where P_i is the implicit deflator of gross capital formation and P_y is the implicit GDP deflator.

The output–capital ratio (Y/K) in equation 9.2 can be written as the product of the capacity utilization rate (u) by the ratio of output to the capital employed (v) as follows:

$$Y/K = u(Y/uK) = uv. \qquad (9.4)$$

Substituting equations 9.3 and 9.4 into equation 9.2 and the result in equation 9.1, we finally get

$$K' = s(1/p)uv - \delta. \qquad (9.5)$$

Equation 9.5 shows that the impact of the savings rate (s) on the growth rate of the capital stock (K') depends on the relative price of investment (p), the degree of capacity utilization (u), and the ratio of output to the capital employed (v). The rate of depreciation (δ) also needs to be taken into account—except that, because it only varies between 0.038 and 0.040 in the series we use, it does not help to explain changes in capital accumulation through time.

In the next section we discuss the empirical construction of the variables s, u, v, and p.

ROLE OF SAVINGS (s)

In view of the importance of the savings rate in explaining the collapse of capital formation, it is fitting to examine the behavior of the two main components of this rate—external and domestic savings—to better understand the evolution of capital formation financing.[4] Table 9.1 shows a breakdown of the financing of gross capital formation, using subperiods characterized by some similarity of parameter values and economic policies (as explained later in this chapter). The breakdown includes gross fixed capital formation (GFCF) and changes in inventories, as well as domestic and foreign savings—all variables measured as ratios to GDP. In contrast to the savings concept to be used later in the decomposition of capital growth, in table 9.1 the change in inventories is part of the investment to be financed.

Table 9.1 Rates of Capital Formation, Savings, and Their Components in Selected Periods

Period	GFCF Rate	Changes in Inventories	Rate of Capital Formation = Total Savings	Foreign Savings	Domestic Savings
1947–1962	14.8	0.7	15.5	0.3	15.3
1963–1967	15.8	1.8	17.6	−0.7	18.3
1968–1973	19.5	1.5	21.0	0.9	20.1
1974–1980	22.6	1.0	23.6	2.6	21.0
1981–1992	19.2	0.1	19.3	−2.5	21.7
1993–1999	17.0	0.5	17.5	1.0	16.5
2000–2011	17.3	0.7	18.0	−1.3	19.3

Source: IPEADATA.

Note: All data listed are rounded percentages of GDP in current values. GFCF, gross fixed capital formation.

In the decomposition of table 9.1, foreign savings is defined in the national accounts as the excess of imports over exports of goods and services, or the net resource transfer from abroad. This is a narrower concept than the balance-of-payments deficit in the current account (which includes net income sent abroad in foreign savings), but it seems more relevant to the analysis of the contribution of foreign capital to GDP growth.[5]

Table 9.1 shows that the 8 percentage point increase in total savings from the immediate post-WWII period (15.5 percent of GDP) to the so-called *fuite en avant* period from 1974 to 1980 (23.6 percent) is explained mainly by higher domestic savings (up from 15.3 to 21.0 percent of GDP).

As also seen in table 9.1, total savings collapsed between the *fuite en avant* period and the long lost decade (1981–1992), having declined by 4.3 percentage points of GDP. Domestic savings varied little. In fact, it rose slightly from 21.0 to 21.7 percent of GDP. It follows that the fall of capital formation financing resulted entirely from a sharp turnaround in the transfer of resources from abroad: from +2.6 percent of GDP between 1974 and 1980 to −2.5 percent of GDP between 1981 and 1992. This change was transmitted to GFCF (which fell to 3.4 percent of GDP). Seen from this perspective, the debt crisis, implying a net outflow of resources to abroad, seems to have been the main culprit behind the fall of GFCF between the two periods.

The fixed investment rate continued to fall in the phase of reforms, from 19.2 percent of GDP between 1981 and 1982 to 17.0 percent of GDP between 1993 and 1999, but now the culprit was the fall of domestic savings (from 21.7 to 16.5 percent of GDP), possibly as a result of the end of the inflation tax plus the pressure of current spending on the government budget that led to a reduction in public investment. In 2000 to 2011, a decrease of foreign savings was more than offset by an increase in domestic savings, raising total savings slightly from 17.5 percent of GDP between 1993 and 1999 to 18.0 percent of GDP between 2000 and 2011.

DEGREE OF CAPACITY UTILIZATION (u)

A usually neglected variable in the growth decomposition in equation 9.6 is the degree of capacity utilization (u). In this case, there was direct information only for the manufacturing industry. The procedure we adopted involves smoothing the movements of capacity use in industry—an activity that is more volatile than the rest of the economy—by incorporating information from other sectors.

According to the estimates shown in figure 9.3, the highest level of capacity utilization occurred in 1961 (99.4 percent) and the lowest in 1992 (86.2 percent). From 2002 on, utilization rates increased, reaching 96.7 percent in 2008 and decreasing slightly to 95.7 percent in 2011.

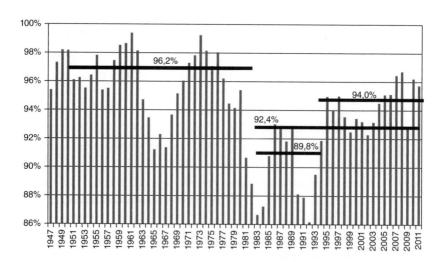

Figure 9.3 **Capacity utilization in the Brazilian economy (u), 1947–2011 (percentage per year).** *Sources:* Authors' elaboration; Bonelli and Bacha (2012).

Figure 9.3 also shows capacity utilization averages in selected subperiods. It is noticeable that the average utilization rate fell from 96.2 percent between 1947 and 1980 to 92.4 percent between 1981 and 2011. Thus, not only did capital and GDP growth collapse after 1980, but average capacity utilization fell almost 4 percentage points as well. Subdividing the years from 1981 to 2011 into two phases, the utilization rate exhibited an upward movement from 89.8 percent between 1981 and 1992 to 94.0 percent between 1993 and 2011, an increase of 4.2 percentage points. Still, capacity utilization remained below the 96.2 percent average recorded from 1947 to 1980.

OUTPUT–CAPITAL IN-USE RATIO (v)

The evolution of the ratio between real GDP and capital in use is shown in figure 9.4. It is characterized by two long declining stretches: the first from 1947 to 1959 (when it falls from 0.8 to 0.62) and the second from 1973 to 1983 (when it falls from 0.61 to 0.46). Toward the end of the series, v increased slightly, from 0.44 between 2001 and 2003 to 0.48 between 2009 and 2011, in tandem with GDP growth.

A neoclassical explanation for the fall of v emphasizes the relationship of this variable with the evolution of the labor–capital ratio. Using a Cobb–Douglas aggregate production function with the usual properties, one can write the output–capital in-use ratio as follows:

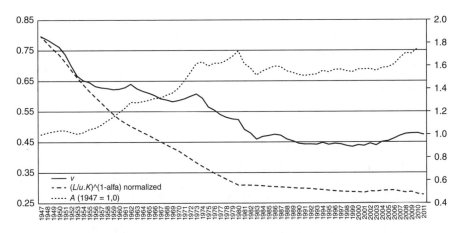

Figure 9.4   Output/capital in-use ratio (v), labor/capital in-use ratio raised to 1 – α, and PTF (A), 1947–2011 (in 2000 prices). *Source:* Authors' elaboration.

$$v = Y/uK = AL^{1-\alpha}(uK)^{\alpha}/uK = A(L/uK)^{1-\alpha},$$

where α is the elasticity of output with respect to capital, L is the labor force, and A is the total factor productivity (TFP). Thus, in this interpretation, v is equal to the product of the rate of technical progress by the labor–capital in-use ratio raised to the power $1 - \alpha$.

Figure 9.4 illustrates the behavior of three variables from 1947 to 2011: v, $(L/uK)^{1-\alpha}$, and A. In this figure, we normalized the expression for the labor–capital in-use ratio, equating it to the value of v in 1947 (both are read on the scale to the left). The series for A also appears with 1947 = 1.0 and should be read in the scale to the right.

Figure 9.4 shows that v declines mostly after the decline of the labor–capital ratio, which is a consequence of capital accumulation that exceeds employment growth until the early 1980s. Total factor productivity growth holds down the decline of v in the initial period. Starting in 1974, total factor productivity grew more slowly, or even decreased, as in the 1980s. After 1980, the pace of capital deepening slowed down and, consequently, the output–capital in-use ratio tended to stabilize. It grew moderately again in the 2000s.

RELATIVE PRICE OF INVESTMENT (p)

The relative price of investment p—the ratio between the implicit deflators of GFCF and GDP—plays a key role in explaining the capital growth plunge. Figure 9.5 shows that the behavior of the relative price of investment in Brazil is peculiar indeed. Aside from an anomalous performance between 1987 and 1994, which we discuss later, it follows a trajectory of continuous expansion. A simple exponential trend line indicates that the relative price of investment grew at a rate of approximately 0.7 percent per year for more than sixty years.

A hypothesis that seems plausible for the anomalous behavior of p during the 1987–1994 period is that after the price unfreezing that followed the failure of the 1986 Cruzado Plan, entrepreneurs adopted a defensive stance against possible future freezes and began reporting to the Vargas Foundation the list price for their machines and building supplies, which tended to be higher than the prices they actually charged. In other words, the initial jump of p in 1987 was simply a statistical error. A great deal of turbulence followed at the end of the decade, both in the country's economy and in the national statistics. Thus, a measurement error, caused

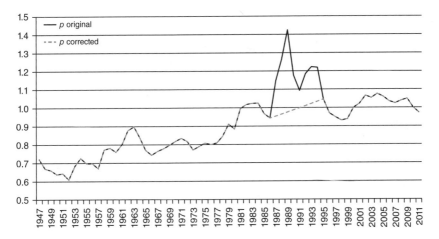

Figure 9.5 Relative price of investment, original and corrected, 1947–2011 (2000 = 1.0). *Sources:* FGV, IBGE, and authors' elaboration.

by the capture of inflated list prices, may have been propagated in subsequent years until a thoroughly new national accounts was created for the period after 1994.

Assuming that measurement errors and changes in the national accounts methodology were behind the anomaly of the p series from 1987 to 1994, we propose henceforth to adopt a correction for this variable. Between 1987 and 1994, we suggest replacing the p series that is obtained from the national accounts by a geometric interpolation of values between 1986 and 1995, as indicated by the dotted line in figure 9.5. Therefore, the corrected series retains all the original values from 1947 to 1986 and from 1995 to 2011, changing only the figures for the intermediate years.[6]

We succeeded in explaining the long-term behavior of the corrected p series by using a multiple regression with three independent variables: the share of imported machines on all machinery and equipment that enters capital formation, the real exchange rate, and a trend. The regression results in table 9.2 have an R^2 of 0.89, denoting an excellent statistical adjustment. The coefficients of all independent variables have the expected signs and plausible values.

The negative coefficient of the share of imported machinery reveals the cost of the import substitution of capital goods. The inclusion of the real exchange rate in the regression is explained by the importance of the import component of investment: the more depreciated the exchange rate, the higher the price of investment relative to GDP. The coefficient

Table 9.2 Regression Statistics with p Corrected as Dependent Variable

Dependent Variable: p Corrected	Coefficient	Standard Error	t-statistic	p value
Intercept	0.6280	0.0326	19.28	0.000
Imported machines/ total machines	−0.1218	0.0501	−2.43	0.018
Real exchange rate	0.1137	0.0287	3.95	0.000
Time trend	0.0058	0.0003	16.95	0.000
R^2	0.8913			
R^2 adjusted	0.8859			
N = 64 (1947–2010) Durbin–Watson statistic	0.6224			

of the time variable implies that there was a progressive rise in the relative price of capital goods in the country, even after allowing for the higher cost of import substitution and the vagaries of the real exchange rate. We believe that this resulted from the low pace of productivity growth in the construction industry: labor productivity in the construction industry grew approximately 1.0 percent per year between 1950 and 2008; for the economy as a whole the rate was 2.3 percent.

CAPITAL GROWTH COLLAPSE DECOMPOSED

In table 9.3, capital growth is decomposed according to the previously obtained equation 9.5. The results follow a periodization that favors the identification of periods with similar characteristics of economic performance and economic policies, namely:

1948–1962: Postwar prosperity and the Kubitschek era
1963–1967: Recession and defeat of democracy
1968–1973: Authoritarian economic miracle
1974–1980: Oil shock and fuite en avant
1981–1992: Debt crisis and lost decade
1993–1999: Real Plan and economic reforms
2000–2011: New macroeconomic regime

Two major periods are clearly characterized in the table: before 1980 and after 1980. Between 1947 and 1980, the growth of the capital stock was strong in all subperiods, reaching 9.8 percent per year in the *fuite en avant*

Table 9.3 Breakdown of Capital Growth (K'): Annual Averages in Selected Periods from 1948 to 2011

Period	K' (% per year)	s (% GDP)	u (%)	v	$1/p$ (= 1.0 in 2000)
1948–1962	8.9	14.8	97.1	0.683	1.415
1963–1967	6.6	15.8	92.6	0.610	1.252
1968–1973	9.6	19.5	96.5	0.593	1.248
1974–1980	9.8	22.6	96.2	0.548	1.201
1981–1992	3.3	19.2	89.8	0.463	1.012
1993–1999	2.3	17.0	93.1	0.442	1.018
2000–2011	2.7	17.3	94.6	0.459	0.969
Total	6.0	17.7	94.4	0.547	1.164

period. Even during the political crisis that ended the Second Republic and initiated the military regime (1963–1967), capital stock growth was relatively high: 6.6 percent per year.

After 1980, capital stock growth fell sharply and did not recover even after the Real Plan conquered hyperinflation in 1994. Part of the responsibility rested on the savings rate (s), which fell more than 3 percentage points as a result of the reduction in foreign savings. The three other factors behind the collapse of capital accumulation were as follows: a decrease in capacity utilization (u) of 6 percentage points, a fall in capital productivity (v) of 8 percentage points, and an increase in the relative price of investment (p) of almost 19 percent. In other words, even after correcting the figures for the relative price of investment as described previously, it continued to be an important determinant in the collapse of capital formation after 1980.

The capital growth rate continued to fall between the long lost decade of 1981 and 1992 and the short phase of reforms between 1993 and 1999. The primary reason for this was a reduction in the domestic savings rate, as explained previously. Finally, between the age of reforms and the growth resumption between 2000 and 2011, a modest acceleration in capital formation occurred that is explained mainly by increases in use of installed capacity and the productivity of capital.

CAPITAL DEEPENING, TFP, AND THE COLLAPSE OF GDP GROWTH

The purpose of this section is to develop a growth decomposition exercise by using an aggregate Cobb–Douglas production function with capital and labor as production factors. Our interest is in the evolution of GDP per worker. The log linearization of a function of this type results in

$$y' = \alpha(uk)' + \text{TFP}', \tag{9.6}$$

where y' is the growth rate of GDP per worker, α is the capital share in GDP, $(uk)'$ is the growth rate of capital employed per worker, and TFP$'$ is the rate of growth of total factor productivity.[7]

Figure 9.6 presents the TFP$'$ series obtained residually from equation 9.6. It can be seen that TFP$'$ varied enormously over time. The average rate of change of TFP varied from a low of -1.0 percent per year in the lost decade (1981–1992) to a high of 3.3 percent per year during the economic miracle period (1968–1973). The average for the entire period was nearly 1 percent per year. After the lost decade, TFP growth resumed, albeit slowly. From 1999 on, total productivity growth was more visible: 1.0 percent per year between 2000 and 2011 (see table 9.4). The breakdown of the sources of GDP per worker growth (y') according to equation 9.6 is presented in table 9.4.

The numbers in table 9.4 reveal much about the relative roles of capital deepening, $(uk)'$, and technical progress, TFP$'$, relative to Brazil's economic growth collapse after 1980. Observe first that, for the period

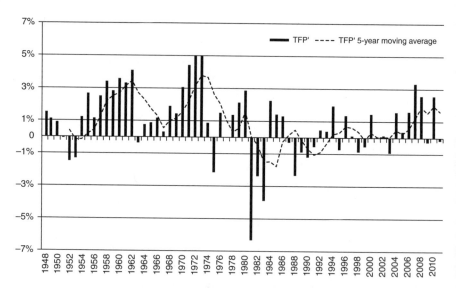

Figure 9.6 Total factor productivity (TFP) yearly growth and five-year averages, 1948–2011 (percentage per year). *Source:* Authors' elaboration.

Table 9.4 Decomposition of GDP per Worker Growth (y'), 1948–2011

Period	y'	TFP$'$	y'-%	$(uk)'$	y'-%
1948–1962	4.40	1.67	0.38	2.73	0.62
1963–1967	2.40	0.50	0.23	1.80	0.77
1968–1973	5.70	3.30	0.58	2.40	0.42
1974–1980	3.60	0.90	0.26	2.70	0.74
1981–1992	−0.80	−1.00	1.37	0.30	−0.37
1993–1999	0.70	0.25	0.35	0.45	0.65
2000–2011	1.20	1.00	0.81	0.20	0.19
1948–2011	2.30	0.85	0.37	1.43	0.63
1948–1980	4.16	1.63	0.39	2.52	0.61
1981–2011	0.31	0.02	0.06	0.29	0.94

a whole (1948–2011), the growth rate of GDP per worker was 2.3 percent per year. Capital deepening accounted for 63 percent of this performance, and TFP$'$ accounted for 37 percent—a similar partition obtained between 1948 and 1980 except for the fact that, in this case, GDP per worker rose 4.2 percent per year. From 1981 to 2011, the growth of GDP per worker sunk to only 0.3 percent per year. A sharp drop in capital deepening was the main ingredient for such poor performance: capital deepening fell from 2.5 percent per year before 1980 to 0.3 percent per year after 1980. Its contribution to the mediocre GDP per worker growth in the latter period rose to 94 percent. This justifies our emphasis on capital accumulation as the main source of Brazil's growth collapse after 1980.

Conversely, it is worth noting that the rate of technical progress also sunk from 1.6 percent per year to nil from the period before 1980 to that after 1980. Moreover (in addition to 1948–1962, when Brazil like the rest of the world benefited from the postwar economic boom), the phases with the highest rates of technical progress were between 1968 and 1973 and 2000 and 2011, when Brazil benefited from policy reforms introduced in the periods that immediately preceded them.[8] Finally, we found that "technical regression" was the dominant factor behind the long lost decade.

CONCLUSIONS

We found a strong association between the GDP and capital stock growth rates after WWII. The usual Granger causality tests suggest that capital growth causes GDP growth even more strongly than GDP growth causes capital growth. The second link has to do with the accelerator; the first is consistent with the predictions of a Solow model outside the steady state.

We proceeded with an accounting-based analysis of the sources of growth both for the capital stock and for GDP per worker. For this purpose, we divided the long period from 1947 to 2011 into seven subperiods characterized by some similarity in parameter behavior and the conduct of economic policy. We focused on the collapse of gross fixed capital formation after 1980, from which Brazil did not fully recover even after overcoming hyperinflation in 1994. For the so-called long lost decade from 1981 to 1992, we observed that little guilt can be attributed to domestic savings. What happened was a collapse of foreign savings as a result of the 1980s debt crisis. Three additional factors behind the collapse of capital accumulation between 1974 and 1980 and 1981 and 1992 were a reduction in capacity utilization, a decline in capital productivity, and, most importantly, a sharp rise in the relative price of investment.

The capital growth rate continued to fall between the long lost decade and the short decade of reforms (1993–1999). Responsibility for this now fell on a reduction in domestic savings and, secondarily, lower capital productivity. Finally, between the age of reforms and the new macroeconomic regime period (2000–2011), a modest acceleration in capital formation occurred that was explained mainly by increases in the use of installed capacity and a higher productivity of capital.

The last step in our review involved an estimation of the roles of capital deepening and technical progress in the evolution of GDP per worker. We found that capital deepening was responsible for nearly two-thirds of GDP per worker growth over the entire post-WWII period (with a similar figure applying to the pre-1980 period). The sharp decline in the growth rates of GDP per worker after 1980 was also found to largely be the result of a collapse in capital accumulation. However, technical progress—probably induced by previous economic reforms—was an important explanation both for the economic miracle (1968–1973) and for the growth recovery between 2000 and 2011. Moreover, the long lost decade was mostly associated with a technical regression induced by the debt crisis and hyperinflation.

Despite a modest recent increase in the output–capital ratio, domestic savings have been too low to allow for growth rates higher than the 4 percent recorded over the past few years. The corollary is that growth can be stifled if access to international financing drops, as it did in 2002 and 2008. Unsurprisingly, we conclude that Brazil's recent slow growth was caused by low rates of investment and domestic savings. If these savings do not increase, the country seems doomed to grow at the modest rates observed in recent years.

POSTSCRIPT

The chapter concludes that despite a modest increase in the output–capital ratio domestic savings are too low to allow for growth rates higher than the 4% recorded until 2011. The experience since then showed this assertion to have been too optimistic.[9]

Without bothering the readers with the details of the construction of the new figures that are still of a preliminary nature (with those for 2014 being only educated guesses), we may synthetize the reasons for being less optimistic about the near future as follows. First, the rise in the output–capital ratio observed up to 2010 reversed itself; this coefficient has returned to values similar to those that prevailed before the commodity boom began in 2004. Second, the labor force growth rate decelerated much faster than we anticipated. Consequently, we now believe that Brazil's potential GDP growth rate (Y') for the next ten years is around 3.3 percent per year.

To see why, let us start with the labor force. From 1948 to 2011, employment grew by a sizable 2.7 percent per year. In the last period we considered in the chapter, 2000 to 2011, employment growth was a respectable 2 percent per year according to our revised estimates. However, after 2011, employment growth decelerated substantially to 1.1 percent per year. Furthermore, new estimates from the 2010 Demographic Census produced by Brazil's Statistical Institute put the growth rate of Brazil's adult population (ages 15 to 65) at approximately 0.9 percent on average over the next ten years. Admitting that a partial reversal of the recent decline in the labor force participation rate may occur, we project employment growth (L') over the next ten years at 1 percent per year. To proceed, we need an estimate for the prospective GDP per worker growth rate, or the growth rate of labor productivity (y').

The growth rate of labor productivity from 2011 to 2014 was only 0.9 percent per year. In terms of the decomposition of this variable in table 9.4, the entire reason for such a lackluster performance was a sharp decline in the growth rate of total factor productivity (TFP'). In fact, for only the second time in our recorded history (the first one being during the lost decade), total factor productivity actually declined by 0.46

percent per year between 2011 and 2014.[10] The contrast with the past could not be sharper: in the entire period from 1948 to 2011, the TFP growth rate was 0.9 percent per year. In the more recent period (2000–2011), the TFP growth rate was a similar 1.0 percent per year. The procyclical behavior of total productivity can be blamed for at least part of the fall. Other likely causes are the loss of impulse coming from abroad (illustrated by the decline in the external terms of trade) and economic policy distortions introduced during Rousseff's presidency. In fact, we still do not know why the TFP growth rate declined sharply during the more recent period. Whatever the cause might be, however, it seems reasonable (if only a little optimistic) to ignore this recent dismal performance and bet that the TFP growth rate of the historical past will reassert itself in the near future, thus generating a contribution to the GDP's growth rate of 1 percent per year.

Finally, the contribution of the growth rate of capital deepening—$\alpha(uk)'$ in table 9.4—to labor productivity growth was 1.3 percent per year between 2011 and 2014, a value near to its historical average (1.4 percent per year between 1948 and 2011). Hence, it seems reasonable to adopt the same figure for the period ahead.

In terms of the equation leading to table 9.4, we have the following decomposition of our new estimate for Brazil's potential yearly GDP growth rate:

$$Y' = L' + y' = L' + \text{TFP}' + \alpha(uk)' = 1\% + 1\% + 1.3\% = 3.3\%.$$

NOTES

1. An extensive version of this chapter (Bonelli and Bacha 2012) discusses statistical sources and procedures in addition to developing themes that are left out of this version.

2. See Bacha and Bonelli (2005). In the present text we also used material from Bonelli and Bacha (2012).

3. For the complete story, see the papers collected in Veloso et al. (2012).

4. It was not possible to split domestic savings between government savings and private savings. The government accounts in the national accounts cannot be used before the 1994 stabilization because, in them, the monetary correction of public debt appears as a current expense, thus generating an absurdly high public sector "dissaving." Previous attempts in the literature at eliminating the monetary correction from the public accounts before 1994 unfortunately generated quite contradictory savings estimates for the government during the period.

5. See Bacha (1992) for a discussion of this topic.

6. In the Brazilian national accounts, the nominal savings rate is calculated residually simply as the product of the price index for investment goods by the volume index of investment. Hence, the correction of the price index series also requires that we correct the nominal savings series for the period between 1987 and 1994. For more details, see Bonelli and Bacha (2012).

7. As explained in Bonelli and Bacha (2012), we adopted the value of 0.46 for the coefficient α. This is almost identical to the value estimated by Considera and Pessôa (2012).

8. For an analysis of the role of the reforms between 1964 and 1967 on the economic miracle period (1968–1973), see Veloso et al. (2008).

9. This postscript was written in October 2014.

10. A decomposition of the growth rate of total factor productivity as a weighted sum of the growth rates of capital productivity and labor productivity shows that its decline was totally explained by a contraction in capital productivity (i.e., in the output–capital in-use ratio).

REFERENCES

Bacha, E. 1992. "External debt, net transfers, and growth in developing countries." *World Development* 20(8): 1183–1192.

Bacha, E. and Bonelli, R. 2005. "Uma interpretação das causas da desaceleração econômica do Brasil." *Revista de Economia Política* 25(3): 163–189.

Bonelli, R. and Bacha, E. 2012. "Crescimento brasileiro revisitado." In *Desenvolvimento econômico: uma perspectiva Brasileira*, edited by F. Veloso, P. C. Ferreira, F. Giambiagi, and S. Pessôa, 236–262. Rio de Janeiro, Brasil: Campus/Elsevier.

Considera, C. and Pessôa, S. 2012. "A distribuição funcional da renda no Brasil." *Texto para Discussão IBRE*. http://www.portalibre.fgv.br.

Veloso, F., Ferreira, P. C., Giambiagi, F., and Pessôa, S., eds. 2012. *Desenvolvimento econômico: uma perspectiva Brasileira*. Rio de Janeiro, Brasil: Campus/Elsevier.

Veloso F., Villela, A., and Giambiagi, F. 2008. "Determinantes do 'milagre' econômico Brasileiro (1968–1973): uma análise empírica." *Revista Brasileira de Economia* 62(2): 221–246.

PART 3

The Real Exchange Rate, Balance of Payments, and Economic Development

Balance-of-Payments Dominance

IMPLICATIONS FOR MACROECONOMIC POLICY

José Antonio Ocampo

A major theme of structuralist economics has been the central role that the balance of payments plays in macroeconomic dynamics (Ocampo et al. 2009). The emphasis on the implications of external gaps and the Dutch disease for growth in developing countries are part of that tradition. However, in this chapter I will refer to a different phenomenon: the heavy influence that the balance of payments exercises on the *short-term* macroeconomic dynamics in developing countries—i.e., the dependence of domestic business cycles on external shocks, positive and negative, that are transmitted through the balance of payments. One of the major features of this dependence is that it also generates strong pressures for macroeconomic policy to behave in a procyclical way.[1] Some of these shocks may be massive and change the long-term trajectory of economic growth; if that is the case, however, they may be understood as structural external gaps.

The close link between external and domestic business cycles in developing countries has old roots. It was evident during the days of the gold (and silver) standard, when countries on the periphery of the world economy were frequently forced to abandon it during crises. However, the aim was always to return to such standards and the associated "rules of the game," which essentially meant procyclical macroeconomic policies. The final collapse of the gold standard during the Great Depression represented a huge paradigmatic break, as Keynesian policy shifted the attention of macroeconomics to *counter*cyclical policies. However, although the center of attention of such policies in the industrial countries came to be the management of aggregate demand through active fiscal and monetary policies, the predominance of external shocks implied that the focus of countercyclical management in developing countries came to be the management of the supply shocks—i.e., constraints on domestic economic activity—associated with the availability of foreign exchange.[2]

The mainstream literature has called "fiscal dominance" a regime in which macroeconomic management is essentially determined by fiscal conditions. Thus, I will call "balance-of-payments dominance" the regime in which the external shocks, both positive and negative, are the essential determinants of short-term macroeconomic dynamics. Under this regime, the balance of payments exercises strong cyclical shocks through trade and the availability and costs of external financing.[3] The latter includes movements in risk spreads (reductions during booms, increases during crises) that reinforce the cyclical effects in the availability of finance and may generate procyclical variations of domestic interest rates. In turn, both trade and the capital account tend to generate cyclical effects on exchange rates (appreciation during booms, depreciation during crises) that have more ambiguous effects. Under these interest and exchange rate pressures, macroeconomic authorities have to fight hard to build the space for effective countercyclical macroeconomic policies.

It is thus not surprising that in the old days (from roughly the 1950s through the 1970s) of state-led industrialization in the developing world (or "import-substituting industrialization" as it is more commonly called), the major instruments of macroeconomic policy focused on managing external shocks, mainly those coming through the trade account but, since the 1970s, also from the capital account. The interventionist apparatus included an array of instruments of protection and export promotion, capital controls, multiple exchange rates (particularly in the early years) and, since the 1960s, the crawling peg, a major Latin American innovation for managing the exchange rates in inflation-prone economies (Frenkel and Rapetti 2011). Most of these instruments were dismantled during the process of economic liberalization. The major one left was the exchange rate, which was made increasingly flexible to accommodate the external shocks that came through the capital account. In several cases, the exchange rate was used to manage domestic policy objectives, particularly to anchor the price level in anti-inflationary programs, in which case it was not even allowed to be an active instrument to manage balance-of-payments shocks.

This chapter will explore the nature and modalities of countercyclical macroeconomic policies under balance-of-payments dominance. In the next section, I deal with the contemporary modalities of this dominance. Then I discuss countercyclical fiscal policies and the space for monetary and exchange rate autonomy in economies subject to such a regime. Given my expertise and background, the Latin American experience is referenced throughout.

THE CONTEMPORARY MODALITIES OF BALANCE-OF-PAYMENTS DOMINANCE

International trade continues to generate cyclical shocks in developing countries.[4] This is particularly true of terms-of-trade variations in commodity-dependent economies. The recent global financial crisis also showed, indeed in a dramatic way, how the economies that specialize in manufacturing and services can be subject to strong cyclical external demand shocks.

However, the dominant feature since the mid-1970s has been the central role that the capital account plays in generating cyclical shocks for those developing countries that have access to private capital markets. Furthermore, whereas fiscal accounts played a principal role in the first contemporary cycle of external financing (from the mid-1970s through the traumatic 1980s), the central feature in recent decades has been the predominance of external private financing and the procyclical effect it has on private sector spending and balance sheets. One of its manifestations has been the frequency of "twin" domestic banking and external crises since the early 1980s, with the liberalizing Southern Cone countries of South America as pioneers in this field.

This phenomenon is, of course, part of the basic tendency of private finance to experience boom and bust cycles, a theme that was central to the Keynesian revolution and developed with particular brilliance by Minsky (1982). Confirmation of this pattern in various settings has been provided, among others, by Kindleberger and Aliber (2005), Reinhart and Rogoff (2009), Akyüz (2011), and Ffrench-Davis and Griffith-Jones (2011). Throughout the business cycle, private agents alternate between "risk appetite" (or, rather, underestimation of risks) and "flight to quality" (risk aversion), to use typical terms in financial parlance. In the case of nonresidents, this is reflected in procyclical finance they provide to domestic agents; in the latter, it is reflected in the alternation in the relative demand for assets denominated in domestic versus foreign currencies, which generate a repatriation of capital during booms followed by capital flight during crises. In turn, opinions and expectations of different agents feed back into one another, generating an alternation of contagion of optimism and pessimism. Asymmetries of information typical of financial markets, risk evaluation models, and certain market practices (benchmarking with competitors) tend to accentuate these trends.

Boom and bust cycles are stronger for those agents that are considered riskier by financial markets and who experience easier availability of finance during booms followed by credit rationing and/or high costs of financing during crises. This is the situation faced by small enterprises and lower-income households even in mature industrial markets. It is also the condition that characterizes emerging and developing countries (including peripherally, Europe during the current crisis) in global financial markets. One way of understanding this phenomenon is that financial integration by developing countries into the global financial market is segmented (Frenkel 2008)—i.e., integration into a market that is segmented by risk categories, with those considered as being riskier subject to deeper boom and bust cycles. As a result, emerging economies experience boom and bust cycles independently of their macroeconomic fundamentals (Calvo and Talvi 2008). Countries that are considered "successful" are inevitably brought into the boom, but this can lead to the accumulation of vulnerabilities that may lead them to crises; if so, they may later turn into pariahs of the global financial world (Ffrench-Davis 2001; Marfán 2005).

Volatility is reflected in the behavior of spreads as well as in the availability and maturity of financing. Risks tend to be more pronounced in developing countries because of the proliferation of maturity and currency mismatches in private sector balance sheets. All forms of financing tend to be cyclical, but this pattern is sharper for short-term financing, which thus tends to be particularly risky (Rodrik and Velasco 2000). A recent diagnosis by the International Monetary Fund (IMF 2011) indicates that the volatility of capital flows has increased over time and is sharper for emerging than it is for advanced economies. Bank and other capital flows are more volatile, followed by portfolio debt flows, but foreign direct investment (FDI) volatility has increased and is now similar to that for portfolio debt flows. In turn, persistence is lowest for portfolio debt flows and has declined for FDI since 2000. In the case of FDI, increasing volatility and lack of persistence may reflect the fact that financial FDI (i.e., borrowing by subsidiary from a parent bank or firm) has increased over time.

Intense short-term movements, such as those produced after the August 1998 Russian moratoria and the September 2008 collapse of Lehman Brothers, are particularly traumatic. However, in practice, the most difficult phenomena to manage in macroeconomic terms are *medium-term* cycles—i.e., those that have tended to last seven to fifteen years. Developing countries have experienced three such cycles since the 1970s and are at the beginning of a fourth: a boom in the second half of the 1970s followed by a collapse in the 1980s; a boom between 1990 and 1997 (shortly interrupted by the December 1994 Mexican crisis) followed by the sequence of emerging market crises that started in East Asia in mid-1997; a boom between 2003 and mid-2008 followed by the global effects of the collapse of Lehman Brothers; and a new boom since mid-2009 (shortly interrupted by events around the world, particularly by the different episodes of the euro crisis).

Historical evidence seems to indicate that the strength of the policies adopted by advanced economies to stabilize financial markets is critical for the length of the downward phase of the cycle. As such, the massive interventions after the collapse of Lehman Brothers were critical for returning to more normal financial conditions in the developing world in a relatively short period of time (approximately a year). The same is true of the massive support to Mexico after its December 1994 crisis (which lasted a few months). In contrast, weak and delayed action after the August 1982 Mexican default and the first stages of the East Asian crisis in the second semester of 1997 led to protracted crises in emerging markets (eight and six years, respectively).

Another factor that has mitigated the strength and length of crises is the reduced external vulnerability of developing countries generated by the combination of massive self-insurance through foreign reserve accumulation and the development of domestic bond markets after the Asian financial crisis, which made governments less dependent on external financing. Both led to the reduced perception of risk, reflected in the low spreads that prevailed between 2004 and 2007. Although this may be understood as a reflection of reduced financial market segmentation, the fact that its counterpart is massive self-insurance through the accumulation of foreign exchange reserves indicates that market segmentation is still a feature of the global economy, but one that can be mitigated by prudential policies.

As indicated previously, the major problems generated by boom and bust cycles are associated with procyclical private sector spending and induced vulnerabilities in balance sheets. However, the major complication is that this is accompanied by the reduced space for traditional countercyclical policies. Given this constraint, the key to appropriate countercyclical management is the expanded availability of policy instruments for managing the domestic effects of external boom and bust cycles. This is particularly so when we understand that stability goes beyond price stability and includes real and financial stability—i.e., avoiding sharp business cycles and domestic financial crises.

This indicates the need for continuing to reflect on the design of countercyclical policies that are appropriate for economies facing balance-of-payments dominance. In the rest of the chapter, I explore three broad set of policies and their capacity to smooth the business cycle: fiscal policies, monetary and exchange rate policies (that because of their linkages must be analyzed simultaneously), and what Epstein et al. (2003) and Ocampo (2008) have called "capital management techniques," which using the terminology en vogue, I will call "macroprudential policies."

COUNTERCYCLICAL FISCAL POLICIES

Fiscal policy can always play a useful countercyclical role, but counteracting the pressures from financial markets and balancing the political considerations that underlie fiscal management is not easy. In countries where commodity prices are an essential source of public sector revenues, one of the best alternatives is to create commodity stabilization funds. Important examples in Latin America are the National Coffee Fund of Colombia (which, however, largely abandoned its stabilization function in the 1990s) and the Chilean copper stabilization funds, but this instrument has spread worldwide, particularly to mineral- and oil-exporting economies. Based on this experience, the UN Economic Commission for Latin America and the Caribbean (ECLAC 2011) proposed creating general stabilization funds for public sector revenues that would absorb the transitory component of such revenues. This should be accompanied by the creation of structural rules for public sector financing, a step taken a decade ago by Chile and most recently replicated by Colombia. This is, of course, no easy task, as GDP trends may not be independent of cyclical fluctuations, particularly in economies experiencing sharp business cycles (Heymann 2000) and in commodity-dependent economies because commodity prices may be subject to short-term fluctuations that may lead to changes in trends. In any case, what the structural rules imply is that public sector finances must be guided by long-term trends. Strictly speaking, what this means is that fiscal policy becomes neutral over the business cycle (i.e., acyclical), implying that it has to be complemented by strict countercyclical instruments.[5] However, to avoid lags in the countercyclical effects of fiscal policy, the best instruments are automatic stabilizers associated with tax and spending policies.

In this regard, the experience of industrial economies is that the best automatic spending stabilizers are those associated with social protection systems, particularly unemployment insurance. The latter may not be an appropriate instrument in developing countries, where informal jobs play an important role in employment generation. Some additional instruments may be needed, particularly emergency employment programs that are automatically triggered during crises. Conditional cash transfers were also used during the recent crisis for this purpose in several countries; however, because these transfers are difficult to reduce during upswings, they cannot be used as a permanent countercyclical tool.

Tax instruments can also play the role of automatic stabilizers. The best case is, of course, a progressive income tax. However, other tax instruments can be useful for that purpose. This is the case for instruments that capture windfall price gains in natural resource exports that are absorbed through the aforementioned commodity stabilization funds. A similar argument can be made for taxing capital inflows during capital account booms. Note that the fiscal argument for the use of this tax, a countercyclical tool, is different from those that will be discussed in the next section that relate to monetary and foreign exchange management. Using similar logic, a countercyclical value-added tax (VAT) could be designed. An alternative used by some countries during the recent crisis was to temporarily reduce some VAT rates to encourage spending.

In any case, countercyclical fiscal policies face both economic and political constraints. In economic terms, the major problem is lack of access to appropriate financing during crises, as well as market (and possibly IMF) pressure to adopt austerity policies to generate "credibility" and in particular to reduce the perceived risk of default. However, if authorities adopt austerity policies during crises, it would be politically impossible to justify maintaining those policies during booms. Thus, austerity during crises generates a vicious circle that leads to the pressure to spend during the succeeding boom, thus generating a procyclical fiscal policy.

In turn, during booms, it is difficult in political terms to justify fiscal austerity to compensate for the "exuberance" of private sector spending (Marfán 2005). This is particularly true if the spending boom benefits high-income groups, whereas cuts in public sector spending affect lower-income recipients, as countercyclical fiscal policy would thus be regarded as regressive in distributive terms. There may also be classic time-inconsistency issues. Particularly, savings during booms may generate pressure to spend them (the pressure Chile faced during the 2003–2008 boom) or to dilapidate them in the form of unsustainable tax cuts (as the United States did after the Clinton era).

Countercyclical fiscal policy can also generate some inefficiencies in public sector spending (e.g., interruptions in public sector investment projects that increase their costs) or long-term inflexibilities (additional social spending during crises that becomes permanent). Furthermore, in political terms, it may be difficult to design countercyclical tax instruments, as reflected in the opposition of commodity exporters to taxes that capture their windfall gains.

For all these reasons, countercyclical fiscal policies are the exception rather than the rule in the developing world. The analysis of cyclical patterns of spending in more than one hundred countries between 1960 and 2003 by Kaminsky et al. (2004) indicated, in fact, that fiscal policies tend to be procyclical in developing countries, particularly in Africa and Latin America, in contrast to the experience of the industrial world. Using these results, Ocampo and Vos (2008) showed that this behavior is associated with lower long-term growth. For Latin America, Martner and Tromben (2003) and Bello and Jiménez (2008) came to similar conclusions regarding the dominance of procyclical fiscal policy in Latin America between 1990 and 2001 and 1990 and 2006, respectively.

Contrary to common perception, this behavior persisted in Latin America during the recent cycle (the 2003–2008 boom and 2009 crisis).[6] Procyclical policies were the rule in most countries, and a few showed persistent expansionary spending policies that implied that they were procyclical during the boom but in a sense turned countercyclical during the crisis. Strict countercyclical policies were followed by only a handful of countries. In fact, a good description of Latin American fiscal patterns over the last two cycles is one in which spending responds with lags to revenues through the business cycle (Ocampo 2011a). Spending was thus moderate during the initial phases of the recent boom but turned very expansionary—i.e., became highly procyclical—toward the end (2006–2008). These spending dynamics were maintained in 2009, thus generating some countercyclical effects. The return to greater austerity in 2010 resulted from the sluggish response to lower revenues but generated a countercyclical effect because of the speedy recovery that took place.

MONETARY AND EXCHANGE RATE AUTONOMY UNDER
BALANCE-OF-PAYMENTS DOMINANCE

There have been numerous examples in recent decades that demonstrate how much influence procyclical pressures during boom and bust cycles in global capital markets have on monetary and exchange rate policies in developing and emerging economies. This is particularly true of monetary policy in economies that have opened their capital accounts and that face strong pressures to reduce interest rates during booms and increase them during crises, following trends in international capital markets. If authorities try to counteract these pressures and manage monetary policy in a countercyclical way, they simply displace the effect toward the foreign exchange market—i.e., they speed up appreciation pressures during booms and depreciation pressures during crises. What this means is that authorities in fact lack policy autonomy and can only choose what procyclical effect from global capital markets they would prefer.[7] This statement must be read in a nuanced way but captures a significant grain of truth.

The effects of exchange rate fluctuations are the most complex, as they generate ambiguous short-term and clearly counterproductive long-term effects. The major countercyclical effect operates through the current account of the balance of payments: exchange rate appreciation during booms leads to a deterioration of the current account, whereas depreciation during crises leads to an improvement in that account; both generate variations in net exports that help stabilize domestic aggregate demand. However, beyond a certain level, these countercyclical effects are actually counterproductive, as there is broad evidence that deterioration in the current account during booms has been a common source of crises: it helps to "absorb" the excess supply of external financing during booms but turns into a major source of vulnerability during crises when capital stops flowing in. In turn, the associated exchange rate volatility generates unstable incentives for investing in the production of tradable goods and services, which are particularly counterproductive in terms of the diversification of the export base.[8] For these reasons, structuralist macroeconomics has taken a negative view of this countercyclical effect of exchange rate movements.[9]

Furthermore, these effects tend to be frequently weaker than the procyclical effects that exchange rate fluctuations also generate through two different channels, and that explain the ambiguous effects that exchange rate fluctuations have over aggregate demand through the business cycle. The first and most important are the effects that exchange rate fluctuations have on private sector balance sheets in economies where the private sector is a net borrower in international capital markets.[10] In this case, appreciation during booms generates capital gains that tend to increase aggregate demand, whereas depreciation during crises generates capital losses and recessionary effects. The second effect is distributive in nature and has been one of the major focuses of the traditional literature on the contractionary effects of devaluation (Krugman and Taylor 1978; Díaz-Alejandro 1963). The simplest way of visualizing them is through the effects of the exchange rate on real wages: appreciation tends to increase real wages, thus generating an expansionary effect if there is a high propensity to consume wage incomes, whereas depreciation during crises generates the opposite effect.

The macroeconomic literature has captured the constraints that authorities face through what has come to be known as the "trilemma" of open economies. Its most important implication is that in countries where the capital account has been opened up, authorities can control the exchange rate or the interest rate, but not both. Prior to the crisis, this led several economists to argue that there is a need for "credible" exchange rate regimes that in their view should either be entirely flexible exchange rates—in which they maintain monetary policy autonomy but give up the management of exchange rates altogether—or "hard" pegs. In the latter case, they really give up both monetary and exchange rate autonomy, indeed creating the modern counterpart of the procyclical "rules of the game" of the gold standard.[11] The system is meant to avoid the destabilizing speculative flows typical of fixed but adjustable rates. However, from historical experience, we know that such destabilizing flows may not be absent and that the collapse of such regimes is indeed chaotic, as was shown by the crumbling of the gold standard during the 1930s and the disorderly breakdown of the Argentinean convertibility regime in the early 2000s.

In contrast, the choice of flexible exchange rates with monetary policies aimed at meeting inflation targets has some countercyclical virtues. Nonetheless, this is true if and only if aggregate domestic demand is the major determinant of inflation.[12] However, as already shown, under balance-of-payments dominance, exchange rate variations can have procyclical effects on aggregate demand. Furthermore, the supply shocks (positive or negative) that exchange rates have on domestic prices run in the opposite direction to those assumed by the inflation-targeting regime and may lead to procyclical policy decisions. Thus, if appreciation reduces the price level during booms, interest rates may not be adjusted at the required magnitude to cool domestic demand; in contrast, the inflationary effect of depreciation may lead to a suboptimal increase in domestic interest rates during crises to cool domestic price inflation. It is not surprising that the theoretical analysis of inflation targeting in open economies has indicated that a strict inflation-targeting regime tends to increase real economic volatility (Svensson 2000).

A "flexible" inflation-targeting regime that also takes into account real volatility can partly correct these problems. However, the foundations of inflation targeting tend to weaken considerably under balance-of-payments dominance due to the fact that aggregate demand and the domestic price level have strong external determinants. As traditional structuralist price analysis indicates, this may be complicated by indexation mechanisms. Inflation targeting also assumes that demand is sensitive to interest rates and that the interest rate set by the central bank affects the overall structure of interest rates in the economy; both assumptions may be inappropriate in many (if not most) developing countries because of inadequately developed domestic financial systems.

For all these reasons, inflation targeting should be replaced by rules that accept that central banks must have multiple objectives. In emerging and developing countries, there should at least be three such objectives: inflation, economic activity (employment), and the exchange rate.[13] There is also broad consensus now that financial stability should be added as a major objective, as it has clear macroeconomic dimensions regardless of whether central banks are the regulatory authority or not. This does not mean that inflation should be a secondary objective, subordinated to or contingent on achieving other objectives; in economies such as those of Latin America that have been prone to inflation, it should be a major one.

Obviously, an alternative reading of the trilemma is that what has to be given up is capital account liberalization. Furthermore, the number of objectives that monetary authorities should have implies that central banks should actively search for more instruments.[14] This is reinforced by the fact that the effectiveness of each individual instrument may be limited, a fact that implies that the number of instruments should generally exceed the number of objectives. This is, in a sense, the essential lesson of macroeconomic management in open economies: the cost of rejecting the use of some instruments is high in economies subject to balance-of-payments dominance. The trade and capital account liberalization process led countries to give up many instruments used in the past to manage external shocks without creating new ones. Furthermore, given the fact that interest rate shocks faced by these economies are procyclical, attempting to counteract such pressures implies that an excessive burden was placed on the exchange rate, which does not always play a countercyclical role.

In the face of these dilemmas, many authorities in emerging and developing countries have pragmatically come to the conclusion that not only are polar exchange rate regimes inappropriate but they also must use a broader set of instruments to manage the challenges typical of balance-of-payments dominance. The two primary instruments have been a more active use of countercyclical variations in foreign exchange reserves, appropriately sterilized, and a return to some form of capital account regulations. Both can be clearly used in a countercyclical way and explain why emerging economies tend to favor "intermediate" foreign exchange rate regimes, particularly administered exchange rate flexibility—and in several countries—highly administered flexibility. On top of this, a new layer of countercyclical instruments for managing prudential regulation has been added. These instruments, together with those associated with the administration of the capital account, have come to be covered under the macroprudential perspective. Interestingly, some analysts also include under this concept some traditional instruments of monetary management that were widely used in the past—particularly reserve requirements on bank deposits—and which several countries had started to use again even before the crisis.[15]

The essential advantage of active foreign exchange reserve management is that it allows, within certain limits, to simultaneously control interest rates and exchange rates (see Frenkel 2007). During booms, this requires sterilized accumulation of foreign exchange reserves that then operate as "self-insurance," enhancing the policy space for a macroeconomic management during the succeeding crisis. Foreign exchange reserve management also helps to smooth out the effects of capital flows on exchange rates and thus the unstable incentives that it generates on the production of tradables. Obviously, sterilized interventions can be costly: at the national level, they can generate losses if the return on the investment of reserves is lower than the costs of capital inflows (which it generally is); for central banks, there may also be losses if the instruments of sterilization are costlier than returns on reserves, including capital gains and losses made on foreign exchange management through the business cycle (a less significant problem in economies with low domestic interest rates).

These costs imply that there may be significant benefits in avoiding excess capital inflows in the first place. The term "control" rather than the most appropriate concept of "regulation" is generally used to refer to interventions in the capital account. Indeed, regulations on capital flows are similar to other types of regulations: they may be quantitative in nature (e.g., prohibitions) or price-based (e.g., reserve requirements on capital inflows). Furthermore, those focused on avoiding excess capital inflows are clearly prudential in character, as they aim at correcting the risks associated with such excess inflows.

Capital account regulations operate in two distinct ways: (1) they improve the liability structure of countries, making them less vulnerable to the greater volatility that characterizes certain flows, and (2) they provide larger space for countercyclical monetary policy. In the latter sense, they enhance macroeconomic policy autonomy. In either case, the literature on this issue indicates that the effects of capital account regulations may be limited and temporary.[16] This does not mean that they should not be used. Rather, it means that they should be used only to the degree necessary to be effective, and that they should be dynamically adjust to compensate for the tendency of financial markets to elude them. Regardless of this, since mechanisms used to evade regulations are costly, they show that regulations are at least partly effective. Among new instruments that can be designed, an attractive one is a reserve requirement on foreign exchange liabilities of both financial and nonfinancial agents that may substitute the traditional reserve requirement on capital inflows. This would also make this instrument more similar to traditional instruments of monetary and prudential regulation, which operate on stocks rather than flows.

The use of capital account regulations with a countercyclical focus can be complemented with domestic prudential regulations, as was suggested by the Bank of International Settlements and ECLAC more than a decade ago and practiced in Spain since 2000.[17] The recent global financial crisis finally compelled authorities to lean toward these instruments. The modality adopted by the Basel Committee in 2010 uses capital as the main countercyclical instrument, but it can be complemented with the countercyclical use of loan loss provisions (the Spanish system) and liquidity requirements, as well as those aimed at moderating the procyclical effects of asset price fluctuations, among others. In emerging and developing countries, an essential ingredient of those regulations must be the management of currency mismatches in portfolios, which tend to generate substantial risks and are one of the basic reasons for the procyclical effects that exchange rate fluctuations may have. Tax provisions can also be used for this purpose, particularly by changing the tax treatment of the external debt service, as suggested by Stiglitz and Bhattarcharya (2000).

The recent empirical literature overwhelmingly favors the view that the reduced external vulnerability was the major reason for the fair performance of developing countries during the recent global financial crises. Depending on the study, the reduced external vulnerability is associated empirically with a combination of five different factors: (1) lower current account deficits, (2) competitive exchange rates, (3) a high level of foreign exchange reserves, (4) reduced short-term external liabilities, and (5) capital account regulations being in place.[18] This confirms the view that balance-of-payments dominance is a major issue that developing countries must learn to manage to improve short-term macroeconomic performance. Other factors such as strong fiscal accounts (where there are major exceptions, including India) and autonomous central banks that follow inflation-targeting rules are less important. Some level of exchange rate flexibility is part of the story, particularly in medium- and large-sized developing countries but, as previously argued, an administered regime in which flexibility is mixed with active countercyclical management of foreign exchange reserves is a better alternative.[19]

CONCLUSIONS

This chapter defines "balance-of-payments dominance" as a macroeconomic regime in which the short-term macroeconomic dynamics is essentially determined by external shocks—positive or negative. I argue that this is the predominant regime in emerging and developing countries. Trade shocks play an important role, but the major procyclical shocks are associated with boom and bust cycles in external financing. Policy challenges are associated not only with the management of such shocks but also with the need for enhancing the space for countercyclical macroeconomic policies, as boom and bust cycles tend to pressure macroeconomic policies to behave in a procyclical way. Countercyclical fiscal policies can play a role but face strong economic and political economy constraints, which explains why fiscal policies tend to be generally procyclical. The best bet is to design policies to reduce external vulnerabilities through a combination of administered exchange rate flexibility, very active foreign exchange reserve management, reduced reliance on external borrowing, and macroprudential regulations, including those that directly affect capital flows.

NOTES

I thank Bilge Erten, Juan Carlos Moreno-Brid, and Martin Rapetti for comments on a previous version of this chapter.

1. I will refer to the shocks generated through the trade or capital account as simply cyclical shocks but will refer to their effects on domestic private or public sector spending as procyclical if they transmit or reinforce the direction of the external shocks. Likewise, I will refer to procyclical policies when those policies reinforce the direction of the shocks. In either case, the policies and effects will become countercyclical when they counteract the direction of the shock.

2. These supply shocks, which affect domestic economic activity through the scarcity of foreign exchange (i.e., make aggregate supply depend on the availability of foreign exchange and not on production capacity), should be differentiated from those that affect the price level, which I will also refer to later.

3. For some countries, variations in the flows of remittances from migrant workers may also be important.

4. Under this heading, I include the so-called "emerging economies," a category that has an unclear definition but will be understood here as the increasing number of developing countries that has access to global private capital markets.

5. This is what Ffrench-Davis (2010) has argued in relation to the Chilean fiscal funds.

6. See, for example, the Inter-American Development Bank (IDB 2008) and Ocampo (2009) for the boom, and IMF (2010) and Ocampo (2011a) for the recent cycle as a whole.

7. There is some similarity here with the view of Robert Mundell regarding monetary policies under a fixed exchange rate regime. According to his now classic view, authorities do not determine the money supply but can change the composition of domestic and foreign exchange assets that the central bank holds.

8. This is, of course, the case only if investors are risk-averse, but I take this to be the general case.

9. See, for example, Frenkel (2007), Ocampo (2003, 2008), Ocampo et al. (2009), and Stiglitz et al. (2006).

10. This may also be true of public sector balance sheets, but those effects can be accommodated in a properly designed countercyclical fiscal policy.

11. This may be said to have affected the European periphery during the recent crisis, but in the case of the peripheral countries that are in the euro area it really reflects the unwillingness of the European Central Bank (ECB) to exercise its countercyclical role, in particular to counteract the increases in risk spreads in those countries

generated by private capital markets. The ECB has referred to this phenomenon as imperfections in the transmission mechanisms of its monetary policy.

12. This reflects the case that the orthodox literature has called the "divine coincidence" that by meeting the inflation targets authorities are able to keep economies at full employment. However, such an outstanding result has been absent even in industrial economies, particularly during the recent global financial crisis. See Blanchard (2012).

13. It is interesting to recall that in the US Federal Reserve System, the exchange rate is not an objective, but monetary authorities have three objectives: maximum employment, inflation, and moderate long-term interest rates.

14. This is a central message of Stiglitz (1998).

15. See in this regard IMF (2010). However, it is useful to differentiate clearly between instruments of monetary and prudential regulation.

16. See, for example, Ocampo (2008) and Ostry et al. (2010).

17. See the review of the debate on this issue in Griffith-Jones and Ocampo (2010) and of the Spanish experience in Saurina (2009).

18. See, for example, Frankel and Saravelos (2010), Llaudes et al. (2010), and Ostry et al. (2010).

19. The classic treatment of intermediate regimes continues to be Williamson (2000).

REFERENCES

Akyüz, Y. 2011. "Capital flows to developing countries in a historical perspective: will the current boom end in a bust?" Research Paper 37. Geneva: South Centre. http://www.southcentre.int/wp-content/uploads/2013/05/RP37_Capital -Flows-to-developing-countries_EN.pdf.

Bello, O. and Jiménez, J. P. 2008. "Política fiscal y ciclo económico en América Latina." Santiago: ECLAC.

Blanchard, O. 2012. "Monetary policy in the wake of the crisis." In *In the wake of crisis: leading economists reassess economic policy*, O. Blanchard, D. Romer, M. Spence, and J. Stiglitz, eds. Cambridge, MA: MIT Press: 7–13.

Calvo, G. and Talvi, E. 2008. "Sudden stop, financial factors and economic collapse: a view from the Latin American frontlines." In *The Washington consensus reconsidered: towards a new global governance*, N. Serra and J. E. Stiglitz, eds. New York, NY: Oxford University Press: 119–149.

Díaz-Alejandro, C. 1963. "A note on the impact of devaluation and the redistributive effect." *Journal of Political Economy* 71(6): 577–580.

ECLAC. 1998. *El pacto fiscal: fortalezas, debilidades, desafíos*. Serie Libros de la CEPAL 47. Santiago: CEPAL.

ECLAC. 2011. *Modalidades de inserción externa y desafíos de política macroeconómica en una economía mundial turbulenta*. Santiago: CEPAL.

Epstein, G., Grabel, I., and Jomo, K. S. 2003. "Capital management techniques in developing countries." In *Challenges to the World Bank and the IMF: developing country perspectives*, A. Buira, ed. London: Anthem Press: 141–174.

Ffrench-Davis, R. 2001. *Financial crises in "successful" emerging economies.* Washington, DC: ECLAC/Brookings Institution.

Ffrench-Davis, R. 2010. "Latin America: the structural fiscal balance policy in Chile: a move toward countercyclical macroeconomics." *Journal of Globalization and Development* 1(1), ISSN (Online) 1948-1837, DOI: 10.2202/1948-1837.1051 (1–16).

Ffrench-Davis, R. and Griffith-Jones, S. 2011. "Taming capital account shocks: managing booms and busts." In *Handbook of Latin American economics*, J. A. Ocampo and J. Ros, eds. New York, NY: Oxford University Press: 161–186.

Frankel, J. and Saravelos, G. 2010. "Are leading indicators of financial crises useful for assessing country vulnerability? Evidence from the 2008–2009 global crisis." NBER Working Paper 16047.

Frenkel, R. 2007. "La sostenibilidad de la política de esterilización monetaria." *Revista de la CEPAL* 93. http://repositorio.cepal.org/bitstream/handle/11362/11221/093031038_es.pdf?sequence=1.

Frenkel, R. 2008. "From the boom in capital inflows to financial traps." In *Capital market liberalization and development*, J. A. Ocampo and J. E. Stiglitz, eds. New York, NY: Oxford University Press: 101–120.

Frenkel, R. and Rapetti, M. 2011. "Exchange rate regimes in Latin America." In *Handbook of Latin American economics*, J. A. Ocampo and J. Ros, eds. New York, NY: Oxford University Press: 187–213.

Griffith-Jones, S. and Ocampo, J. A. 2010. *Building on the counter-cyclical consensus: a policy agenda.* Washington, DC: The Intergovernmental Group of Twenty-Four on International Monetary Affairs and Development.

Heymann, D. 2000. "Grandes perturbaciones macroeconómicas, expectativas y respuestas de política." *Revista de la CEPAL* 70. http://repositorio.cepal.org/bitstream/handle/11362/12197/070013029_es.pdf?sequence=1.

IDB 2008. "All that glitters may not be gold: assessing Latin America's recent macroeconomic performance." Washington, DC: Author.

IMF 2010. "Regional economic outlook, Western Hemisphere: heating up in the south, cooler in the north." Washington, DC: Author.

IMF 2011. "World economic outlook." Washington, DC: Author.

Kaminsky, G. L., Reinhart, C. M., and Végh, C. A. 2004. "When it rains, it pours: pro-cyclical capital flows and macroeconomic policies." NBER Working Paper 10780. http://www.nber.org/papers/w10780.pdf.

Kindleberger, C. P. and Aliber, R. 2005. *Manias, panics, and crashes: a history of financial crises*, 5th ed. New York, NY: Wiley.

Krugman, P. and Taylor, L. 1978. "Contractionary effects of devaluations." *Journal of International Economics* 8, (3): 445–456. DOI:10.1016/0022-1996(78)90007-7.

Llaudes, R., Salman, F., and Chivakul, M. 2010. "The impact of the Great Recession on emerging markets." IMF Working Paper WP/10/237. https://www.imf.org/external/pubs/ft/wp/2010/wp10237.pdf.

Marfán, M. 2005. "La eficacia de la política fiscal y los déficit privados: un enfoque macroeconómico." In *Más allá de las reformas: dinámica estructural y vulnerabilidad macroeconómica*, J. A. Ocampo, ed. Bogotá: ECLAC/World Bank/Alfaomega.

Martner, R. and Tromben, V. 2003. "Tax reforms and fiscal stabilization in Latin America." In *Tax Policy, Public Finance Workshop Proceedings* (pp. 140–171). Rome: Banca d'Italia Research Department.

Minsky, H. P. 1982. *Can "it" happen again? Essays on instability and finance.* Armonk, NY: M.E. Sharpe.

Ocampo, J. A. 2003. "Capital account and counter-cyclical prudential regulations in developing countries." In *From capital surges to drought: seeking stability for emerging markets*, R. Ffrench-Davis and S. Griffith-Jones, eds. London: Palgrave Macmillan: 217–244.

Ocampo, J. A. 2008. "A broad view of macroeconomic stability." In *The Washington consensus reconsidered*, edited by N. Serra and J. E. Stiglitz, chap. 6. New York, NY: Oxford University Press.

Ocampo, J. A. 2009. "Latin America and the global financial crisis." *Cambridge Journal of Economics* 33(4): 703–724.

Ocampo, J. A. 2011a. "¿Cómo fue el desempeño de América Latina durante la crisis financiera global?" *Ensayos Económicos* 61/62. Banco Central de la República Argentina. http://www.bcra.gov.ar/pdfs/investigaciones/61_62_Ocampo.pdf.

Ocampo, J. A. and Vos, R. 2008. *Uneven economic development.* London: Zed Books.

Ocampo, J. A., Rada, C., and Taylor, L. 2009. *Growth and policy in developing countries: a structuralist approach.* New York, NY: Columbia University Press.

Ostry, J. D., Ghosh, A. R., Habermeir, K., Chamon, M., Qureshi, M. S., and Reinhardt, D. B. S. 2010. "Capital inflows: the role of controls." IMF Staff Position Note SPN/10/04. https://www.imf.org/external/pubs/ft/spn/2010/spn1004.pdf.

Reinhart, C. and Rogoff, K. 2009. *This time is different: eight centuries of financial folly.* Princeton, NJ: Princeton University Press.

Rodrik, D. and Velasco, A. 2000. "Short-term capital flows." In *Proceedings of the Annual World Bank Conference on Development Economics 1999* (pp. 59–90). Washington, DC: World Bank.

Saurina, J. 2009. "Dynamic provisioning, the experience of Spain." World Bank, Financial and Private Sector Development Vice-Presidency, Policy Note 7.

Stiglitz, J. E. 1998. "More instruments and broader goals: moving toward the post-Washington Consensus." UNU-WIDER, 2nd Annual Lecture. Helsinky: WIDER.

Stiglitz, J. E. and Bhattacharya, A. 2000. "The underpinnings of a stable and equitable global financial system: from old debates to a new paradigm." In *Proceedings of the Annual World Bank Conference on Development Economics 1999* (pp. 91–130). Washington, DC: World Bank.

Stiglitz, J. E., Ocampo, J. A., Spiegel, S., Ffrench-Davis, R., and Nayyar, D. 2006. *Stability with growth: macroeconomics, liberalization, and development.* New York, NY: Oxford University Press for the Initiative for Policy Dialogue, Columbia University.

Svensson, L. E. O. 2000. "Open-economy inflation targeting." *Journal of International Economics* 50(1): 155–183.

Williamson, J. 2000. *Exchange rate regimes for emerging markets: reviving the intermediate option.* Washington, DC: Institution for International Economics, Policy Analysis in International Economics.

CHAPTER 11

The Real Exchange Rate, the Real Wage, and Growth

A FORMAL ANALYSIS OF THE "DEVELOPMENT CHANNEL"

Jaime Ros

Traditional macroeconomic analysis suggests that a higher real exchange rate (RER) has a positive effect on the balance-of-payments constrained level of economic activity, provided, of course, that the Marshall–Lerner condition is fulfilled. Recent, mostly empirical studies have suggested the existence of a growth, rather than level, effect on output of a higher RER. Indeed, the relationship between the real exchange rate and the rate of economic growth has been receiving a great deal of attention in recent years after the extraordinarily high growth rates achieved by countries that have deliberately undervalued their real exchange rates and the slow growth rates experienced by several countries with overvalued exchange rates. The first case is illustrated by China's experience (see Razmi et al. 2012) and—in the Latin American context—to a lesser extent Argentina's, whereas the second case can be seen in Mexico's experience (see Blecker 2009; Ibarra 2010; Moreno-Brid and Ros 2012). This relationship has been the subject of a large and increasing number of empirical studies and significantly less theoretical discussions.

One objective of this chapter is to contribute to an understanding of how and why the real exchange rate may affect long-run growth. To achieve this objective, the chapter relies on the "development channel" highlighted in Frenkel and Ros (2006) in the analysis of the relationship between the RER and employment in Latin America. This channel is implicitly or explicitly present in Balassa (1971) and Kaldor (1971), both of whom studied and advocated export-led growth (see Frenkel and Ros 2006). Another aim is to clarify the short- and long-run relationships between the RER and the real wage. A higher RER almost inevitably implies a lower real wage in the short run. At the same time, by promoting investment in sectors where productivity increases endogenously with output and capital accumulation, a higher RER may imply a higher real wage in the long run. The opposite is true for real exchange appreciation. Krugman (1987) and Ros and Skott (1998) discussed how a transitorily higher real wage that results from a real exchange rate appreciation can lead to a permanent long-run reduction of the real wage in the presence of dynamic economies of scale.

The chapter is organized as follows. The first section reviews the empirical studies that have shown a relationship between exchange rate misalignment and slow growth and between undervaluation and fast growth and the suggested explanations of these relationships. The second section presents an analytical framework that draws on the contributions of Nicholas Kaldor and Joan Robinson to the theory of economic growth. In this framework, a depreciated real exchange rate contributes to a higher level of employment and higher real wages in the long run and, under certain conditions, to faster long-term growth through its effects on the profitability of investment. The key condition is the presence of increasing returns to scale in the traded goods sector.

EMPIRICAL FINDINGS AND SUGGESTED MECHANISMS

By now there are many empirical studies that have found negative correlations between exchange rate misalignment and growth—the more overvalued the currency, the lower the per capita growth rate—or positive correlations between undervaluation and its correlates on the one hand and growth on the other. Cavallo et al. (1990) presented cross-country regressions among developing countries from 1960 to 1983 that showed a negative correlation between per capita GDP growth and a measure of (policy-induced) misalignment of the RER, as well as a measure of RER instability. Dollar (1992) found a significant, negative relationship between distortion in the RER and per capita GDP growth between 1976 and 1985 for a group of developing countries after controlling for the effects of RER variability and level of investment. Thus, for example, African countries with the highest degree of overvaluation were the slowest to grow, whereas Asian countries with the lowest degree of distortion were the fastest (with Latin American countries falling in between). Razin and Collins (1997) found nonlinearities in the relationship between misalignment and growth: only very high overvaluations seemed to be associated with slower growth, whereas moderate to high (but not very high) undervaluations were associated with high growth. The analysis referred to ninety-three countries from 1975 to 1992 and controlled for a number of indicators of initial conditions, the external environment and macroeconomic policy. The estimates implied that a 10 percent overvaluation was associated with a decline in real per capita GDP growth of 0.6 percent. Polterovich and Popov (2002) presented cross-country regressions that showed that the rapid accumulation of foreign exchange reserves, associated with policies intended to sustain depreciated exchange rates, contributed to export-led growth. Countries with rapidly growing foreign exchange reserves to GDP ratios exhibited higher investment–GDP ratios, higher trade–GDP ratios, higher capital productivity, and higher rates of growth. Acemoglu et al. (2003) found that overvaluation of the RER was the only macroeconomic variable (the others being government consumption and the average rate of inflation) that had a negative effect on growth after controlling for institutional variables and initial GDP per capita from 1970 to 1998. Prasad et al. (2007) showed with a wide sample of developing countries between 1970 and 2004 a positive association between growth rates and current accounts in the balance of payments (even after controlling for standard determinants of growth) and between growth and real exchange rates. In terms of magnitude, their results suggested that in the short run, a 1 percent increase in the degree of overvaluation accompanied a decline in growth of about 0.4 percent. Overvaluation is measured as the deviation of the exchange rate from purchasing power parity after accounting for differences in incomes (Balassa–Samuelson effect). Levy Yeyati and Sturzenegger (2009) found that there is an effect of exchange rate intervention on growth; i.e., depreciated exchange rates seem to induce higher growth. Gala (2008) used a panel of fifty-eight developing countries from 1960 to 1999 and showed a negative association between overvaluation and per capita GDP growth after controlling for the initial level of income and structural and macroeconomic characteristics. The estimates implied that a 10 percent undervaluation was associated with a per capita GDP growth up to 0.15 percent higher. Rodrik (2008) reached similar results for a sample of 184 countries and found that the link between undervaluation and growth was particularly strong among developing countries. Razmi et al. (2012) found a positive effect of the real exchange rate on investment growth, especially among developing countries, in a set of 153 countries between 1960 and 2004. Rapetti et al. (2012) confirmed these results and showed that the effects of currency undervaluation on growth were larger and more robust in developing economies.

There are a number of suggested mechanisms through which the RER influences growth. Ros and Skott (1998) emphasized the profitability effects of the real exchange rate on capital accumulation. Under the presence of increasing returns to scale in the traded goods sector, the profitability squeeze produced by overvaluation can lead the economy to a lower-level equilibrium after a period of contraction and falling real wages. Similarly, Polterovich and Popov (2002) pointed to the positive effects on investment of the higher profitability in the traded goods sectors. The impact of investment on growth is amplified by the higher productivity of the invested capital, mostly in sectors subject to international competition. Frenkel (2004) and Frenkel and Ros (2006) highlighted the development channel that operates through the profitability and expansion of the traded goods sector as the development of tradable activities generates economies of specialization and learning externalities that are capitalized by less dynamic sectors. Gala (2008) also highlighted the profitability channel, as well as the role of technological change, in the context of a neo-Keynesian model of profit-led growth. Rodrik (2008) emphasized the expansion of the traded goods sector; in his view, a depreciated RER is the next best policy that can help to overcome the institutional and market failures that particularly affect that sector. Razmi et al. (2012) viewed the real exchange as an instrument for reconciling a sustainable trade balance with a target rate of accumulation: given a target for the trade balance, a real depreciation is required to achieve a higher rate of accumulation to transfer domestic expenditure away from tradable goods and allow for increased capital good imports necessary for a higher investment. Porcile and Lima (2010) presented a similar mechanism in the balance-of-payments constrained growth model. By contrast, Levy Yeyati and Sturzenegger (2009) argued that the effect, rather than through a boost to the tradable goods sector via import substitution or export growth, works largely through the increase of domestic savings. Devaluation, as in Diaz Alejandro's (1963) classic analysis, redistributes income from low-income, low-savings propensity workers to high-income capitalists, which in turn boosts overall savings. In small and medium firms with limited access to finance, this increases internal funds with a positive effect on investment. The increase in overall savings also tends to lower the cost of capital for large companies that fund their investments in capital markets.

SHORT- AND LONG-RUN EFFECTS OF THE REAL EXCHANGE RATE ON GROWTH AND REAL WAGES

A SMALL OPEN-ECONOMY MODEL: BASIC ASSUMPTIONS

The economy considered produces a single tradable good, and firms face given terms of trade in international markets and are price takers in the domestic market. This small open-economy assumption is, in my view, an appropriate analytical framework for the typical developing economy whose growth for the most part leaves the terms of trade that it faces in international markets unaffected.

Firms maximize profits equal to $PY - WL$, where P is the domestic price equal to the international price times a constant nominal exchange rate equal to one, W is the nominal wage, Y is output, and L is labor input. Firms maximize profits, taking nominal wages and prices as given, subject to a production function constraint $Y = A\,F\,(K, L)$, where K is capital input. The level of productivity (A) is, for the time being, taken as exogenously given and constant over time. From the first-order condition for profit maximization, we have the equality between the real wage and the marginal product of labor:

$$W/P = F'(L). \tag{11.1}$$

The determination of employment is derived from equation 11.1. Indeed, solving this equation for L yields $L = L\,(A, W/P, K)$, which shows the level of employment determined by the capital stock, the real wage, and the level of productivity, with L_A, $L_K > 0$ and $L_{W/P} < 0$. This level of employment (and output) is therefore independent of domestic demand. Firms do not increase production in response to higher domestic demand (given the real wage, W/P); rather, they adjust it by reducing exports and increasing sales in the domestic market. The reason is that they face a perfectly elastic demand for exports. Indeed, if they increased production in response to higher domestic demand, their marginal cost would exceed the price of exports. This would induce firms to reduce their exports until the marginal cost of production was again equal to the price of exports. This means that a higher domestic demand fully crowds out exports. A higher level of foreign demand, by contrast, to the extent that it increases the international price of exports, has a positive effect on employment and output given the nominal wage. The same effect results from a devaluation of the nominal exchange rate because it increases domestic and export prices in domestic currency.

With respect to the demand side, we assume there are no savings out of wages and let s_π be the propensity to save out profits. Consumption (C) is then determined as $PC = WL + (1 - s_\pi) (PY - WL)$, where we are assuming away, for simplicity, imports of consumption goods. Investment has a domestic (I_d) and imported component (M_k). Thus, $P_I I = PI_d + P_m M_k$, where P_I is the price of capital goods and $M_k = mI$, so that there is a fixed amount ($m < 1$) of complementary imports per unit of total investment.

INTERACTIONS BETWEEN PROFITABILITY AND ACCUMULATION IN THE MEDIUM TERM

We now derive two relationships between the profit rate and the rate of accumulation such that, in a steady state, profit expectations are fulfilled and the rates of growth of output and the capital stock are constant and, as we shall see in figure 11.1, equal to Robinson's "desired rate of accumulation" (Robinson 1962). Note first that combining the definition of the profit rate with equation 11.1 implies

$$r = \alpha(P/P_I)\upsilon \quad \upsilon = \upsilon (A, W/P) \ \upsilon_A > 0, \upsilon_{W/P} < 0, \tag{11.2}$$

where α is the profit share in output (assumed constant) and υ is the output–capital ratio (Y/K). The profit rate is thus a decreasing function of the real wage and of the ratio of capital goods prices to export prices (P_I/P), i.e., an increasing function of the country's terms of trade, and is independent of the rate of accumulation.[1] Equation 11.2 is thus the equation of the horizontal line in figure 11.1.[2]

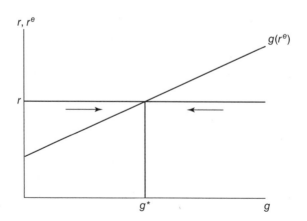

Figure 11.1 **The warranted growth rate.**

The second relationship is a rate of accumulation function that makes the rate of accumulation depend on the propensity to invest (β) and the expected profit rate (r^e) (à la Robinson 1962), as well as a risk-adjusted international profit rate (r^*):

$$g = \beta \, (r^e - r^*), \qquad\qquad (11.3)$$

which implies that with $r = r^e$, $r = (g/\beta) + r^*$. In a steady state, $r^e = r$. Figure 11.1 shows the determination of the steady-state values of g and r. At the intersection of the two lines, corresponding to equations 11.2 and 11.3, the rate of accumulation generates a profit rate that only equals the expected profit rate that induced this rate of accumulation.[3] This desired or equilibrium rate of accumulation is analogous to Harrod's warranted growth rate, because in the present open-economy context it is such that the investment forthcoming at the equilibrium profit rate generates additional productive capacity such that the increase in domestic demand leaves the composition of total output between exports and domestic sales unchanged. Thus, on the warranted growth path, exports and domestic demand grow at the same rate, equal to the rate of growth of productive capacity.

Above the $g(r^e)$ line (given by equation 11.3), the profit rate is higher than expected and investment decisions will be revised upward, whereas below the line the rate of profit is lower than expected and the rate of accumulation increases. With continuous market clearing on the goods market and in the absence of labor supply constraints, the economy converges through the r line to the stable equilibrium at the intersection of the r and g (r^e) lines.

SHORT- AND LONG-RUN EFFECTS OF A REAL DEVALUATION IN THE ABSENCE OF TECHNICAL PROGRESS

Consider the effects of a devaluation of the real exchange rate (a higher P/W). This shifts the r line up, moving the economy toward a new equilibrium path with a higher growth rate and lower real wage.[4] The increase in growth holds only for a short- or medium-run period, however, in which we can neglect changes in nominal wages. To examine what happens beyond this short period, we have to consider the adjustment of nominal wages and the real exchange rate that will occur as a consequence of labor market conditions.

First, consider the determinants of the rate of wage inflation. We adopt here a structuralist specification that makes the growth rate of nominal wages (w) depend on the rate of domestic price inflation (π) and the gap between a target (or bargained) real wage (ω) and the real consumption wage effectively received by workers (W/P):

$$w = \pi + \lambda(\omega - W/P) \qquad \omega = \omega\,(L/N))\,\omega' > 0. \qquad (11.4)$$

Further, we assume that the target real wage is an inverse function of the unemployment rate (i.e., an increasing function of the employment rate L/N, where N is the total labor force). This inverse relationship is supported by empirical research on the "wage curve" that establishes a negative relationship across regions and sectors between wage levels and unemployment (see Blanchflower and Oswald 1994, 2005). The wage inflation equation is thus similar to a Phillips curve equation augmented by the effects of expected price inflation. Indeed, as long as the nominal exchange rate is constant and foreign inflation is zero, current price inflation is nil, and current inflation coincides with expected inflation. Equation 11.4 can also be interpreted as showing the dynamic behavior of the real consumption wage ($w - \pi$) as an inverse function of its level: a higher real wage implies a slower growth of nominal wages in relation to domestic prices. The feedback effect on the growth of the real wage is thus negative.

Consider now the dynamic behavior of the employment rate over time. Assuming a Cobb–Douglas production function $Y = AK^{\alpha}L^{1-\alpha}$ and solving equation 11.1 for the level of employment (L) yields $L = [A\,(1 - \alpha)/(W/P)]^{1/\alpha}\,K$. Taking logs in this employment equation and differentiating with respect to time and then subtracting the rate of growth of the labor force (n) from both sides of the equation, we have

$$l - n = g - (1/\alpha)\,(w - \pi) - n \qquad g = g\,(W/P) \qquad g' < 0, \qquad (11.5)$$

where l is the rate of growth of employment and π is the rate of price inflation. In equation 11.5, g, the rate of capital accumulation, equal to the rate of growth of the capital stock assuming no depreciation of capital, is determined by equations 11.2 and 11.3 under the assumption $r = r^e$. We express this equilibrium rate of accumulation as an inverse function of the real wage. Other variables and parameters that affect the equilibrium rate of accumulation are the propensity to invest, the level of productivity, and the risk-adjusted international profit rate. Note that because the growth of the real wage in equation 11.4 is an increasing function of the employment rate, equation 11.5 shows the rate of change of the employment rate ($l - n$) as an inverse function of its level.

Consider now the dynamic adjustments in real wages and the employment rate. Setting $w = \pi$ in equation 11.4, we obtain the equation of a locus of $(L/N, W/P)$ combinations along which the real wage is stationary:

$$\lambda \left[\omega(L/N) - W/P\right] = 0.$$

In $(L/N, W/P)$ space, this is an upward-sloping schedule: a higher employment rate tends to raise w above π, and this requires a higher real wage, which reduces w, to maintain stability of the real wage. Because the feedback effect of the real wage on its rate of change is negative (and thus stabilizing), the real wage falls when above the locus and increases when below it (see figure 11.2). The position of the schedule is determined by labor market parameters (the ω (.) function).

Substituting equation 11.4 into 11.5 and setting $l = n$, we obtain a locus of $(L/N, W/P)$ combinations along which the employment rate is stationary:

$$g\,(W/P) - (1/\alpha)\,\lambda\,\left[\omega(L/N) - W/P)\right] - n = 0 \quad g' < 0 \quad \omega' > 0.$$

This schedule can have a negative or positive slope. The reason is that a higher real wage has two effects on the rate of growth of employment. First, it reduces employment growth through its negative effect on the rate of accumulation. Second, it increases employment growth through its negative effect on the growth of real wages. In figure 11.2, I assume that the first effect is stronger than the second, which is why the schedule slopes downward: the negative effect on employment growth of a higher real wage requires a lower employment rate (which, by reducing wage

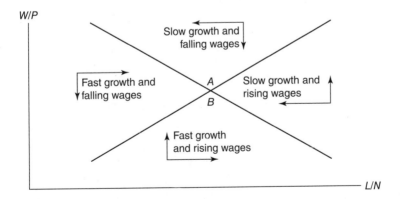

Figure 11.2 Long-term dynamic adjustments.

growth, increases employment growth) to keep the employment rate stable (see the appendix at the end of this chapter for further analysis). The position of the schedule is determined by parameters, such as the propensity to invest, which affects the g (.) function and labor market parameters that affect the λ (.) and ω (.) functions. Because the feedback effect of the employment rate on its growth (given by $l - n$) is stabilizing, the employment rate increases when the economy is to the right of the schedule and falls when it is to the left.

The two schedules of real wage and employment stability divide the $(W/P, L/N)$ space into four regions, as depicted in figure 11.2. As shown in the diagram, provided that the long-run equilibrium at the intersection of the two schedules is stable, the economy converges to a steady state in which the rate of capital accumulation is equal to Harrod's natural rate (the growth rate of the labor force, n, under our present assumptions), whereas the output–capital ratio, employment rate, real exchange rate, and real wages all remain constant over time. The appendix discusses the stability conditions.

It is clear from this analysis that the short-run effects of devaluation on growth and real wages will be reversed in the long run under our present assumptions. Indeed, consider in figure 11.2 the effects of a devaluation starting from a long-run equilibrium at point A with $g = n$. The economy moves to point B in the short run into the region of increasing employment and rising wages. The gains in employment are temporary and reversible, however, because they are eventually offset by higher wages that make the economy converge, through oscillations, to the initial long-term equilibrium at point A, in which the rate of capital accumulation is equal to the natural rate, and real wages and the real exchange rate are equal to their initial values.

LONG-RUN EFFECTS OF A REAL DEVALUATION IN THE PRESENCE OF ENDOGENOUS TECHNICAL PROGRESS

We now extend the model to consider changes in productivity (A). Note that these changes will now affect labor demand, the output–capital ratio, and the rate of profit, all of which are increasing functions of A, as well as the capital–labor ratio, which is a decreasing function of A. The evolution of A over time responds to a productivity growth function (or "technical progress function" in Kaldor's terminology) that is based on the contributions of Kaldor and Robinson to the theory of economic growth. Kaldor indicates three sources of increasing returns. The first, of a static nature, are the economies of scale that result from the three-dimensional nature of space.[5] The other two sources refer to two aspects of specialization: the substitution of direct for indirect labor (i.e., an increase in the capital–labor ratio), and learning by doing, a source of technological externalities.[6] As a result of the last two aspects, in Kaldor's (1975) view, productivity increases are endogenous to the process of capital accumulation per worker.

For Robinson, productivity growth is influenced by labor and goods market conditions. Firms speed up the diffusion of new technologies in response to shortages in the labor market by adopting new techniques that reduce labor costs.[7] As Robinson puts it: "Even more important than speeding up discoveries is the speeding up of the rate at which innovations are diffused. When entrepreneurs find themselves in a situation where potential markets are expanding but labor hard to find, they have every motive to increase productivity" (Robinson 1956: 96).

We put together these ideas by assuming the following productivity growth function:

$$\rho = \mu\,(g-1) + \psi\,(l-n). \qquad (11.6)$$

This function makes the rate of productivity growth (ρ) depend on the rate of growth of the capital labor ratio ($g-1$, á la Kaldor), and on the excess of employment growth over the growth of the labor force ($l-n$, a la Robinson).

In the views of Kaldor and Robinson, technical change has a strong element of irreversibility. This is what Kaldor meant by "dynamic" in the expression "dynamic economies of scale." If this is the case, in equation 11.6, $\mu\,(g-l) = 0$ if $g < l$, and $\psi\,(l-n) = 0$ if $l < n$. We shall consider also the case of reversible productivity changes in which equation 11.6 holds without restrictions.

A second change is that we modify the wage inflation equation as follows. We assume as before that the target real wage is determined by labor market conditions (the employment rate, L/N). However, to simplify the analysis and clarify the processes of adjustment, I assume that nominal wages increase beyond the rate of domestic inflation only when the target wage is above the actual real wage. Otherwise, if the real consumption wage is above the target real wage, nominal wages grow exactly at the rate of price inflation (and not below it). The target real wage is then really a threshold that triggers wage inflation (above price inflation) only when the actual wage falls below it (for a similar specification, see Basu's formalization of Kalecki's model of inflation in Basu [1997]). Equation 11.4 is thus replaced by

$$w = \pi + \lambda\ (\omega - W/P) \qquad \omega = \omega\ (L/N),\ \omega' > 0 \qquad \text{for } \omega > W/P$$

and

$$w = \pi \quad \text{for } \omega \leq W/P. \tag{11.7}$$

Consider now, under the present assumptions, the effects of a devaluation starting from an initial long-term equilibrium at point A in figures 11.3 and 11.4. Suppose that the initial employment rate is so low that the real wage is above the threshold wage so that nominal wages are constant (because with the given nominal exchange rate, domestic inflation is nil). Thus, the economy is on a warranted path that is also a long-term equilibrium with $g = l$ and $l = n$. K/L and L/N are thus also constant. Because $\rho = 0$, at this equilibrium the level of productivity is also constant.

Now suppose that P increases as a result of a devaluation. The real wage falls and the r line shifts upward. The profit rate and the rate of accumulation increase toward a new warranted path at point B. Because the rate of accumulation increases, employment growth increases above the growth of the labor force. The employment rate increases, but the capital labor ratio falls (as a result of the positive employment effect of the fall in the product wage). Suppose that initially nominal wages do not change because although the real wage falls as a consequence of devaluation it remains above the threshold wage given the initially very low employment rate (this will be true, of course, provided that the devaluation is not so large as to

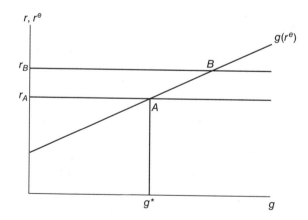

Figure 11.3   Short- and long-term effects of a real devaluation.

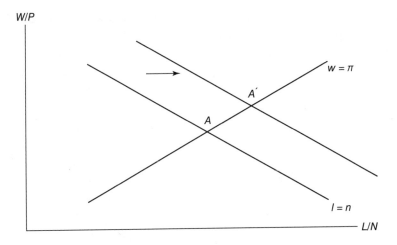

Figure 11.4 Long-term dynamic adjustments with irreversible productivity changes.

reduce the real wage below the threshold). In the new warranted path, the employment rate increases, and because of its effect on productivity, the r line will keep shifting up toward a still higher warranted growth rate.[8]

There will come a point, at a sufficiently high employment rate, at which the threshold wage will become higher than the real wage. At this point, nominal and real wages start increasing, bringing about a fall in the rates of profit and capital accumulation. Employment growth therefore falls as a result of both the fall in the rate of capital accumulation and the positive growth of wages. This process brings employment growth back into equality with the growth of the labor force. At the point at which employment growth is again equal to the growth of the labor force, the employment rate stops increasing. However, at this higher employment rate, nominal wages may (or may not) continue to grow. There are several possibilities.

Suppose that wages continue to grow because at the employment rate considered the target wage is above the real wage. As wages increase, the growth of employment falls below the growth of the labor force, causing the employment rate to fall. The target wage thus falls until wage growth is again zero. If at this point the rates of capital accumulation and employment growth are lower than the rate of labor force growth, the employment rate continues to fall. With reversible productivity changes, productivity falls, and it is conceivable that the resulting fall in the profit rate brings the economy back to point A. In terms of the diagram in

(L/N, W/P) space, the shifts in the schedule of employment stability that took place as a result of the changes in productivity are completely reversed, and the economy returns to the initial long-run equilibrium.

A second possibility is that when wage growth falls back to zero, the employment rate stabilizes at a higher level than the initial one. In this case, the economy will converge to a long-run equilibrium that features the same rates of profit and capital accumulation as the initial equilibrium (the economy goes back to point A in figure 11.3) but at higher levels of (1) productivity, (2) the capital–labor ratio, and (3) the employment rate, all of which increased during the process of adjustment. In terms of figure 11.4, the higher level of productivity shifts the schedule of employment stability to the right, and the economy converges to a new long-run equilibrium at point A′, with a higher employment rate and higher real wage. (Because productivity and the capital–labor ratio are higher than their initial values, it is easily verified from the labor demand function that the real wage, W/P, is higher.) So, even with reversible productivity changes, it is possible for the devaluation to have positive long-term effects on real wages and the employment rate. In this case, what prevents the return to the initial long-term equilibrium at point A is the fact that nominal wages do not fall once the threshold wage is brought back below the actual wage and, therefore, the capital–labor ratio and level of productivity do not continue to fall.

With irreversible productivity changes, the technical changes and new technologies introduced as a result of the increase in the employment rate after the devaluation and the increase in the rates of profit and capital accumulation will unambiguously shift the schedule of employment stability to the right as a result of the increase in the level of productivity during the adjustment process. This leads the economy to a new long-run equilibrium at A′ in figure 11.4, with a higher employment rate and higher real wages. In figure 11.3, in (r, g) space, the r (g) line shifts back to its initial position as a result of the increase in real wages.

What if the target wage is an increasing function of the level of productivity? Suppose equation 11.7 is replaced by

$$w = \pi + \lambda\,(\omega - W/P) \quad \omega = \omega\,(L/N, A), \omega_1, \omega_2 > 0 \quad \text{for } \omega > W/P$$

$$\text{and}$$

$$w = \pi \qquad \text{for } \omega \leq W/P. \tag{11.8}$$

A real devaluation can now have a long-term growth effect. In this case, wages do not stabilize as the employment rate falls and reduces the target wage. Rather, it is possible that the negative effect of wage growth on employment growth is compensated by a higher rate of capital accumulation that results from the higher profit rate. At the same time, the negative effect of wage increases on the profit rate is compensated by the positive effect on productivity growth of the rate of accumulation being higher than employment growth (precisely because wage growth is positive). The economy then converges to a new long-term equilibrium with a rate of capital accumulation higher than the growth of employment and a positive rate of growth of wages. It is a long-term equilibrium that, compared with the initial one, features a higher rate of accumulation and faster growth of real wages, faster productivity growth, and a constant employment rate. Unlike what happens in the previous cases, as productivity increases over time, the target wage keeps increasing, continually disturbing the equality with actual wages and causing the latter to grow over time. In $(L/N, W/P)$ space, the shifts to the right of the schedule of employment stability are accompanied by upward shifts of the schedule of wage stability, which keep the employment rate constant and real wages increasing. In (r, g) space, the economy converges to a warranted path in which the rate of capital accumulation is higher than the rate of growth of the labor force and output per worker continually increases as a result of productivity growth equal to $\rho = \mu(g - 1)$. Thus, on the long-run equilibrium path, the economy no longer grows at the rate of growth of the labor force. The output growth rate is no longer exogenous; it is equal to $(\mu + \alpha)g + (1 - \alpha - \mu)\, n$ and that of output per worker is $(\mu + \alpha)\, (g - n)$, where g is the warranted growth rate constrained by the propensity to invest. The warranted rate of capital accumulation is now a determinant of the natural rate.

CONCLUSIONS

The models presented in this chapter aimed at giving a theoretical foundation to the profitability or development channel postulated in the empirical literature on the real exchange rate and growth. They also sought to answer the question of what happens with the long-run effects of a real devaluation on real wages in the presence of the profitability channel and endogenous technical change.

In the models presented, a higher real exchange rate is favorable to capital accumulation and employment growth in the short run because it reduces the product wage in the traded goods sector with a positive effect on the sector's profitability. In the absence of technical progress, the gains in employment as a result of the higher rate of accumulation are reversed in the long run while the real wage returns to its initial value. With endogenous productivity change, the employment gains are not reversed, and the steady-state value of the real wage increases as a result of the higher employment rate (which favors the diffusion of new technologies that reduce labor costs) and the higher capital–labor ratio that, through embodied technical progress and technological externalities, increases the economy's productivity.

This appendix presents a fuller analysis of the stability of the long-run equilibrium. For simplicity we leave aside technical progress. The analysis of long-run adjustments and the resulting equilibrium involves a system of two differential equations. The first, showing the dynamic behavior of the real wage, is derived from the wage inflation equation and can be expressed in reduced form in the following equation:

$$(\hat{W/P}) = F(L/N, W/P) \qquad\qquad F_1 > 0, F_2 < 0.$$

The second equation, showing the dynamic behavior of the employment rate, has the following reduced form:

$$(\hat{L/N}) = G(L/N, W/P) \qquad\qquad G_1 < 0, G_2\ ?$$

The sign restrictions on the partial derivatives follow from the analysis in the text. They imply that the locus of real wage stability, $(\hat{W/P}) = 0$, is positively sloped, whereas the locus of employment stability, $(\hat{L/N}) = 0$, may be positively or negatively sloped depending on whether the effect of W/P on $(\hat{L/N})$ is positive or negative. The effect of a higher W/P is to reduce wage inflation, which tends to increase the employment growth rate (making G_2 positive), but a higher W/P reduces v, the output–capital ratio (as exports and the volume of output fall), which has a negative effect on the rate of capital accumulation and the growth of employment (making G_2 negative). We must therefore distinguish two cases: (1) $G_2 < 0$, yielding a negatively sloped $(\hat{L/N}) = 0$ locus; and (2) $G_2 > 0$, yielding a positively sloped locus.

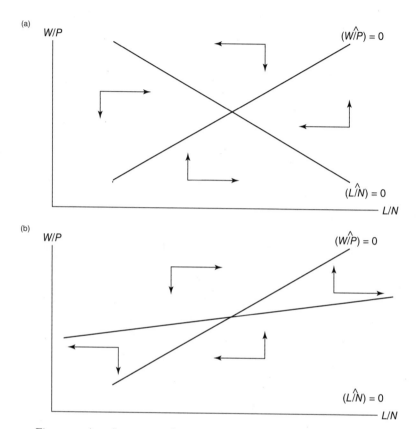

Figure 11.A.1   Long-term dynamic adjustments.

Case 1 is depicted in figure 11.A1a, which reproduces figure 11.2. It can be shown easily that given the sign restrictions of the partial derivatives, the system has a negative trace and positive determinant. The equilibrium is thus stable and the economy converges in the long run to the intersection between the two loci.

Case 2 may feature instability if G_2 is very large, i.e., if the effect of a real wage fall on wage inflation is very strong. In this case, as shown in figure 11.A1b, the slope of the $(\hat{L/N}) = 0$ locus is positive and less than the slope of the $(\hat{W/P}) = 0$ locus. The intersection is then a saddle point. The instability can be explained with the example of a devaluation starting from an initial long-run equilibrium. The resulting fall in the real wage triggers a rapid process of wage inflation, so rapid that the positive effect on employment growth that results from the higher profitability is offset by the negative effect on employment growth that arises from wage growth. The employment rate then falls, moving the economy away from the initial long-run equilibrium. By contrast, if G_2 is positive but relatively small so that the $(\hat{L/N}) = 0$ locus is steeper than the $(\hat{W/P}) = 0$ locus, the economy converges to the long-run equilibrium with a warranted growth rate equal to the natural rate.

NOTES

I am grateful to Carlos Ibarra, Carlo Panico, and Martín Rapetti for comments on a previous version of this chapter. The usual caveat applies.

1. In this economy, the goods market equilibrium condition can be expressed as savings per unit of capital ($s_\pi r$) equals the sum of investment and net exports per unit of capital $((1 - m) g + x)$, where r is the profit rate equal to $(PY - WL)/P_I K$, g is the rate of capital accumulation (I/K), and x is the exports–capital ratio. This goods market equilibrium condition does not establish, however, a relationship between the rate of profit and the rate of accumulation. The profit rate is unaffected by the rate of capital accumulation. The reason is that changes in the rate of accumulation, which affect domestic demand, are reflected in changes in the exports–capital ratio through the mechanism previously discussed, leaving the rate of profit unaffected.

2. Note that the r line is horizontal under the assumption of perfect competition in both the foreign and domestic markets. With imperfect competition in the domestic market, the r line would slope upward because an increase in the rate of accumulation, by increasing domestic sales, shifts the composition of firms' sales from exports to the more profitable domestic market.

3. In Robinson's words, this is the desired rate of accumulation, "a rate of accumulation which is generating just the expectation of profit that is required to cause it to be maintained" (Robinson 1962, p. 130, in Sen 1970)

4. Note that in this model the profit rate increases as a result of an increase in the output–capital ratio (the average productivity of capital) and not as a result of a redistribution against wage earners (employment increases in the same proportion as real wages fall).

5. In this respect, Kaldor gives the example of a pipeline: when a stretch (of unitary length) of a pipeline is constructed, the increase in output (the liquid transported) is greater than the increase in inputs (the materials used to build the cylinder). This example was meant to represent different types of plant-level economies of scale that follow directly from an increase in production.

6. These are directly taken from the arguments of Allyn Young and depend on the process of division of labor. See Lavezzi (2003).

7. For a formalization of Robinson's views, see Bhaduri (2006), Dutt (2006), and Dutt and Ros (2007).

8. In the case of reversible technical changes, this requires that the initial fall in the capital–labor ratio does not offset the positive effects on productivity of the increasing employment rate.

REFERENCES

Acemoglu, D., Johnson, S., Thaicharoen, Y., and Robinson, J. 2003. "Institutional causes, macroeconomic symptoms: volatility, crisis and growth." *Journal of Monetary Economics* 50(January 1): 49–123.

Balassa, B. 1971. "Trade policies in developing countries." *American Economic Review* 61(2): 178–187.

Basu, K. 1997. *Analytical development economics. The less developed economy revisited.* Cambridge: MIT Press.

Bhaduri, A. 2006. "Endogenous economic growth: a new approach." *Cambridge Journal of Economics* 30(1): 69–83.

Blanchflower, D. and Oswald, A. 1994. *The wage curve.* Cambridge, MA: MIT Press.

Blanchflower, D. and Oswald, A. 2005. "The wage curve reloaded." NBER Working Paper 11338. http://www.nber.org/papers/w11338.pdf.

Blecker, R. 2009. "External shocks, structural change, and economic growth in Mexico, 1979–2007." *World Development* 37(7): 1274–1284.

Cavallo, D. F., Cottani, J. A., and Kahn, M. S. 1990. "Real exchange rate behavior and economic performance in LDCs." *Economic Development and Cultural Change* 39(October): 61–76.

Diaz-Alejandro, C. F. D. 1963. "A note on the impact of devaluation and the redistributive effect." *Journal of Political Economy* 71(6): 577–580.

Dollar, D. 1992. "Outward-oriented developing economies really do grow more rapidly: evidence from 95 LDCs, 1976–1985." *Economic Development and Cultural Change* 40(3): 523–544.

Dutt, A. 2006. "Aggregate demand, aggregate supply, and economic growth. *International Review of Applied Economics* 20(3): 319–336.

Dutt, A. and Ros, J. 2007. "Aggregate demand shocks and economic growth." *Structural Change and Economic Dynamics* 18(1): 75–99.

Frenkel, R. 2004. "Real exchange rate and employment in Argentina, Brazil, Chile and Mexico." Paper prepared for the G24. http://policydialogue.org/files/events/Frenkel_Exchange_Rate_Employment.pdf.

Frenkel, R. and Ros, J. 2006. "Unemployment and the real exchange rate in Latin America." *World Development* 34(4): 631–646.

Gala, P. 2008. "Real exchange rate levels and economic development: theoretical analysis and econometric evidence." *Cambridge Journal of Economics* 32(2): 273–288.

Ibarra, C. 2010. "Capital flows, real exchange rate, and growth constraints in Mexico." Unpublished manuscript. Department of Economics, Universidad de las Américas, Mexico City.

Kaldor, N. 1971. "Conflicts in national economic objectives." *Economic Journal* 81(321): 1–16.

Kaldor, N. 1975. "What is wrong with economic theory" *Quarterly Journal of Economics* 89(3): 347–357.

Krugman, P. 1987. "The narrow moving band, the Dutch disease, and the competitiveness consequences of Mrs. Thatcher: Notes on trade in the presence of dynamic scale economies." *Journal of Development Economics* 27(1–2): 41–55.

Lavezzi, A. 2003. "Smith, Marshall and Young on division of labor and economic growth." *European Journal of the History of Economic Thought* 10(1): 81–108.

Levy Yeyati, E. and Sturzenegger, F. 2009. "Fear of appreciation: exchange rate policy as a development strategy." In *Monetary policy frameworks for emerging markets*, edited by G. Hammond, R. Kanbur, and E. Prasad, chap. 5. Cheltenham, UK: Edward Elgar Publishing.

Moreno-Brid, J. C. and Ros, J. 2010. *Desarrollo y crecimiento en la economía Mexicana. Una perspectiva histórica*. Mexico City: Fondo de Cultura Económica.

Polterovich, V. and Popov, V. 2002. "Accumulation of foreign exchange reserves and long term growth." New Economic School working paper.

Porcile, G. and Lima, G. T. 2010. "Real exchange rate and elasticity of labor supply in a balance-of-payments-constrained macro dynamics." *Cambridge Journal of Economics* 34(6): 1019–1039.

Prasad, E., Rajan, R., and Subramanian, A. 2007. "Foreign capital and economic growth." *Brookings Papers on Economic Activity*. http://www.brookings.edu/-/media/Files/Programs/ES/BPEA/2007_1_bpea_papers/2007a_bpea_prasad.pdf.

Rapetti, M., Skott, P., and Razmi, A. 2012. "The real exchange rate and economic growth: are developing countries special?" *International Review of Applied Economics* 26(6): 735–753.

Razin, O. and Collins, S. 1997. "Real exchange rate misalignments and growth." NBER Working Paper 6174. http://www.nber.org/papers/w6174.pdf.

Razmi, A., Rapetti, M., and Skott, P. 2012. "The real exchange rate and economic development." *Structural Change and Economic Dynamics* 23(2): 151–169.

Robinson, J. 1956. *Accumulation of capital*. London: Macmillan

Robinson, J. 1962. "A model of accumulation." In *Essays in the theory of economic growth*, A. Sen, ed. New York, NY: Macmillan, 1970: 34–59.

Rodrik, D. 2008. "The real exchange rate and economic growth." *Brookings Papers on Economic Activity*. http://www.brookings.edu/-/media/projects/bpea/fall-2008/2008b_bpea_rodrik.pdf.

Ros, J. and Skott, P. 1998. "Dynamic effects of trade liberalization and currency overvaluation under conditions of increasing returns." *The Manchester School* 66(4): 466–489.

Sen, A. 1970, ed. *Growth economics*. New York: Penguin.

CHAPTER 12

The Real Exchange Rate and Economic Growth

SOME OBSERVATIONS ON THE POSSIBLE CHANNELS

Martín Rapetti

The idea that a stable and competitive real exchange rate (RER) is favorable for economic development now has a respectable status in policy and academic circles.[1] A recent body of empirical research that documents a strong association between the level and volatility of the RER and economic growth has contributed a great deal to consolidating this view. Research has mostly relied on a variety of econometric techniques applied to large cross-country data sets. Although the documented positive effects of both RER competitiveness and stability on growth seem to be robust empirical findings, the mechanisms that drive these associations still remain unclear. Several explanations have been proposed, but theoretical examination and empirical validation of these explanations have only just begun.

The purpose of this chapter is to explore the merits and weaknesses of the proposed channels in light of recent empirical research. In the section that follows, I summarize the main empirical findings that have emerged from the econometric analyses of the association between the RER and economic growth. In the next section, I move on to discuss the mechanisms that might explain this association and then how the proposed mechanisms relate to the empirical findings under review. I close the chapter with some remarks and possible avenues for future research.

It is no mystery how the theme of this chapter relates to Roberto Frenkel's work. Frenkel has been among the most outspoken leaders and pioneers who have argued that developing countries should strive to maintain a stable and competitive RER for development purposes. His work on this subject has been extensive, insightful, and influential.

THE RER IN GROWTH REGRESSIONS

Recent empirical analyses of the association between RER levels and economic growth have mostly been carried out through growth regressions.[2] Finding a measure of the level of the RER to be placed on the right-hand side of a growth regression is not straightforward. To be meaningful, it needs to be comparable across countries (i.e., cross-section analysis), across time (i.e., time-series analysis), or both (i.e., panel data analysis). To address these complications, the standard strategy has been to construct "RER misalignment" indexes, which are used as right-hand variables in the regressions.

Because a misalignment index is the ratio of actual to "equilibrium" RERs, a critical step in this methodology is defining and estimating the latter. There are two standard notions of equilibrium RER in the literature.[3] One is linked to Balassa (1964) and Samuelson's (1964) observations that in small open economies purchasing power parity (PPP) somewhat holds for tradable prices and that nontradable prices tend to be lower in less developed countries because real wages in those countries are also lower. According to the Balassa–Samuelson hypothesis, equilibrium RERs in developed countries tend to be lower than in developing countries. As a hypothesis for long-run behavior of RERs, it has supporting evidence (Taylor and Taylor 2004).

A second approach follows the popular view pioneered by Meade (1951) and suggests that the equilibrium level of the RER is one consistent with the simultaneous attainment of internal and external balance. The most troublesome aspect of this approach relates to the appropriate definition of "external balance." In many cases, this is pragmatically defined as a situation in which the current account is financed by "sustainable" net capital inflows (Hinkle and Montiel 1999), which is also a vague concept. According to this view, the equilibrium RER is determined by long-run economic fundamentals that affect external sustainability, including the net foreign asset position, terms of trade, productivity, the degree of trade openness, and government consumption.

In line with these theoretical views, two empirical approaches have been followed to construct misalignment indexes. One approach defines the equilibrium RER as the purchasing power parity level adjusted by the Balassa–Samuelson effect (PPP-based). PPP-based equilibrium RERs are estimated through equations such as the one presented below in equation 12.1, in which the level of the RER (q) is regressed by some measure of the degree of economic development, usually the GDP per capita (Y):

$$\ln q = \alpha_1 + \beta_1 \ln Y + \epsilon \tag{12.1}$$

with $\alpha_1 > 0$ and $\beta_1 < 0$. The fact that β_1 is a negative value indicates that the equilibrium RER lowers with higher degrees of economic development as predicted by the Balassa–Samuelson effect.

The other empirical strategy relies on either single-equation or general equilibrium macroeconometric models, in which the estimated equilibrium RER depends on economic fundamentals (fundamentals-based). In a single-equation framework, its empirical estimation is similar to equation 12.1, but the number of regressors is extended to include—in addition to the Balassa–Samuelson effect—a measure of degree of trade openness, the net foreign asset position, the terms of trade, and the ratio of government consumption over GDP. A fundamentals-based estimation is represented by equation 12.2, which coincides with equation 12.1, except for the vectors X and v that include the additional regressors and their corresponding parameters:

$$\ln q = \alpha_2 + \beta_2 \ln Y + vX + \varepsilon. \tag{12.2}$$

In cross-section estimations, the variables and error terms in equations 12.1 and 12.2 appear with a subscript i, which indicates the country. In panel data environments, an additional subscript t is included to indicate the time period. Panel data estimations also include period fixed effects.

The misalignment index is then constructed as the ratio of actual to equilibrium RER ($m = q/q^*$), with q^* estimated either through equations 12.1 or 12.2. When the exchange rate is defined as the domestic price of a foreign currency—as in this chapter—values of the misalignment index higher (lower) than 1 imply that the RER is undervalued (overvalued). Defined in this way, the misalignment index can also be called the RER undervaluation index, and with the inverse definition of the exchange rate, the RER overvaluation index.[4]

The growth regression literature provides substantial evidence that higher RER levels tend to be associated with higher GDP per capita growth rates. This association seems robust to changes in the estimation technique (cross-section ordinary least squares, panel data [fixed and random effects], dynamic panel data [generalized method of moments], nonlinear panels, and panel cointegration techniques), number of control variables, and data sources for both the dependent and independent variables (Penn World Tables, International Financial Statistics, World Development Indicators, Maddison Project Database). This literature has also shown that RER volatility—typically measured as the standard deviation or coefficient of variation of the RER—is negatively associated with GDP growth.

A comprehensive survey of this literature is beyond the scope of this chapter. There are a number of issues, however, that are worth discussing in some detail because they are important for the subsequent analysis presented later. These issues involve whether the observed positive association between RER levels and economic growth varies (1) across countries and periods, (2) between cases of RER overvaluation and RER undervaluation, and (3) between indexes of misalignment used. I briefly discuss these issues in the sections that follow.

COUNTRIES AND PERIODS

Many studies have analyzed the association between the RER and economic growth in samples exclusively composed of developing countries: e.g., Cottani et al. (1990), Dollar (1992), and Gala (2008). Others analyzed samples that also include a relatively small number of developed countries: e.g., Razin and Collins (1999) and Aguirre and Calderón (2005). Rodrik (2008) explicitly tested whether the association occurs only in developing countries. He used a PPP-based index of RER undervaluation in a fixed-effects model for a panel of up to one hundred eighty-four countries between 1960 and 2004. He defined developing countries as those with a GDP per capita less than $6,000 and found that the positive relationship between RER undervaluation and economic growth is stronger and more significant for developing countries than it is for developed ones. Rapetti et al. (2012) replicated Rodrik's work and showed that if the threshold is instead selected from anywhere in the $9,000 to $15,000 range, the estimated effect of RER undervaluation on growth will also be large and highly significant for developed countries. To address the issue in more detail, Rapetti et al. (2012) developed a series of alternative classification criteria and empirical strategies to evaluate the existence of asymmetries among groups of countries. They found that the effect of currency undervaluation on growth is indeed larger and more robust for developing economies.

Many studies used sample periods starting after 1980. This might raise the issue of whether the documented association is exclusive of the so-called "second financial globalization era." Rodrik (2008) estimated the effect of undervaluation on growth in developing countries for two distinct periods (1950–1979 and 1980–2004) and found that it was significant in both with virtually identical magnitudes. Using several alternative definitions of developing countries, Rapetti et al. (2012) attained results that were similar to Rodrik's, even when dividing the sample in an alternative split for the pre- and postglobalization eras (1950–1974 and 1975–2004). Extending the analysis for a substantially longer period, Di Nino et al. (2011) also found supporting evidence that the relationship is strong for developing countries and weak for advanced countries in both the pre-and post-World War II period (1861–1939 vs. 1950–2009).

ASYMMETRIES

The first studies to analyze the relationship between RER misalignments and economic growth were motivated by the idea that RER overvaluation hinders growth. For instance, Cottani et al. (1990) used a fundamentals-based index of RER overvaluation in a cross-section regression for twenty-four developing countries between 1960 and 1983 and found a statistically significant negative relationship between the variables. Dollar (1992) also found a robust negative relationship between a PPP-based RER overvaluation index and economic growth in a cross-section study for ninety-five developing countries between 1976 and 1985. A common reading of these results is that RER misalignment—not just overvaluation—hurts economic growth.

More recently, researchers have begun to investigate more carefully whether the effects of RER overvaluation and undervaluation are asymmetric. Razin and Collins (1999) constructed a fundamentals-based index of RER overvaluation and used it for a pooled sample of ninety-three developed and developing countries over sixteen- to eighteen-year periods since 1975. They found that overvaluation hurts growth whereas undervaluation favors it. The effect of overvaluation seems stronger though. Aguirre and Calderón (2005) found that the estimated coefficients of their misalignment indexes were larger for cases of overvaluation than those of undervaluation; here again, however, the positive effect of undervaluation on growth was significant both statistically and economically. Rodrik (2008) found that overvaluation hurts growth, undervaluation favors growth, and no significant difference could be seen in terms of the size of each effect. Rapetti et al. (2012) found results similar to Rodrik's, although the effect of overvaluation was slightly higher in absolute terms than that of undervaluation. Bereau et al. (2012) used a panel nonlinear technique—i.e., a panel smooth transition regression model—to capture whether there are asymmetries between RER undervaluation and over-valuation. They found robust evidence that undervaluation accelerates and overvaluation decelerates growth.

MISALIGNMENT INDEXES

An important conclusion that emerges from the empirical literature is that the positive association between RER levels and growth does not seem to depend on the way the misalignment index is constructed. Aguirre and Calderón (2005) developed three fundamentals-based indexes of RER overvaluation using panel cointegration and time series techniques for a panel of sixty developed and developing countries between 1965 and 2003. They found that GDP per capita growth correlated negatively with each index developed. They also obtained very similar results when replacing the fundamentals-based indexes with a PPP-based index.

MacDonald and Vieira (2010) estimated seven equilibrium RERs using fixed-effects and random-effects models for a panel of ninety countries between 1980 and 2004. They used different combinations of regressors (GDP per capita, net foreign assets, terms of trade, and government consumption) in their estimations. They then constructed a PPP-based undervaluation index similar to Rodrik's and six fundamentals-based undervaluation indexes. In all cases, they found a significant and positive correlation with economic growth, which was stronger for developing and emerging countries. The estimated effect of RER undervaluation on growth was very similar with the seven indexes.

The results in Aguirre and Calderón (2005) and MacDonald and Vieira (2010) suggest that in practice the estimation of PPP- and funda-mentals-based equilibrium RERs are very similar. Berg and Miao (2010) addressed this issue explicitly. They used Penn World Tables 6.3 data to estimate a fixed-effect model for a PPP-based undervaluation index simi-lar to equation 12.1 and for a fundamentals-based undervaluation index similar to equation 12.2—using the terms of trade, the degree of open-ness, and government consumption and investment (both as a share of GDP) as additional regressors. They found that the two indexes were virtually indistinguishable from one other; the correlation coefficient between them was 0.96.

In summary, the evidence gathered from the growth regression litera-ture suggests first that the effect of RER misalignment on growth comes in the form of undervaluation stimulating growth and overvaluation hurting it. The negative effect of the latter is likely to be stronger in absolute terms than that of the former. These effects are especially attributable to the experience of developing countries, and there is no evidence that the documented effects correspond to a specific historical period. Finally, although they have different theoretical backgrounds and implications, PPP-based and fundamentals-based misalignment indexes seem to be empirically identical.

POSSIBLE MECHANISMS BEHIND THE POSITIVE ASSOCIATION BETWEEN RER AND GROWTH

Recent research has been much more successful at establishing a robust positive association between RER levels and economic growth than it has been at uncovering the mechanisms behind it. Although there might be some room for debate, it seems to be widely accepted that the causality behind the documented correlation runs from RER levels to economic growth. Everyday experience shows that governments use a variety of instruments, including exchange rate, monetary, fiscal, incomes, and capital management policies, to manage the level and evolution of the RER with real objectives. Thus, the relevant question is not one of causality but rather one that attempts to pinpoint the mechanism that explains why undervalued (overvalued) RER levels would favor (hurt) economic growth. Several possible mechanisms have been proposed in the literature. I briefly discuss four of them.[5]

The first is what Berg and Miao (2010) call the "Washington Consensus" view, which states that a RER misalignment implies some sort of macroeconomic disequilibrium that by itself is bad for growth. Presumably anchored in Walrasian general equilibrium theory, this view suggests that a misaligned RER is a disequilibrium value of a relative price that induces an inefficient allocation of resources that lowers economic growth. Although it has been inspired by cases of RER overvaluation, this view considers that RER undervaluation also has deleterious effects on growth. The evidence gathered in econometric studies of the association between the RER and economic growth goes against the Washington Consensus view. As previously discussed, this literature has robustly found that whereas RER overvaluation tends to hinder growth, RER undervaluation stimulates it.

Another proposed mechanism suggests that higher RER levels tend to increase the saving rate that, in turn, translates into faster capital accumulation and growth. The main weakness of the "saving channel" is theoretical: it is unclear how higher RER levels would affect growth via changes in the saving rate. Using an intertemporal optimization framework, Montiel and Serven (2009) could not identify a mechanism through which changes in the RER level affect the saving rate. Their baseline model shows that a rise in the equilibrium value of the RER leads to a permanent increase in income and consumption, leaving the saving rate unchanged.

Razmi et al. (2012) developed a structuralist framework to show that higher RER levels help accelerate capital accumulation and economic growth in a small open economy. In their baseline model, the saving rate depended on functional income distribution. A rise in the RER allowed for a higher rate of capital accumulation but had an ambiguous effect on the wage share and the aggregate saving rate.

Levy Yeyati and Sturzenegger (2009) also related the RER and the saving rate to distributional changes. A transition to a higher RER typically reduces real wages and transfers income from workers to firms. Following the seminal contribution by Díaz-Alejandro (1963), if workers have a propensity to spend greater than firms, this redistribution increases the saving rate. It is not clear, however, that the redistribution must raise accumulation. As the original analysis of Díaz-Alejandro showed, a RER devaluation that leads to higher savings can be contractionary. This issue has been examined extensively in Kaleckian models (e.g., Blecker 1989; Bhaduri and Marglin 1990), in which it was shown that both expansionary and contractionary cases are possible.

There is one more theoretical challenge in addition to those already mentioned: it is not clear in these accounts why higher saving and investment rates require not merely higher but undervalued (i.e., above equilibrium) RER levels as found in the empirical literature.

I call the third proposed mechanism the "macro-prudential channel" because it focuses on how foreign capital movements to developing countries in the context of financial globalization affect economic performance through transitory RER misalignments. The extreme form of this mechanism arises when RER overvaluation caused by capital inflows leads to currency and financial crises with long-lasting negative impacts on growth. A number of developing countries—mostly in Latin America—have experienced this type of boom and bust episode.[6] Many began with the implementation of macroeconomic stabilization programs that combined fixed or semi-fixed exchange rates, liberalized current and capital accounts, and the deregulation of domestic financial markets. In a first phase, the combination of these elements stimulated capital inflows that appreciated the RER, expanded economic activity, and induced current account deficits.

In many cases, a consumption boom ensued without an increase in the investment rate. Even when investment did increase, the appreciation of the RER favored investment in nontradable activities with little increase in the export capacity that was required to repay foreign debt.

In a second phase, the excessive external borrowing raised concerns about the sustainability of the fixed exchange rate regimes and triggered speculative attacks against the domestic currencies. The effect of capital outflows was typically contractionary. The domestic banking systems— which were short in foreign currency and long in local assets—faced liquidity problems and in many cases went bankrupt, exacerbating the negative impact on economic activity. In cases in which the collapse of the financial system was severe and the external debt burden very high, the crises had long-lasting effects on economic growth. Clear examples of these dynamics are the stabilization programs based on active crawling pegs (the so-called *tablitas*) in Argentina, Chile, and Uruguay during the late 1970s that ended up in severe debt crises that crippled growth during the "lost decade" of the 1980s. Other stabilization programs that led to crises occurred in Mexico (1994–1995), Brazil (1998–1999), Argentina (2001–2002), and Uruguay (2002). Taylor (1998) suggested that cyclical dynamics of this nature were also observed in the Southeast Asian crises of 1997 and 1998, and Bagnai (2012) argued similarly for the current crisis in Southern Europe.

Historical records support this mechanism in the case of RER overvaluation and low or negative growth; whether it can also account for the observed positive association between undervalued RERs and higher growth is more controversial. Several authors have indicated that undervalued RERs help stabilize long-term growth by limiting external debt accumulation and avoiding contractionary effects of sudden stops (Prasad et al. 2007). Undervalued RERs typically generate current account surpluses and facilitate foreign exchange reserve accumulation. Current account surpluses and large stocks of foreign exchange reserves in turn operate as an insurance against international financial instability and sudden stops. Recent research seems to support this view. Aizenman and Lee (2007) found evidence suggesting that international reserve accumulation in emerging markets has been carried out as a self-insurance strategy to protect the economy from sudden stops. Polterovich and Popov (2003) and Levi Yeyati and Sturzenegger (2009) found a positive correlation between foreign reserve accumulation and RER levels and reserve accumulation and economic growth. Similarly, Prasad et al. (2007) found that current account balances are highly and positively associated with both undervalued RERs and economic growth.

The macro-prudential channel is somewhat related to the saving channel. The former states that international capital markets operate with many imperfections that negatively affect long-term economic performance, particularly in developing countries. Consequently, these countries need to establish safe linkages with the international markets to minimize their reliance on foreign savings. A higher RER helps to reduce domestic absorption of tradables while promoting domestic production of tradables, thus lowering foreign savings.

Notice, however, the important differences between both channels. The saving channel focuses primarily on the level of savings and assumes that higher saving rates translate into higher capital accumulation and growth. As mentioned previously, the necessary link that connects saving rates, investment, and RER levels has not been adequately established in theoretical terms. The macro-prudential channel focuses on the composition of savings, highlighting the imperfections of international capital markets and their potential negative effects on growth.

The fourth mechanism can be referred to as the "tradable-led growth channel." Essentially, this mechanism sees economic development as a process characterized by a rapid and intense structural transformation from low- to high-productivity activities that are largely tradable. "Modern" tradables have traditionally been associated with manufacturing, but some services (e.g., software) and knowledge-intensive agricultural activities (e.g., seed production) are also now recognized as being a part of this group. The tradable-led growth channel can be seen as consisting of three broad elements. First, modern tradable activities are intrinsically more productive or operate under some sort of increasing returns to scale. Second, given this trait, the reallocation of (current and future) resources to these activities—i.e., structural change—accelerates GDP per capita growth. Third, accumulation in these activities depends on their profitability, which in turn depends on the level of the RER. Rapid capital accumulation requires a sufficiently competitive (undervalued) RER to compensate for the market failures caused by the increasing returns.

A large number of specific mechanisms have been advanced using this general logic. For instance, Rodrik (2008) indicated that modern tradable activities are affected disproportionally by market and institutional failures. Using an endogenous growth model, he showed that the resulting misallocation of resources toward nontradables leads to slower economic growth; an undervalued RER can be a second-best policy that compensates for the market and institutional failures, improves tradable profitability, and accelerates economic growth.

Several other economists have recognized the important interplay between RER levels and market failures in economic development. Learning externalities, for instance, imply that infant industries can benefit from temporary protection against foreign competition via a transitory RER undervaluation (Ros 2001). Similarly, temporary RER overvaluation can lead to deindustrialization and lower growth—as in the Dutch disease case—when tradable firms' production is subject to some form of increasing returns to scale (e.g., Krugman 1987; Ros and Skott 1998). The opposite case—transitory RER undervaluation—can spur a virtuous dynamics of structural change and economic development (Rapetti 2013). Models of export-led growth have emphasized positive externalities that are not equally prevalent in nonexport activities; policies that reallocate resources to export industries therefore promote higher growth in these models (e.g., de Melo and Robinson 1992).

Another popular mechanism emphasizes that the lack of foreign exchange may constrain economic growth in developing countries. This idea has a long tradition in structuralist economics, at the UN Economic Commission for Latin America and the Caribbean,[7] and in the balance-of-payments–constrained growth literature initiated by Thirwall (1979). In some accounts within these traditions, it has been emphasized that higher (lower) RER levels tend to relax (exacerbate) the balance-of-payments constraint and thus accelerate (decelerate) growth.[8] Although based on a somewhat different rationale, this mechanism can be considered part of a broadly defined tradable-led growth channel. Both channels share the view that economic development concurs with the expansion of tradable activities and that higher RERs favor their profitability and consequently capital accumulation and economic growth.[9]

AN EVALUATION OF THE PROPOSED CHANNELS IN LIGHT OF THE EMPIRICAL EVIDENCE

The prediction of the Washington Consensus view that undervalued RERs affect economic growth negatively collides with empirical evidence that shows the exact opposite. No persuasive mechanism has been proposed within the saving channel. Thus, in this section, I consider the other two proposed mechanisms: the macro-prudential channel and the tradable-led growth channel. I evaluate both of them in light of the empirical findings discussed previously.

The macro-prudential channel posits that the failures in the international capital markets affect developing countries in the form of excessive volatility, sudden stops, and external crises. Thus, lowering the reliance on foreign savings can enhance economic growth in these countries. Because it lowers the demand of foreign savings, this view predicts that a higher RER level should accelerate growth in developing countries.

Fundamentals-based misalignment indexes are adequate for empirically assessing this mechanism. The equilibrium level of the RER estimated for these indexes is the one that allows the economy to achieve internal and external balances simultaneously. Its level is determined by a sustainable (or equilibrium) flow of foreign savings. Because developing countries need to demand less-than-equilibrium foreign finance to protect themselves from international capital market failures, the macro-prudential channel would predict that undervalued (overvalued) RERs enhance (hurt) economic growth in developing countries. The empirical evidence reviewed earlier supports this prediction. It is important to note, however, that econometric evidence suggests that the documented positive association between RER levels and growth holds for developing countries not only in the second globalization period (i.e., since roughly the mid-1970s) but also before it. Thus, the macro-prudential channel explains at best only part of observed associations. Another explanation is needed.

I now turn to the question of how to empirically evaluate the tradable-led growth channel. Recall that it consists of three related elements. Modern tradable activities are special because they operate under some sort of increasing returns to scale. As a result, a relative expansion of these activities compared with others accelerates GDP per capita growth. Their expansion, in turn, depends on the level of the RER because it determines the profit rate of tradables. For simplicity, the latter can be stated formally as the rate of capital accumulation in the tradable activities (g_T) being a positive function of their profit rate (r_T) relative to the profit rate in the foreign country (r_T^*):

$$g_T = g(r_T / r_T^*) \qquad \text{with } g' > 0. \qquad (12.3)$$

The parity between profit rates in the home and foreign country $(r_T = r_T^*)$ implies

$$\frac{P_T Y_T - W L_T}{P_T K_T} = \frac{P_T^* Y_T^* - W^* L_T^*}{P_T^* K_T^*}, \qquad (12.4)$$

where P_T is the price of tradable goods (including capital goods), Y_T is tradable goods output, W is the nominal wage rate, K_T is the capital stock in the tradable goods sector, and the asterisk (*) refers to the foreign country. Assuming that technology for tradable production is similar in both countries—meaning that the output–capital ratios are the same—the law of one price holds for tradables, and labor is homogeneous across sectors within countries, the parity condition expressed in equation 12.4 implies the intuitive result that relative wages expressed in common currency need to be proportional to the ratio of tradable labor productivities for the profit rate parity to hold:

$$q_W \equiv \frac{E W^*}{W} = \frac{Y_T^* / L_T^*}{Y_T / L_T} \equiv \frac{1}{y_T}, \qquad (12.5)$$

where E is the nominal exchange rate, q_W is the foreign to domestic wage ratio expressed in common currency, and y_T is the relative labor productivity in tradables. The RER is defined as the relative price between baskets of goods and services produced or consumed in different countries expressed in the same currency:

$$q \equiv \frac{E P^*}{P}, \qquad (12.6)$$

where P^* and P are foreign and domestic price indexes. Both price indexes in equation 12.6 comprise tradable and nontradable prices. Assuming that the law of one price holds for tradables and that the weighting scheme of P and P^* are similar, we get

$$q = \left(\frac{E P_T^*}{P_T} \right)^{1-\theta} \left(\frac{E P_N^*}{P_N} \right)^{\theta} = \left(\frac{E P_N^*}{P_N} \right)^{\theta}, \qquad (12.7)$$

where P_N is the price of nontradables and θ and $1 - \theta$ are the shares of nontradables and tradables in both price indexes, respectively. Nontradable prices are largely determined by the nominal wage rate, typically in some sort of imperfect competition environment. Thus, further assuming that nontradable prices are determined by a markup (μ) over average costs, equation 12.7 turns into

$$q = \left(\frac{(1+\mu^*)EW^*}{(1+\mu)W} \frac{Y_N / L_N}{Y_N^* / L_N^*} \right)^{\theta} = (\delta y_N q_W)^{\theta}, \quad (12.8)$$

where δ is the foreign-to-domestic markup factor ratio and y_N is the relative labor productivity in nontradables. Given that δ and y_N are relatively stable in the short and medium run, equation 12.8 reveals the intuitive result that the behavior of RER is largely determined by the evolution of relative wages (q_W) over such time horizons.

Plugging equation 12.5 into 12.8, we obtain the level of RER that is compatible with the parity between the tradable profit rates in the home and the foreign country, which is referred to as $\bar{q}$:

$$\bar{q} = \left(\delta \frac{y_N}{y_T} \right)^{\theta}. \quad (12.9)$$

The Balassa–Samuelson effect rests on the observation that rich countries have far greater relative labor productivity in tradable than in nontradable activities compared to poorer countries. The Balassa–Samuelson effect thus predicts that the value of y_N / y_T in equation 12.9 and consequently the level of $\bar{q}$ would tend to decrease with the level of the GDP per capita of the home country. This means that the PPP-based equilibrium RERs of the empirical literature discussed previously (see specifically equation 12.1) coincides with the estimation of $\bar{q}$ under the assumption that δ is constant.[10] Consequently, a PPP-based misalignment index can be interpreted as an index of the degree of deviation of the tradable profit rate in the home country relative to the foreign country. This is an adequate index to empirically evaluate the tradable-led growth channel.

When the actual level of the RER equals $\bar{q}$ (i.e., when the PPP-based misalignment index is equal to 1), the profit rate of tradables in the home country is the same as in the foreign country (i.e., the United States in the empirical literature). Would modern tradable activities in developing countries grow at rates that could catch up with such a RER level? There are at least two reasons to expect a negative answer. First, the derivation of $\bar{q}$ only considered relative labor productivities of home and foreign tradable firms. There are a number of elements external to the firms that make total tradable productivity in developing countries lower than in developed countries. A lack of adequate communication and transportation infrastructure, worse public services, and lower aggregate productivity of the economy operate as further drawbacks for tradable productivity in developing countries that need to be compensated for. Second, even when adjusting for these elements it is likely that profit rates in developing countries will need to pay a (risk) premium over those paid in developed countries. Consequently, there are good reasons to expect that only an undervalued RER level—i.e., actual RER higher than $\bar{q}$—would offer proper incentives (i.e., $r_t > r_t^*$) to expand modern tradable activities in developing countries. In other words, a tradable-led growth mechanism would predict that RER undervaluation (overvaluation), measured through a PPP-based misalignment index, would accelerate (decelerate) economic growth in developing countries. As reviewed previously, the empirical evidence gathered in the growth regression literature strongly supports this prediction.

CONCLUDING REMARKS

During the last decade, a large number of studies have analyzed the relationship between RER levels and economic growth. At this moment, the empirical evidence that has emerged from this research effort strongly suggests that whereas RER undervaluation favors economic growth, RER overvaluation hurts it. These effects have been observed in developing countries in the pre- and postfinancial globalization periods. These findings have passed a large number of robustness checks, including changes in the econometric techniques and data sets used. Thus, the positive effect of RER levels on economic growth in developing countries can be regarded as a strong empirical observation. It is the mechanism(s) involved that remains debatable.

In this chapter, I analyzed the mechanisms that have been proposed in the literature. My take is that two of them adjust to the empirical findings best: the macro-prudential channel and the tradable-led growth channel. A drawback of the former is that it predicts that undervalued (overvalued) RERs favor (hurt) growth in developing countries only in the globalization period (since the 1970s). Evidence, however, shows that the association is also observed in the preglobalization period. The tradable-led growth channel does not distinguish between periods, thus better fitting the evidence. This does not mean that the macro-prudential channel does not hold any water. A higher-than-equilibrium RER is a type of macro-prudential policy that reduces the probability of sudden stops and crises. Because the mechanisms are not mutually exclusive, both might have some explanatory power.

In addition to the difference in terms of time periods, it is not possible to determine which explanation is more adequate. In a growth econometric setup, the two channels must be evaluated with different misalignment indexes: the macro-prudential channel with a fundamentals-based index and the tradable-led growth channel with a PPP-based index. Because the estimations of equilibrium RERs in both cases end up becoming indistinguishable from one another, it is not possible to discriminate between the two channels from a growth regression. Because most research on the association between the RER and economic growth has been conducted through growth econometric analysis, other strategies need to be explored in the future. In this regard, much could be learned from the detailed study of specific episodes of growth acceleration triggered by stable and competitive RER strategies.

NOTES

I thank Jaime Ros, Ricardo Ffrench-Davis, Roxana Maurizio, and Emiliano Libman for their helpful comments.

1. I follow the definition of nominal exchange rate as the domestic price of a foreign currency. Consequently, a higher RER implies a more competitive or depreciated domestic currency in real terms.

2. Other strategies, such as case and episode studies or historical narratives, have also been used. For studies of growth episodes, see Hausmann et al. (2005) and Freund and Pierola (2012). For historical analyses of specific cases in Latin America, see Frenkel and Rapetti (2008, 2012).

3. For a critical assessment of the notion of exchange rate equilibrium, see Taylor (2004).

4. This would be defining the nominal exchange rate as the units of foreign currency exchanged for one unit of domestic currency.

5. A slightly different classification of the mechanisms is presented in Skott et al. (2012).

6. Frenkel (1983) pioneered the analysis and formalization of this kind of dynamics. See also Frenkel and Rapetti (2009).

7. See chapter 10, this volume: "Balance-of-Payments Dominance: Its Implications for Macroeconomic Policy" by José Antonio Ocampo.

8. Porcile and Lima (2010) and Razmi et al. (2012) are recent examples.

9. It could even be argued that tradable production also operates under some broad form of increasing returns in the external-constrained growth story. The expansion of tradable activities generates a positive externality by raising the net supply of foreign exchange and thus providing the rest of the economic sectors foreign exchange at a relatively lower cost. Given that exporters do not internalize the positive external effect of supplying additional units of foreign exchange, an undervalued RER is required.

10. Applying natural logs to equation 12.9 and substituting y_N / y_T by Y^{-1}—the simplest way of modeling the inverse relationship between y_N / y_T and the GDP per capita as predicted by the Balassa and Samuelson effect—yields equation 12.1, with $\alpha_1 = \theta ln\delta$ and $\beta_1 = -\theta$. It is important to notice that given that $\theta > 0$, it follows that $\beta_1 < 0$, as consistently observed in the empirical literature.

REFERENCES

Aguirre, A. and Calderón, C. 2005 "Real exchange rate misalignments and economic performance." Central Bank of Chile Working Paper 315. http://www.bcentral.cl /estudios/documentos-trabajo/pdf/dtbc315.pdf.

Aizenman, J. and Lee, J. 2007. "International reserves: precautionary versus mercantilist views, theory and evidence." *Open Economies Review* 18(2): 191–214.

Bagnai, A. 2012. "Unhappy families are all alike: Minskyan cycles, Kaldorian growth, and the eurozone peripheral crises." Iniciativa para la Transparencia Financiera documento técnico. http://www.itf.org.ar/pdf/documentos/87_2012.pdf.

Balassa, B. 1964. "The purchasing power parity doctrine: a reappraisal." *Journal of Political Economy* 72(6): 584–596.

Bereau, S., López Villavicencio, A., and Mignon, V. 2012. "Currency misalignment and growth: a new look using nonlinear panel data methods." *Applied Economics* 44 (27): 3503–3511.

Berg, A. and Miao, Y. 2010. "The real exchange rate and growth revisited: the Washington Consensus strikes back?" International Monetary Fund Working Paper 10/58. https://www.imf.org/external/pubs/ft/wp/2010/wp1058.pdf.

Bhaduri, A. and Marglin, S. 1990. "Unemployment and the real wage: the economic basis for contesting political ideologies." *Cambridge Journal of Economics* 14(4): 375–393.

Blecker, R. 1989. "International competition, income distribution and economic growth." *Cambridge Journal of Economics* 13(3): 395–412.

Cottani, J., Cavallo, D., and Khan, S. M. 1990. "Real exchange rate behavior and economic performance in LDCs." *Economic Development and Cultural Change* 39(1): 61–76.

de Melo, J. and Robinson, S. 1992. "Productivity and externalities: models of export-led growth." *Journal of International Trade and Economic Development* 1(1): 41–68.

Díaz-Alejandro, C. F. D. 1963. "A note on the impact of devaluation and the redistributive effect." *Journal of Political Economy* 71(6): 577–580.

Di Nino, V., Eichengreen, B., and Sbracia, M. 2011. "Real exchange rates, trade, and growth: Italy 1861–2011." Bank of Italy, Economic Research and International

Relations Area Working Paper 10. http://www.bancaditalia.it/pubblicazioni /quaderni-storia/2011-0010/QSEn_10.pdf.

Dollar, D. 1992. "Outward-oriented developing economies really do grow more rapidly: evidence from 95 LDCs, 1976–1985." *Economic Development and Cultural Change* 40(3): 523–544.

Frenkel, R. 1983. "Mercado financiero, expectativas cambiarias y movimientos de capital." *El Trimestre Económico* 200(4): 2041–2076.

Frenkel, R. and Rapetti, M. 2008. "Five years of stable and competitive real exchange rate in Argentina." *International Review of Applied Economics* 22(2): 215–226.

Frenkel, R. and Rapetti, M. 2009. "A developing country view of the current global crisis: what should not be forgotten and what should be done." *Cambridge Journal of Economics* 33(4): 685–702.

Frenkel, R. and Rapetti, M. 2012. "Exchange rate regimes in the major Latin American countries since the 1950s: lessons from history." *Journal of Iberian and Latin American Economic History* 30(1): 157–188.

Freund, C. and Denisse Pierola, M. 2012. "Export surges." *Journal of Development Economics* 97(2): 387–395.

Gala, P. 2008. "Real exchange rate levels and economic development: theoretical analysis and econometric evidence." *Cambridge Journal of Economics* 32(2): 273–288.

Hausmann, R., Pritchett, L., and Rodrik, D. 2005. "Growth accelerations." *Journal of Economic Growth* 10(4): 303–329.

Hinkle, L. E and Montiel, P. J. 1999. *Exchange rate misalignment: concepts and measurement for developing countries.* New York, NY: Oxford University Press.

Krugman, P. 1987. "The narrow moving band, the Dutch disease, and the competitive consequences of Mrs. Thatcher." *Journal of Development Economics* 27(1-2): 41–55.

Levy Yeyati, E. and Sturzenegger, F. 2009. "Fear of appreciation: exchange rate policy as a development strategy." In *Monetary policy frameworks for emerging markets*, edited by G. Hammond, R. Kanbur, and E. Prasad, 69–94. Northampton, UK: Edward Elgar.

MacDonald, R. and Vieira, F. 2010. "A panel data investigation of real exchange rate misalignment and growth." CESifo Working Paper 3061. http://core.ac.uk /download/pdf/6409241.pdf.

Meade, J. 1951. *The theory of international economic policy: the balance of payments.* New York, NY: Oxford University Press.

Montiel, P. and Serven, L. 2009. "Real exchange rates, saving, and growth: is there a link?" Commission on Growth and Development Working Paper 46. http:// siteresources.worldbank.org/EXTPREMNET/Resources/489960-1338997241035 /Growth_Commission_Working_Paper_46_Real_Exchange_Rates_Saving _Growth_Link.pdf.

Polterovich, V. and Popov, V. 2003. "Accumulation of foreign exchange reserves and long term growth." MPRA Paper 20069. University Library of Munich, Germany.

Porcile, G. and Lima, G. T. 2010. "Real exchange rate and elasticity of labor supply in a balance-of-payments-constrained macrodynamics." *Cambridge Journal of Economics* 34(6): 1019–1039.

Prasad, E. S., Rajan, R. G., and Subramanian, A. 2007. "Foreign capital and economic growth." *Brookings Papers on Economic Activity* 38(1): 153–230.

Rapetti, M. 2013. "Macroeconomic policy coordination in a competitive real exchange rate strategy for development." *Journal of Globalization and Development* 3(2): 1–31.

Rapetti, M., Skott, P., and Razmi, A. 2012. "The real exchange rate and economic growth: are developing countries special?" *International Review of Applied Economics* 26(6): 735–753.

Razin, O. and Collins, S. M. 1999. "Real exchange rate misalignments and growth." In *The economics of globalization: policy perspectives from public economics*, edited by A. Razin and E. Sadka, pp. 59–83. Cambridge, UK: Cambridge University Press.

Razmi, A., Rapetti, M., and Skott, P. 2012. "The real exchange rate and economic development." *Structural Change and Economic Dynamics* 23(2): 151–169.

Rodrik, D. 2008. "The real exchange rate and economic growth." *Brookings Papers on Economic Activity* 39(2): 365–439.

Ros, J. 2001. *Development theory and the economics of growth*. Ann Arbor: University of Michigan Press.

Ros, J. and Skott, P. 1998. "Dynamic effects of trade liberalization and currency overvaluation under conditions of increasing returns." *The Manchester School* 66(4): 466–489.

Samuelson, P. 1964. "Theoretical notes on trade problems." *Review of Economics and Statistics* 46(2): 145–154.

Skott, P., Rapetti, M., and Razmi, A. 2012. "Real exchange rates and the long-run effects of aggregate demand in economies with underemployment." University of Massachusetts Amherst Working Paper 2012–06. http://www.umass.edu/economics/publications/2012-06.pdf.

Taylor, A. and Taylor, M. 2004. "The purchasing power parity debate." *Journal of Economic Perspectives* 18(4): 135–158.

Taylor, L. 1998. "Capital market crises: liberalisation, fixed exchange rates and market-driven destabilisation." *Cambridge Journal of Economics* 22(6): 663–676.

Taylor, L. 2004. "Exchange rate indeterminacy in portfolio balance, Mundell–Fleming and uncovered interest rate parity models." *Cambridge Journal of Economics* 28(2): 205–227.

Thirwall, A. 1979. "The balance of payments constraint as an explanation of international growth rate differences." *Banca Nazionale del Lavoro Quarterly Review* 32(128): 45–53.

PART 4

Finance and Crises

Capitalism and Financial Crises

A LONG-TERM PERSPECTIVE

Andrés Solimano

Capitalism has a considerable capacity for creating material wealth and spurring technical innovations, but this process is often far from smooth. In fact, it has been shown historically (and continues to be shown) that wealth creation often comes along with inequality, booms, recessions, and recurrent financial crises.

Financial crises, a theme of great interest to Roberto Frenkel throughout his professional life, are costly in several respects.[1] They stop the normal flow of credit (the lifeblood of any economic system) and deepen recessions, creating unemployment, reducing real wages, and leading to wealth destruction. Economic and financial crises were behind the rise of nationalism and xenophobia in Europe in the 1920s and 1930s and accompanied the turn to authoritarianism in Latin America in the 1970s and 1980s. Today, in crisis-ridden Europe, we see again the emergence of xenophobic parties trying to mobilize in their favor the social discontent and frustration associated with high unemployment and diminished expectations.

The financial crisis of 2008 and 2009 in the United States and Europe has challenged the view that the world is divided between a financially stable core (the mature capitalist economies of North America and Europe) and a chronically unstable periphery (developing countries in Latin America, Africa, and Asia). This time the crisis also hit the core and its closer periphery formed by countries such as Iceland, Ireland, Portugal, Greece, Spain, and Italy, while developing countries have continued to grow at respectable rates after 2008.

The recent spate of financial crises in advanced capitalist countries is, in a sense, also a crisis of economic theory built around the assumption of what neoclassical theory has termed the "rational economic man." A variety of free market theories such as the efficient financial market hypothesis, monetarism, supply-side economics, and the real business cycle have been very influential in shaping the views and policies of central banks and finance ministers since the 1970s and 1980s, with generally deleterious effects on the economy and society.

Economic and financial crises come in a variety of different shapes, but all involve a disruption of the "normal" workings of an economy. Several types of crises can be identified, such as (1) a crisis of "overproduction" that involves unused productive capacity and unemployment of labor; (2) an inflationary crisis accompanied by high fiscal and balance-of-payments deficits and massive exchange rate depreciation; and (3) a crisis with an important financial component that involves the illiquidity or insolvency of banks, a debt crisis, "sudden stops" in the inflows of external financing and defaults, and the rescheduling of outstanding public and private debt.

This chapter is organized into three sections. The first section takes a look at several episodes of economic and financial crises throughout the nineteenth, twentieth, and early twenty-first centuries. The second section interprets the historical perspective on crises regarding links between macro conditions and financial instability, the nature of the social contract, and various regularities in the causal factors of different crises and the role of debt in prolonging them. The third section examines the current (mis)direction of mainstream economic analysis and points to the flaws of the International Monetary Fund (IMF) in the run up to the 2008–2009 crises along with the pitfalls of austerity. The chapter ends with some final remarks.

ECONOMIC AND FINANCIAL CRISES FROM THE NINETEENTH TO TWENTY-FIRST CENTURIES: A BRIEF OVERVIEW

The historical evidence shows that the incidence of financial crises was higher in the eras of *unregulated capitalism*: from the long nineteenth century up to 1913 (*liberal capitalism*) and the second wave of globalization that has been in place since the 1970 and 1980s, which could be considered *neoliberal capitalism*. In contrast, the frequency of financial crises with international contagion effects was severely reduced or disappeared altogether during the period of regulated capitalism that was characteristic of the Bretton Woods period (1944–1971). This regime of regulated capitalism constrained private capital movements at international levels and promoted national policies designed to guarantee full employment and economic security and universal access to education, health, housing, and pensions through the welfare state in advanced capitalist economies.

In contrast, neoliberal capitalism has promoted the relocation of production toward low-wage countries; the privatization of state-owned enterprises, banks, and social services; and the expansion of global financial markets. As a result of these policies, income and wealth are now primarily in the hands of global and national economic elites—and at unprecedented levels (Solimano 2014).

THE FIRST WAVE OF GLOBALIZATION (CA.1870–1913)

The British Empire, the hegemonic power of the long nineteenth century, fostered free trade and free capital mobility under its own rules. London was the financial center of the world, and the British pound (sterling) was the dominant currency under the international gold standard. Economic historians have called the period from ca. 1870 to 1913 the "first wave of globalization." This period also saw large flows of international migration between Europe and the New World during a time when virtually no passports or visas existed—the "age of mass migration"—(Hatton and Williamson 1998; Solimano 2010a).

The first wave of globalization, spurred on by the gold standard, was an age of low inflation in the price of goods and services; nevertheless, it was also a period of speculative bubbles in asset prices and financial crashes. In fact, banking and debt crises were pervasive both in the center of the world economy and in Latin America, Asia, the offshore British colonies, Russia, and others (periphery). In most cases, the crises were followed by a contraction in economic activity, unemployment, and bankruptcies of firms and banks. Noted episodes included the debt crisis that took place after the French–Prussian War, the long recession from 1873 to 1896, the Baring crisis of the 1890s, and the panic of 1907. Earlier crises in the nineteenth century were the 1825–1826 crises in London and the crises of 1837 and 1857 in the United States.[2]

THE INTERWAR YEARS

The sophisticated and financially interconnected world that preceded 1914 came to an abrupt and tragic end with the outbreak of World War I.

The war interrupted the process of economic integration of labor and financial markets across countries (with its benefits and costs) that characterized the first wave of globalization. After the war, the main European empires collapsed: the Romanov dynasty after the Russian Revolution of 1917, the Ottoman Empire, the Austro–Hungarian Empire of the Habsburg monarchy, and the Kaiser in Germany (Solimano 1991, 2010a).

The 1920s and 1930s were very unstable decades. This was a period of deglobalization, high inflation, exchange rate volatility, disintegration of capital markets, financial crisis, depression, and political turbulence. In the early 1920s, the monetization of big fiscal deficits in Austria, Hungary, Germany, and Poland led to high and explosive inflation along with massive depreciations of the domestic currency. Recomposing a stable economic and geopolitical equilibrium proved to be exceedingly complicated.

War reparations, imposed against Germany by the Treaty of Versailles and denounced in 1919 by John Maynard Keynes in his book *The Economic Consequences of Peace,* severely injured the Weimar Republic and paved the way for the rise of Nazism by fostering national resentment. In most European countries, workers' movements engaged in distributive conflicts with rich economic elites who did not want to lose their economic privileges. In this socioeconomic and international context, the margin for adopting coherent macro policies was rapidly eroding. The restoration of the economic order of the *belle époque* (period before 1914) was virtually impossible after major shocks such as the stock market crash of 1929, the Great Depression, and the massive bank failures of the early 1930s.

THE BRETTON WOODS SYSTEM OF 1945–1971/1973

After World War II, new institutions were needed at domestic and international levels to avoid further self-destruction of capitalism and to support economic reconstruction in Europe and decolonization and development in the periphery of the world economy. For that purpose, the British and Americans agreed to the creation of the United Nations to preserve international peace and the Bretton Woods Institutions formed by the IMF and the International Bank for Reconstruction and Development (the World Bank) to ensure global economic stability and development. The IMF received the mandate to provide financing and policy assistance for an orderly resolution of balance-of-payments imbalances of deficit and surplus countries. In turn, the World Bank was to support capital formation (initially) in Europe and in developing countries. Both institutions were located in Washington, DC, close to the US Department of the Treasury.

At the domestic level, the emerging system of regulated capitalism in the United States and Europe rested on four main pillars: (1) active macroeconomic policies designed to dampen the business cycle and ensure full employment; (2) the welfare state (less so in the United States) aimed at providing universal social protection and access to education, health, housing, and pensions to the majority of the population; (3) controlled private capital markets at national and international levels under a system of fixed exchange rates; and (4) a reasonable balance of power between organizations representing the interests of capital and labor unions.

The period between 1950 and 1973 saw steady growth and moderate inflation and came along with a low frequency of financial crisis, high employment, economic security, and reasonable social peace. This era has been called the "golden age of capitalism" or "age of shared prosperity."

NEOLIBERAL GLOBALIZATION

In the late 1960s and early 1970s, the post-World War II consensus of full employment, control of capital flows, the welfare state, and balanced relations between capital and labor started to show signs of exhaustion. Keynesianism was on the retreat, whereas monetarism and neoliberalism were on the rise. Through their writings and/or personally, Milton Friedman and Friedrich Hayek convinced key political leaders such as Margaret Thatcher, Ronald Reagan, and Augusto Pinochet that the way to progress was based on free markets, deregulation, privatization, and international integration. In the United States and United Kingdom, "shared prosperity" between capital and labor had to be sacrificed for the needs of neoliberalism. To enable this, the power and influence of labor unions had to be abridged and capital strengthened. In the case of Pinochet, democracy was sacrificed in the name of the free market and to repress social movements and left-wing parties.

Major changes took place in the international monetary system during the 1970s. A key turning point in the shift from a world of fixed exchange rates to a system of flexible exchange rates among main currencies was the abandonment of the free convertibility of the US dollar to gold in 1971. The exit from the "dollar window" was not smooth, and the two oil shocks of 1973 and 1979 further complicated the transition to an orderly system of flexible exchange rates.

The world economy became much more open to capital movement and trade than in any previous decade since the belle époque. Global capital markets expanded further with the reduction of capital controls and, quite significantly, the collapse of communism in the late 1980s and early 1990s and the active promotion of free market economics by the US government, the World Bank, the IMF, and mainstream academia.

A distinctive feature of the second wave of globalization has been the high frequency of financial crises that involved debt defaults and debt rescheduling. This was a period of a number of financial and political crises around the globe: the debt crisis of Latin America in the 1980s that affected Mexico, Brazil, Chile, Argentina, Peru, and other countries in the region and the debt problems of the Philippines and Turkey in the 1980s. At the same time, financial problems were also present in advanced capitalist countries: in the United States, there were some 1,400 savings and loans institution and 1,300 commercial bank failures between 1984 and 1991 (Reinhart and Rogoff 2009). In October 1987, a precipitous decline in the US stock market resembled the infamous stock market crash of October 1929, and in the Far East, significant banking problems emerged in Japan between 1989 and 1990.

Europe was not shielded from instability either. Scandinavian countries, for example, had problems with their banks in the early 1990s, and the Exchange Rate Mechanism suffered severe strain in 1992 and 1993 when the Bank of England had to let the sterling depreciate in the face of insurmountable speculation against the currency, a move that also affected the Italian lira, the French franc, and other European currencies.

In Mexico, a currency crisis erupted before the presidential election of 1994 that was contained through a mega-loan (by the standards of the time) of $50 billion provided by the US government.[3] In 1997, the crisis spread to Korea, Thailand, Indonesia, and other countries of the region that suffered currency crises, financial turbulence, and recession in what was known as the East Asian financial crisis. In turn, post–Soviet Russia underwent a sharp depreciation of the ruble and a banking crisis in 1998. In the same year, the Long-Term Capital Management Fund in the United States, despite having some Nobel laureates on their advisory staff, failed.

In Ecuador, a full-blown banking and currency crisis developed in 1999 that led in early 2000 to the replacement of the national currency, the sucre, by the US dollar as the legal tender in a bold move aimed at arresting explosive monetary instability.[4] In 2001 and 2002, Argentina was affected by severe financial and macroeconomic crises when the country abandoned a ten-year-old currency board that had established a one-to-one parity between the Argentinean peso and the US dollar. To cope with the crisis, the government expropriated deposits in failed banks—an action known as the *corralito*. Another serious macrofinancial crisis erupted in Turkey in 2000 and 2001 that was accompanied by large fiscal deficits, a fragile banking system, high inflation, and unstable exchange rates (Yeldan 2002).

In the mid-to-late 1990s, the US economy experienced a rapid increase in the share price of technology firms—the "dot-com bubble"—that eventually burst in 2000. To jump-start the economy, the Federal Reserve lowered interest rates, which contributed to creating a new price bubble, this time in the real estate market.

The continued expansion of complex financial instruments (derivatives, debt equity swaps, collateralized debt obligations) littered the portfolios of banks and other financial intermediaries with toxic assets and further complicated the management of the 2008–2009 crisis—which turned out to be the worst crisis since the early 1930s. What took place in the United States also had serious reverberations in Europe, which has suffered severe stagnation and economic contraction in the countries most affected by the crisis for half a decade. Average unemployment rates have been more than 25 percent of the labor force in Spain and Greece, while at the same time youth unemployment has climbed to 55 percent.

INTERPRETING THE FINANCIAL CRISIS EXPERIENCE

From a historical perspective, the series of financial crises over the last quarter century have resembled both the episodes of the first wave of globalization (ca. 1870–1914) and the financial turbulence of the late 1920s and early 1930s.

It is worth noting that the two spells of globalization—the late nineteenth and early twentieth and late twentieth and early twenty-first centuries, respectively—displayed apparently stable macroeconomic conditions of low inflation and steady growth. However, these macroeconomic outcomes did not sufficiently guarantee financial stability during these two eras.

Complacency with tranquil macroeconomic conditions and neglect of incubating financial crises were behind the crash of 2008–2009. Advanced capitalist countries largely underestimated the possibility of financial crises that had been so frequent in developing countries and emerging economies. The prevailing view among central banks, finance ministers, and mainstream macroeconomists was that the global economy was enjoying a "Great Moderation." Many papers were written in the 1990s and 2000s that claimed that we were living in a new state of macroeconomic stability thanks to the wisdom and prudence of central banks and finance ministers. Reality showed, however, the mystifying nature of those claims.

As mentioned before, the instability of the 1920s and 1930s is also relevant for understanding the recent spate of crises. The unchecked financial speculation of the second half of the 1920s preceded the wave of bank failures of the early 1930s; likewise, the financial speculation of the early and mid-2000s preceded the financial crash of 2008–2009. In turn, wild trajectories in asset prices were present both in the roaring 1920s and in the many crises of the 1990s and 2000s.

Financial crises develop under a certain sociopolitical context. The pre-1914 social contract was dominated by capital—an alliance of big banks and big corporations that was so vividly described by authors such as Hobson (1902) and Hilferding (1910). In contrast, labor unions were relatively weak, and social legislation was light. Nearly a century later, during the neoliberal era of the late twentieth century, the social contract was also strongly biased in favor of capital, particularly the financial capital that dominated the interests of industry, workers, and the middle class.

In the 1970s, conservatives primarily in the United Kingdom and United States blamed strong labor unions and accommodative macro policies for their state of stagflation and relative economic decay. In contrast, in the 2000s, the problem was that capital was too strong. After two decades of deregulation, privatization, and financialization that led to high profits for capital owners and financial speculators, the deregulation frenzy proved to be highly destabilizing for the economy and society as a whole.

In the 1920s and 1930s, achieving a stable socioeconomic equilibrium proved to be very difficult. Labor unions and communist parties battled fascism and Nazism in Europe, engendering social conflict and, along with the Great Depression of the early 1930s, this contributed to change the course of economic policies away from internationalism towards protectionism. In the 2010s, the rise of extremist right-wing political parties again showed that severe economic crises, high unemployment, and economic insecurity can engender intolerant and aggressive social responses against immigrants and the integrationist framework of the European Union.

REGULARITIES IN FINANCIAL CRISIS[5]

The varieties of financial crises I have reviewed herein provide greater context and added depth for studying the factors that cause financial crises and for discussing possible ways of averting them. Some common patterns and regularities can be highlighted:

1. Crises need to be viewed in historical and systemic terms. They are manifestations of some fundamental malfunctioning of the economic system and, indirectly, of the institutional and political framework surrounding it. The historical record shows that crises are more common in periods of integrated capital markets, high corporate power, and weak regulation of financial markets.
2. There is a wide variety of "igniting factor(s)" of financial crises such as new innovations, railway development, urbanization, the end of war, and the discovery of valuable natural resources (nineteenth and early twentieth centuries). In the neoliberal era (late twentieth and early twenty-first centuries), relevant igniting factors include financial liberalization, privatization, and information technology breakthroughs.
3. Financial crises can occur under a broad variety of monetary and exchange rate regimes. The financial crises of the first wave of globalization developed under the gold standard; the financial crises in the second wave of globalization developed under flexible exchange rates in a fiat money system and under a monetary union (the euro area). In emerging economies and developing countries, financial crises have taken place under fixed exchange rates, currency boards, and adjustable pegs. Moreover, several financial crises occurred under situations of large fiscal imbalances, whereas other crises stemmed from imbalances in the private sector rather than in the public sector.
4. Economic cycles tend to be amplified when accompanied by unsustainable increases in credit and debt, making the burst after a boom more severe and the recovery more protracted. Fisher (1933) underscored this point.[6]
5. Central banks and regulators often have a hard time detecting a bubble in asset prices and then acting accordingly. However, refraining to intervene during the development of a price bubble can prolong an unsustainable cycle and make it more difficult from which to recover when bubbles prickle.

6. The political economy of financial crises suggests that in elite-dominated capitalism, cozy relations often develop among politicians, public policy officials, and bankers, and the interests of financial elites can receive undue importance relative to the interest of depositors, savers, and the population at large that bear most of the costs of financial crises. In the boom phase of the cycle, financial elites push for deregulation, whereas in the crash phase they ask for generous rescue packages.

7. Debt defaults and forced rescheduling through history have been common features in the aftermath of financial crashes. They are often adopted after governments attempt to generate resource surpluses to serve external debts and can come at high social costs in terms of growth and employment losses and cuts in real wages and social benefits.

THE DISTURBING STATE OF ECONOMIC SCIENCE

Economic and financial crises present important challenges for neoclassical economic theory. In this paradigm, the economy is viewed as a set of interlocking markets with effective mechanisms, i.e., prices, for correcting disequilibria. The underlying assumption is that individuals are "rational" and can weigh the benefits and costs of their decisions. The world is seen as an arena of optimal choices, rational expectations, and efficient financial markets. In contrast, crises can show how the destructive forces of myopia, short horizons, manias, manipulative behavior, and other patterns of irrational human behavior startlingly depart from the ideal of self-correcting markets as often articulated in mainstream economics textbooks.

In recent decades, economists have become very influential in formulating policy, although in several parts of the world the economic record of their advice in terms of growth, equality, and financial stability is far from encouraging. Economics has become a field increasingly detached from reality—a dry subject obsessed with "formalization," such as the use of mathematic formulas and models to understand complex social phenomena. Formal models are prized over realism, relevance, and common sense. In a sign of the times, teaching and research in economics have sharply departed from the old classic traditions of situating economic analysis in its proper historical, institutional, and political contexts. Decontextualization may lead to serious mistakes in policy making and induce researchers to spend their time and talent on issues of lesser interest and relevance.

Economists who rationalize individualism and greed and who promote narrow concepts of rationality seem very odd to common people. Unfortunately, this is the standard training economists have been receiving in the last thirty years or so from economics departments at universities in the United States. This tendency has also grown rapidly in Europe, the Organization for Economic Cooperation and Development, and a score of developing countries.

An example along these lines is that, despite the ample historical and current evidence of irrationality in the behavior of financial markets and the devastating effects of financial crises, economists and financial theorists since the 1970s have looked for ways to demonstrate that financial markets are, essentially, efficient mechanisms for allocating savings for productive uses and effective tools for properly pricing risk.[7,8]

The quest to demonstrate the inherent rationality of financial markets represented a strong departure from the views and writings of Keynes, who himself was both a successful participant in the stock market and a privileged witness and actor of the volatile and crisis-prone decades of the 1920s and 1930s. Those real-world experiences strongly shaped his views and led him to stress the role of "animal spirits" and volatile expectations in economic processes rather than optimal pecuniary calculation. Keynes made the analogy of the stock markets with a casino and recommended *not* entrusting financial markets with the delicate task of guiding intertemporal resource allocation in the economy.

THE IMF

Key actors in the financial drama of recent years were the IMF and central banks. The failure of the IMF to anticipate the 2008–2009 financial crisis and enforce its surveillance mandate on large member countries running sizeable fiscal imbalances and with excessive bank leverage (such as the United States and the United Kingdom) point to a discouraging role of the IMF in the run up to the crisis. In particular, the IMF refrained from explicitly warning that a financial crisis was a real possibility in those economies. In addition, its role in imposing very costly austerity programs on medium-sized economies such as Greece, Spain, Portugal, and Ireland has further affected the credibility and public appreciation of the institution. The IMF should revise its conceptual framework—which underestimates the economy-wide risks of financial vulnerability—to focus more on traditional macroeconomic aggregates. Moreover, the IMF is (rightly) perceived as complacent when it comes to fiscal imbalance runs in large and powerful countries but rough and uncompromising with small (powerless) and medium-sized economies when they have to adopt adjustment programs.

In the meantime, the IMF research department has begun questioning what may have gone wrong with the type of macroeconomics it practiced.[9] Furthermore, the IMF's Independent Evaluation Office, which reports to the board of directors and not directly to management, has acknowledged in various reports the lack of diversity in conceptual approaches and a deeply ingrained in-house corporate culture largely unwilling to consider alternative approaches in macroeconomics.[10] The fact that unregulated market economies are prone to experience financial crises is rarely mentioned explicitly in IMF reports. These crises are considered more as outside events rather than endogenous outcomes of economies with large macro imbalances and insufficiently regulated financial systems.

CENTRAL BANKS

Several central banks have recently adopted the view—reflected in their formal chart of objectives—that the control of inflation in the prices of goods and services (but *not* inflation of asset prices) is their only mandate other than guaranteeing normal internal and external payments. Traditionally, important targets such as contributing to full employment and real exchange rate stability have either been excluded from their list of mandates or considered as secondary in importance.

Central bank policy formulation is increasingly informed by stochastic dynamic general equilibrium (DSGE) models. This family of empirical macro models is based on the assumptions of optimizing and forward-looking agents, rational expectations, and market clearing.[11] Common sense and economic realities would suggest that models resting on these premises will hardly be the most appropriate analytical and empirical tools for analyzing financial cycles of destabilization and crises and for proposing appropriate policies for restoring stability and growth. The DSGE strategy of modeling and empirical calibration has serious drawbacks. First, it is apparent that these models may be more useful (if at all) for simulating incremental policy changes and small shocks than they would be for exploring the causes and consequences of boom-and-bust cycles, recessions, and financial crises, which create significant disturbances when the whole economy, or large markets therein, is out of equilibrium. Second, it is unclear how well these models deal with volatile expectations, herding effects, large departures of asset prices from fundamentals, and other disequilibrium paths. Third, an additional shortcoming of this family of models is its strong built-in tendency to quickly restore equilibrium in the wake of large shocks.

CONCLUDING REMARKS

Financial crises need to be understood in a historical perspective and in systemic terms rather than as isolated episodes resulting from unchecked greed by economic agents or because of massive mistakes of economic calculation by financial participants in the market, albeit these elements have also been present. Historically, financial crises have occurred more frequently during periods of unregulated capitalism, both in its liberal and neoliberal varieties of the last 200 years. In contrast, financial crises with international propagation effects were virtually absent in the era of regulated capitalism (from the early 1950s to the early 1970s).

The notion that we were living in an era of "Great Moderation" was promoted by mainstream macroeconomists and policy officials of advanced economies in the 1990s and 2000s. However, the 2008–2009 crisis showed that low inflation and relatively steady growth were not sufficient conditions for guaranteeing financial stability and ensuring lasting prosperity, a situation also present in the first wave of globalization of the late nineteenth century. In turn, at the level of financial sector policy, the influence of the efficient market hypothesis was significant in the United States, the United Kingdom, and in other nations. In hindsight, it is clear that this doctrine encouraged complacency with financial market excesses such as high leverage, the proliferation of complex financial instruments, and the growing indebtedness of families, firms, and government—all factors that helped to trigger the financial crisis.

The recent episodes of irrationalities and volatility of financial markets have cast serious doubts on the validity and relevance of the efficient market hypothesis. A sensible macrofinancial research agenda in the years ahead should focus on better understanding the role played by financial accelerators, changes in expectations, bounded rationality, and herd behavior in propagating financial shocks and then reverting to financial distress and recession. We also need to know more about the behavior of hedge funds and derivatives and the nature of the political connections between large financial intermediaries and government.

The 2008–2009 crisis also highlights the urgent need for revising the dominant ways of conducting research, teaching, and offering policy advice by economists. Policy makers are informed by a profession that holds an idealized view of markets, omniscient consumers and producers, and stable expectations that bear little resemblance to the real world. No wonder serious policy mistakes are made and costly crises erupt that affect the lives of millions.

This chapter also highlights the serious conceptual and operational flaws of two key institutions in charge of monetary and financial stability—the IMF and central banks—and highlights the need for more democratic control of the latter and for curbing the power of the former in dictating the terms of austerity programs around the world.

Repeated bailouts of commercial banks and large financial intermediaries have reduced the legitimacy of financial capitalism, increasingly viewed as a system in which profits are privatized in booming years and losses are socialized during crises. This illegitimacy crisis is also relevant to recent austerity programs in peripheral Europe and in the past to Latin America and other continents in which the cost of adjustment is mostly borne by workers, the middle class, public sector employees, youth, and the elderly, while shielding rich economic elites from the effects of austerity imposed by governments and international organizations that represent the interests of rich creditors.

NOTES

Comments by Ramiro Albrieu, Martín Rapetti, Mario Damill, and Guillermo Rozenwurcel on an earlier draft are appreciated.

1. See, for example, Frenkel and Rapetti (2009).

2. There is a vast literature on this period: for example, Musson (1959), Marichal (1989), Bordo and Meissner (2005), Brunner and Carr (2007), Reinhart and Rogoff (2009), Newbold (1932), and Solimano (2014).

3. The exchange rate and financial crises in Mexico were also accompanied by political instability. Early in 1994, there was the Zapatista uprising in the south of the country, and in March of that year Luis Donaldo Colosio, the presidential candidate of the PRI, Partido Revolucionario Institucional, was assassinated under circumstances that remain unclear.

4. Constitutionally elected President Jamil Mahuad, who officially announced the dollarization in 1999, was toppled in January 2000 by a conspiracy of army generals who were assisted by a radicalized indigenous movement. See Beckerman and Solimano (2002).

5. This section draws from Solimano (2014).

6. For recent treatments of the role of debt in economic cycles, see Reinert (2012).

7. The efficient markets hypothesis became the theoretical justification for the deregulation and development of national and global capital markets in the 1970s and 1980s. It posits that in buying and selling assets, investors and market participants use all relevant information—the random walk hypothesis for asset prices—in making their financial decisions. In that sense these decisions are "rational."

The theory could be somewhat relevant for an individual investor, but applying it for inferring rational outcomes in macro markets is bound to be a largely misguided claim; for expositions and evaluations of the efficient markets hypothesis, see Beechey et al. (2000), Fama (1970), and Samuelson (1965).

8. Alan Greenspan, chairman of the US Federal Reserve between 1987 and 2006, believed in the efficient markets theory and proclaimed, before the 2008 crisis, that financial markets have strong self-equilibrating mechanisms. The massive market failures evidenced since 2007 in advanced capitalist countries of North America and Europe have reduced the credibility of this theory.

9. See, for example, Blanchard et al. (2010).

10. The Independent Evaluation Office has made the point that the IMF's research on macroeconomics and finance before the 2008–2009 crisis largely ignored the work of important scholars such as Hyman Minsky on instability and fragility in financial markets (the author is rarely cited in the IMF's research and policy papers in the years before 2007–2008). See Solimano (2010b).

11. In a concession to realism, these models incorporate in their practical applications (light) Keynesian features such as price stickiness and nominal rigidities of wages and other "frictions."

REFERENCES

Beckerman, P. and Solimano, A. 2002. *Crisis and dollarization in Ecuador*. Washington, DC: World Bank.

Beechey, M., Gruen, D., and Vickrey, J. 2000. "The efficient markets hypothesis: a survey." Reserve Bank of Australia Research Discussion Paper 2001–01. http://www.rba.gov.au/publications/rdp/2000/pdf/rdp2000-01.pdf.

Blanchard, O., Dell'Ariccia, G., and Mauro, P. 2010. "Rethinking macroeconomic policy." International Monetary Fund Staff Position Note SPN/10/03. https://www.imf.org/external/pubs/ft/spn/2010/spn1003.pdf.

Bordo, M. and Meissner, C. 2005. "Financial crises, 1880–1913: the role of foreign currency debt." National Bureau of Economic Research Working Paper 11173. http://www.nber.org/papers/w11173.pdf.

Brunner, R. F. and Carr, S. D. 2007. *The panic of 1907: lessons learned from the market's perfect storm*. Hoboken, NJ: John Wiley & Sons.

Fama, E. 1970. "Efficient capital markets: a review of theory and empirical work." *Journal of Finance* 25(2): 383–417.

Fisher, I. 1933. "The debt-deflation theory of great depressions." *Econometrica* 1(4): 337–357.

Frenkel, R. and Rapetti, M. 2009. "A developing country view of the current global crisis: what should not be forgotten and what should be done." *Cambridge Journal of Economics* 33(4): 685–702.

Hatton, T. G., and Williamson, J. G. 2005. *The age of mass migration. Causes and economic impact.* New York: Oxford University Press.

Hilferding, R. 1910. *Finance capital: a study of the latest phase of capitalist development,* T. Bottomore and P. Kegan, eds. London: Routledge.

Hobson, J. A. 1902. *Imperialism: a study.* New York, NY: James Pott and Co.

Marichal, C. 1989. *A century of debt crises in Latin America: from independence to the Great Depression, 1820–1930.* Princeton, NJ: Princeton University Press.

Musson, A. E. 1959. "The Great Depression in Britain, 1873–1896." *Journal of Economic History* 19(2): 199–228.

Newbold, J. T. W. 1932. "The beginnings of world crisis, 1873–1896." *Economic History* 2(7): 425–551.

Reinert, E. S. 2012. "Mechanisms of financial crises in growth and collapse: Hammurabi, Schumpeter, Perez, and Minsky." The Other Canon Foundation and Tallinn University of Technology Working Papers in Technology Governance and Economic Dynamics 39. http://hum.ttu.ee/wp/paper39.pdf.

Reinhart, C. and Rogoff, K. 2009. *This time is different: eight centuries of financial folly.* Princeton, NJ: Princeton University Press.

Samuelson, P. 1965. "Proof that properly anticipated prices fluctuate randomly." *Industrial Management Review* 6: 41–49.

Solimano, A. 1991. "The economies of Central and Eastern Europe: an historical and international perspective. In *Reforming Central and Eastern European economies: initial results and challenges,* edited by V. Corbo, F. Coricelli, and J. Bossak, 9–23. Washington, DC: World Bank.

Solimano, A. 2010a. *International migration in an age of crises and globalization.* Cambridge, UK: Cambridge University Press.

Solimano, A. 2010b. "Financial IMF research on macro-financial linkages: context, relevance, and diversity of approaches." Paper prepared for the Independent Evaluation Office of the International Monetary Fund. http://www.itf.org.ar/pdf /documentos/79-2011.pdf.

Solimano, A. 2012. *Chile and the neoliberal trap: the post-Pinochet era.* Cambridge, UK: Cambridge University Press.

Solimano, A. 2014. *Elites, crisis and economic democracy.* New York, NY: Oxford University Press.

Yeldan, E. 2002. "Behind the 2000/2001 Turkish crisis: stability, credibility, and governance, for whom? Paper prepared for the Department of Economics, Bilkent University, Ankara, Turkey. http://yeldane.bilkent.edu.tr/Chennai_Yeldan2002 .pdf.

CHAPTER 14

Financial Crises, Institutions, and the Macroeconomy

José María Fanelli

This chapter analyzes the linkages among the macroeconomy, institutions, and financial intermediation in the context of financial crises. A key motivation for the analysis is the question of "perverse" interactions among financial disequilibria, macroeconomic imbalances, and the stability of economic institutions, all of which are typical during crises. These interactions delay the return to normality and, under certain conditions, may even induce irreversible changes. On the financial side, we frequently observe permanent reversions in the process of financial development, whereas on the real side, the probability that the economy is mired in a low-growth trap or long-lasting period of recession increases, as was the case of the "lost decade" in Latin America in the 1980s and Japan in the 1990s. The analysis basically refers to emerging economies, but some aspects are also relevant to advanced countries.

Traditionally, financial analyses tended to focus on the study of efficiency and equilibrium. As a consequence, too little effort was invested in the specification and description of the economic institutions that support market transactions. This made it difficult to analyze systemic instability and conflicts over property rights—phenomena that usually accompany financial crises. The lack of specification of the institutional framework creates a gap between microeconomics and macroeconomics and, in the case of the analysis of crises, makes it necessary to establish sounder macrofoundations for microeconomics (Fanelli and Frenkel 1995; Fanelli 2011).

The approach to these issues has changed substantially in the last two decades thanks to the contributions of institutional analysis and the political economy literature. Institutional economics allows us to define the notion of economic systems more precisely, facilitating the study of disequilibria that originate from systemic failures. Based on the political economy approach, in turn, it is possible to clarify the linkages between conflict and economic decisions and to show the role of institutions as a device for managing conflict and easing cooperation (North 1995; Acemoglu 2008).

One important purpose of this chapter is to show that the institutional and political economy literature can help us to better understand financial crises for two reasons: first, financial crises involve conflicts over property rights and changes in income and wealth distribution that have the potential to generate systemic instability; second, crises undermine the credibility of economic institutions and therefore create dysfunctionalities that can, in turn, give rise to systemic coordination failures.

Our analytical framework includes contributions from finance, institutional economics, macroeconomics, and political economy. The first section discusses the concept of the economic system. The approach is much more abstract than the rest of the chapter and synthesizes the issues that are discussed in more detail in Fanelli (2012). The main purpose is to show the connections between institutions and organizations and the way in which they come together to form an economic system. We will use the notion of economic systems to analyze why crises create systemic dysfunctionalities. The concepts are general and can be applied to other dimensions in addition to the financial system. The second section examines the anatomy and functions of financial intermediation, and the third presents financial dysfunctions from a systemic perspective and explores the linkages among financial intermediation, property rights, and financial instability. The chapter ends with a summary of the main conclusions.

ECONOMIC SYSTEMS AND CRISES

In this section, we discuss a notion of economic systems that sets institutions and organizations at center stage and is suitable for analyzing the systemic dysfunctions associated with financial crises. An important purpose is to show the linkages among cooperation, conflict, coordination, and institutions and the way in which such linkages are formed, thus enabling the economic system to perform its functions. Based on this analysis, we will be able to define what "systemic dysfunction" means. For the sake of brevity we will use some diagrams.[1]

The two basic restrictions that economic agents face are scarcity and uncertainty. To deal with these restrictions agents specialize and cooperate in different tasks. Cooperation, however, gives rise to conflicts that concern just how much effort should be invested and the way in which benefits will be shared. Thus, although cooperation can help increase welfare, it may also increase costs by introducing a new type of risk associated with strategic uncertainty: How will the other party behave? The diagram in figure 14.1 will be useful in organizing our arguments.

Cooperation must be organized, and conflicts may arise during the process that could make bargaining become necessary (see figure 14.1). To narrow uncertainty and the costs of negotiating, it is necessary to establish rules aimed at creating restrictions and incentives that generate predictable behavioral routines (Milgrom and Roberts 1992). Such rules are embodied in institutional frameworks that comprise codes, laws, regulations, and resolutions structured in hierarchies (see Ostrom 2007). A key purpose of this framework is to provide models for structuring and managing organizations, which are the "places" where specialized agents cooperate and use society's resources. The basic organizational models are hierarchies, markets, and households (see Gibbons 2000).

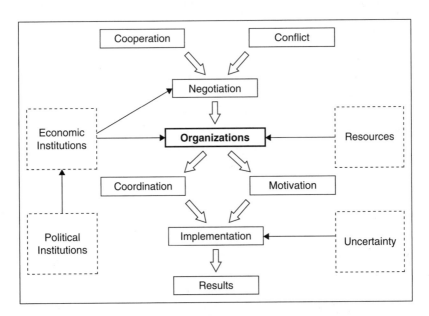

Figure 14.1 Cooperation, conflict, and organizations. *Source:* **Fanelli (2012).**

Whereas some institutions develop spontaneously, modern institutional frameworks emerge from negotiation processes regulated by political institutions that are senior to economic institutions (Scartascini et al. 2010). The establishment of an institutional framework may require the investment of a large amount of resources, but the fixed costs incurred can easily be amortized: the same set of rules can be used repeatedly to coordinate a large set of activities. The consumption of the services provided by the rule does not create rivalry: if a firm uses the law of corporations to establish itself, this does not prevent another organization from also using the same law. Of course, this creates an incentive problem (free riding): the incentives to invest in efforts to develop the institutional framework will be weak if agents can use them without paying the costs. This is why citizens must pay taxes and vote, whereas foreigners are excluded from enjoying certain rights.

As indicated in figure 14.1, for cooperation to be feasible, the rules of the game should be able to coordinate (plan activities, supply information) and provide incentives for agents to behave as expected in relation to cooperative activities. Still, in a stochastic world, there will be uncertainty in regard to the results, and uncertainty may or may not take the form of risk (see Knight 1921).

Organizations do not exist in isolation: the division of labor binds them, generating complementarities. Therefore, an additional problem is achieving the coordination of activities between organizations that are managed independently. To what extent can we expect decisions to be made in a decentralized manner by various individuals and organizations that lead to optimal results? To tackle this problem, the institutional framework should not only provide organizational models for specific activities but also for collective action aimed at solving systemic problems, such as low-growth traps, unemployment, and macroeconomic instability. The organizational models that are required in this case are economic policy regimes and regulatory bodies that specialize in solving failures concerning coordination and motivation that go beyond the scope of a microeconomic organization's decisions.

Based on what has been discussed previously, we can now define an economic system as a structure of organizations whose purpose is to facilitate the use of resources and the tasks of cooperation and conflict management that are inherent to economic activities. These organizations are brought together through an institutional framework that seeks to ensure the functionality of the organizations and the economic system as a whole.

A crisis, in turn, can be defined as a postshock situation in which the institutional framework and existing organizations cannot ensure that the system will continue to perform its functions: to enable cooperation and to handle conflicts in a cost-effective way.

Based on these definitions and figure 14.1, the anatomy of a crisis could be synthesized as follows:

1. A shock occurs and, as a consequence, strategic uncertainty is augmented because the institutional and organizational models in use to coordinate, motivate, and implement decisions and actions that can cushion the consequences of the shock and restore equilibrium are not effective. The dysfunctions occur both within and between organizations, generating spillover effects (externalities).

2. Coordination failures and spillovers generate systemic instability. Among the most common sources of such instability are as follows:
   - Job losses and increased unemployment that negatively affect aggregate demand and the level of conflict in labor relations.
   - Unforeseen changes in the agents' balance sheets that result in excessive leverage and the increased likelihood of substantial losses of income and wealth.
   - Deterioration in the expectation of appropriability of the benefits of investment and increase the risk of borrowing, which retracts investment and durable consumption.
   - Deterioration in the functionality of organizations: the lack of funding liquidity and the fall in the number of transactions that eventually result in the disappearance of some markets, raising idle capacity.

3. To organize cooperation activities and resolve disputes under the new conditions, the agents are forced to resort to negotiation beyond routine.

4. Systemic instability and conflicts undermine the credibility of existing institutions because of the following:
   - The agents affected by the crisis push for changes in the rules of the game to mitigate the undesirable effects on their jobs, income, and balance sheets.
   - Politicians perceive that something should be done to restore the functionality of the system. The government makes changes in the policy regime and regulations designed to disable the factors that are causing systemic instability and conflicts.

5. The agents perceive that there is likely to be "unusual" income and wealth transfers associated with changes in the rules of the game and take such a

fact into account when making a decision; the agents adopt strategies that seek to minimize risks, such as increasing demand for liquidity and safe assets with the resulting depression of aggregate demand.

6. The crisis invades the sphere of politics. In addition to single-exit strategies, agents resort to voice and collective action to change institutions. Because the ability for collective action depends on the details of the political situation and the ability of institutions to channel claims and negotiations, the outcomes in relation to changing rules and wealth transfers are difficult to predict, and strategic uncertainty is exacerbated.

7. Because the crisis affects institutions and institutional change shows path dependency (Aoki 2001; Bodie and Merton 2005), the crisis has nonergodic effects (i.e., induces structural changes). Empirically, the effects are expressed as irreversible changes in the stocks of wealth and their distribution.

In short, many of the deleterious consequences of crises originate from the fact that when systemic dysfunctionalities occur, agents foresee that the rules will change, producing lasting effects on their wealth, and act accordingly to hedge that risk. The essential factor that causes the changes in the pattern of crisis behavior vis-à-vis normal circumstances is that existing rules in a crisis environment are not taken for granted, and hence, the role of institutions concerning the coordination and motivation of agents' behavior weakens, and strategic uncertainty increases. When the institutions that regulate financial intermediation are not credible, the goal of using resources efficiently tends to be displaced by the goal of protecting wealth and income. This is only natural if financial property rights are perceived to be shaky and unemployment is rising. We must consider that the level of strategic uncertainty can be very high in a context in which the characteristics of the changes in the rules of the game depend on political negotiations among groups with different and heterogeneous means for achieving their political goals and/or protecting their economic interests.

INSTITUTIONS, ORGANIZATIONS, AND THE FUNCTIONS OF FINANCIAL INTERMEDIATION

Based on the conceptual framework presented in the previous section, we will now discuss the linkages between institutions and financial crises.

The separation of ownership from control over an asset is a necessary condition for financial transactions to take place. In the case of a loan, for example, the creditor renounces control of the asset in favor of the debtor. Consequently, financial transactions can give rise to high transaction costs associated with agency problems. The costs are associated not only with designing an appropriate contract but also with ex-post negotiations that will be a function of the efficiency of systemic factors, such as the efficiency of the courts, corruption, and so on. In addition, financial transactions are intensive in the use of information. On the one hand, gathering and processing information can be very costly; on the other hand, information has characteristics of a public good that can distort the incentives to produce it, giving rise to severe market failures. Countries with high macro volatility experience an additional problem: information becomes obsolete quickly, and the associated risks may be difficult to manage.

Financial activities involve complicated agency problems and use information intensively. Hence, financial intermediation is conducted by a large number of organizations that are specialized in dealing with agency and information issues. Their network ranges from the issuers of financial instruments to investors who demand them and a large number of organizations responsible for designing the contracts and identifying the parties, securing payments, and enforcing regulations. Figure 14.2 shows the anatomy and functions of financial intermediation.

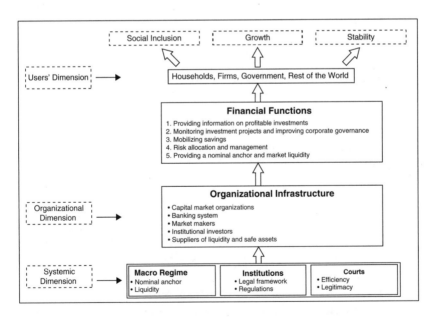

Figure 14.2 Anatomy and functions of financial intermediation.

The rectangle labeled "financial functions," appearing at the center of the figure, shows the role of the financial system, which, according to Levine (2004), can be grouped into five categories:

1. Providing information on profitable investments
2. Monitoring investment projects and improving corporate governance
3. Mobilizing savings
4. Risk allocation and management
5. Providing a nominal anchor and market liquidity

In essence, the first three categories refer to the intermediation process between savings and investment; the last two refer to the management of risk and liquidity.

The arrows at the top of figure 14.2 indicate that these functions are relevant to three goals that are valuable to users and society: social inclusion, economic growth, and macroeconomic stability. The financial system creates value because it helps to improve the performance of the economic system in these three aspects. The link between financial intermediation and stability was studied mainly by macroeconomists who were interested in the role of the financial system as a provider of liquidity and nominal anchor for contracts (Keynes 1936; Gurley and Shaw 1960; Patinkin 1965; Tirole 2010), as well as a source of distortions and crises (Keynes 1936; Minsky 1975; Rajan 2005). The influence of the financial system on growth has been analyzed primarily by researchers interested in developing economies (McKinnon 1973; Shaw 1973; Levine 2004). The analysis of the impact of financial intermediation on social inclusion is more recent (see Duflo 2011).

As shown in figure 14.2, the elements involved in the intermediation process can be studied based on three dimensions: user, organizational, and systemic.

THE USERS' DIMENSION

The ultimate users of financial services are firms, households, different tiers of the government, and the rest of the world. To be sure, to analyze specific issues, users can be classified in different ways, as is the case with demographics that emphasize the financial relationship among generations. These agents may act as demanders and suppliers of financial assets, and their balance sheets will show asset/liability structures with different characteristics with regard to liquidity, credit risk, or currency risk. The role of the financial system is to design and supply a set of useful instruments that can satisfy the preferences of these users in the cheapest way; i.e., the financial system must minimize transaction costs while efficiently managing the risks involved.

ORGANIZATIONAL DIMENSION

If users conducted financial transactions individually, the transaction and information costs would be high. Organizations specialized in financial transactions can exploit scale and scope economies as well as develop new technologies and increasingly efficient organizational schemes. To reflect this, we have drawn a rectangle that represents the organizational "infrastructure" that is necessary to facilitate transactions in financial markets. The organizations and actors involved in the infrastructure are highly specialized, and their activities are complementary. However, because decision making is largely decentralized, coordination problems arise. The "invisible hand" of the market can only partially solve these problems given the pervasive presence of agency problems and the fact that the activity is information-intensive and information has public good characteristics. To overcome the deficiencies associated with market failures, a large part of financial intermediation activities are organized via hierarchies rather than markets. In addition, both markets and hierarchical organizations are tightly regulated. Markets, organizations, and regulatory institutions make up the financial system. Following Milgrom and Roberts (1992), financial transaction costs can be defined as the costs incurred by society to make the financial system work.

The transaction costs incurred by organizations operating as financial intermediaries absorb resources that must be subtracted from other productive activities. This is true even when transactions are made via markets: market makers, for example, must finance their stocks of financial assets and bear important risks. Indeed, the very fact that resources are allocated to fund financial intermediation indicates that such intermediation creates value. Although no "new" good is created when a transaction is made, value arises from the fact that mutual benefits of trade that would have otherwise gone unexploited are actually realized. Thus, the financial system's main task is to create value by reducing transaction costs, and the organizations that act as intermediaries do so by exploiting two sources of cost reduction: specialization in the services they provide and economies of scale and scope. Intermediary organizations can obtain low-cost information by exploiting economies of scale in information research and processing. These organizations also have comparative advantages in monitoring the use of funds and evaluating the quality of corporate governance. They also play a key role in mobilizing and agglomerating the resources of small savers. For example, mutual funds give agents access to well-diversified portfolios without losing liquidity.

Economies of scale can dramatically reduce the average cost of financial services by reducing the incidence of fixed costs, lowering the costs of learning, and taking advantage of the positive external economies generated in interactions among specialized agents. The reduction in transaction costs in the capital markets typically takes the form of lower margins between buying and selling prices of assets and lower charges for the brokerage and custody of securities. In the banking system, cost reductions take the form of decreases in the spread between borrowing and lending rates and lower fees on transactions. In emerging countries, a key failure is the lack of scale, which increases fixed costs and constrains learning and the accumulation of expertise.

There is no unique relationship between financial functions and the organizations responsible for carrying them out. The characteristics of the latter are highly dependent on the institutional context within which transactions take place. For example, some systems are based on financial markets and others on banks. In addition, organizational structures are constantly evolving. Financial intermediation is a highly dynamic activity regarding learning and innovation. Likewise, changes in the institutional framework and the real economy generate new financial demands.

Even though financial organizations compete in several segments in which they produce services that are close substitutes, it is also true that the different segments of the financial system meet operational functions that complement one another and form networks. Also, these organizations contribute to good corporate governance by monitoring investment projects and contract enforcement, both of which are crucial for avoiding coordination failures. To be sure, the advantages of scale and increasing returns have a dark side: they can generate structures in which some players have market power.

One characteristic feature of weak financial systems is the underdevelopment of certain organizations that occupy central places in the network of complementary financial activities, such as market makers, institutional investors, insurance firms, and providers of liquid and safe assets.

When markets are small and illiquid, the information that prices provide is unreliable; the volatility of asset values is greater and increases the probability that disequilibria will give rise to strong, destabilizing spillover effects. Under such circumstances, very negative interactions between market liquidity and funding liquidity often occur.

Market makers are a source of positive externalities because they maintain and expand market liquidity. In times of high volatility this function deteriorates because market makers are reluctant to operate with a large stock of assets because of the high risk involved. The more volatile the economy, the greater the risk of acting as a market maker; therefore, the return required to engage in the activity is higher. Volatility thus becomes a cause of increased transaction costs to the extent that it induces reductions in the scale of operation of the market makers.

Institutional investors have the central role of structuring funds that are adapted to the users' demands with regard to return, risk, liquidity, and duration. As the activities of institutional investors increase the number of transactions, these investors contribute to increasing market liquidity and improving the ability of market prices to reveal the characteristics of the economy, enhancing the markets' informational efficiency. When institutional investors are weak, as is frequently the case in emerging economies, it is typically a consequence of the poor development of some segments of the financial system, such as banks or insurance companies. Additionally, it may be difficult to structure portfolios efficiently because of the lack of diversity, scale, and liquidity in equity markets and because of the underdevelopment of the derivatives markets, both of which can keep investors from achieving a reasonable degree of diversification in their portfolios.

The 2008–2009 financial crisis in the developed world highlighted the importance of the financial organizations that issue safe assets. This activity is mainly carried out by the government through the central bank and the issuance of treasury instruments. Safe assets have two critical functions. The first is to inform the market what the risk-free interest rate is, which "anchors" the structure of interest rates. The second is to provide papers with high market liquidity. These papers are necessary for structuring portfolios with certain characteristics in the case of institutional investors. The lack of safe assets can seriously affect financial stability and generate runs against the local currency.

The downgrade of the sovereign debt of several governments that resulted from the global crisis created a shortage of safe assets, which can be used as a way of hedging against systemic risk. Thus, in countries with systemic risk, such as the case of Spain in the post-2008 period, the flight to quality not only took the form of an increase in the demand for safe assets but also that of a capital outflow. This connection between the lack of safe assets and capital outflows was already well-known in emerging countries where, in the 1990s for example, flight to quality took the form of a run on the banks, falling prices of risky assets, and capital flight. In Argentina, where credibility is a structural problem, a good proportion of the financial portfolios accounted for dollar bills, deposits in foreign banks, and US Treasury bonds. The demand for these assets by Argentine savers reflects the inability of the domestic financial system to issue safe assets. Far from reflecting a "cultural trait," hoarding dollars is the counterpart of financial underdevelopment: because no asset can be used as a hedge against macroeconomic and systemic risks, the agents rely on dollarized assets.

The linkage between the demand for safe assets and capital outflows has negative consequences for macroeconomic volatility because it generates the threat of sudden reversals in the direction of capital movements ("sudden stops"): under normal circumstances, risk aversion is low, as is the value of hedging against systemic instability, and the reduced demand for safe foreign assets does not foster capital outflows. The opposite is true when macroeconomic conditions deteriorate. In a crisis scenario, there can be a dramatic increase in outflows. When this happens, institutional investors and banks face serious difficulties in complying with prudential regulations and building efficient portfolios because of the sudden increase in the price of a basic input—the safe asset. Just as a sudden increase in the price of imports can dislocate value chains, a lack of safe assets can disorganize the intermediation network.

SYSTEMIC DIMENSION

Since financial activities are complementary and market failures exist, coordination failures at the level of the system can occur and lead to either suboptimal equilibria or situations in which transactions are made at disequilibrium prices, giving rise to destabilizing forces. In the first case, the system can find itself caught in an inefficiency trap and, in the second, "false" prices can cause strong wealth transfers that affect agents' balance sheets, giving rise to undesired, excessive levels of leverage. Traps and instability generated by false prices can have marked effects on all the performance indicators mentioned previously: growth, macroeconomic stability, and social inclusion. They can also erode the quality of the organizational infrastructure if the banks' capitalization is diluted, if market makers face excessive risks associated with their activities, or if the sustainability of the government debt is in question. When users perceive these systemic imbalances, their risk aversion increases, thus feeding liquidity preferences.

Acting at the financial system level has to do with collective rather than individual actions, and institutions get involved because they are essential for the organization of collective action. The most important among the institutions that comply with this function are shown in figure 14.2: the macroeconomic regime, the institutional framework that regulates financial activities, and the judicial system.

The legal and regulatory framework is relevant to financial relations because it has a role in creating the conditions for the smooth functioning of markets, preserving good corporate governance, and ensuring credibility. If those who manage the shareholders' equity in a corporation are unreliable, this will be reflected in the reluctance of investors to invest in stocks or bonds issued by private corporations. The same applies to government bonds if the authorities discretionally change the conditions. Contract enforcement is critical. If the legal and regulatory framework is unreliable, transactions do not take place, and markets shrink or disappear. In particular, the supply of long-term credit becomes very scarce . When markets for long-term financial relations disappear, financial organizations cannot provide the long-term instruments that pension funds, insurance companies, or the government needs.

FINANCIAL DYSFUNCTIONS AND CRISES

To assess the ability of a given financial system to meet the five functions of finance that we have identified is a complex task. The task is simplified if we assume, first, that transaction costs are low and originate from frictions in the functioning of a system that has as a unique and inherently stable equilibrium, and, second, if we adopt the Pareto efficiency criterion to evaluate the functionality of the system. Beyond its applicability under normal circumstances, these assumptions are overly restrictive for a context of crisis. A necessary first step in this regard is to distinguish between financial normality and financial crisis.

FINANCIAL NORMALITY

Financial normality occurs when the institutional framework and macro-economy are stable, property rights are well-defined, and conflict resolution is based on well-established, well-known routines. In Fanelli (2012), we called the resource base—physical, human, and the stock of knowledge—the "hardware" of the economy and the institutional framework the "software." Using such classification, we can say that during periods of stability the agents make decisions and act as if the software that governs the transactions had the same ontological status as the hardware. Hence, when carrying out financial and monetary transactions, the rules that govern such transactions become "second nature."

The function of the financial software is to minimize the transaction costs that the parties must incur because of the existence of frictions. Under normal conditions, given that the software changes very slowly, the agents will correctly predict the transaction costs they will have to pay. Not surprisingly, during the Great Moderation, financial and monetary theory in developed countries was dominated by this view. Frictions were added more or less ad hoc to an equilibrium approach rooted in the general equilibrium paradigm to explain certain abnormalities or "puzzles," such as credit rationing or the existence of money.

FINANCIAL CRISIS

We have argued that in crisis events the rules become unstable and affect the credibility of the institutional framework. Concerning financial decisions, agents will anticipate that macroeconomic and financial instability could force major changes in regulations with probable redefinitions of property rights that will affect the net worth and liquidity of many agents. In such a context, a rational agent will internalize the fact that changes in the institutional environment might occur and that, as a consequence, the software of the economic system will no longer be as firm as the hardware.

The uncertainty about the "true" balance sheets and financial condition of borrowers and banks will restrict the set of agents that are able to issue safe, high-quality assets. In addition, there will be greater uncertainty about the ability to meet the terms of existing contracts and the real value of nominal debt because of the uncertainty about the future value of money in real terms. The transaction costs that will be incurred ex-post to complete a financial transaction will be difficult to calculate ex-ante insofar as they will depend on the speed and degree of difficulty in resolving conflicts that entail complex negotiations.

If conflicts over property rights become more frequent and widespread, transaction costs for the system as a whole will not only increase but will also become more volatile. Two very important facts associated with this type of scenario are as follows: first, there is an increase in the demand for safe assets, which are defined as those assets that are more suitable for preserving property rights and for providing a hedge against the volatility of transaction costs; second, the goal of maximizing the value of the agent's net worth—the allocation problem—tends to be dominated by the goal of preserving property rights. These factors negatively affect investment and increase risk aversion.

The significant differences that exist between normal and crisis situations suggest that to evaluate the functionality of the financial system, i.e., its ability to meet the five functions analyzed, the traditional efficiency criterion should be supplemented with criteria that consider the role of property rights and macroeconomic stability.

Taking into account the three dimensions of the financial system, we can now define three conditions for evaluating the functionality.

MICROECONOMIC EFFICIENCY CONDITION

An efficient financial system should operate with minimum transaction costs given the restrictions associated with the resource endowment, technology, information, and institutions. When this occurs, all potentially beneficial financial transactions—i.e., those able to generate net benefits after considering minimal transaction costs—are conducted. Such transactions are made via markets or hierarchies, and the choice will be made to minimize transaction costs. If some markets are missing or underdeveloped, the cause will not be irrationality on the part of users but the impossibility of organizing the financial transaction to obtain a net benefit given the constraints.

SYSTEMIC EFFICIENCY CONDITION

The decentralized choices that seek to minimize transaction costs for each organization do not necessarily result in the minimization of the cost to keep the overall system working. System efficiency is key not only for the efficiency of individual organizations but also in compelling those organizations to complement one another in positive ways. This raises the question of systemic coordination: there might be more than one equilibrium, and one might be better than the rest.

A frequent factor that leads to a bad equilibrium is the lack of stability of the institutional framework as a result of discretionary changes in regulations, insufficient transparency, and corruption. When institutions are unstable and not credible, ceding control over the assets' property in a financial transaction is too risky because of the lack of guarantees. Hence, in a crisis situation risks increase, and financial transactions that would be profitable for both parties under normal circumstances will remain unexploited. A direct consequence of this is that the number of transactions will fall, and intermediation will become more expensive because markets and organizations lose scale, and the lack of scale increases transaction costs. This can produce a shallow finance trap: intermediation costs are high because the scale of operation is low, and the scale is low because the costs of making transactions are excessive. Thus, the effects of excessive systemic risk that originate from institutional weaknesses are tantamount to instituting a tax on all financial activities.

Another factor that could lead to an inefficient equilibrium is that the authorities responsible for discovering better ways of coordinating the system fail because of insufficient knowledge or incentives to carry out the task. When the problem concerns either the credibility of the rules or weak incentives for coordinating agents in a better equilibrium, a strategy to improve the efficiency of the system would be necessary to change the rules of the game, which requires collective action.

In summary, efficiency has two aspects: microeconomic and systemic. The former depends on the efficiency of individual organizations and the latter on collective action, which has to design and enforce a set of economic institutions suitable for setting the system on a "good" equilibrium path.

SYSTEMIC STABILITY CONDITION

A financial system should create the conditions for ensuring its own stability. Note, however, that a system that is stable may not always be efficient. When caught in a shallow finance trap, the system is stable but not at its most efficient.

A basic requirement that a system must fulfill to be stable is the aggregate consistency condition: given property rights, the sum of agents' claims on assets must not exceed the total value of existing wealth. To satisfy this requirement, the value of existing financial instruments should be in line with economic fundamentals. Hence, after a shock occurs, prices should first adjust flexibly toward equilibrium; the eventual conflicts over property rights and contracts associated with unforeseen changes in the balance sheets should then be quickly and efficiently negotiated to obtain the same results that would be obtained in a zero-transaction-cost economy.

A financial system undergoing a crisis period does not meet this aggregative condition of stability and, as a consequence, conflicts over property rights tend to take center stage. Distributional conflicts are exacerbated in crises precisely because the sum of the claims over the wealth of the parties involved exceeds the value of existing wealth. In a banking crisis, the claims of depositors are often greater than the bank's total assets, which mean the latter's net worth becomes negative. In a debt crisis—as a consequence of the bailouts of banks and/or prior over-indebtedness—government debt frequently becomes unsustainable, and governments default because they are unable to generate the required fiscal surpluses. Conflicts over property rights exist in both normal and crisis situations, but the specific difference is that in the second case conflicts are widespread, and transaction costs become higher and difficult to foresee.

In mathematical terms, we can say that in a crisis situation the parameters that define the model of the economy are inconsistent with stability. Therefore, to restore stability, it is necessary to change the value of some parameters. To that end, it is frequently necessary to change the rules of the game to restore the consistency between the value of wealth and the sum of claims on it. It is necessary to adapt the software to the restrictions posed by the hardware. To be sure, this implies that the process of restoring stability will generate winners and losers, giving rise to political economy problems that will call for the involvement of the polity.

Conflicts over property rights increase strategic uncertainty and induce macroeconomic disequilibria that frequently compel the authorities to implement procyclical policies that prioritize the restoration of consistent property rights rather than employment. An additional factor that generates procyclical forces is that those who can spend or lend to riskier borrowers prefer to demand safe assets because of the anticipated instability in the rules and the uncertain future tax burden given the governments' increasing deficit.

It follows then that the sooner the conflicts concerning property rights are resolved, the sooner the crisis will be overcome. A key obstacle for quick resolution, however, is that policy measures—such as a default on public debt, devaluation of the currency, or bailout of the banking system—can induce strong redistribution effects that place the question of legitimacy at center stage. In other words, there will be a trade-off between the time it takes to resolve the crisis and political legitimacy, and it is the polity rather than policy makers that deal with this type of dilemma (Hausman and McPherson 1996; Sabatier 2007).

Beyond stability, crises are also related to the other two criteria of functionality. When financial organizations cannot minimize transaction costs or the economy falls into a shallow finance trap, agents are more exposed to shocks because there will be fewer instruments for managing risks.

Crises can have deleterious effects on efficiency in the short and medium run because they usually transform both financial organizations and the linkages between them. When transaction costs vary, adaptive changes occur in the structure of markets and organizations based on hierarchies (banks, regulatory bodies) to respond optimally to the signals of the new environment. The process of organizational restructuring not only impinges on micro and system efficiency but can also delay or accelerate the resolution of the crisis. This implies that the system's ability for organizational engineering influences the speed of overcoming the crisis. Engineering ability depends on both the ability of individual organizations and the ability to act collectively at the systemic and institutional levels to reduce the likelihood of systemic coordination failures. To account for these types of phenomena, the assumption that transaction costs are a given and small can be a particularly misleading argument for explaining decision making in a crisis environment, i.e., to account for the way in which agents' expectations about the evolution of the software of the system impinges on their choices. From this point of view, we need not only microfoundations for macroeconomics but also macrofoundations for microeconomics.

Two implications of the previous argument should be stressed. First, the development of the financial system should show path dependency to the extent that its trajectory heavily depends on the evolution of the institutional and organizational infrastructure that supports financial transactions (Greif and Kingston 2011). Second, because the different parts of the financial system are complementary, organizational and institutional disarray that impinges on financial transactions should induce strong spillover effects. If this is true, it should be very difficult to form expectations about the outcome of a crisis insofar as it is difficult to determine what the probability distribution of future events will be, or worse, what the future events could be. In this regard, the notion of system helps highlight the interactions between the micro and macro dimensions: because of spillover effects associated with systemic dysfunctions, agents will take into account whether the environment in which they are making decisions is typical of crises.

CONCLUSIONS

In this chapter, I have analyzed the linkages among financial crises, the macroeconomy, and institutions, taking into account the contributions of the institutional and political economy literature. The main purpose was to examine the role of property rights and conflicts in the context of financial stress. The main conclusions can be synthesized as follows.

During a crisis period, conflicts refer to the distribution of income flows and the existing stocks of wealth; the resolution of such conflicts entails bargaining processes that can endure, especially if negotiations refer to property rights over assets.

Conflicts and negotiations take place in different arenas—formal and informal organizations, the public sphere, congress, and the courts—and may influence the course of institutional change to the extent that the process of bargaining and conflict resolution may include changes in the rules of the game (regulations, laws). In such a context it will be hard to foresee what the future rules of the game will be.

Because the institutional framework is structured hierarchically, the higher the institutions reformed are in the hierarchical order, the higher the uncertainty concerning strategic decisions will be because the range of decisions affected will be broader.

The results of the negotiations may have significant impacts on the private agents' balance sheet composition and net worth. When the outcome of the conflict-and-bargaining process has systemic consequences, governments always become involved—directly or indirectly—and, consequently, the crisis will also affect the government's balance sheets.

The consequences for the agents' net worth can be difficult to foresee. When a crisis erupts, it might be clear that "some" property rights will be affected insofar as we see that the claims over assets exceed the present value of future returns under normal conditions. Likewise, some categories of taxpayers will have to bear a higher tax burden to finance the crisis. But as negotiations develop, it will be difficult for the potential lenders to predict what the potential borrowers' ability to pay will be and for the taxpayers to foresee their future tax burden.

Under these circumstances, decision makers will be inclined to take a wait-and-see attitude. They will change the way they react based on the instability of the rules of the game and the uncertainty about the "actual" state of the balance sheets. This means that the patterns that guide decisions under "normal" and "crisis" scenarios will differ substantially.

As a consequence of the wait-and-see attitude and the uncertainty concerning balance sheets, all sorts of spillover effects will be at work: the investment rate will fall, liquidity preference will be stronger because banks will find it difficult to preserve liquidity, and unemployment will rise. This normally creates macroeconomic disequilibria and systemic dysfunctions, and macroeconomic policies become involved in the crisis-resolution process because the goal of such policies is to address coordination failures at the level of the economic system.

Macroeconomic policies' goals, however, are different in a crisis situation. One key goal of macroeconomic management during a crisis period is managing the disequilibria to ensure a minimum degree of macroeconomic and political stability while a new set of consistent property rights is being negotiated. In general, primary goals during a crisis are to reduce the negative effects on employment and to keep the monetary and financial system working while negotiations over property rights and, eventually, the implementation of reforms in the rules of the game proceed. For example, the central bank typically concentrates on maintaining acceptable levels of funding and market liquidity even though it cannot reduce the excessive leverage of the private sector in the short run; or the treasury runs sizable deficits to avoid an escalation in unemployment, although the sustainability of the public sector's debt might be under scrutiny.

The resolution of a crisis requires a new situation in which property rights are consistent in the aggregate, stable, and reasonably well-defined, while markets are clear. To achieve this, the visible hand of the polity must work together with the invisible hand of the market. This creates a causal link that goes from the economy to the institutional framework.

The literature on institutions focuses on the causal factors that go from institutions to the economy. It assumes that once institutions are in place, they will shape decisions. However, when the crisis makes the set of decisions that result from the existing institutional framework inconsistent, it might be necessary to change parts of such a framework. This point was to a certain extent overlooked in the literature because of the identification of suboptimal results with suboptimal equilibria. However, when a crisis occurs and the existing rules of the game cannot deliver consistent outcomes, the ensuing disequilibria and spillover effects—including distributional ones—may result in pure instability or in the absence of any equilibrium. When this occurs, the rules of the game become dysfunctional, and it becomes necessary to reform the normative framework to deactivate the sources of instability or to define a new equilibrium if none—either good or bad—exists.

The institutional status quo can be deemed inadequate because of the emergence of economic dysfunctionalities, but, frequently, reform proposals are also motivated by the fact that the system's legitimacy falls under question because of the effects of the crisis on employment and distribution. This suggests that the analysis of crises can reveal the channels through which economic factors influence the polity and, therefore, institutional change.

Political institutions, which are senior to economic institutions, have to provide two key elements: first, they must establish mechanisms for reforming the rules of the economic game; second, they must make it possible to evaluate the results of the functioning of the economic system in light of widely shared social values, which is critical for preserving the system's legitimacy.

Social inclusion, growth, and stability are key standards in this regard. Economic analysis has given excessive weight to efficiency. In addition to the degree of efficiency, the notion of functionality takes into consideration whether the system can preserve itself (if it is stable), whether it can grow, and whether it can achieve a minimum degree of legitimacy (i.e., a consensus on wealth distribution as well as environmental issues).

I conclude with a few remarks on normality, crisis, and research in economics. In times of crisis, the research resources allocated to study disequilibrium and systemic dysfunctionalities increase, and economists of great talent feel attracted to the issue. When stability reigns, however, interest wanes, and the research funds tend to fade away. Only a group of researchers interested in the analysis of "rare" phenomena study monetary and financial instability. In light of this fact, it comes as no surprise that a large part of the most relevant contributions to the knowledge of coordination failures and spillover effects occurred in times of crisis. Good examples in this regard are the controversy between Thomas Tooke and Henry Thornton at the beginning of the nineteenth century that contributed to clarifying the role of money and credit; the discovery of the liquidity trap and the Fisher and Pigou effects as a consequence of the attempt to account for the crisis of the 1930s; and the crises in emerging countries in the 1990s that (1) brought about significant progress in how the process of financial deregulation and integration in the global capital markets is understood and (2) gave rise to the concepts of sudden stop, contagion, and twin crises. It is reasonable to conjecture, then, that the efforts to understand the subprime crisis and the ensuing instability will significantly increase our knowledge of the causes and consequences of financial failures.

Two main sources of progress in economic knowledge are the problems that arise from the internal logic of ongoing research programs and the demands that stem from public policies. During normal, stable periods, the research agenda tends to be dominated by the problems that have to do with the academic research program, whereas during turbulent periods the practical problems related to economic policy tend to be dominant. In this sense, because crises typically occur after a period of normality, economists are ill-prepared to meet the social demands for public policies that can tackle crisis management and resolution. Under these circumstances, we frequently observe that approaches and authors that had been forgotten or discredited return to center stage. The best example today is Hyman Minsky's view of the role that credit plays in modern capitalism, which has regained popularity after the subprime crisis. Of course, Minsky never lost popularity in the emerging world, where episodes of financial instability have been so common under the aegis of the second globalization regime.

From the previous argument, it follows that to improve the ability to deal with crises, it would be necessary, on the one hand, to improve the linkages between the academic research agenda and the research agenda that center on problems originating from the demands of economic and political actors and, on the other hand, to maintain the analysis of instability and systemic dysfunctionality on the research agenda even during normal times.

To a great extent, the theoretical progress in institutional economics, the role of information, and transaction costs in finance have been the consequence of the internal logic of various research programs that were underway in the last quarter of the twentieth century. But the newly produced knowledge of these issues was applied for different reasons in different contexts, including both normality and crises. In what has to do with crisis episodes, the most interesting and novel contributions originated in the application of the new knowledge to the analysis of financial and macroeconomic instability in emerging countries, frequently associated with the attempts of sweeping market-oriented institutional reforms. This is only natural. There was a strong social demand to understand episodes such as the institutional transformations that followed the fall of the Berlin Wall, the reform processes inspired in the Washington Consensus, and the financial crises provoked by the failure of financial liberalization. A good part of the efforts were made by the research departments of multilateral organizations such as the World Bank and International Monetary Fund, regional banks, and research centers in developing countries (see Fanelli and McMahon 2006; Fanelli, 2007). To account for the financial instability episodes and reforms in developing countries, the mainstream approach to macroeconomics, money, and finance had to be adapted. Reforms are essentially systemic in nature, and the mainstream approach focuses mainly on the effects that "frictions"—linked to information and agency problems—have on the equilibrium properties of stable economies. Given that developed countries enjoyed the extended Great Moderation period, the incentives for studying instability and crises were weak, and the research agenda was basically led by the puzzles generated by the internal logic of the research programs underway, which had their roots in the general equilibrium research agenda. Beyond financial developments in the emerging world, however, when the Great Moderation was suddenly displaced by the Great Recession and the threat of global crisis, it was evident that economic researchers had probably overinvested in the analysis of stable economies. In this regard, my discussion of the phenomena associated with financial crises, based on the analysis of emerging financial instability, might be useful in exploring the research issues that will probably gain more importance on the research agenda of financial problems.

NOTE

1. See Fanelli (2012) for a detailed discussion of these issues.

REFERENCES

Acemoglu, D. 2008. "Growth and institutions." In *The new Palgrave dictionary of economics*, edited by S. Durlauf and L. E. Blume New York, NY: Palgrave Macmillan.

Aoki, M. 2001. *Toward a comparative institutional analysis*. Cambridge, MA: MIT Press.

Bodie, Z. and Merton, R. C. 2005. "Design of financial systems: towards a synthesis of function and structure." *Journal of Investment Management* 3(1): 1–23.

Duflo, E. 2011. "Balancing growth with equity: the view from development." Paper prepared for the Economic Policy Symposium, Jackson Hole, WY. http://www.kansascityfed.org/publicat/sympos/2011/gd1.pdf.

Fanelli, J. M. 2007. *Understanding market reform in Latin America: similar reforms, diverse constituencies, varied results*. New York, NY: Palgrave Macmillan.

Fanelli, J. M. 2011. "Domestic financial development in Latin America." In *The Oxford handbook of Latin American economics*, edited by J. A. Ocampo and J. Ros, 241–265. New York: Oxford University Press.

Fanelli, J. M. 2012. *La Argentina y el desarrollo económico en el siglo XXI ¿Cómo pensarlo? ¿Qué tenemos? ¿Qué necesitamos?* Buenos Aires: Siglo XXI Editores.

Fanelli, J. M. and Frenkel, R. 1995. "Micro-macro interactions in economic development." *UNCTAD Review* July: 129–155.

Fanelli, J. M. and McMahon, G., eds. 2006. *Understanding market reforms*, vol. 2. New York, NY: Palgrave Macmillan.

Gibbons, R. 2000. "Why organizations are such a mess (and what an economist might do about it)." Paper prepared for doctoral text on organizational economics. http://web.mit.edu/rgibbons/www/Org_mess.pdf.

Greif, A. and Kingston, C. 2011. "Institutions: rules or equilibria?" In *Political economy of institutions, democracy, and voting*, edited by N. Schofield and G. Caballero, 13–43. Berlin: Springer Verlag.

Gurley, J. G. and Shaw, E. S. 1960. *Money in a theory of finance.* Washington, DC: Brookings Institution.

Hausman, D. M. and McPherson, M. 1996. *Economic analysis and moral philosophy.* Cambridge, UK: Cambridge University Press.

Keynes, J. M. 1936. *The general theory of employment, interest, and money.* London: Palgrave Macmillan.

Knight, F. H. 1921. *Risk, uncertainty and profit.* Boston, MA: Hart, Schaffner & Marx.

Levine, R. 2004. "Finance and growth: theory and evidence." In *Handbook of economic growth*, edited by P. Aghion and S. Durlauf, 865–934. Amsterdam: Elsevier.

McKinnon, R. I. 1973. *Money and capital in economic development.* Washington, DC: Brookings Institution.

Milgrom, P. and Roberts, J. 1992. *Economics, organization and management.* Englewood Cliffs, NJ: Prentice Hall.

Minsky, H. P. 1975. *John Maynard Keynes.* New York: Columbia University Press.

North, D. 1995. *Instituciones, cambio institucional y desempeño económico.* México City: Fondo de Cultura Económica.

Ostrom, E. 2007. "Institutional rational choice: an assessment of the institutional analysis and development framework." In *Theories of the policy process*, P. A. Sabatier, ed. Cambridge, MA: Westview Press.

Patinkin, D. 1965. *Money, interest, and prices*, 2nd ed. New York, NY: Harper & Row.

Rajan, R. G. 2005. "Has financial development made the world riskier?" National Bureau of Economic Research Working Paper 11728. http://www.nber.org/papers/w11728.pdf.

Sabatier, P. A. 2007. *Theories of the policy process.* Cambridge, MA: Westview Press.

Scartascini, C., Spiller, P., Stein, E., and Tommasi, M., eds. 2010. *El juego político en América Latina ¿Cómo se deciden las políticas públicas?* Bogotá, Colombia: BID-Mayol Ediciones.

Shaw, E. S. 1973. *Financial deepening in economic development.* New York, NY: Oxford University Press.

Tirole, J. 2010. "Illiquidity and all its friends." Bank for International Settlements Working Paper 303. http://www.bis.org/publ/work303.pdf.

CHAPTER 15

United States Size Distribution and the Macroeconomy 1986–2009

Lance Taylor, Armon Rezai, Rishabh Kumar,
Nelson Barbosa, and Laura Carvalho

This chapter is about severe limitations in reducing income inequality in the United States. In model simulations, when they are applied at politically "reasonable" levels, standard policy tools such as increased taxes on high-income households, higher transfers to people with low incomes, and raising wages at the bottom do not reduce rich versus poor inequality by very much.

The basic reason is that consistent macroeconomic accounting shows that there are three income redistribution flows on the order of 10 percent of GDP. The first two are fiscal tax/transfer payments (broadly progressive) and financial transactions (regressive). The last is an increase over two decades by 10 percent of GDP in the share of primary incomes expropriated by the top 1 percent of income recipients. In a macroeconomically consistent framework incorporating the size distribution of income, we show that policy interventions such as those already mentioned cannot reverse this historically large and unrequited income transfer.

For ease in presentation, the household size distribution has been rescaled to the national income and product accounts (NIPA). It is summarized by a metric (the Palma ratio) that—as opposed to the standard Gini coefficient—emphasizes the disparity in incomes between the "poor" (say households in the bottom one or two quintiles of the size distribution of income) and the "rich" (the top decile or top percentile). The ratio has trended strongly upward over time.

To trace macroeconomic and distributive linkages, we use a simple, static demand-driven macro model based on a social accounting matrix (SAM) that enfolds meso-level data on key distributive variables (types of

Table 15.1 US Consolidated (Aggregate) Social Accounting Matrix (% GDP)

2008		Current Expenditures					Capital Expenditures			
		HH and NPI	BUS	GOV	ROW	INT and DIV	HH	BUS	GOV	Total
Uses of total supply		70.22		16.66	12.92		3.70	10.90	3.48	117.89
HH and NPI	67.82		0.26	12.89	0.00	15.15				96.12
Wages and salaries	45.80									
Employer contributions	10.65									
Proprietors' and rental income	9.30									
CCA	2.06									
Transfers			0.26	12.89						
INT and DIV received		15.15				15.15				
BUS	23.22				1.89	19.22				44.33
Surplus plus statistical discrepancy	14.48									
CCA	8.73									
Transfers										
INT and DIV received					1.89	19.22				
GOV	8.96		17.58	2.67	0.13	0.81				30.16
Net indirect taxes and operating surplus	6.79									
CCA	2.18									
Direct tax, transfers, etc.			10.64	2.67	0.13					

	HHs and NPIs	BUS	GOV	ROW	INT and DIV	Total
Contributions received	6.94					23.83
INT and DIV received					17.89	
ROW	0.46	0.63	0.43		0.81	4.42
Imports	0.46	0.63	0.43			
Transfers	0.46	0.63	0.43			
INT and DIV received			2.80	4.10	4.42	39.60
INT and DIV disbursed	1.80	30.90	2.80	4.10	4.42	39.60
Total expenditures	90.07	34.47	32.78	19.04	39.60	234.04
Levels of net lending						
HHs and NPIs	6.05		3.70	-3.70		2.35
BUS	9.87	-2.62		-10.90		-1.04
GOV			-3.48		-6.10	
ROW		4.78			4.78	
INT and DIV					0.00	0.00
Total	96.12	44.33	30.16	23.83	39.60	
GDP	117.89				14291.5	39.08
Palma ratio (top 1 vs. bottom 40)			3.70	-3.70	-10.90	3.48 10.90 -3.48

Note: BUS, business; CCA, capital consumption allowances; DIV, dividends; GOV, government; HH, households; INT, interest; NPI, nonprofit institutions; ROW, rest of the world.

income, including transfers received, taxes paid, consumption, and savings) for swaths of the size distribution into the NIPA system. Basically, we rescaled available data to fabricate a representation of the size distribution consistent with the NIPA from the Bureau of Economic Analysis (the BEA accounts are themselves a fabrication). The numbers provide a broad-brush representation of the distributive situation for the period from 1986 to 2009. For the model simulations we focused on 2008, a relatively "normal" year for the economy.

We begin the presentation with a review of the US size distribution in the context of the SAM, shedding light on how relatively large fiscal and financial transfer payments and unequal income flows fit into the macro system. Then we go on to simulation results. The chapter concludes with an addendum that discusses the Republican "Path to Prosperity" budget proposal in the House of Representatives; there are also two appendices at the end of the chapter that detail how we put the accounting together and set out the specification of the model, respectively.

THE US ECONOMY AS TRANSFER UNION

To borrow a phrase from Europe, the US economy is a "transfer union" (although of modest proportion compared to European practice). Through both financial and fiscal channels, money flows of well over 10 percent of GDP (or $1.5 trillion) are transferred among different groups of economic actors. The SAM in table 15.1 illustrates the magnitudes scaled to GDP in 2008. The accounting rules are straightforward. Sums of corresponding rows and columns should be equal; the sums of "institutional" sectors' levels of savings and investment toward the bottom (savings with a positive sign and investment with a negative) are equal at 18.1 percent of GDP as the condition for the overall balance.

The sectors included are households and nonprofit institutions, corporate business (nonfinancial and financial), the overall government sector (federal, state, and local), and the rest of the world. For accounting purposes, a fictional financial sector also appears. It collects interest and dividends disbursed by the other sectors as sources of income in a row and redistributes them in the corresponding column.[1]

The first column gives a cost breakdown of total supply, or GDP plus imports. Supply amounts to 117.9 percent of a GDP of $14291.5 trillion. The first row shows how it is split between current and capital expenditures (the latter rows show that households, business, and government all invest in inventories and/or physical capital). Imports are included in the first column as opposed to the first row (with a negative sign) because their costs when they cross the frontier are incorporated into the value of total supply. The other columns and rows respectively present sectoral uses and sources of incomes.

In the first column, the CCA entries represent capital consumption allowances or depreciation by sector. They have to be included on the cost side because depreciation makes up part of the investment outlays in the first row.

For the household sector, wages and salaries and employer contributions (to insurance and pension funds) are usually lumped together as "labor compensation." Sleight of hand, however, is involved. As shown in bold, the contributions paid as a cost of employment amount to 10.7 percent of GDP, but then 6.9 percent is passed back to the government (essentially as an employment tax) in its row for contributions received. Wages and salaries alone give a better measure of take-home pay before direct taxes. They make up only 45.8 percent of GDP.

Second, in addition to the employee contributions, other main sources of government income are indirect taxes (plus minor surpluses of government enterprises) and direct taxes, including 10.6 percent from households (shown in italics). But then in the column for government outlays, households receive 12.9 percent of GDP as transfers (also in italics). Although 12.9 percent is small by the European standard of roughly 20 percent, it does signal that a substantial share of GDP is recycled through the direct tax/transfer system. The other major outlay is 16.7 percent of GDP ($2.387 trillion) for government purchases of goods and services.

Third, the business sector (including financial business) pays 30.9 percent of GDP to the fictional financial sector as interest and dividends (shown in bold and italics). Reflecting the volume of transactions among US financial firms, it gets 19.2 percent back (also in bold and italics). The corresponding numbers in 1986 were 27.3 percent and 17.1 percent, with the increase over 22 years indicating the increasing role of finance in the economy.

The household sector is the other main recipient of financial flows at 15.2 percent (with a 1.8 percent outlay; also shown in bold and italics). In effect, there is a net financial transfer from business to households of the same magnitude as the fiscal transfer. As will be seen, the impact of these transfers on the economies of households differs markedly across the size distribution of incomes.

Total government expenditures are 32.8 percent of GDP, whereas revenues are 30.2 percent; i.e., the overall government sector dissaves 2.6 percent of GDP in its row for net lending. Negative government savings is reported as the *current* deficit in the simulations we present later in the chapter. Adding investment expenditure of 3.5 percent boosts government net borrowing or the overall deficit to 6.1 percent of GDP (or $872 billion according to the BEA's estimates).

The rest of the world's income from US imports is 17.9 percent; its purchases of exports are 12.9 percent. After taking transfers and financial flows into account, "foreign savings" (or the US current account deficit) is 4.8 percent of GDP or $686 billion.

Looking at the overall picture of net lending flows, the household sector saved more than it invested in 2008 (although the pattern varied notably across the size distribution). Business was a net borrower of 1 percent of GDP.

SIZE DISTRIBUTION AND THE ROLE OF THE TOP 1 PERCENT

Figure 15.1 gives a broad-brush picture of the US size distribution of income for 2008, scaled to fit the NIPA numbers in table 15.1.[2] We split households into four groups: those in the bottom two quintiles of the size distribution with a mean income per household of $42,850 (right-hand scale); those between the 41st and 90th percentiles with a mean income of $106,590; the 91st to 99th percentiles with $278,320; and the top percentile at $2,140,460. Sources of incomes are as in table 15.1, i.e., wages and salaries,

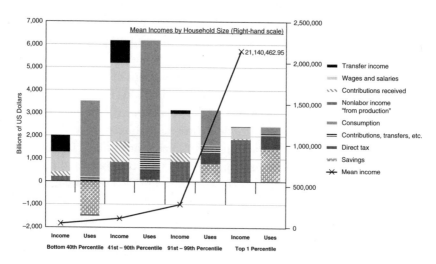

Figure 15.1   US income and expenditure distribution by household size.

social contributions received, transfers received, and "other" (including interest and dividends, proprietors' and rental incomes, and CCA).

These income flows do *not* include capital gains, which do not figure in the NIPA system.[3] For the top two groups they generated substantial incomes: $337,700 for the top 1 percent and $61,600 for the next group down. Other groups on average received less than $1,000 (around $100 at the bottom). In more prosperous years, the top 1 percent received greater than $500,000 from this source.

One way of thinking about the degree of inequality in the United States is in terms of a Palma ratio of the mean incomes of the top 1 percent to the bottom 40 percent.[4] Figure 15.2 shows the ratio for disposable income (total income minus social contributions to the government, interest paid out, and direct taxes) on the right-hand scale. The other curves are shares of the four income groups in GDP (left-hand scale).

Note that the top 1 percent steadily increased its GDP share from 5 percent to nearly 15 percent over two decades (the third major transfer mentioned previously), whereas shares of the other groups have been stable or declined. The Palma ratio (solid black line) nearly doubled. If 80 percent of capital gains ("post-tax") are added to disposable income, the ratio reached a level of nearly 50 percent before the financial crisis; it dropped off somewhat thereafter. Pointing out that income inequality has increased markedly in the United States is scarcely novel. How the current situation fits into national accounting, however, is of considerable interest.

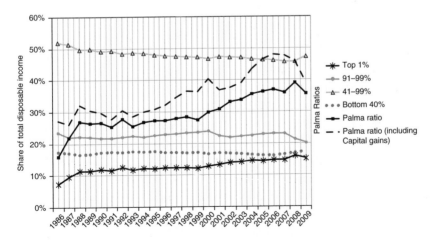

Figure 15.2   Share of disposable income for household groups.

SOURCES AND USES OF INCOMES

Returning to figure 15.1, for each group the left-hand bars show sources of incomes (again, these estimates are consistent with the totals in table 15.1). The ones to the right indicate how incomes are used. There are striking differences across income groups.

The 46.9 million households in the bottom two quintiles spend more than they receive. This extra outlay is represented by the segments of their right-hand bar below the horizontal axis, which signal dissaving and negative direct taxes. In the Bureau of Labor Statistics (BLS), consumer expenditure data in the bottom two quintiles have had consistently negative savings levels for two decades. There are many plausible explanations—clandestine payments, defaulted personal debt, family support, etc.—but the pattern is clear in available data. Above the axis, the two outlays are for consumption and social contributions sent to the government in line with table 15.1.

On the income side to the left, poor households receive modest social contributions and nonlabor income. The big items are labor income and transfers. Transfers are a bit smaller than wages. Both series have run closely together since 1986 (transfers were larger until 1995).

The pattern for the top 1 percent (1.1 million households) is entirely different. Transfers and employer contributions make a minimal contribution to income. Wages and salaries are a significant source (approaching $500,000 per year), but the lion's share comes from proprietors' incomes and interest and dividends. Both check in at around $800,000. Uses of income include consumption, social contributions, and direct taxes of $585,000. Savings of roughly 10 percent of GDP accounts for the rest.

In passing, note that there are approximately 43 times as many low- as high-income households, whereas the relatively rich have 50 times the average income of the poor. The share of GDP of the top 1 percent is higher than the share of the bottom 40 percent.

For the middle class, 58 million households between the 41st and 90th percentiles, income from labor (wages and contributions) is the dominant source. They also receive transfers (the total is about the same as for the bottom two quintiles) and nonlabor incomes. The bulk of their income is devoted to consumption, with modest direct taxes and very low but positive savings.

The pattern for the 91st and 99th percentiles is transitional between the groups on either side. Wages and salaries are their major source of income. Transfers are less important than for the middle class, whereas nonlabor income has a higher share. These 11.3 million households pay more in direct taxes than the middle class and have positive savings, but consumption still accounts for roughly half of their income.

MODEL SIMULATIONS

A simple comparative static macro model at best gives a bird's-eye view of possible impacts of policy changes, especially since the US tax and transfer system is extremely complicated (in Europe transfers are typically directed routed through the public sector as opposed to an ad hoc maze of specific programs). Nevertheless, some insights can be gleaned. Table 15.2 presents macrolevel impacts of shocks to the system.[5] Table 15.3 shows distributive implications for disposable incomes and numbers of households. We consider the impacts of fiscal expansion (without and with higher taxation), higher taxes linked with increased transfers, and wage increases for low-income groups.

As emphasized in connection with figure 15.1, there are significant differences across the size distribution in household savings behavior— average rates are negative at the bottom and positive at the top. The simulations reported here are all based on average saving rates. Modifications such as setting the marginal savings rate to zero at the bottom do not affect the results very strongly.

Row B in the tables shows the effects of an increase of 100 (billion dollars) of government purchases of goods and services from an initial level of 2,381. GDP increases by 102, signaling a modest multiplier for GDP (the multiplier for total supply is 1.2). Both the fiscal and foreign deficits go up. On the distributive side, numbers of households in all groups increase—this response is a proxy for higher employment generated by fiscal spending. An increase in government expenditure G of 4.1 percent generates a rise of 0.7 percent in "employment," again a modest increment. The model specification treats direct taxes and transfers as lump sum, fixed in real terms. Hence, the percentage increases in mean disposable incomes for each group are less than total incomes, which leads to a modest average income loss across the board.[6]

The highest-income households and the group just below pay direct taxes of 586 and 490, respectively (a total of 1,076). Suppose that their (lump sum) direct taxes are increased by more than 20 percent to 150 and 100, "offset" by an extra 250 in government spending (a 10.5 percent increase). Row C in table 15.2 shows that GDP expands and the fiscal deficit decreases. As seen in table 15.3, employment rises, whereas mean disposable income goes down for all four income groups (in part for the reasons discussed previously). The 9 percent decrease for the richest group is especially visible, and the Palma ratio falls by 8 percent.

This simulation focuses on reducing inequality by cutting disposable incomes at the top. A 20 percent tax hike, however, may well be politically out of bounds as of 2015, even though it could readily be based on wealth, capital gains, or the large financial flows illustrated in table 15.1. Still, a 9 percent reduction in income as a result of the tax increase does not go very far toward offsetting the 300 percent increase in real average income that the top 1 percent enjoyed between 1986 and 2008.

Row D shows the effects of a more modest tax increase at the top combined with higher transfers to low-income groups; i.e., taxes are raised on high savers transfers, increased for a group with negative savings. This package is expansionary, raises disposable incomes at the bottom, and reduces incomes at the top. It cuts the fiscal deficit. A larger version would cut further into the Palma ratio by reducing the numerator and raising the denominator. Taxing the rich with offsetting transfers to the poor looks like an effective means for ameliorating inequality overall. Nevertheless, the Palma metric does not fall by very much. Raising transfers to the bottom from 708 toward a "European" level of 1,100 would require a 50 percent tax hike at the top, imposition of a value-added tax, or perhaps a combination thereof.

In contrast, row E concentrates on the denominator by raising money wages for the bottom two quintiles (by 10 percent at the bottom and 5 percent for the second quintile), broadly in line with the minimum wage increases analyzed by the Congressional Budget Office (CBO 2014). As shown in table 15.2, there is a 0.55 percent increase in real GDP as a result of higher consumption demand, and the GDP deflator goes up by 0.7 percent. Table 15.3 reports a 3 percent increase in disposable income for the bottom two quintiles, with the other groups decreasing slightly. The Palma ratio falls from 39 to a bit less than 38. Potential offsets to the wage increase should also be considered.

The US transfer system effectively "taxes" income increases at the bottom of the size distribution by reducing benefits. A rough estimate of the tax rate is 30 percent (CBO 2014). Row F in the tables shows that the low-income wage increase is less expansionary and redistributive when this limitation is taken into account.

The usual objection to a minimum wage increase is that firms will cut back on employment (or raise labor productivity) in response. Row G shows that bringing this possibility into play reduces increases in GDP

Table 15.2 Macroeconomic Impacts of Policy Shifts: Level Changes

Policy		Real GDP[a] (%)	GDP Deflator (%)	Government Deficit[a] (%)	Current Account Deficit[a] (%)
A	Initial level	14291.5	1	374.56	683.778
B	Government spending increase by 100	102.2 (0.72)	0 (0.00)	90.45 (24.15)	18.279 (2.67)
C	Government spending increase by 250; tax increase by 100 and 150 for top two	161.5 (1.13)	0 (0.00)	−13.67 (−3.86)	28.879 (4.22)
D	Tax increase by 50 on top two groups and transfer to bottom	154.7 (1.08)	0 (0.00)	−13.58 (−3.63)	27.664 (4.05)
E	Wage increase by 10% for bottom 20% and by 5% for next 20%	79.2 (0.55)	0.0071 (0.71)	−10.65 (−2.84)	16.625 (2.43)
F	Wage increase with a 30% marginal tax rate on low incomes	39.4 (0.28)	0.0071 (0.71)	−27.32 (−7.29)	9.468 (1.38)
G	Wage increase and 30% marginal tax rate with an employment elasticity of $\sigma = -0.5$	5.1 (0.04)	0.0127 (1.27)	−19.36 (−5.17)	4.68 (0.68)
H	Wage increase with a falling markup	80.9 (0.57)	0.00678 (0.68)	−11.05 (−2.95)	16.911 (2.47)
I	Wage increase and falling markup with a 30% marginal tax rate on low incomes	41.1 (0.29)	0.00678 (0.68)	−27.72 (−7.40)	9.756 (1.43)
J	Wage increase, falling markup, 30% marginal tax, and employment elasticity of $\sigma = -0.5$	18.9 (0.14)	0.01035 (1.04)	−22.64 (−6.04)	7.029 (1.03)

[a] Billions of US dollars.

Table 15.3 Level Changes in Distribution from Policy Shifts

| | Policy | Bottom 40th Percentile | | 41st–90th Percentile | | 91st–99th Percentile | | Top 1 Percentile | | Palma Ratio |
		Mean Disposable Income ('000 USD)	Household Size (Millions of Households)	Mean Disposable Income ('000 USD)	Household Size (Millions of Households)	Mean Disposable Income ('000 USD)	Household Size (Millions of Households)	Mean Disposable Income ('000 USD)	Household Size (Millions of Households)	
A	*Initial Level*	39.41	46.93	86.11	57.95	206.29	11.26	1538.17	1.13	39.03
B	Govt spending increase by 100	-0.26 (-0.66%)	0.34 (0.72%)	-0.57 (-0.67%)	0.41 (0.71%)	-1.29 (-0.63%)	0.08 (0.72%)	-5.15 (-0.33%)	0.01 (0.72%)	0.13 (0.33%)
C	Govt spending increase by 250, increase tax by 100 and 150 for top two	-0.41 (-1.04%)	0.53 (1.13%)	-0.90 (-1.05%)	0.65 (1.13%)	-10.81 (-5.24%)	0.13 (1.13%)	-139.37 (-9.06%)	0.01 (1.13%)	-3.16 (-8.10%)
D	Increase tax by 50 on top two groups and transfer to bottom	1.71 (4.35%)	0.51 (1.08%)	-0.83 (-0.96%)	0.60 (1.04%)	-6.34 (-3.07%)	0.12 (1.08%)	-51.54 (-3.35%)	0.01 (1.08%)	-2.88 (-7.38%)
E	Raise wage by 10% for bottom 20% and by 5% for next 20%	1.23 (3.12%)	0.26 (0.55%)	-0.36 (-0.42%)	0.32 (0.55%)	-1.05 (-0.51%)	0.06 (0.55%)	-2.32 (-0.15%)	0.01 (0.55%)	-1.24 (-3.17%)

F	Wage increase with a 30% marginal tax rate on low incomes	0.91 (2.30%)	0.13 (0.27%)	−0.31 (−0.36%)	0.16 (0.28%)	−0.55 (−0.27%)	0.03 (0.28%)	−0.33 (−0.02%)	0.00 (0.28%)	−0.88 (−2.27%)
G	Wage increase and 30% marginal tax rate with an employment elasticity of σ = −0.5	1.08 (2.75%)	0.02 (0.04%)	0.13 (0.15%)	0.02 (0.04%)	−0.15 (−0.07%)	0.00 (0.04%)	2.73 (0.18%)	0.00 (0.04%)	−0.98 (−2.50%)
H	Wage increase with a falling markup	1.22 (3.10%)	0.27 (0.57%)	−0.37 (−0.43%)	0.33 (0.57%)	−1.07 (−0.52%)	0.06 (0.57%)	−2.47 (−0.16%)	0.01 (0.57%)	−1.23 (−3.16%)
I	Wage increase and falling markup with a 30% marginal tax rate on low incomes	0.90 (2.27%)	0.13 (0.29%)	−0.15 (−0.17%)	0.17 (0.29%)	−0.57 (−0.28%)	0.03 (0.29%)	−0.48 (−0.03%)	0.00 (0.29%)	−0.88 (−2.25%)
J	Wage increase, falling markup, 30% marginal tax and employment elasticity of σ = −0.5	1.01 (2.56%)	0.06 (0.13%)	0.02 (0.02%)	0.08 (0.13%)	−0.31 (−0.15%)	0.01 (0.13%)	6.54 (0.43%)	0.00 (−0.19%)	−0.81 (−2.08%)

and employment. Because of the latter effect, average disposable income of the bottom group goes up.

Firms might also adjust to the wage increase by reducing markups. Row H shows stronger expansion, less inflation, and stronger real income gains.

All effects are combined in row J. Raising low-income wages seems to be beneficial, but in overall macroeconomic terms the changes are minimal, in the range of a few percent of initial levels of the relevant variables.

BOTTOM LINE

This last observation illustrates the fundamental message of this chapter. Policy initiatives within "feasible" limits will not strongly affect distribution in the US economy. Modifying taxes and transfers within the 10 percent of output that could be manipulated by the government or increasing wages at the bottom by 10 percent (or even 20 percent) simply cannot offset the shift of 10 percent of GDP toward the top income group that occurred after the 1980s.[7] Only major social changes—"expropriating the expropriators" to use an old expression—could begin to accomplish that task.

ADDENDUM: "THE PATH TO PROSPERITY"

Row D in tables 15.2 and 15.3 illustrates the effects of raising taxes on high savers at the top of the size distribution and transferring money to low savers at the bottom. The Republican 2015 budget proposal in the House of Representatives follows the opposite course. On an annual basis, the basic idea is to cut transfers across the board by approximately $500 billion and to cut taxes for the top two groups by $50 billion each. The transfer reduction is impressive at 27 percent of the initial level; the tax cuts are approximately 10 percent.

Not surprisingly, in a demand-driven model GDP falls by approximately 5 percent. The current government deficit drops from 374.6 to 38. To get to a "balanced budget" or zero government net borrowing (equals current savings minus investment), there would have to be a reduction of 690 (29 percent) in current government spending. GDP would end up falling by 9 percent.

These numbers show that the "Path to Prosperity" leads toward depression, as it must in an economy in which expenditure determines income. Presumably, prosperity could be created if reduced net borrowing by the government were to flow automatically into higher capital formation and growth. Despite the current House majority's faith in Say's law, capitalist economies do not work that way.

National Accounting and Size Distribution of Income

Based on the sources listed in table 15.A.1, the construction of a data set that integrates the size distribution into the NIPA took place as outlined in the following seven steps:

1. Annual data from the NIPA system were restated as SAMs. In principle it should be straightforward to restate national accounts in the form of a SAM, but this step is not normally taken by the Bureau of Economic Analysis.

2. The CBO definitions of income flows were adjusted for rough consistency with the definitions in NIPA (the major arbitrary assumption was to assign one-half each of "other income" flows to financial incomes and wages).

3. For each year in the sample, shares of total income (including transfers) and taxes for the seven household categories were calculated as ratios of flows at the group level to the corresponding totals in the CBO data set.

4. These income shares were then applied to each year's NIPA totals of wages, transfer, financial, and proprietors' incomes to estimate flow levels for the seven income groups. A NIPA-consistent distribution of total income across groups also came out of this calculation.

5. CBO-based shares were used to distribute total NIPA outlays for direct taxes, social insurance, and finance across all seven groups.

6. Shares of total consumption by quintile (adjusted to be consistent with NIPA definitions) from the BLS data were calculated and then applied to NIPA total consumption. Savings flows by quintile could then be calculated as the differences between income levels and outlays for consumption, finance, and taxes.

7. Savings data by quintile were extrapolated to estimate levels for the 81 to 90 percent, 91 to 99 percent, and the top 1 percent income groups. Consumption levels for these groups followed residually.

Table 15.A.1 Data Sources

Source	Website
CBO (2012)	http://www.cbo.gov/publication/43373
BEA (2009)	http://www.bea.gov/iTable/index_nipa.cfm
BLS (2009)	http://www.bls.gov/cex/csxstnd.htm#2009

Note: CBO, Congressional Budget Office; BEA, Bureau of Economic Analysis; BLS, Bureau of Labor Statistics.

Model Specification

We put together a simple comparative static simulation model to examine how distributive changes and the macroeconomy interact.

The basic setup makes output a function of effective demand, with the price level determined by costs. We begin on the side of costs, starting with labor. For the United States, one has to deal with the vagaries of labor taxation. The "basic" wage flow for household group i is $\tilde{W}_i$, the sum of "wages and salaries," and "employer contributions to employee funds" from the SAM. If Φ_i is the ratio of that group's "employer contributions for government social insurance" to $\tilde{W}_i$, then $W_i = (1 + \Phi_i)\tilde{W}_i$ is the total labor cost for group i.

The corresponding "wage" or labor payment (total payments received divided by number L_i of households in the group) is $w_i = W_i/L_i$ and $b_i = L_i/X$. All of this abstracts from household structure, participation rates, etc., but it is a place to start. The groups are defined by the base year levels of income that define boundaries between boxes such as quintiles, deciles, etc. Tax/transfer policies would shift incomes up or down in the boxes, with repercussions on the level of economic activity. Individual households of course may move into or out of a box when their income levels change. Our simulations focus on changes of income levels within boxes, ignoring possible movements across boundaries.

In an alternative specification adopted when low income w_i changes, we allow for "substitution" among different types of labor:

$$b_i = \gamma_i (w_i/Z)^{-\sigma},$$

with Z set by a constant elasticity of substitution cost function

$$Z = [\Sigma \gamma_i (w_i)^{1-\sigma}]^{1/(1-\sigma)}.$$

In most simulations, we assume that the elasticity of substitution is zero: $\sigma = 0$. In this case, total per unit labor cost faced by business becomes $Z = \sum w_i b_i$, with b_i constant.

With P as the price of output (not quite equal to the GDP deflator), the overall cost decomposition is

$$PX = \tau PX + eaP^* X + \Xi PX + ZX + \Pi PX,$$

where τ is the ratio of the sum of nonlabor indirect taxes (minus subsidies), government CCA, and surplus of government enterprises to output. The exchange rate is e, a is the import/output ratio, and P^* is a price index for the rest of the world. The term ΞPX is the sum of household proprietors' income, rental income, and CCA. Indirect taxes, imports, and proprietors' incomes, etc., are assumed to be proportional to output. Total profits are ΠPX.

For the baseline scenarios (with zero elasticity of substitution), this formulation leads naturally to a markup equation for P based on per unit costs of labor and imports:

$$P = (Z + eaP^*) / (1 - \tau - \Xi - \Pi).$$

If $\rho = eP^*/P$ is an index of the real exchange rate, we add a constant elasticity function for price dependency of the import coefficient:

$$a = \alpha \rho^{-\gamma},$$

with $\gamma > 0$, which can be solved jointly with the cost function to determine the price level in the economy (in the simulations discussed below, $\gamma = 0.75$). Econometric evidence of minimum wage increases on the aggregate price level suggests very small effects (compared to price levels of goods of low-wage industries). To capture this low (minimum) wage elasticity of the GDP deflator, the markup is endogenized in some simulations by assuming $\Pi = Z_0 Z^{\psi_1}$, with $\psi_1 = -0.1$.

With prices specified, now look at income and expenditure accounts, omitting various small items that might be included on one side of the accounts as "other" net (positive or negative) income or expenditure O_i.

Begin with households. Total household income is

$$Y_H = \sum Y_i,$$

with income for group i as

$$Y_i = w_i b_i X + \xi_i PX + PQ_i + U_i + O_i.$$

That is, in addition to "wages" $w_i b_i X$, household income includes proprietors' (plus rental and CCA) income $\xi_i PX$, the value of "real" government transfers PQ_i, financial receipts U_i (interest and dividends), and other net receipts O_i (from the business and rest-of-world sectors). The condition $\sum \xi_i = \Xi$ applies.

Uses of income for group i are

$$Y_i = PC_i + \Gamma_i \tilde{W}_i + PT_i + R_i + S_i \,,$$

with C_i as consumption, $\Gamma_i \tilde{W}_i$ as the sum of "contributions" (for social insurance) and transfers to government, PT_i as direct taxes (so that T_i is a "real" tax level), R_i as financial payments, and S_i as savings.

We note that transfers, financial receipts, direct taxes, and financial payments are all treated as lump sum flows. This is the simplest way to build them in and allows us to emphasize the shifts in income distribution.

We need consumption functions for C_i. The main argument is disposable income,

$$D_i = Y_i - \Gamma_i \tilde{W}_i - PT_i - R_i \,,$$

which will be affected by taxes and transfers along with wage levels.

Of course,

$$C = \sum C_i.$$

We set up consumption functions in the form

$$PC_i = A_i + (1 - s_i) D_i \,,$$

with s_i as the group marginal savings rates. The A_i and s_i parameters were adjusted to "calibrate" consumption levels to those in the SAM. In the standard specification, marginal savings rates are set to equal average rates. For the bottom two quintiles, where consumption exceeds income, this implies negative autonomous consumption. In a second specification, a nonnegativity constraint is imposed on these A_i.

Business derives income from profits and interest to yield

$$Y_B = \Pi PX + U_B.$$

Net operating surplus is

$$N_B = Y_B - P\Delta_B \,,$$

with Δ_B as real capital consumption plus the statistical discrepancy. Spending is

$$Y_B = N_B + P_{\ B} = PT_B + R_B + S_B + O_B,$$

with T_B as direct tax, R_B as financial payments, and O_B as omitted smaller payments. Savings S_B will be the balancing item.

We use an investment function linear in output, output growth, and net operating surplus

$$I_B = \iota_1 X + \iota_2 N_B,$$

with $\iota_1 = i_X + \iota_g g_X$ capturing the effects of the level and growth of output on business investment as described in Fazzari et al. (2008).

Government's income is

$$Y_G = \tau PX + \sum \Gamma_i \tilde{W}_i + P(\sum T_i + T_B) + U_G,$$

with U_G including the CCA and profits of enterprises. Its uses of income are

$$Y_G = PG + \sum PQ_i + R_G + S_G + O_G,$$

with R_G as interest payments and O_G as omitted flows. Savings S_G or the fiscal surplus is the balancing item.

Rest-of-world income is

$$Y_R = eaP^* X + U_R,$$

with the payment U_R coming from the financial sector. Its income uses are

$$Y_R = PE + R_R + S_R + O_R,$$

with R_R as payments to the financial sector, O_R as omitted flows, and S_R as "foreign savings" or the current account deficit. Exports E are a constant elasticity function of unit labor cost Z (following Storm and Naastepad [2012], we set the elasticity to -0.12).

For the financial sector we have

$$\sum R_i + R_B + R_G + R_R = \sum U_i + U_G + U_R + S_F.$$

In equilibrium the sum of omitted flows has to equal zero:

$$\sum O_i + O_B + O_G + O_R + O_F = 0.$$

To solve the model we need the macro-balance relationship

$$\sum C_i + (I_H + I_B + I_G) + G + E - X = 0,$$

incorporating behavioral relationships for household consumption levels, business and household investment, and imports and exports. It is simplest to treat G and I_G (but not government dissaving S_G) as exogenous policy variables. Multipliers with respect to G are output, 1.20; fiscal deficit, 0.90; and trade deficit, 0.18. All values are in the conventional range for simple demand-driven models.

Nominal GDP can be defined as

$$VQ = (P - eP^* a)X = (P - a)X,$$

with V as the GDP deflator; X, P, and a as levels of output, price, and the import/output coefficient in any simulation, respectively; and $e = P^* = 1$ initially. Real GDP is

$$Q = (1 - a)X,$$

so the deflator becomes

$$V = (P - a)/(1 - a).$$

NOTES

This work was supported by INET and is based on a version forthcoming in the Review of Keynesian Economics. We thank Duncan Foley for ongoing comments, and the publisher and the editors for their permission to reproduce it here.

1. In principle, the national accounts can always be formulated as a SAM. In practice, they are rarely if ever set out in matrix form. We constructed table 15.1 from the accounts published by the BEA.

2. As discussed in appendix 15.1, we used data from the CBO (2012) report on the size distribution and the Bureau of Labor Statistics Consumer Expenditure Survey (BLS 2009) to put together the estimates in the diagram.

3. Capital gains can be inferred from changes of wealth over some period in the flow of funds accounts or directly from income tax data.

4. In fact, Palma (2011) suggests using the income of the top 10 percent in the numerator, but we chose the top percentile to underline the large degree of inequality in the United States.

5. Recall from the previous discussion that the numbers in table 15.1 report the current fiscal deficit at a level of 374.6 in the base year. Adding investment spending of 497.2 sets overall government borrowing to 871.8 or 6.1 percent of GDP.

6. The specification is not unreasonable. Many households in the bottom two quintiles rely on prefixed income transfers such as Social Security. Presumably, over time, disposable income would rise more or less in line with GDP as transfers ratchet up.

7. This observation is not model-specific. Given the accounting underlying table 15.1 and figures 15.1 and 15.2, even a highly neoclassical model would yield outcomes similar to those reported here.

REFERENCES

BEA 2009. "National data: GDP and personal income." http://www.bea.gov/iTable/index_nipa.cfm.

BLS 2009. "Consumer expenditure survey." http://www.bls.gov/cex/csxstnd.htm#2009.

CBO 2012. "The distribution of household income and federal taxes, 2008 and 2009. http://www.cbo.gov/publication/43373.

CBO 2014. "The effects of a minimum-wage increase on employment and family income." http://www.cbo.gov/publication/44995.

Fazzari, S., Ferri, P., and Greenberg, E. 2008. "Cash flow, investment, and Keynes-Minsky cycles." *Journal of Economic Behavior & Organization* 65: 555–572.

Palma, J. G. 2011. "Homogeneous middle vs. heterogeneous tails and the end of the 'inverted U': it's all about the share of the rich." *Development and Change* 42: 87–153.

Storm, S., and Naastepad, C. W. M. 2012. *Macroeconomics beyond the NAIRU.* Cambridge, MA: Harvard University Press.

CHAPTER 16

Sovereign Credit Risk in Latin America and Global Common Factors

Manuel Agosin and Juan Díaz-Maureira

The financial crisis associated with the bursting of the real estate bubble in the United States and some European countries led to the worst financial crisis the world economy has known since the Great Depression and is already widely being referred to as the Great Recession. This crisis, which entered its worst phase after the collapse of Lehman Brothers on September 15, 2008, generated an acute liquidity shortage in the entire global financial system, led to a collapse in stock markets across the world and, in 2009, to a sharp contraction in output in most countries.

Thus, the bankruptcy of Lehman Brothers is seen as the key signal that triggered the potential collapse of the global financial system (saved only by decisive official intervention in most of the large economies of the world). This shock caused the sovereign risk indicators of individual countries to rise sharply, regardless of their individual fundamentals. The impact was particularly acute in emerging economies, which experienced a simultaneous drying up in their access to external financial resources or what Calvo et al. (2008) called a "systemic sudden stop."

Even emerging economies with stable economic and political fundamentals were severely affected by the global financial crisis that began toward the end of 2008. For example, countries such as Brazil and Chile, whose ample international reserves and/or fiscal savings reduced to practically zero the probability that they would not honor their debt commitments, also experienced a steep increase in their indicators of sovereign risk.

This stylized fact suggests that, during a crisis, financial risk indicators of developing economies do not respond to changes in variables that are specific to a particular country and are instead determined by global financial factors that are common to all economies.

The objective of this chapter is to measure the impact that such global factors have over the idiosyncratic financial risks of a set of Latin American countries for which complete sovereign risk data have been available since the beginning of 2007. Sovereign risk spreads, which had been declining prior to early 2007, indicating growing risk appetite in international financial markets, began to trend upward in the beginning of 2007, perhaps as risk appetite showed signs of reverting. During the first phase, this trend was very gradual, but, as the crisis in the United States and European financial markets began to gather speed, sovereign credit spreads rapidly widened for all Latin American countries. They peaked toward the end of January 2009 and from then on began gradually returning to the levels experienced in early 2007 (see figure 16.1 for a sample of Latin American countries). Spreads for these countries began to drift upward again with the intensification of the European sovereign debt crisis.

We use two measures of sovereign risk. The first is the Emerging Markets Bond Index (EMBI) spreads compiled by J.P. Morgan and reported by Bloomberg on a daily basis. A country's EMBI is determined in basis points (hundredths of one percentage point) and is expressed as the minimum return that a sovereign from a given country must offer for investors to purchase its bonds. It is estimated as the difference between the yield on domestic sovereign bonds in US dollars and the rate on US Treasury thirty-year bonds (an investment considered riskless).

The second indicator we use is the credit default swap (CDS) on a sovereign's debt. The CDS is an instrument to hedge default risk and is

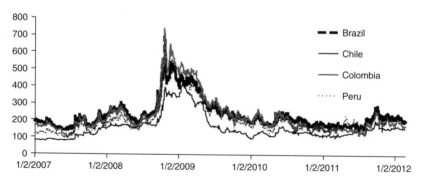

Figure 16.1 Daily Emerging Markets Bond Index spreads for selected countries in Latin America, January 2, 2007–February 23, 2012 (basis points). *Source*: Bloomberg.

akin to the payment of an insurance premium on the default of a given financial instrument—in our case sovereign bonds of Latin American countries. Our database includes fifteen countries in Latin America (there were fewer countries with data available for CDSs). We use daily data for the period from January 2, 2007 through February 23, 2012.

To identify the existence of a common factor and to estimate its value, we use two methodologies: principal components and a Kalman filter. Our research yields three principal results. First, there is robust evidence that there exists a common factor in the evolution of sovereign risk premia for the countries considered in the study. This common factor explains roughly 90 to 95 percent of the variation in our two indicators of sovereign risk. Second, the common factor becomes a much more important explanatory factor after the Lehman bankruptcy. In technical terms, the use of a Kalman filter allows us to show that the common factor itself shifts upward significantly after the Lehman episode. Third, we calculate the long-run, stationary-state values of the sovereign credit risk indicators, and these conform to conventional notions of sovereign risk (as reflected in credit ratings).

Despite the relevance of sovereign credit risk on a country's ability to borrow in international markets (and the costs associated with such borrowing), empirical studies in the international literature on the subject have been scarce. Some studies have focused on estimating the impact of macroeconomic fundamentals on sovereign credit risk in emerging economies (Edwards 1986; Kamin and von Kleist 1999; Zhang 2008). Other research efforts share with this chapter the attempt to quantify the common factors that explain the co-movement of sovereign risk in a group of economies. For example, Délano and Selaive (2005) applied the methodology of principal components and used the EMBI as an approximation to sovereign risk in nineteen developing economies. They found that, for the period from 1998 to 2004, common factors explained a large share of the variation in the daily EMBI spreads of these countries. Using CDS data, Pan and Singleton (2008) found that the CDSs of Mexico, Turkey, and South Korea shared an important relationship with the VIX index of the United States (the VIX index is a popular measure of the implied volatility of S&P 500 index options). Longstaff et al. (2011), applying principal components to monthly averages of CDS data for twenty-six countries from October 2000 through January 2010, found that 64 percent of the volatility of CDSs was explained by a common factor.

Our study is close in spirit to Délano and Selaive (2005) and Longstaff et al. (2011). However, it differs in three fundamental ways. First, our research utilizes both EMBI and CDS data, whereas Délano and Selaive (2005) used only EMBI data and Longstaff et al. (2011) only CDS data. Second, we explore the wealth of information contained in the daily frequency of both series of data, rather than monthly averages, used in Longstaff et al. (2011). Third, we used two econometric techniques to detect the existence of common factors: principal components and a Kalman filter. Délano and Selaive (2005) and Longstaff et al. (2011) used only principal components. In addition, we approximate the unobservable common factor by an observed variable (the TED spread, defined as the difference between LIBOR and the interest rate on Treasury bills, both with a maturity of three months) and explore the plausibility that the daily spread data and the coefficient that links the spread to the proxy for the unobservable common factor exhibited breaks after the Lehman credit event.

The chapter is organized in the following manner. The first section presents the data and derives some stylized facts from their examination. The second section contains the principal results, and the last section provides some conclusions.

THE DATA

As already noted, we use two measures of sovereign financial risk. The first one is the spread on the EMBI for each country, calculated by J.P. Morgan. The exact calculation of a country's EMBI spread considers a package of similar assets from a given sovereign. Therefore, the EMBI spread should be considered a reasonable approximation of the measurement of country risk, but it cannot be observed in the markets themselves. Table 16.1 summarizes the descriptive statistics for these data.

The second indicator is the CDS on sovereign debt. As already noted, the CDS is an instrument used to hedge the risk of default on specific debt instruments. A CDS is the yearly premium, expressed in basis points, on insuring against the default of a debt instrument (in our case, a sovereign bond) worth US$10,000, with a given maturity. We use CDSs on five-year bonds.

To understand how a CDS operates, consider the following example. An investor A purchases a government X's bond with a five-year maturity and face value of US$10,000. To insure against X's default, investor A decides to

Table 16.1 Daily EMBI Spreads for Fifteen Latin American Countries, January 2, 2007 to February 23, 2012: Descriptive Statistics (Basis Points)

Country	Mean	SD	Min	Max
Argentina	753	416	185	1,965
Brazil	236	85	138	688
Chile	160	73	78	411
Colombia	229	109	95	741
Costa Rica	226	129	63	657
Dominican Republic	517	345	122	1,785
Ecuador	1,177	968	538	5,069
El Salvador	353	165	99	928
Guatemala	282	127	114	751
Jamaica	605	243	222	1,324
Mexico	211	92	89	627
Panama	221	106	114	648
Peru	213	97	95	653
Uruguay	286	150	133	907
Venezuela	960	414	183	1,887

Source: Bloomberg's.

purchase a CDS from hedge fund B for a price, say, of US$100 (1 percent of the face value of the bond), which must be paid once a year on a specified date. If government X defaults at any time before the maturity of the bond, hedge fund B must make restitution of the face value of the bond to investor B, who in turn hands over the bond to hedge fund B. In some cases, where there is a debt restructuring, B pays A the difference between the restructured and face value of the bond. In the case of any "credit event" (inability or unwillingness of government X to pay the face value of the bond), investor A stops making yearly premium payments on the CDS.

The CDS is a more accurate reflection than the EMBI sovereign credit spread of the probability perceived by the market that a government may not honor its debt obligations. The sample available for CDSs is smaller than that for the EMBI. There are only nine Latin American countries for which CDS data are available daily. The data we used is from February 2, 2007 to February 23, 2012. Table 16.2 summarizes the descriptive statistics of CDS data.

Table 16.2 Credit Default Swaps on Sovereign Latin American Debt, February 2, 2007 to February 23, 2012: Descriptive Statistics (Basis Points)

Country	Mean	SD	Min	Max
Argentina	1,111	1,005	183	4,689
Brazil	150	79	62	586
Chile	88	60	12	323
Colombia	169	84	65	600
Ecuador	2,039	1,676	534	4,432
Mexico	143	91	28	601
Panama	158	89	61	587
Peru	156	83	60	586
Venezuela	1,019	596	151	3,239

Source: Bloomberg's.

IDENTIFYING THE COMMON FACTOR

In this section, we present the results of estimating the relevance of a common factor underlying the evolution of the risk indicators for all Latin American countries. We used two methodologies to estimate a unobservable common factor: the methodology of principal components and an estimation using a Kalman filter. For technical details on the Kalman filter methodology, see Geweke (1977), Sargent and Sims (1977), Watson and Engle (1983), and Stock and Watson (1989). It should be noted that the Kalman filter methodology works well when the number of endogenous variables is small; as N grows the number of parameters exceed the number that can be estimated. For full technical details, see Hamilton (1994) and Lütkepohl (2005).

Before analyzing the results, it is important to discuss a significant technical issue related to the stationarity of the risk indicators. When applying the standard unit root tests found in the time-series literature, one would conclude that the CDS series is I(1); in other words, the series must be differenced once to make it stationary, and estimations should proceed with these latter data. This was what Longstaff et al. (2011) did. However, it is difficult to think that, from an economic standpoint, the CDS could be an I(1) series. The basic argument in considering the CDS a stationary variable is that it is associated with the probability of default. In fact, this probability can be calculated from the CDS. Since the probability of default must be between zero and one, the CDS series cannot diverge after a shock. Why, then, do unit root tests conclude that CDS series are I(1)? The explanation probably lies in the fact that we have very short series and that their available length does not allow us to observe their true dynamics. Therefore, in our estimation, we used level indicators of risk.

We were able to estimate the common factor for the EMBI by applying the methodology of common factors. We have 20,745 observations (15 countries, with 1,383 daily observations for each country). We estimate an equation by maximum likelihood of the following type:

$$SP_{i,t} = \alpha_i + \beta_i CF_t + \mu_{i,t},$$

where $SP_{i,t}$ is the EMBI spread for country i on day t, CF_t is the common factor we want to estimate, and $u_{i,t}$ is an error term with the usual properties. We estimate the common factor and two parameters for each country: a constant (α_i) and a coefficient β_i. The latter measures the sensitivity of the country's EMBI spread to the common factor. The econometric estimates of the coefficients of the equation and common factor were obtained using maximum likelihood estimators.

The coefficients α_i can be interpreted as the long-run idiosyncratic country risk: when $F_t = 0$, $\mu_{i,t} = 0$, and $SP_{i,t} = \alpha_i$ for all t. In other words, in the absence of individual country shocks and no changes in international financial markets that affect the spreads of individual countries, the latter should be equal to α.

Principal component analysis shows that there is only one significant common factor in the EMBI spread data set.[1] The estimated common factor is shown in figure 16.2. As can be seen from casual inspection, the common factor is very similar in its time profile to that of the individual EMBI spread series.

With the estimates of the common factor, we can calculate the correlations between the common factor and each country's EMBI spreads. Table 16.3 shows that the correlation coefficients between the common factor and the individual-country EMBI spreads and the share of the variance not associated with the common factor for the sample as a whole, both for 2007 and for the pre- and post-Lehman periods. The average correlation coefficient is extremely high and, for most countries, above 90 percent. Additionally, the idiosyncratic shock of the model (i.e., the share of the variance in the spread not associated with the common factor) explains a relatively low percentage of the total variance of the

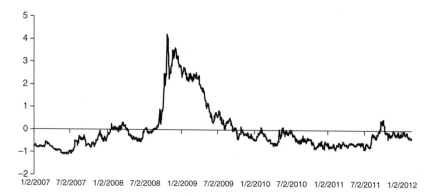

Figure 16.2   Unobservable common factor in Emerging Market Bond Index spreads of fifteen Latin American countries, estimated by principal components (maximum likelihood). *Source*: Authors' calculations.

EMBI spreads for each of the countries considered, with the exception of Venezuela, Ecuador, Argentina (pre-Lehman), and Jamaica (in 2007). Post-Lehman, the correlation coefficients for all countries increase considerably, even for the outliers.

Even though these four countries' sovereign risk premiums are correlated with the common factor, they are less influenced by it and determined to a greater degree by other, unspecified country-specific factors. We interpret these to be variables that make these countries' debt instruments less attractive for international investors than similar instruments in other Latin American countries. At any rate, the results of our econometric exercise correspond with conventional wisdom: Venezuela, Ecuador, Argentina, and Jamaica have pursued policies that are unfriendly toward foreign financial investors and have a track record for repudiating their debts.

We also estimated a model of common factors using a Kalman filter both for the full sample and for the pre- and post-Lehman subsamples (see table 16.4). The exogenous variable was still the EMBI spread, and we estimated the same specification as previously outlined; this time, however, we modeled the common factor as a linear function of a dummy variable with value zero before September 15, 2008, and unity afterward. This binary variable attempts to capture the effect on the common factor of the Lehman bankruptcy. The common factor estimated with this

Table 16.3 Correlation Between the Common Factor Estimated Through Principal Components and Individual Country EMBI Spreads and Variance Not Associated with the Common Factor

Country	Full Sample		2007 Data Only		Before September 15, 2008		After September 15, 2008	
	Correlation	Variance (%)	Correlation	Variance (%)	Correlation	Variance (%)	Correlation	Variance (%)
Argentina	0.97	7	0.75	44	0.89	21	0.97	5
Brazil	0.96	7	0.88	23	0.93	14	0.98	5
Chile	0.96	9	0.9	19	0.95	9	0.97	6
Colombia	0.96	7	0.9	19	0.92	16	0.98	5
Costa Rica	0.95	9	0.97	6	0.97	5	0.98	4
Dominican Republic	0.98	4	0.97	6	0.95	10	0.97	5
Ecuador	0.91	18	-0.16	97	-0.16	98	0.92	15
El Salvador	0.94	11	0.95	10	0.95	10	0.96	7
Guatemala	0.97	5	0.96	9	0.98	4	0.97	6
Jamaica	0.94	12	0.85	28	0.95	10	0.95	10
Mexico	0.99	3	0.95	9	0.97	5	0.98	3
Panama	0.98	4	0.96	8	0.97	6	0.99	2
Peru	0.98	4	0.97	5	0.96	8	0.98	4
Uruguay	0.96	8	0.96	9	0.98	3	0.98	4
Venezuela	0.74	45	0.88	23	0.93	13	0.83	32

Table 16.4 Estimation of the Model of Common Factors with a Kalman Filter, with the Full Sample Using the Lehman Dummy and Pre- and Post-Lehman Samples, an Endogenous Variable, and the EMBI Spread (Maximum Likelihood Estimations)

Country		Full Sample		Before September 15, 2008		After September 15, 2008	
		Coefficient	SE	Coefficient	SE	Coefficient	SE
Dummy		0.8	0.1				
Argentina	β	364.6	8.1	124.9	5.6	392.1	9.9
	α	569.7	18	420.1	7	917.7	13.6
Brazil	β	79.1	1.6	36	1.3	95.4	2.3
	α	196.5	3.8	203.5	1.8	252.4	3.2
Chile	β	65.5	1.4	36.2	1.4	77.2	2
	α	126.8	3.2	129.3	1.8	174.9	2.7
Colombia	β	101.6	2	40	1.5	123.3	3
	α	178	4.9	186.1	2	250.4	4.2
Costa Rica	β	117.8	2.4	63.4	2.2	143.5	3.6
	α	166.7	5.7	186.2	3.1	245.5	4.9
Dominican Republic	β	313	6.5	112.9	4.4	356.3	8.9
	α	359.3	15.2	299.7	5.8	624.1	12.3
Ecuador	β	808	19.4	−9	3.8	984.2	28.2
	α	770.7	40.8	659.5	3.8	1,433	36.5

El Salvador	β	139.1	3.3	58.1	2.2	141.5	3.8
	α	283.4	7	206.6	2.9	425.9	5
Guatemala	β	113.9	2.4	44.1	1.5	130.2	3.4
	α	225.1	5.5	207.2	2.1	319.6	4.6
Jamaica	β	205.2	4.8	87.8	3.4	209.7	5.6
	α	501.4	10.3	391.1	4.5	710.1	7.5
Mexico	β	84.5	1.7	34.4	1.2	94.7	2.3
	α	168.7	4.1	150	1.7	241.5	3.2
Panama	β	99.3	1.9	36.1	1.3	121.3	2.9
	α	170.9	4.7	178.9	1.7	241.6	4.1
Peru	β	90.4	1.8	35.5	1.3	105.1	2.6
	α	167.8	4.3	160	1.7	239.5	3.6
Uruguay	β	139	2.8	58	2	171.6	4.1
	α	215.6	6.7	236.3	2.8	309.9	5.8
Venezuela	β	256.2	9.5	151.4	6.1	179.2	6.3
	α	831.2	15.5	451.8	8	1,211.20	7.6
Log likelihood		-109,850.1		-30,415.6		71,982.60	
Observations		1,343		444		899	

Note: The number of observations refers to observations per country. We used observations for those days on which we had observations for all countries.

methodology is very similar to the values obtained with the principal components methodology. In fact, the correlation coefficient between both series is 0.98.

The estimated coefficient for the dummy variable (Lehman effect) is positive and highly significant. Its value is 0.8. In other words, the common factor rises by 0.8 post-Lehman. The impact on the country EMBIs depends on β. For example, the Lehman event added approximately 65 basis points to the Brazilian EMBI and 250 to the Dominican Republic's.

These results are interesting on various counts. As noted, the coefficient of the common factor is highly significant for all countries included in the sample. The range of variation is from 65 for Chile to 808 for Ecuador. Transforming the common factor into basis points by multiplying it by 100, means that a basis point increase of one in the common factor was, on average, associated during this period with a basis point change of 0.65 in Chile's sovereign spread and 8.08 in Ecuador's.[2,3]

Although this is more conjecture than something we can definitively show with a statistical test, the size of the common factor appears to be correlated to the degree of creditworthiness, level of income per capita, and size of the countries concerned. The most creditworthy countries in the sample according to "objective" data on sovereign spreads or "subjective" credit ratings (Chile, Brazil, Mexico, and Colombia) have the lowest estimated β, whereas Ecuador, Argentina, the Dominican Republic, and Venezuela have the highest.

The estimated alphas track perceived notions of creditworthiness, corroborating the analytical conclusion that they estimate long-term idiosyncratic country risk factors. Thus, at the lower end, the constant for Chile is estimated to be 126 basis points, whereas it rises to 831 for Venezuela, 771 for Ecuador, and 570 for Argentina. This suggests that, despite the co-movement of spreads across the region, investors appear to differentiate between different issuers of sovereign debt in ways that conventional wisdom suggests they would.

The results with the two subsamples also lend credence to the hypothesis that the effect of the common factor on country EMBI spreads rose very sharply after Lehman. All β were significantly higher post-Lehman. In addition, α, which one might take to reflect "pure" country risk, also rose significantly. Thus, adverse shocks in international capital markets (such as Lehman) seem to have two impacts on sovereign risk spreads: (1) it makes all spreads more sensitive to risk appetite/aversion in international markets, and (2) it tends to push up all spreads independently of the co-movement factor.

Rather than trying to estimate the unobservable common factor, an attempt was made to approximate it using an observed variable. We use the TED spread, defined as the difference between LIBOR and the interest rate on Treasury bills (both with a maturity of three months). We estimate ordinary least squares equations for each country, in which the sovereign spread (EMBI) is the dependent variable that incorporated the following explanatory variables: the value of the TED spread lagged one day (to account for a possible codetermination of the TED spread and the EMBI spreads), the Lehman dummy, and an interactive variable between the lagged TED spread and the Lehman dummy. Again, we estimate the model with the full sample and with the two subsamples (pre- and post-Lehman). The results are shown in table 16.5.

The results show that, for almost all countries in the sample, the TED spread has a positive, high (with point estimates in the range of 0.4 to 0.5), and significant impact on the individual sovereign spread of each country. In most countries, the Lehman dummy adds a significant and quantitatively important number of basis points to the post-Lehman constant. The interactive variable is also quite significant. The coefficient that links the TED spread to countries' sovereign spreads rose sharply after the Lehman collapse. In most countries, the coefficient exceeded unity after September 15, 2008, which means that, post-Lehman, a one-point increase in the TED spread— our measure of international financial risk appetite/aversion—led, on average, to more than a one-point increase in country EMBI spreads.

The exceptions are Ecuador (negative coefficient for the TED spread pre-Lehman) and Venezuela (negative effect of Lehman on the coefficient that links the TED spread and the EMBI spread).

The results obtained with the use of the EMBI spreads are pretty robust to changes in the measure of sovereign risk. One may object that the way the EMBI as constructed biased the results in favor of the hypothesis that there is a common factor that accounts for the co-movement of individual country risk measures. The EMBI spreads were built using the interest rate on thirty-year US Treasury bonds. That is, this latter interest rate was subtracted from the interest rate on national bonds to arrive at the EMBI spread. Therefore, by construction, a change in US interest rates will affect all the measured EMBI spreads at the same time.[4]

As an alternative, we apply the same econometric models to country CDS as the dependent variable. The estimated common factor using CDSs is almost identical to the one using EMBI spreads. As shown in table 16.6, there is a high correlation between the common factor,

Table 16.5 Ordinary Least Squares Estimation of Model for EMBI Country Spreads Using TED Spreads, the Lehman Dummy, and an Interaction Between Them as Explanatory Variables, February 2, 2007 to February 23, 2012 (1,284 Observations)

Country	Variable	Coefficient	SE	Country	Variable	Coefficient	SE	Country	Variable	Coefficient	SE
Argentina	TED	1.6	0.1	Ecuador	TED	-0.5	0.1	Uruguay	TED	0.6	0.0
	Dummy	463.9	19.8		Dummy	234.6	46.0		Dummy	37.3	7.8
	Interaction	1.1	0.3		Interaction	6.8	0.8		Interaction	0.7	0.1
	Constant	239.9	11.8		Constant	713.9	10.5		Constant	167.6	4.4
	R^2	0.6			R^2	0.4			R^2	0.6	
Brazil	TED	0.4	0.0	El Salvador	TED	0.6	0.0	Venezuela	TED	2.2	0.1
	Dummy	29.4	4.3		Dummy	209.0	7.8		Dummy	922.8	14.7
	Interaction	0.4	0.1		Interaction	0.4	0.1		Interaction	-1.2	0.2
	Constant	161.6	2.9		Constant	141.3	4.5		Constant	204.3	11.1
	R^2	0.6			R^2	0.6			R^2	0.8	
Chile	TED	0.5	0.0	Guatemala	TED	0.5	0.0				
	Dummy	53.1	3.9		Dummy	97.8	6.3				
	Interaction	0.1	0.1		Interaction	0.4	0.1				
	Constant	76.4	2.6		Constant	149.2	3.2				
	R^2	0.5			R^2	0.5					

Colombia				Jamaica		
TED	0.4	0.0		TED	1.3	0.1
Dummy	33.2	5.5		Dummy	355.1	11.6
Interaction	0.6	0.1		Interaction	0.1	0.2
Constant	140.8	3.4		Constant	252.9	6.8
R^2	0.6			R^2	0.6	
Costa Rica				Mexico		
TED	0.8	0.0		TED	0.4	0.0
Dummy	61.3	6.9		Dummy	76.9	4.3
Interaction	0.3	0.1		Interaction	0.4	0.1
Constant	98.8	4.0		Constant	108.6	2.4
R^2	0.5			R^2	0.6	
Dominican Republic				Peru		
TED	1.2	0.1		TED	0.4	0.0
Dummy	247.5	17.1		Dummy	60.0	4.4
Interaction	1.5	0.3		Interaction	0.4	0.1
Constant	166.7	9.0		Constant	112.6	2.4
R^2	0.6			R^2	0.7	

Source: Authors' calculations based on Bloomberg data.

Table 16.6 Correlation Between the Individual Country Credit Default Swaps and the Common Factor, Estimated with Principal Components and the Variance Not Associated with the Common Factor

Country	Full Sample		2007 Data Only		Before September 15, 2008		After September 15, 2008	
	Correlation	Variance (%)	Correlation	Variance (%)	Correlation	Variance (%)	Correlation	Variance (%)
Argentina	0.95	10	0.95	10	0.88	23	0.95	10
Brazil	0.99	2	0.9	19	0.94	12	0.99	3
Chile	0.96	8	0.82	32	0.93	13	0.96	7
Colombia	0.97	6	0.96	8	0.96	8	0.98	3
Ecuador	-0.25	94	-0.14	98	-0.21	95	-0.74	45
Mexico	0.99	3	0.99	2	0.98	3	0.99	3
Panama	0.98	4	0.99	2	0.99	2	0.99	3
Peru	0.98	3	0.98	4	0.93	14	0.98	3
Venezuela	0.88	22	0.91	16	0.92	15	0.89	21

estimated via principal components, and the country CDSs. The only country that did not follow this pattern was Ecuador, where, in fact, the correlation was negative. All correlation coefficients rise significantly post-Lehman, and only Ecuador and Venezuela exhibit a high variance in their CDSs not associated with the common factor. For the full sample, the variance of Ecuador's CDS explained by the idiosyncratic shock is 95 percent. For Venezuela's, it is 19 percent.

Finally, following the same procedure as we did for the EMBI spread, we estimate the common factor through a Kalman filter, with the individual country daily CDS as the endogenous variable and using as an additional variable the Lehman dummy. The results are shown in table 16.7.[5]

The results are very similar to those obtained using the sovereign EMBI spread (shown in table 16.4). The Lehman shock added an estimate of 0.9 basis points to the common factor that explained all CDSs. The estimated common factor is a highly significant determinant of the country CDSs, and its coefficient has an absolute value of between 52 (Chile) and 852 (Argentina). The only anomalous result was Ecuador, where the common factor had a negative (and significant) coefficient. At the same time, Ecuador exhibits a huge constant (the estimate of the long-run idiosyncratic risk) of 2,304 basis points. Data availability do not allow for an estimation of the parameters of all countries for the pre-Lehman subsample.[6] However, both are much higher for the post-Lehman period than for the sample as a whole. Again, adverse credit market shocks affect negatively both the level of the CDSs and the extent to which they respond to changes in international financial market conditions.

CONCLUSIONS

Using a sample of Latin American countries from just before the onset of the financial crisis to the beginning of 2012, this chapter has shown that there is a large element of co-movement in the variables that are conventionally used to measure sovereign credit risk: the EMBI spread and the CDS on sovereign debt. If the EMBI spread or the CDS on a country's sovereign paper reflected the inherent risk of investing in its bonds, one should not expect that changes in these variables would be correlated across countries. To put it a different way, nothing in the fundamentals of a country such as Chile seem to justify the enormous swings in its EMBI spread (or in its sovereign CDS): its EMBI spread went from

Table 16.7 Estimation of the Common Factor Model for Country Credit Default Swaps Through a Kalman Filter, with a Lehman Dummy Using the Full and Post-Lehman Samples (Maximum Likelihood Estimations)

Country		Full Sample		After September 15, 2008	
		Coefficient	SE	Coefficient	SE
	Dummy	0.9	0.1		
Argentina	β	851.5	19.4	995.9	27.3
	α	590.2	43.4	1,421.3	36
Brazil	β	72.4	1.4	85.4	2.1
	α	105.4	3.5	169.9	2.9
Chile	β	51.7	1.1	53.9	1.4
	α	56.3	2.6	111.8	1.9
Colombia	β	76.4	1.5	94.7	2.2
	α	121.9	3.8	183.7	3.2
Ecuador	β	−432.6	41.8	−1,138.6	47.9
	α	2,303.7	55	2,710.1	54.9
Mexico	β	81.7	1.7	90.1	2.2
	α	93.2	4	175.9	3
Panama	β	81.2	1.6	99.7	2.4
	α	107.9	4	175.5	3.3
Peru	β	75.8	1.5	88.6	2.2
	α	109.6	3.7	178.2	3
Venezuela	β	458.7	12.2	433.7	13.6
	α	738.8	24.7	1,299.8	17
Log likelihood		−66,726.1		−442,88.9	
Observations		1,320		899	

Note: The number of observations refers to observations per country. We used observations for those days on which we had observations for all countries.

78 basis points at the beginning of 2007 to 410 at the end of January 2009 and back to 90 basis points at the end of December 2009. These gyrations have more to do with changes in risk appetite and liquidity conditions on international financial markets than with changes in domestic fundamentals.

We attempted to measure the common factor behind the variations in the EMBI spreads and CDSs and to estimate its impact on sovereign spreads in three different ways. One was principal component analysis. The second was the use of a Kalman filter and the introduction of a dummy to reflect the effect of the Lehman collapse. In the third set of regressions, we use the TED spread as a proxy for the unobservable common factor and estimate its impact on EMBI spreads before and after Lehman.

We find that the presumption for the existence of a common factor is strong and substantiated by the data. The estimated common factor and its proxy (the TED spread) are highly significant variables that explained variations in EMBI spreads and CDSs. In addition, we find that the Lehman episode had two distinct effects on country credit risk: a constant effect, by adding basis points to the risk measures, and a trend effect, by raising the value of the common factor. In the regressions using the TED spread as the explanatory variable, the coefficient associated with this proxy for the common factor rises sharply post-Lehman. In other words, the impact of Lehman seems to have been to make all Latin American sovereign paper riskier (demanding higher interest rates) and more sensitive to international risk appetite and liquidity conditions.

This is not to say that country fundamentals play no role in determining the level of risk valuations, whether measured by the EMBI spreads or CDSs. They do. Generally speaking, the constants in our econometric exercises do seem to reflect a ranking according to perceived country risk, with Chile, Brazil, Mexico, and Colombia at the low end of the spectrum and countries such as Ecuador, Venezuela, or Argentina at the higher end. However, even these measures of long-run country risk are influenced by international factors: they experience discrete and significant upward movements when international liquidity and risk appetite diminish abruptly.

What does this mean for policy? In the first place, international financial market conditions are fundamental in determining market access and the price a country must pay to borrow internationally, independent of the quality of its policy making or future prospects. This would suggest that a measure of protection against the effects of Lehman-like episodes, whether through building up reserves or a sovereign wealth fund, is a good idea. Second, countries integrating into international financial markets have to be aware of its dangers. Low interest rates and easy access do not mean that a country has "made it" into the ranks of creditworthy countries. Therefore, treading with care in the brave new world of international financial integration is highly advisable.

NOTES

1. We retain components with eigenvalues greater than one (the Kaiser–Guttman criterion).

2. One should also add a constant so that the common factor never falls below zero. This, of course, does not alter the analysis in this paragraph, because such a constant, multiplied by the coefficients attached to the common factor, simply shifts by the same amount as the constants estimated for each country.

3. The level of 100 in the normalized common factor is estimated to have been reached just after the Lehman event (at the end of October 2008). Roughly a month later it was at 300.

4. It should be noted, however, that the bias involved runs counter to the findings shown in table 16.5: a fall in the US Treasury bond rate will cause all EMBIs to rise. In other words, the built-in relationship between the US interest rate (a component of the common factor) and the EMBI spreads is negative. Our findings show a significantly positive relationship between the common factor and the EMBI spreads. This means that, if anything, by using the EMBIs, we could be underestimating the impact of the common factor.

5. Note that CDS data are not available for all countries. Therefore, the countries included in table 16.7 are Argentina, Brazil, Chile, Colombia, Ecuador, Mexico, Panama, Peru, and Venezuela.

6. For some days there are no quotes for several countries. The parameters are estimated with a balanced panel, so the absence of data for one or more countries eliminates the possibility of using the data available for other countries.

REFERENCES

Calvo, G., Izquierdo, A., and Mejía, L. F. 2008. "Systemic sudden stops: the relevance of balance-sheet effects and financial integration." National Bureau of Economic Research Working Paper 14026. http://www.nber.org/papers/w14026.pdf.

De Jong, P. 1988. "The likelihood for a state space model." *Biometrika* 75(1): 165–169.

Délano, V. and Selaive, J. 2005. "Spreads soberanos: una aproximación factorial." Banco Central de Chile Documentos de Trabajo 309. www.bcentral.cl/estudios/documentos-trabajo/pdf/dtbc309.pdf.

Edwards, S. 1986. "The pricing of bonds and bank loans in international markets: an empirical analysis of developing countries' foreign borrowing." *European Economic Review* 30(3): 565–589.

Geweke, J. 1977. "The dynamic factor analysis of economic time series models." In *Latent variables in socioeconomic models*, D. J. Aigner and A. S. Goldberger, eds. Amsterdam: North-Holland: 124–145.

Hamilton, J. 1994. *Time series analysis*. Princeton, NJ: Princeton University Press.

Kamin, S. and von Kleist, K. 1999. "The evolution and determinants of emerging market credit spreads in the 1990s." Bank for International Settlements Working Paper 68. www.bis.org/publ/work68.pdf.

Longstaff, F., Pan, J., Pedersen, L., and Singleton, K. 2011. "How sovereign is sovereign credit risk?" *American Economic Journal: Macroeconomics* 3(2):75–103.

Lütkepohl, H. 2005. *New introduction to multiple time series analysis.* Berlin: Springer-Verlag.

Pan, J. and Singleton, K. 2008. "Default and recovery implicit in the term structure of sovereign CDS spreads." *The Journal of Finance* 63(5):2345–2384.

Sargent, T. J. and Sims, C. A. 1977. "Business cycle modeling without pretending to have too much a priori economic theory." In *New methods in business cycle research: proceedings from a conference,* C. A. Sims, ed. Minneapolis, MN: Federal Reserve Bank of Minneapolis: 83–104.

Stock, J. H. and Watson, M. W. 1989. "New indexes of coincident and leading economic indicators." In *NBER macroeconomics annual,* vol. 4, edited by O. J. Blanchard and S. Fischer, 351–394. Cambridge, MA: MIT Press.

Watson, M. W. and Engle, R. F. 1983. "Alternative algorithms for the estimation of dynamic factor: MIMIC and varying coefficient regression models." *Journal of Econometrics* 23(3): 385–400.

Zhang, F. X. 2008. "Market expectations and default risk premium in credit default swap prices: a study of Argentine default." *Journal of Fixed Income* 18(1): 37–55.

PART 5

Approaches to Development

Cognitive Dissonance

POSTWAR ECONOMIC DEVELOPMENT STRATEGIES AND BRETTON WOODS
INTERNATIONAL FINANCIAL STABILITY

Jan Kregel

DOES DEVELOPMENT ECONOMICS EXIST?

One of the most debated questions in economics is whether developing economies require a special theory and policy. Prebisch (1950) was among the first to argue that the mainstream economics of developed countries is not applicable to developing countries in South America. In his view, an alternative theory was required to understand the problems that faced developing countries in the Southern Hemisphere. Hirschman (1981) criticized what he called "monoeconomics," by which he meant the mistaken application of one uniform theory to the development problems of both developed and industrialized economies. Kaldor (1964) adopted a similar position, noting that the International Monetary Fund's (IMF) application to developing economies of policies designed for developed countries could produce perverse and undesired results.

The opposite view is represented by John Williamson's enunciation of the "Washington Consensus," designed to be the death knell of "development" economics. Williamson (1989) simply reiterated a prior criticism by Lal (1983) directed at Albert Hirschman and other "pioneers" of development who he claimed had forsaken traditional economic theory in their analysis of developing countries. Lal attacked development economists' policies as mere "theoretical curiosities" based on a perversion of orthodox economic principles held to be applicable in developing economies only and that "falsely deny the universal applicability of rational economic behavior . . . on which standard economic theory relies for its results" (Toye 1993: 95). Even worse, in Lal's view, these economists favored policies of domestic industrialization based on the argument that the "case for free trade is invalid for developing economies" (95).

But this simply echoed a long tradition. For example, John Coppock, a US State Department economist, referred to his work on development policy for the United Nations in its formative years as follows: "most of us . . . felt that economic problems are economic problems wherever they happen to be. You wanted to know the facts of a particular country and situation, of course, but detailed knowledge of a particular country wouldn't make much difference as to exchange rate policy or the investment situation or trade regulations and so on" (in UN Oral History Project, cited in Toye and Toye [2004: 26, 306]).

It is important to recognize that Lal was simply applying to traditional development theory (which, in the early postwar years, was basically Keynesian) the "counterrevolution" against Keynesian economics proposed by Milton Friedman and Harry Johnson and supported by the political revolution led by Margaret Thatcher and Ronald Reagan. Set off by Little et al.'s (1970) Organization for Economic Cooperation and Development (OECD) study of trade and industry in developing countries that attacked the efficacy of protection in promoting growth and extended by the work of Krueger (1974) on the perverse rent-seeking incentives created by industrial protection, the counterrevolution called for a removal of the state from active participation in economic decision making, opening of domestic markets to external competition, and deregulation of domestic markets as the basis for eliminating the errors and inconsistencies in government regulations in support of development.

Thus, Williamson could correctly claim that his proposed Consensus contained nothing novel but was based on "ideas that had long been regarded as orthodox so far as OECD countries are concerned" (Williamson 2002: 2). The Consensus was also meant to counter what Williamson characterized, echoing Lal's earlier assessment of traditional development theory, as "a sort of global apartheid which claimed that developing countries came from a different universe" (Williamson 2002: 2). The implication was that the difficulties faced by Latin American economies in the 1980s resulted largely from the failed attempt by development economists to formulate and apply policies that were specific to the context of the region.

BRETTON WOODS, INTERNATIONAL FINANCIAL STABILITY, AND INTERNATIONAL IMBALANCES

It is interesting that a similar debate over the role of the international financial system to be designed at Bretton Woods never occurred. Indeed, in the discussions over the postwar economic and financial structure, the debate was between those countries that were most interested in promoting local and global full employment and thus most likely to be in structural deficit—basically the United Kingdom—and a country that was experiencing positive expansion and what seemed to be a structural external surplus—the United States. The debate was thus over the policies appropriate for eliminating these imbalances in the absence of what was believed to be the automatic mechanism of the gold standard.

The fear of the deficit countries was that the need to maintain stable exchange rates would require them to sacrifice full employment policy, whereas the surplus countries were more concerned about the inflationary impact of the measures that would be required to maintain exchange rate stability. Thus, the UK position proposed by Keynes was for a "symmetric" adjustment mechanism in which both surplus and deficit countries would be obliged to cooperate, whereas the US position proposed by Harry Dexter White was for a "stabilization" fund in which the deficit country would be provided bridge financing to preserve exchange rate stability while introducing policies to reduce external imbalances.

Developing countries were not well represented at Bretton Woods; indeed, many were not yet in existence, and the question of the impact of the international financial system on development was hardly discussed except at the last minute with the addition of the last word to the title of the International Bank for Reconstruction and Development (IBRD). There was no discussion of the implications for developing countries of the decision to promote stable exchange rates and to use the IMF's short-term stabilization funds to employ policies to reduce or eliminate deficits. The implicit assumption behind the system was that members would on average have balanced external positions, because this is what would be required for maintaining exchange rate stability. This also implicitly applied to developing countries that would become members of the IMF.

In contrast, consideration of development policies was left primarily to UN agencies in the early postwar period. Their analysis of the problems that faced developing countries was based on the presumption of scarcity in domestic savings and financial resources. Thus, the problem of development was conceived as providing flows of financial resources from developed to developing countries. The first UN development decade (Stokke 2009) that set a growth objective of 5 percent for developing countries therefore concluded that this would require a transfer of 1 percent of developed country GDP to developing countries.

The US program of support for Latin America in the 1960s, the Alliance for Progress, was also predicated on inducing capital flows from the United States to Latin America.

Few economists noted that this approach to development contradicted the principles of the Bretton Woods institutions because it would require sustained balance-of-payments surpluses in developed countries that corresponded to the capital outflows to developing countries—and conversely for developing countries to run balance-of-payments deficits that corresponded to the acquisition of industrial imports from developed countries. However, if international financial stability required stable exchange rates, this meant that the size of the deficits that could be run by developing countries would be limited by conditions of international financial stability and not by the needs of developing countries. Indeed, the very policies that would be required to preserve exchange stability would be designed to reduce the development possibilities of developing countries.

But the presumption of external equilibrium was not the only component of cognitive dissonance between development policies and international financial stability. When internal adjustment policies supported by IMF conditionality were unable to produce a reversal of external disequilibrium, countries were required to introduce a currency realignment. Although Keynes argued that the new international system would require substantial exchange rate flexibility, his concerns—apart from granting countries the ability to adjust exchange rates within 10 percent of parity without reference to the IMF and to introduce restrictions on trade under the scarce currency clause—were rejected (Skidelsky 2000).

However, the efficacy of devaluation in producing external balance was already known to require very precise elasticity conditions (summarized in the Marshall–Lerner conditions). Although it was not obvious that these conditions applied to developed countries—indeed, it was generally believed that the United Kingdom on the one hand and the reconstructing economies on the other did not satisfy the conditions—whether they would be satisfied in developing countries was never considered. It seems reasonable a priori that they would not have been met, and much of Prebisch's (1950) arguments concerning the negative impact of the declining terms of trade were couched in terms of the impossibility for developing countries to meet those elasticity conditions.

The postwar international financial system was thus designed on the presumption of external equilibrium across countries, in which deficit countries would be primarily responsible for external adjustment through internal demand policies and, when that was not sufficient, to use exchange rate depreciation to reinforce the impact of contractionary fiscal policies. Conversely, international development policy was formulated on the presumption that sustained surpluses of the developed countries would be available to finance deficits of the developing countries in support of sustained expansion and the inapplicability of exchange rate adjustment as a measure of influencing external balances.

That these two visions of the postwar financial system were inconsistent does not seem to have occurred to the IMF, IBRD, or United Nations, each of which is respectively responsible for exchange rate stability and economic development. In this context, Prebisch's concerns can be seen as a recognition of this inconsistency, whereas the emergence of the Washington Consensus can be seen as a resolution of this cognitive dissonance in official policy by rejecting the need for any special conditions and policies for developing countries.

This internal inconsistency represented a major obstacle for developing countries and ignored a major problem: international debt. Because foreign exchange would be required to pay for the excess of imports of necessary consumption goods and capital goods over exports required for the development plans, these plans required positive net resource flows encouraged by early UN development policy. Over time, however, these flows generate debt service outflows that increase the current account deficit to increase unless the trade deficit is reduced to accommodate a fixed level of capital inflows and lead to a reduced impact on development. Alternatively, foreign capital inflows would have to increase to accommodate the rising current account deficit caused by the increased debt service payments on capital factor services accounts for any given level of the goods account deficit, leading to an ever-increasing level of external debt. Neither solution would be compatible with the stability of the international system conceived at Bretton Woods.

THE STABILITY OF GROWTH WITH FOREIGN SAVINGS: A PONZI SCHEME

As Domar (1950) has shown, a development strategy based on net imports financed by foreign capital inflows can only exist with a stable ratio of debt to GDP if the interest rates paid for foreign capital are equal to or less than the rate of increase of lending by foreigners. If interest rates are higher than the rate of increase of inflows, the policy will eventually and automatically become self-reversing as the current account becomes dominated by interest and profit remittances that exceed capital inflows.

In the context of the cognitive dissonance between stability of the international financial system and development, it is interesting to note that the Domar conditions for a sustained long-term development strategy based on sustained external financing are equivalent to the conditions required for a successful Ponzi financing scheme. As long as the rate of increase in inflows from new investors in a pyramid or Ponzi scheme is equal to or greater than the rate of interest paid to existing investors in the scheme, there is no difficulty in maintaining the scheme. However, such schemes are eventually condemned to failure because of the increasing absolute size of the net debt stock. Domar's condition only refers to the ratio of debt to GDP, not its absolute size.

External financing cannot provide developing countries with a permanent development strategy unless the rate of increase of export earnings is equal to the rate of interest on the outstanding debt. However, if the foreign borrowing is not used for expenditures that create net foreign exchange earnings (it makes little difference if this is domestic infrastructure investments or purchases of basic or luxury consumption goods or military equipment), the country's development planning will be subject to maintaining the steady rate of increase in capital inflows and will become a hostage to international financial markets. But even if foreign borrowing is used to expand export potential, any external event that causes the rate of increase in inflows to fall off will create domestic instability and require domestic adjustments to reduce dependence on external resources, which usually leads to a financial crisis through failure to meet financial commitments. At the same time, to make foreign lenders confident in the country's ability to meet foreign commitments, policies that enhance the short-term ability to pay, such as building up foreign exchange reserves or reducing external dependence by reducing domestic growth to produce a stronger export performance and fiscal balance, must be implemented. However, these policies are also self-defeating from the point of view of positive development, because they either reduce the capital inflows that can be maintained on a permanent basis or reduce the growth of per capita incomes. External financing as a source of a long-term development strategy is thus a double-edged sword that must be managed judiciously if it is to contribute to development rather than becoming a source of persistent financial instability and crisis.

The international financial system's prejudice in favor of limited external imbalances, however, is as much of an impediment.

DEVELOPMENT SCENARIOS BASED ON EXTERNAL RESOURCES

The hazard of relying on external flows for development in the presence of a presumption of international financial stability under Bretton Woods should be interpreted carefully. There are three possible general cases:

Case 1, in which the rate of interest on foreign borrowing exceeds the rate of increase of capital outflows: Domar's (1950) argument is made by comparing unchanged rates of change over time. Based on this assumption, it is possible to conclude that whenever the assumed constant servicing rate on foreign borrowing over time is above the prevailing and assumed constant rate of increase of inflows, the borrowing country will experience continually rising external debt stocks and an eventual crisis and reversal of net resource flows that may lock the economy into a low-level debt trap. A sustained development policy based on external capital is not viable under these conditions.

Case 2, in which the rate of increase of capital inflows is equal to or greater than the rate of interest on foreign borrowing: Even if the Domar sustainability condition is met and the assumed constant servicing rate is equal to or below the assumed constant rate of increase in capital inflows, it will still be true that external debt stocks will rise continuously, and the borrowing economy will be subject to increasing financial fragility and financial crisis because a small internal or external shock that causes an increase in its net goods account deficit through either a fall off in export volumes or prices or an increase in export volumes or prices. In addition, a reduction in the rate of increase in capital inflows or an increase in the rate of interest on foreign loans will lead to a reversion to case 1.

Case 3, in which a rate of increase in capital inflows and interest rates vary over time: Indeed, the normal case is for both the rate of debt servicing and the rate of capital inflows to be highly volatile. Capital surges can bring about sharp changes in flows that push the rate of increase in inflows above the servicing rate. But such surges also bring about a bunching of repayments in the future and create a large accumulation of nonrepatriated profits that can be rapidly reversed when capital flows fall off to rates below the servicing rate, thus aggravating the reversal of resource flows. These fluctuations will be further aggravated if the tenor of lending is particularly short term, as this will increase the variability of both the rate of increase of inflows and the rate of interest.

For case 1, it is clear that the problem lies with the disparity between the rate of interest and the rate of increase of capital inflows and can be remedied by action to reduce the former or increase the latter. It is interesting that the period of greatest success of external financing occurred when international capital flows were intermediated by the multilateral financial institutions at preferential interest rates with long maturities or through grants-in-aid. However, the international financial system and the reform of its architecture seem to have consistently moved away from this framework to restore a system of private financial flows at market rates that are generally believed to have caused repeated breakdowns of the international system, which the multilateral institutions were created to prevent.

For case 2, where the strategy may be sustainable, the basic problem is implementing a transitional policy that allows for the use of positive resource flows to create domestic productive capacity for exports that allows the borrower to grow at its maximum potential rate without pushing the economy into financial crisis. For a development policy based on external flows to be successful, the external resources would have to be dedicated to the creation of a competitive industrial sector to increase manufactured goods exports, allowing increased total imports for a given rate of capital inflows and eventually allowing exports to shift to covering debt service, allowing the rate of capital inflows to decline *pari passu* until the current account went into deficit, external debt was fully repaid, and the country became a capital exporter with reverse capital flows.

However, with free international capital markets, a smooth transition of this nature is unlikely because success makes the country a more attractive and less risky investment destination, so there will be a tendency for flows to increase, making some sort of controls necessary. The goal is to reach an end state in which net export surpluses of goods and services are sufficient for repaying foreign borrowing. This policy must thus have as components a policy of export promotion, as well as a policy of controlling the rate of increase of foreign borrowing and ensuring that the tenor of the borrowing is the same as the length of the development plan. Thus, policies that increase the maturity and repayment structure of the lending may be as important as policies that ensure low interest rates.

The alternatives would be for foreign investors to automatically reinvest interest and dividends or to avoid the use of fixed interest rate instruments. Domar suggested that the simplest and most obvious remedy lies "not in abstaining from foreign investment which the world needs badly, but in reducing the interest rate on public lending to a minimum consistent with the preservation of international dignity; surely we don't need the interest as income" (Domar 1950: 133). Although these alternatives were meant to provide a safety cushion in the form of financial resources, Domar's comment suggests another approach in terms of a cushion determined by the difference between the interest rate paid on foreign lending and the rate of increase in foreign borrowing; i.e., the cushion should be greater than, say, two standard deviations of the rate of increase in capital inflows. Prebisch's report to the First United Nations Conference on Trade and Development (UNCTAD 1964) suggested another form of safety cushion: the creation of a fund to provide compensatory finance that would be in the form of noninterest-bearing grants in amounts calculated to compensate countries for their terms of trade losses.

Another alternative, given by Ohlin (1995), is to recognize that deregulated open competitive internal markets and sustained international capital inflows are neither necessary nor sufficient conditions for a successful development strategy. He noted that there is

> sometimes an indignant presumption that there should always be a net transfer to developing countries in order to help them to import more than they exported. Behind this presumption there is the old idea that countries in the course of their development should be capital importers until they mature and become capital exporters. This, however, does not mean that they should receive positive net transfers, borrowing more than they pay in interest and dividends. . . . If export performance and the returns on the use of foreign resources are adequate, foreign debts and investments can be serviced without the aid of new loans.
>
> (OHLIN 1995:3)

LONG-TERM DEBT SUSTAINABLE DEVELOPMENT SCENARIOS

These observations suggest that the problem might be resolved by specifying what might be called a long-term "debt-sustainable" development scenario (Kregel 2004, 2007), which could be divided into three stages. In the first, the Domar stability condition would be met for approximately twenty years while the country invests in production and export capacities and positive net inflows are maintained. This would be followed by a second stage of approximately ten years, in which the newly created capacity allows exports to grow more rapidly than the overall economy and a steady reduction in the rate of net capital inflows. This would be followed by a third stage, in which net capital flows are reversed and the accumulated stock of external debt is gradually repaid as productivity, net exports, and the external surplus increase. After approximately fifty years the country would become a net foreign lender.

This ideal debt-sustainable scenario will face three problem stages. The first stage is when debt ratios may well exceed values associated with short-term sustainability. If borrowing is truncated for this reason, the entire development process is jeopardized.

If the second stage is reached, experience suggests that successful income and export expansion will make the country more attractive to international investors, causing an increase rather than a decrease in the rate of capital inflows. This could be accompanied by an inappropriate appreciation of the exchange rate that may threaten the further development of domestic export capacity. It is at this stage that some management of capital inflows may be required to balance the needs of borrowers and lenders.

The third stage is when private markets in general will not lend for fifty-year terms that such a scenario requires, so that the lending will have to continue to have a large official component or be intermediated by an international financial institution that lends under concessional terms. This is particularly important in the first stage when debt ratios may far exceed what are considered acceptable short-term limits.

Early studies by the IBRD (e.g., Avramovic 1958, 1964) also recognized the importance of assessing debt servicing capacity over long periods of time, although in practice it gave importance to short-term adjustments in domestic resource use. This approach of viewing debt sustainability over the entire development process was eventually abandoned. This "growth-cum-debt" approach shares many commonalities with the three-stage debt-sustainable scenario outlined previously.

In the first stage, savings start from a level that is too low to finance domestic investment requirements so that the country has to borrow to finance part of its investment and to meet service on the debt accumulated in the process. In the second stage of the process, savings have grown sufficiently to finance domestic investment but cannot yet meet the entire burden of interest and amortization payments on the accumulated debt, including the payment of foreign currency on the external debt burden. Thus, debt continues to grow, but at a slower pace than in the first stage because some of the increasing savings can be used to meet debt service. As the third stage begins, domestic savings are sufficient for financing domestic investment and for meeting the interest on accumulated debt. As the country begins to generate a surplus of savings above domestic investment and interest payments, it can start to pay down debt while maintaining a satisfactory momentum of economic development. The borrower eventually pays back all the interest costs that it has postponed from earlier periods, and the growth-cum-debt cycle is complete; foreign capital has also been repaid after earning interest throughout the period of its employment in the borrowing country.

However, the success of this cycle depends on a sequence of economic adjustments that take place over time. In the initial period of import substitution, aid flows are used to support the structural change of the economy through development of newly diversified export sectors with rapidly rising and less volatile export earnings that eventually produce the funds required to meet debt service.

The key to this approach is whether debt can be repaid over the full development cycle rather than whether debt service can be met in any particular period of time. Indeed, it is premised on the fact that debt service will not be met over the early periods in which short-term debt ratios will be continuously deteriorating. Its success depends on the provision of financing through these early periods. In addition, it requires that the long-term growth of income produces internal savings, that the government can mobilize these increased savings in the form of fiscal revenues, and that the increased domestic resources can be transferred through the appropriate adjustment of the external balance. Sustained growth and income depend on growth in savings, and the growth in savings depends on growth in income. Similarly, a sustained growth in income cannot be achieved unless the foreign trade sector of the economy develops fast enough to provide the external earnings that are needed to satisfy growing import requirements and to finance other external outlays. The required rate of export growth will of course vary from country to country depending on its dependence on natural resources. This approach to debt sustainability thus requires the design of a long-term national development strategy that by the end of the process eliminates the necessity for additional borrowing and debt service through increasing per capita incomes and export earnings on a sustained basis.

The bottom line is that the international financial system has to be capable of accepting sustained and substantial international imbalances to provide the funding of such scenarios, as well as allowing developing countries to practice policies that produce the required export earnings to generate the funds required to meet debt service and debt repayment. And here the discussion recalls the cognitive dissonance described previously, because the international financial system was designed to prevent the existence of such sustained imbalances and continues to promote and encourage policies to eliminate them.

This approach is not original. It is very similar to that developed in the early work of Avramovic (1958, 1964) at the IBRD on long-term aspects of debt sustainability. Although these studies first analyzed the short-term aspects of the problem, it was noted that "the logical sequence appears to be from the long-run growth problem to the temporary deviations, which occasionally interrupt the trend" (Avramovic 1964: 9), because "continuing growth in per capita production and the underlying process of rapid accumulation of productive capital is the basic long-run condition of debt servicing capacity" (Avramovic 1964: 11). It was for this reason that short-term indicators such as debt service ratios were considered to lack any theory that would support them as meaningful indicators of the long-run aspect of debt servicing capacity. A similar analysis of long-term indebtedness and international imbalances as conditions for development can also be found in Dunkman (1933).

A similar approach is also taken by Marcelo Diamand in his theory of external bottlenecks as the impediment to developing countries with unbalanced productive structures, such as monocommodity exporters, to operate a successful development strategy (Diamand 1978). Diamand argued that a basic external bottleneck is the limited capacity of developed countries to absorb developing country exports or alternatively to produce exports that are competitive in international markets. He noted that although traditional theory presumes that shortages created by bottlenecks will be eliminated by price adjustments imposed by the market mechanism, this adjustment mechanism would transfer income to the producers of scarce items and have an impact on real wages. If wages are near subsistence, as is the case in large portions of the population of developing countries, this will simply lead to an increase in labor costs that will offset the initial price adjustment mechanism. The only adjustment possible then becomes an adjustment in quantities, i.e., a reduction in national income that reduces the demand for the scarce commodity to its natural supply.

EXPORT EXPANSION AND EXCHANGE RATE POLICY

The three-stage scenario described above raised the question of how to induce the required expansion of exports. As Kaldor noted, the basic problem that faces developing countries is not an inability to produce manufactured goods but an inability to produce them at levels of productivity that allow them to be competitive in international markets, i.e., the same problem identified by Diamand (1978) as a bottleneck. And this is the problem of relative prices. For a primary commodity producing developing country

> the first measure should thus consist in restructuring the industrial exchange rates for exports. The starting point must be an exchange rate adequate for the primary sector. But there is no reason why this primary exchange rate for exports should coincide with the nominal exchange rate. The nominal exchange rate can be based on a more expensive dollar, reconstructing the primary exchange rate for exports, which had been set as a starting point by means of the application of adequate export duties. Thus, we would have two basic exchange rates. On the one hand, the nominal rate, which would be used for financial transactions, industrial exports and, with the corresponding import duties (much lower than in the conventional system), also for imports. On the other hand, we would have the primary exchange rate for exports, determined by the nominal rate less export duties. This reform would bring the nominal exchange rate substantially closer to the structure of industrial costs and would improve the possibility to export manufactured goods.
>
> (DIAMAND 1978:31)

Kaldor made a similar point:

> When import requirements exceed the capacity to export on account of high domestic costs, this is generally taken as evidence of over-valuation of the currency. . . . but it is essential to understand that that it is not the kind of overvaluation that could be "cured" by any uniform adjustment of the exchange rate. This is because the exchange rate

which would make it possible for an under-developed country to develop export markets in manufactured products would mean a considerable under-valuation of its currency in terms or primary commodities which form the great bulk of its exports; and the rise in export proceeds in the primary sector which follows a devaluation tends to generate an inflation in domestic costs and prices that soon neutralizes any initially beneficial effects on the export costs of manufacturers. . . . The rise in the domestic price of export crops is bound, sooner or later, to lead to a corresponding rise in the local prices of food. And since, at the levels of income characteristic of under-developed countries, money wages in industry will be closely correlated to the price of food, a rise in earnings from primary exports will tend to bring about a corresponding advance in the level of money costs in manufacturing production.

(KALDOR 1964:186–187)

As a consequence, "there is no *single* rate of exchange which is capable . . . of securing equilibrium between domestic costs of production and the prices, or the level of costs, in foreign markets," and, in agreement with Diamand, "There is no way out of this dilemma except by some system of dual exchange rates, or some system of combined taxes and subsidies which produce the same effect as dual exchange rates" (Kaldor 1964: 187–188).

Thus, the successful implementation of the three-stage scenarios presented previously would require a system of dual or multiple exchange rates in addition to the presumption of sustained imbalances as being inconsistent with the Bretton Woods framework of international financial stability.

However, if dual exchange rates are a necessary condition, it also follows that the use of exchange depreciation to provide stability and eliminate imbalances will not only be ineffective but also prevent successful development. As Kaldor notes,

the periodic efforts of . . . the I.M.F. to secure an alleviation of the balance of payments problems of particular under-developed countries by the introduction of more "realistic" exchange rates . . . have proved so misguided. In most of these cases . . . devaluation has been followed by a new wave of inflation, which has swallowed up the stimulus to exports afforded by the devaluation, within a relative short period. The diagnosis that has led to such recommendations has been based on the false analogy from the situation of industrialized countries whose export prices are cost-determined to that of primary producers whose export costs are price-determined.

(KALDOR 1964:187–188)

CONCLUSION

The Bretton Woods framework for international trade and financial stability was thus predicated on application to developed countries at a similar stage of development and with similar productive structures. It implicitly precluded the implementation of any development strategy that relied on developing the manufacturing sector by imports from developed countries that produced substantial international imbalances. This is because it was predicated on a rough balance in external positions over time to preserve exchange rate stability.

The presumption of exchange rate stability and the preclusion of dual exchange rates prevented developing countries from overcoming cost disadvantages in their nascent export sectors; in addition, the use of devaluation as a tool for eliminating external imbalances also worked against the ability of developing countries to develop the foreign exchange through exports that were necessary for financing the development of manufacturing.

The international financial system developed at Bretton Woods may have been appropriate for developed countries; it was a positive impediment to developing countries' attempts to embark on a strategy of industrial catching up.

REFERENCES

Avramovic, D. 1958. *Debt servicing capacity and postwar growth in international indebtedness*. Baltimore, MD: Johns Hopkins University Press.

Avramovic, D. 1964. *Economic growth and external debt*. Baltimore, MD: International Bank for Reconstruction and Development.

Diamand, M. 1978. "Towards a change in the economic paradigm through the experience of developing countries." *Journal of Development Economics* 5(1): 19–53.

Domar, E. 1950. "The effect of foreign investments on the balance of payments." *American Economic Review American Economic Review* 40(5): 805–826.

Dunkman, W. 1933. *Quantitative credit control*. New York, NY: Columbia University Press.

Hirschman, A. 1981. *Essays in trespassing*. Cambridge, UK: Cambridge University Press.

Kaldor, N. 1964. "Dual exchange rates and economic development." *Essays on Economic Policy* 2: 178–200.

Kregel, J. A. 2004. "External financing for development and international financial instability." The G-24 Discussion Paper Series 32. http://unctad.org/en/docs /gdsmdpbg2420048_en.pdf.

Kregel, J. A. 2007. "Rethinking debt sustainability in the context of the millennium development goals." *Banca Nazionale Quarterly Review* 60(242): 225–248.

Kregel, J. A. 2008. "The discrete charm of the Washington Consensus." *Journal of Post Keynesian Economics* 30(4): 541–560.

Krueger, A. 1974. "The political economy of the rent-seeking society." *American Economic Review* 64(3): 291–303.

Lal, D. 1983. "The poverty of development economics." Hobart Paper 16. London: Institute of Economic Affairs.

Little, I., Scitovsky, T., and Scott, M. 1970. *Industry and trade in some developing countries: a comparative study*. London: Oxford University Press.

Prebisch, R. 1950. *The economic development of Latin America and its principal problems*. Santiago: United Nations Economic Commission for Latin America.

Ohlin, G. 1995. "The negative net transfers of the World Bank." In *International monetary and financial issues for the 1990s*, vol. 5. New York, NY: UNCTAD: 1–13.

Skidelsky, R. 2000. *John Maynard Keynes fighting for Britain, 1937–1946*. London: Macmillan.

Stokke, O. 2009. *The UN and development: from aid to cooperation*. Bloomington: Indiana University Press.

Toye, J. 1993. *Dilemmas of development*, 2nd ed. Oxford, UK: Blackwell.

Toye, J. and Toye, R. 2004. *The UN and global political economy*. Bloomington: Indiana University Press.

UNCTAD 1964. "Towards a new trade policy for development." In *Proceedings of the United Nations Conference on Trade and Development*, vol. II, March 23–June 16, Geneva, Switzerland.

Williamson, J. 1989. "What Washington means by policy reform." In *Latin American adjustment: how much has happened?* J. Williamson, ed. Washington, DC: Institute for International Economics: 5–20.

Williamson, J. 2002. "Did the Washington Consensus fail?" Outline of speech at the Center for Strategic & International Studies, Washington, DC. http://www2.econ .iastate.edu/classes/econ502/tesfatsion/WashingtonConsensus.JWilliamson2002 .pdf.

CHAPTER 18

New Developmentalism as a Weberian Ideal Type

Luiz Carlos Bresser-Pereira

The idea of "new developmentalism" appeared in Brazil in the beginning of the 2000s as an alternative both to neoliberal orthodoxy, which had prevailed throughout the world for almost thirty years, and to old or classical developmentalism, which characterized many developing countries after World War II. Classical developmentalism or the structuralist development theory is a system of ideas that the pioneers elaborated upon on the basis of the canonical works of Prebisch (1949), Nurkse (1953), and Lewis (1954) and that was applied to countries that were on the threshold of their industrial and capitalist revolutions. Fifty years later, in the context of globalization, a quite different economic and political world, the developing countries had industrialized and become middle-income and democratic. They needed, therefore, a new critique of the conventional economic theory, new economic models and new policy proposals for economic and social reforms aimed not only at economic development but also social inclusion. The new developmentalism that began to emerge in Latin America in the 2000s was a response both to these demands and to the failure of the Washington Consensus and, more broadly, of the thirty neoliberal years of capitalism (1979–2008).

In 2003, I introduced the concept of new developmentalism, placing it in opposition both to the Washington Consensus and to classical developmentalism.[1] In doing so, I reflected, and endeavored to renew, the critique of neoliberal orthodoxy framed by a number of first-rate economists, among them Roberto Frenkel. Soon, a large group of post-Keynesian and structuralist economists joined us, and in 2010 eighty of the world's most eminent development macroeconomists and political economists discussed and approved a document titled "Ten Theses on

New Developmentalism."[2] Robert Frenkel was one of the most authoritative voices in this debate.[3] New developmentalism thus became an alternative strategy to the Washington Consensus and to old developmentalism, and, with the ten theses, also became an institution, an ensemble of defined and shared diagnoses, ideas, and policies. It became on the one hand what Max Weber called an "ideal type"—an abstract and systemic description of economic, social, and political phenomena.[4] On the other hand, as an increasing number of left-wing politicians and developmentalists were elected in the region, we witnessed once again, after the interregnum of the neoliberal years, the building of a developmental state.

New developmentalism conceived as an ideal type is not, therefore, simply a list of policies. In addition to being an informal national development strategy, it is a new theoretical framework to understand development macroeconomics; it is a summing up of values, goals, models, policies, laws and, chiefly, understandings and commitments that engender investment opportunities for entrepreneurs and improve the living standards of the population; it is a form of state—the developmental state; it is the fruit of a developmental class coalition or political pact.

In any society, some kind of consensus on the policies adopted is crucial. When these policies and their underlying ideas are not imposed but, rather, freely adopted by society, we might assume that, despite the problems of representation or agency, there is a social agreement or developmental political pact. In democracies, the implementation of new developmentalism entails the government's reliance upon the support of the people and part of the elite—an ample support base that brings the social classes together.

New developmentalism does not exist anywhere in pure form. The governments of developing countries often embrace ineffective and unreliable policies, regardless of whether they reflect the ideas of old-developmental, neoliberal orthodox, or new-developmental economists. But when there is a developmental social agreement, and a nation espouses a developmental strategy that resembles the one already outlined, we might say that this nation is building a new-developmental state and is actually realizing its development. The existence of a social agreement does not mean the presence of complete consensus. Liberal and dependent elites and external interests—the classic opponents of the developmental state—will persist in opposing its main features, namely the strategic role played by the state in advancing development and reducing inequalities, the priority assigned to development, and the emphasis placed on the social and environmental setting. Nor is a social agreement on development within the class coalition necessarily permanent. Support for development has to be constantly rebuilt because it is always vulnerable to being eroded or destroyed. When this happens, the way for class struggle, liberal domination, and social repression is open.

The new developmental state is a form of state adapted to global capitalism, i.e., to a stage of capitalism in which economic competition among nations is of the essence. The role of the state is to create investment opportunities, to invest when necessary, and to regulate the market, the financial market in particular, in order to ensure growth with price stability and financial stability. I understand development to signify not only as increasing economic growth and industrialization but also as a reduction in social inequalities and an improvement in the living standards of the population.

In this chapter I will summarize these new ideas, contrasting them both to old developmentalism and neoliberal orthodoxy. Instead of distinguishing between policies (new developmentalism) and theory (structuralist development macroeconomics), I will bring economic policies and theory under the name of "new developmentalism." I do not thereby mean to say that the distinction between policies and theory is not useful. It seems to me, however, that insofar as we think of new developmentalism not only as a national development strategy but also as a historical ideal type, merging the theoretical and policy aspects is fruitful.

CLASSICAL DEVELOPMENTALISM, NEOLIBERAL ORTHODOXY, AND NEW DEVELOPMENTALISM

Scope. Classical developmentalism was applied to countries that were beginning their industrial revolution; neoliberal orthodoxy aims to be applicable to all kinds of countries; new developmentalism applies to middle-income countries that have already concluded their capitalist revolution.

The state in production. Classical developmentalism ascribed to the state an important role in production—in neoliberal orthodoxy, none; new developmentalism limits an active role of the state to the monopolistic or near-monopolistic sectors, in particular to infrastructure sectors, mining, and public services; approximately 20 percent of total investment should be undertaken by the state.

Strategic role of the state. Both old and new developmentalism assign a strategic role to the state in defining and implementing, jointly with society, a national developmental strategy; neoliberal orthodoxy limits the role of the state to ensuring property rights, contracts, and antitrust enforcement.

Planning. Classical developmentalism ascribed a fundamental role to economic planning; neoliberal orthodoxy rejects it; new developmentalism divides the economy into a competitive and monopolistic sector that comprises infrastructure, public services, base industry, and large-scale mining; whereas for the latter planning is required, for the former coordination alone does the job satisfactorily.

Fiscal accountability. Both new and old developmentalism and neoliberal orthodoxy recommend resorting to limited budget deficits in times of crisis; all three, therefore, espouse fiscal accountability. However, whereas developmentalists are always menaced by vulgar Keynesianism, which recommends increasing public spending in response to almost every difficulty, neoliberal orthodoxy is menaced by an equally vulgar predisposition to treat reductions in public spending as a kind of panacea.

Interest rate and exchange rate. Classical developmentalism paid little attention to the interest rate, the exchange rate, or the formulation of macroeconomic policies and emphasized industrial policy (whose scope was broad enough to include macroeconomic issues such as the effective exchange rate determined by import tariffs and export subsidies); neoliberal orthodoxy pays no attention to either the interest rate or the exchange rate because it assumes that these macroeconomic prices are correctly determined by the market. New developmentalism rejects this assumption and affirms that in developing countries the interest rate tends to be excessively high because it is abused as an instrument for controlling inflation and because policy makers justify their policy by asserting that it is a cure to "financial repression" that would exist in developing countries. As for the exchange rate, which plays a central role in structuralist development macroeconomics, new developmentalism affirms that the exchange rate tends to be cyclically and chronically overvalued as a result of Dutch disease and the excessive capital inflow caused by high interest rates, the policy of relying on foreign savings to generate growth, the use of the exchange rate as an anchor, and exchange rate populism (i.e., the practice adopted by many vote-seeking politicians of fixing the exchange rate, which in the short run reduces inflation and artificially increases wages).

Dutch disease. Classical developmentalism recognized the significance of Dutch disease and attempted to offset it by means of multiple exchange rate regimes or the combination of import tariffs and export subsidies; neoliberal orthodoxy ignores it; new developmentalism clearly defines Dutch disease, regarding it as a permanent overvaluation of the exchange rate caused by Ricardian rents that allow for the export of commodities at a substantially higher exchange rate than the rate that other tradable industries need to be competitive.

Domestic market- or export-led development. Development is *domestic market-led* when import substitution industrialization prevails and the import–export coefficient is falling, and, if this fall is the outcome of the appreciation of the exchange rate, wages will increase more than profits; development is *export-led* when the import–export coefficient is increasing, and, if this increase is a consequence of depreciation of the exchange rate, profits will increase more than wages; development is *balanced* when GDP, exports, wages, and profits increase approximately at the same rate. Old developmentalism did not maintain that developing countries were likely to export manufactured goods and advocated import substitution, which did not cause wages to increase more than profits except in the short periods of exchange rate appreciation; neoliberal orthodoxy ignores this discussion and asserts that the law of comparative advantage in international trade will determine the growth model; new developmentalism assumes that the import substitution strategy expired long ago for middle-income countries, that the imports coefficient should be reasonably steady and, therefore, if the growth rate is considered satisfactory, development should neither be domestic market-led or export-led but, rather, balanced; the strategy should be temporarily export-led only if necessary to correct the exchange rate to increase the investment rate and to achieve a desired higher growth rate.[5] In a state of equilibrium in which the exchange rate is in the industrial equilibrium and the investment rate and the growth rate are regarded as satisfactory, wages, profits, exports, GDP, and GDP per capita will grow at an approximately equivalent rate, and the rate of profit will also be constant at a satisfactory level, while wages increase with productivity; growth will be balanced. Often, however, the exchange rate is overvalued, and it becomes necessary to depreciate it. In this case, exports and profits will grow more rapidly than wages for a while, but soon the exchange rate will reach the industrial equilibrium, depreciation will stop, and wages will again increase with productivity while the rate of profit turns again satisfactory, but now wages as well as GDP per capita will increase faster than before the depreciation and before the exchange rate was chronically overvalued.

Competitive exchange rate. Classical developmentalism did not pay attention to the need of a competitive exchange rate because it was oriented to the domestic market and to the growth of manufacturing industries, which were protected from international competition; neoliberal orthodoxy assumes that the exchange rate determined by the market is normally competitive; new developmentalism asserts that the market, if working properly, tends to lead the exchange rate to "current-account equilibrium" (that which intertemporarily balances the country's current account), but where Dutch disease has taken hold (which is the case in most developing countries, including the fast-growing Asian countries), the actual equilibrium exchange rate, the effectively competitive rate, is the "industrial equilibrium exchange rate," i.e., the exchange rate that allows tradable industries to be competitive by utilizing state-of-the-art technology.

Inflation. Classical developmentalism embraced the theory of structural inflation based on supply bottlenecks and accepted inflation of up to 20 percent a year; neoliberal orthodoxy does not see any grounds for developing countries to run inflation rates that exceed international standards; new developmentalism concurs with neoliberal orthodoxy in the case of countries that are already middle income, because in this circumstance the supply bottlenecks are no longer relevant, but distinguishes accelerating from maintaining and sanctioning factors and stresses that when inflation has an inertial component contraction of demand is ineffective in controlling it.

Protection or industrial equilibrium exchange rate? Old developmentalism advocated high customs duties and multiple exchange rates to protect an infant manufacturing industry; neoliberal orthodoxy rejects any kind of protection. New developmentalism supposes on the one hand that in middle-income countries industries are no longer infant and sees no grounds for protection, but it underlines that import tariffs are often not protectionist but a way of partially neutralizing Dutch disease; on the other hand, it stresses that import tariffs and the exchange rate are partial substitutes and requires a competitive exchange rate.[6]

Foreign constraint. Classical developmentalism believed in the existence of an external structural restriction to economic growth—namely a permanent scarcity of dollars or other reserve currencies—that stems from an income elasticity of demand for industrial goods greater than one, whereas the income elasticity of primary goods in rich countries is smaller than one, thus justifying relying on foreign savings for growth; neoliberal orthodoxy strongly supports the thesis because it is interested, on the one hand, in the existence of a chronic current account deficit and therefore a chronically overvalued exchange rate in developing countries, and, on the other hand, in financing developing countries with loans and direct investment. New developmentalism rejects the pessimism of old developmentalism in relation to the elasticities problem and asserts that, first, they have never been so crucial and, second, that its importance wanes to the extent that a country begins to export manufactured goods. It is true that countries often face a "shortage of dollars," but this shortage results from the fact that the exchange rate tends to be chronically overvalued in developing countries rather than from unfavorable elasticities.

Growth with domestic savings. In principle, new developmentalism rejects growth with foreign savings—the standard recommendation that liberal orthodoxy makes to developing countries, which classical developmentalism accepted. Only in special circumstances, such as when investment opportunities are high, the country is already growing fast, or the marginal propensity falls, will new developmentalism accept it. The rejection derives, first, from the fact that there is not an effective foreign constraint; second, that current account deficits (foreign savings) lead to increased financial fragility and a financial currency crisis; third, that capital inflows caused by the current account deficits appreciate the local currency and generally involve a high rate of replacement of domestic savings by foreign savings; fourth, that when a country has Dutch disease, its neutralization (putting the exchange rate in the industrial equilibrium level) implies a current account surplus, not a deficit.

Fixed or floating exchange rate. Classical developmentalism accepted the regime of fixed exchange rates enshrined in the Bretton Woods agreement and defended by Keynes; neoliberal orthodoxy pursues the *free float*, which is likely to end in financial crisis; new developmentalism rejects the strict fix or float dichotomy and, grounded in the tendency of the exchange rate to be cyclically overvalued, seeks a strongly administered floating exchange rate; for that it recommends the purchase and sale of reserves, capital controls, and—to offset Dutch disease—a variable tax on exports of the products that generate it. Such a tax would be the equivalent of the industrial equilibrium exchange rate minus the current account equilibrium exchange rate, which, by shifting the supply curve in relation to the exchange rate, leads the exchange rate to the industrial equilibrium.

Social development. Classical developmentalism was usually part of the development strategy of authoritarian regimes involved in the national and industrial revolutions of their countries; it advocated a better income distribution but did not prescribe any social welfare policy; neoliberal orthodoxy is concerned only with free trade because the market will take care of the rest; new developmentalism is usually implemented in new democracies and should also be a "social" developmentalism—a developmentalism concerned with a more egalitarian distribution of benefits in society.

TWO APPLICATIONS

Understood in the terms described in the previous section, new developmentalism implies a surprising and remarkable policy prescription: developing countries should avoid current account deficits in their search for growth; they should not attempt to grow by relying on foreign savings or foreign financing. Financing development is of the essence (both Schumpeterian innovation and Keynesian investment are grounded in credit), but credit should be in *national* currency. Foreign finance, in principle, is of no advantage to a country unless it comes with technology or opens opportunities for exports. The great foreign debt crisis of the 1980s revealed that the growth strategy that relied on foreign currency was a big mistake, a mistake sponsored by rich countries that were eager to become creditors and achieve either high interest rates or high profit rates from their loans and direct investments by occupying their domestic markets. The crisis was fostered in developing countries by the misleading thesis of a "foreign structural constraint" to be overcome by resorting to foreign savings. In fact, there is a foreign constraint only if the exchange rate is overvalued—a chronic phenomenon in developing countries. But the harm caused by foreign currency indebtedness is not limited to the crises it triggers. Actually, it comes about in three stages: first, it appreciates the national currency, artificially increases wages and consumption, and entails a high rate of substitution of internal savings by foreign savings; second, it causes financial fragility, renders the country dependent, and drives it to the practice of "confidence building"—of doing everything its creditors demand, which usually runs counter to its national interest; and finally, third, after the credit bubble has been inflated and multinational corporations and banks have earned huge profits from high interest rates, and trader, high bonus, creditors lose confidence, debt rollover is suspended, and a balance-of-payments financial crisis breaks.

These three stages are part of the classic history of developing countries—always indebted, almost always suffering from low growth rates, and always vulnerable to a balance-of-payments crisis. It is the history of the countries that do not seek to offset the tendency of their exchange rates to be cyclically as well as chronically overvalued; and thus, instead of pursuing equilibrium or a current account surplus, they opt for foreign debt. Quite different is the case of the developmental Asian countries that attempt to grow by relying on their own resources, because they are aware that "capital is made at home."

In most cases, developing countries grow faster if they run current account surpluses and thus help finance the rich countries. The Dutch disease model explains this remarkable truth. For a country to offset Dutch disease (or the "natural resources curse"), it needs to shift its exchange rate from current account equilibrium (which clears its current account) to industrial equilibrium (the exchange rate that allows industries that utilize state-of-the-art technology to be competitive). The country should establish an export tax or retention that equals the industrial equilibrium exchange rate minus the current account equilibrium exchange rate, but exporters will bear no cost because they will be rewarded by the exchange depreciation, which is caused by shifting the supply curve in relation to the exchange rate. If it achieves this shift—something that is feasible but not particularly easy—the country will, by definition, have a current account surplus and the rich countries a current account deficit. At this industrial equilibrium exchange rate, which plays the role of a "light switch," the efficient enterprises of the country will be connected to international demand, while the possibly less efficient enterprises in foreign countries that export to this country will be disconnected.

Developing countries, therefore, should not attempt to grow by relying on foreign savings, because a current account deficit indicates exchange overvaluation even when there is no Dutch disease—and even greater overvaluation when there is. Generally, when a country seeks to grow by relying on foreign savings, i.e., with current account deficits, the capital inflows necessary to finance the deficit appreciates the exchange rate and artificially increases real wages because, even when it takes the form of direct investment, it increases consumption more than investment. As a result, in addition to having to send profits and interest payments abroad, the country ends up facing the threat of a balance-of-payments crisis.

In the 1990s, neoliberal hegemony was so great that even the developmental Asian countries such as South Korea, Thailand, Malaysia, and Indonesia forgot that capital is made at home, became externally indebted despite having kept their budgets balanced, and experienced severe balance-of-payments crises. The lesson learned by those countries is even more pertinent for countries such as Brazil and Argentina, which suffer from Dutch disease, however moderately. These countries will grow faster if they keep their current accounts in modest surplus.

CONCLUSION

The economic objective of middle-income countries is to achieve the level of well-being enjoyed by rich countries; their social goal is to make their societies less unequal. Whereas liberal orthodox strategy is rarely compatible with long-term growth and classical developmentalism undergoes a severe crisis since the 1970s, new developmentalism offers a new theoretical framework and suggests a way to achieve that goal, but does not guarantee success. The more developed a developing country already is, the more likely it is to succeed, because it already made its industrial revolution and relies on a better-structured society and state. This is reason why middle-income countries face less difficulties in being governed than poor countries, but we should not underestimate the difficulties that middle-income countries face.

A new-developmental state does not need to embrace all the models and policies presented here—which together can be envisaged as an ideal type—but it has to hold onto a national development strategy supported by a developmental political pact. The government of such a state has a strategic role in investment and in the planning of monopolistic sectors, macroeconomic policy (especially in relation to the exchange rate), the regulation of financial markets, and the social or distributive policies aimed at building up what is not just a developmental state but a social welfare state as well.

NOTES

1. For a report on the emergence of new developmentalism and development structuralist macroeconomics, see Bresser-Pereira (2011).

2. See www.tenthesesonnewdevelopmentalism.org.

3. See Frenkel (2006, 2007, 2008) for some of his contributions to new developmentalism.

4. According to Max Weber (1917: 90), "an ideal type is formed by the one-sided accentuation of one or more points of view and by the synthesis of a great many

diffuse, discrete, more or less present and occasionally absent concrete individual phenomena, which are arranged according to those one-sided emphasized viewpoints into
a unified analytical construct."

5. According to Bhaduri and Marglin's wage-led model (1990) that assumed
import substitution, inequality would decrease, but, in real terms, in the periods that
prevailed, the import substitution model inequality tended to increase, not decrease.

6. It is a partial form of neutralizing Dutch disease because it only neutralizes it on
the import side, not the export side.

REFERENCES

Bhaduri, A. and Marglin, S. 1990. "Unemployment and the real wages: the economic
basis for contesting political ideologies." *Cambridge Journal of Economics* 14(4):
375–393.

Bresser-Pereira, L. C. 2011. "An account of new developmentalism and its structuralist
macroeconomics." *Brazilian Journal of Political Economy* 31(3): 493–502.

Frenkel, R. 2006. "An alternative to inflation targeting in Latin America: macroeconomic
policies focused on employment." *Journal of Post-Keynesian Economics* 28(4): 573–591.

Frenkel, R. 2007. "The sustainability of monetary sterilization policies." *CEPAL
Review* 93: 29–36.

Frenkel, R. 2008. "The competitive real exchange-rate regime, inflation and monetary
policy." *CEPAL Review* 96: 191–201.

Lewis, A. W. 1954. "Economic development with unlimited supply of labor." *The
Manchester School* 22(2): 139–191.

Nurkse, R. 1953. *Problems of capital formation in underdeveloped countries.* Oxford,
UK: Basil Blackwell.

Prebisch, R. 1949. "El desarrollo económico de América Latina e sus principales prob-
lemas." *Revista Brasileira de Economia* 3(4): 47–111.

Weber, M. 1917/1997. *The methodology of the social sciences*, E. Shils and H. A. Finch,
eds. New York: Free Press.

Mario Damill is senior researcher at the Center for the Study of State and Society (CEDES), member of the National Council of Scientific and Technological Research (CONICET), and professor of macroeconomics at the University of Buenos Aires, Argentina. His research focuses on macroeconomic and financial policies in Argentina and Latin America.

Martín Rapetti is an associate researcher at the Center for the Study of State and Society (CEDES), an assistant researcher at the National Council of Scientific and Technological Research (CONICET), and professor at the University of Buenos Aires, Argentina. His research focuses on macroeconomics, finance, and development.

Guillermo Rozenwurcel is principal researcher at the National Council of Scientific and Technological Research (CONICET) and visiting fellow at CEDES. He is also the Director at Centro de iDeAS- UNSAM (National University of San Martin) and professor at the School of Economics (UBA) and the School of Politics and Government (UNSAM). His research focuses on macroeconomics, money and finance, development, and Latin American economics.

Daniel Kampel is a visiting researcher in the economics department of CEDES. He has done consulting work in various areas of the national state (Ministry of Economy, House of Representatives), the province of Buenos Aires (Senate), and the city of Buenos Aires (Ministry of Finance).

Daniel Heymann is director of the Interdisciplinary Institute of Political Economy of Buenos Aires (IIEP-BAIRES). He teaches courses and lectures at numerous national and international universities. His main research areas are macroeconomics, economic development, and models of complex systems in economics. A full member of the National Academy of Economic Sciences, he was coordinator of macroeconomic analysis of the Office of ECLAC Buenos Aires.

Francisco Roldán is a Ph.D. candidate in economics at New York University. His research focuses on macroeconomics of crises and the consequences of extreme uncertainty.

Julio Dreizzen is professor of corporate finance at the University of Buenos Aires, member of the board of directors of Banco Hipotecario, and CFO of IMPSA. He served as Undersecretary of Finance at the Ministry of the Economy of Argentina, executive director of Galicia Capital Markets, member of the board of directors of the Central Bank of Argentina, and deputy executive director of the IMF.

Omar Chisari is professor at the Universidad Argentina de la Empresa and member of the National Council of Scientific and Technological Research (CONICET). He was president of the Association of Economists of Argentina and serves as vice president of the National Academy of Economic Sciences of Argentina. He works on theoretical microeconomics, regulatory economics, and computable general equilibrium.

Gustavo Ferro is a researcher at the National Council of Scientific and Technological Research (CONICET) and professor at the Universidad Argentina de la Empresa (UADE). He works on regulatory economics, applied microeconomics, and comparative efficiency measurement. He has been a consultant for IABD, the World Bank, ECLAC-UN, and UNDP.

Juan Pablo Vila Martínez is assistant professor at the University of Buenos Aires and Universidad Argentina de la Empresa (UADE).

Oscar Dancourt is professor at the Pontifical Catholic University of Peru. He was a member of the board of directors and president of the Central Bank of Peru. His research focuses on macroeconomics and monetary and financial economics.

Ricardo Ffrench-Davis is professor at the University of Chile, National Prize in Social Sciences. He has written about 150 scholarly articles and 21 books on macroeconomics, development, and Latin American economics.

Gustavo Cañonero is managing director and head of economic research for emerging markets at Deutsche Bank. He worked at Salomon Brothers, the International Monetary Fund, the Argentine Ministry of Finance, and the Center for the Study of State and Society (CEDES).

Carlos Winograd is research fellow and professor at the Paris School of Economics and associate professor at the University of Paris-Evry V d'Essone. He was Secretary of State for Competition, Regulation, and Consumer Affairs of Argentina. He has done consulting work for multilateral institutions, governments, and the corporate sector on macroeconomics, strategy, mergers and acquisitions, litigation, and antitrust regulation.

Roxana Maurizio is a professor at the University of General Sarmiento and researcher at the National Council for Science and Technology (CONICET). She also works as a consultant for national and international organizations (ILO, ECLAC, the World Bank, UNDP). Her areas of interest are labor economics, income distribution, poverty, and social policies in Latin America.

Edmar Bacha is founding partner and director of the Casa das Garças Institute of Economic Policy Studies in Rio de Janeiro. He was previously a member of the Brazilian government in various capacities, including the formulation and implementation of the Real stabilization plan. He taught at several Brazilian and U.S. universities and has written many scholarly articles and books on the Brazilian economy and the international economy.

Regis Bonelli is senior researcher at Instituto Brasileiro de Economia (IBRE), Fundação Getulio Vargas (FGV), and associate researcher at Casa das Garças. He was director-general at IBGE (Brazilian Institute of Geography and Statistics); research director, IPEA (Institute of Applied Economic Research); and executive director at BNDES (National Development Bank).

José Antonio Ocampo is professor and director of the Economic and Political Development Concentration in the School of International and Public Affairs and co-president of the Initiative for Policy Dialogue at Columbia University. He is also chair of the Committee for Development Policy of the United Nations Economic and Social Council (ECOSOC). He has served in numerous positions at the United Nations and in his native Colombia, including UN Under-Secretary-General for Economic and Social Affairs, Executive Secretary of the ECLAC, and Minister of Finance of Colombia.

Jaime Ros is professor of economics at the National University of Mexico and emeritus professor at the University of Notre Dame. He specializes in development economics with special reference to Mexico and Latin America. He has written several scholarly articles and books.

Andrés Solimano is founder and chairman of the International Center for Globalization and Development (CIGLOB) based in Santiago, Chile. He is associate professor at Catholic University of Chile and has been country director at the World Bank, executive director at the Inter-American Development Bank, regional advisor at the United Nations Economic Commission for Latin America and the Caribbean, and director of FLACSO-Chile. His main research topics include inequality, international migration, global capitalism, political economy, and macroeconomic and development policy.

José María Fanelli is senior researcher at CEDES and National Council for Scientific and Technical Research (CONICET) and professor at the University of Buenos Aires and San Andrés University. He has been a consultant for ECLAC, IADB, The G-24, UNCTAD, IDRC, and GDN. He specializes in macroeconomics, money, and finance.

Lance Taylor has been a professor in the economics departments at Harvard, the Massachusetts Institute of Technology, and the New School for Social Research, among other institutions. He has published widely in the areas of macroeconomics, development economics, and economic theory.

Armon Rezai is an assistant professor at the Vienna University of Economics and Business and an external research affiliate at the Oxford Centre for the Analysis of Resource Rich Economies of Oxford University. His work focuses on growth and distribution, and climate change.

Rishabh Kumar is a Ph.D. student in the department of economics at the New School for Social Research.

Laura Carvalho is assistant professor in the department of economics of the University of Sao Paulo. Her research focuses on income distribution and economic growth, macroeconomics, and development.

Nelson Barbosa-Filho is professor at the Getulio Vargas Foundation and the Federal University of Rio de Janeiro, Brazil, and currently Minister of Budget, Planning, and Management of Brazil.

Manuel Agosin is dean of the School of Economics and Business of the University of Chile. He has been an economic advisor to several Latin American governments and a consultant to the United Nations, the Inter-American Development Bank, and the Latin American Reserve Fund. He works on macroeconomics, finance, trade, and development.

Juan Díaz-Maureira is an instructor of the department of economics at the University of Chile and economist at the Central Bank of Chile. His research focuses on econometrics and macroeconomics.

Jan Kregel is a senior scholar at the Levy Economics Institute of Bard College. He holds the position of professor of development finance at the Tallinn University of Technology. He is a life fellow of the Royal Economic Society (UK) and an elected member of the Società Italiana degli Economisti, Miembro Distinguido y de Honor of the Asociación Nacional de Economistas y Contadores de Cuba, and Member of the Italian Accademia Nazionale dei Lincei. He received the Veblen-Commons Prize of the Association for Evolutionary Economics in 2011.

Luiz Carlos Bresser-Pereira is an emeritus professor at the Getulio Vargas Foundation. He was Finance Minister and Minister of Federal Administration of Brazil. He has written several scholarly articles and books on macroeconomics and development.

INDEX

Page number in *italics* indicate figures.

accumulated inventories, 44*n*4
AD curve, 94
ad valorem taxes, 60, 63, 80
aggregate consistency condition, 302–3
aggregate demand, in Chile, *120, 120*–21
aggregate supply curve. *See* AS curve
Alliance for Progress, 360
animal spirits, 138, 281
anti-inflationary policies, 9–10, 14, 101
Argentina: business climate in,
   153–56; capital flight events in,
   58–59; Central Bank of, 16, 66;
   CGE model and, 58, 65–68, *67*;
   convertibility in, 15; CPI and, 139;
   crawling peg in, 135, 258; credit
   growth in, 136, *142–44*, 142–46,
   146; disequilibria in, 134–39, 141,
   143–44, 146–49, *147, 149*; economic
   crisis in, 277; economic recovery
   of, 16; employment composition
   in, 161, *162–68*, 164, 166; financial
   intermediation in, 143–44, *144*;
   foreign exchange reserves of, 141;
   Frenkel in, xiv–xvi, 3; hourly labor
   income in, *167–68*, 169; income
   segmentation in, *172–74*; inflation
   in, xvii–xviii, 2, 10–14, 47, 144–45,
   148; investment in, 148–56, *149–55*;
   labor informality in, 161, *162–68*,

164, 166, 169, *172–74, 176*, 176–77,
178–80, 179–81, 185*n*5; minimum
wage in, 179, 186*n*10; monetization
in, 144, 146; *La noche de los bastones
largos* in, xiv, xxviii*n*1; problem-
oriented research on, xvii; property
rights in, 153–56; regulation in,
153–56; RER in, 14–17; reserves of,
141; risk premia in, xxiii, 134–36,
138–42, *140–41*, 146, 149, 153,
156, 157*n*5; savings in, 153–56,
154–55; sovereign risk in, 136–39,
141, 146–49, *147, 149, 337–38*, 340,
341–42, 344, 346, 348, 349, *350*, 351
AS (aggregate supply) curve, 91, 93,
95–96, 104*n*30
ATT. *See* average treatment effect on the
treated
austerity policies, 217–18, 281, 284
Austral Plan, xvi
automatic spending stabilizers, 217
average treatment effect on the treated
(ATT), 174

bailouts, 284
balance of payments: BP curve and,
88–91; devaluation improving,
93; economic crises and, 5–6, 83;
economic development and, 360;

balance of payments (*continued*)
MABP and, 7–8; monetary policy
and, 83, 88–91, 93–98, 100–101,
135, 216, 219–25; portfolio model of,
7–8; RER influencing, 229, 231–32
balance-of-payments dominance: capital
account and, 213, 217, 219–23;
contemporary modalities of, 213–16;
countercyclical approach and, 211–12,
216–20, 222–25, 225*n*2, 225*nn*11–
12; cyclical shocks in, 212–13, 222,
224, 225*n*2; defined, 212, 224; in
developing countries, 211–15, 217–
19, 221–24; exchange rate and, 216,
219–25; fiscal policies and, 216–18;
macroprudential policies and, 216;
monetary policies and, 216, 219–25;
overview of, xxiv, 211–13, 224–25;
supply shocks and, 212, 220–21,
225*n*3; taxation and, 217–18, 224
Balassa–Samuelson effect, 130*n*4,
251–52, 263, 266*n*11
Banco de la Provincia de Buenos Aires, xvi
banking system, interest rates of, 84–85
between effect, 180, 185
Bolivia: employment composition in,
161–62, *162–68*, 164, 166; hourly
labor income in, *167–68*; income
segmentation in, *172–74*; labor
informality in, 161–62, *162–68*, 164,
166, *172–74*, 176, *176*, *178–80*
boom and bust: cycles, 4, 213–16,
217–18, 279; globalization and,
257–58
booms: commodity, 142–43, *143*, 146;
savings during, 218
BP curve, 88–91, 93, 95–96, 98–99
Brazil: capacity utilization in, *196*,
196–97; capital deepening in, 201–3,
202–3, 206; capital growth collapse
of, 188–89, 200–204, *201–3*; capital
growth decomposition in, 192–204,
193, *195–97*, *199–203*; credit growth
in, 136, 142, *144*, 145, *146*; debt
defaults of, 191; economic growth

of, xxiii–xxiv, 188–206, *189*, *193*,
195–97, *199–203*, 205–6; economic
miracle of, 190; employment
composition in, 161, *162–68*, 164,
166; external shocks in, 192; foreign
exchange reserves of, 145; future
growth rate of, 205–6; GDP of, 188,
189, 190, 192–99, *193*, *201*, 201–6,
203; historical sketch of, 189–92;
hourly labor income in, *167–68*;
hyperinflation in, 191; income
segmentation in, *172–74*; investment
in, 190–94, 196, 198–201, *199*,
204–5, 207*n*6; labor informality
in, 161, *162–68*, 164, 166, *172–74*,
176, 176–77, *178–80*, 179–81,
185*n*5; minimum wage in, 179; new
developmentalism in, 373; output–
capital in-use ratio in, 197–98, *198*;
savings in, 194–96, *195*, 206*n*4,
207*n*6; sovereign risk in, 333, *334*,
337–38, 341–42, 344, *346*, 348, *350*,
351; TFP in, 198, 202–3, *202–3*,
205–6; wage indexing in, 191
Brazilian Development Bank, 50
Bretton Woods, 379; capitalism and,
274–75; developing countries at,
359; economic development and,
xxvii, 358–61, 363, 371; financial
crises and, 274–75
British Empire, 273
bubbles: dot-com, 277; failure to detect,
279
business climate, in Argentina, 153–56

capacity utilization, *196*, 196–97
capital account: balance-of-payments
dominance and, 213, 217, 219–23;
cyclical shocks generated by, 213;
liberalization, 221–22; regulation,
115, 223
capital accumulation: formal sector
unemployment influenced by, 60;
profitability interacting with, *234*,
234–35; rates, 232, *234*, 234–36,

238–39, 241–45, 247n4; RER influencing, 232, 234–44, 247n2, 247n4, 257

capital deepening, in Brazil, 201–3, 202–3, 206

capital flight, 58–59

capital flows, foreign debt determining, 89–91

capital gains, 317, 331n4

capital growth: capacity utilization and, 196, 196–97; capital deepening and, 201–3, 202–3, 206; collapse, 188–89, 200–204, 201–3; decomposition, 192–204, 193, 195–97, 199–203; GDP related to, 192–94, 193; output–capital in-use ratio in, 197–98, 198; relative price of investment and, 198–200, 199–200; savings influencing, 194–96, 195

capitalism: bailouts in, 284; Bretton Woods system and, 274–75; elite-dominated, 280, 284; financial crises and, xxvi, 271–84; global, 273, 375; IMF and, 272, 274–75, 281–82; in interwar years, 273–74; liberal, 272; Path to Prosperity and, 324; regulated, 272, 275; unregulated, 272. See also neoliberal capitalism

capital–labor ratio, 238–39, 242, 244, 247n9

capital mobility: imperfect, 105n37; perfect, 62; unemployment and, 61–62. See also international capital mobility

capital outflows: in development scenarios, 363; external shocks and, 94–97, 96; safe assets linked to, 298

cash constraints: on input purchases, 30–37, 33–34, 36; none, 29–30

CDS. See credit default swap

Center for the Study of the State and Society (CEDES), xv–xvi

Central Bank of Argentina, 16, 66

central banks, financial crises and, 279, 282–84

CGE model. See computable general equilibrium model

Chile: aggregate demand in, 120, 120–21; capital account regulations in, 115; copper in, 117–19, 120, 123, 125–29, 131n15; countercyclical approach to, xxii, 113–17, 119, 122–23, 127–28; CPI in, 130n7, 131n10; crawling peg in, 258; democracy in, 113–14, 117; dictatorship in, 113, 117; disequilibrium in, 124–27, 125; employment composition in, 161, 162–68, 164, 166; external balances in, 118–19, 119; external shocks in, 111–12, 118, 123; food basket in, 121, 130n7; Frenkel in, xv; GDP of, 111–20, 116, 120, 122–25, 125, 128–29; hourly labor income in, 167–68, 169; income segmentation in, 172–74; investment in, 152, 152; labor informality in, 161, 162–68, 164, 166, 169, 172–74, 176, 176–77, 178–80, 179–80; macroeconomic imbalance in, 127–29; minimum wage in, 179; neoliberalism in, 117, 126; since 1973, 112–17, 116; output capacity used in, 123–24; overview of, 111–12, 129–30; productivity gaps in, 130n2; recovery of, 123–30, 125; reforms, 111–14, 117, 122, 129–30, 131n22; RER in, xxii, 111, 116–17, 124–27, 125, 129, 130n4, 131n16; resource allocation in, 132n23; sovereign risk in, 333, 334, 337–38, 341–42, 344, 346, 348, 349–50, 350; taxation in, 122, 128, 131n21; 2008–2009 crisis impacting, 111–12, 118–23, 119–20, 130

classical developmentalism, 373–80

clean floating regime, 97

cognitive dissonance, in economic development, 360–62, 368

Colombia: National Coffee Fund of, 216; sovereign risk in, 334, 337–38, 341–42, 344, 347–48, 350, 351

commodity boom, 142–43, *143*, 146
commodity stabilization funds, 216
comparative analysis, xx, 3
competitive exchange rate, 378
composition effect, 180, 185
computable general equilibrium (CGE)
    model: Argentine data in, 58, 65–68,
    67; computational experiments
    with, *69*, 69–77, *71–77*; elements
    of, 62–65; for structural and
    institutional parameters, xxi, 58,
    62–68, *67*, 70, 74, 81*n*5
Concertación Democrática (Democratic
    Coalition), 113
conditional operation in *t* + 1, 41–43,
    43
confidence building, 380
conflict: cooperation and, *289*, 289–91;
    in financial crises, *289*, 289–91,
    300–301, 303–5
constrained input purchases: cash
    constraints on, 30–37, *33–34, 36*;
    inventory management and, 30–37,
    33–34, 36; restricted current output
    and, 32–35, *33–34, 37, 38*; in *t*,
    41–43, *43*; unrestricted current
    output and, 31–32, 35–36, *36*
constrained production in *t*, 40–41, *42*
consumer price index (CPI): Argentina
    and, 139; in Chile, 130*n*7, 131*n*10;
    wages indexed to, 70–71, *74–77*, 79
control, regulation and, 223
cooperation, conflict and, *289*, 289–91
copper, 117–19, *120*, 123, 125–29,
    131*n*15
Corporacion Andina de Fomento, 50
corporate credit, 50
Costa Rica: employment composition
    in, 161, *162–68*, 164, 166; hourly
    labor income in, 167–68, *167–68*;
    income segmentation in, *172–74*;
    labor informality in, 161, *162–68*,
    164, 166–68, *172–74, 176*, 177,
    178–80; sovereign risk in, *337*,
    341–42, 347

countercyclical approach: balance-of-
    payments dominance and, 211–12,
    216–20, 222–25, 225*n*2, 225*nn*11–
    12; to Chilean economy, xxii,
    113–17, 119, 122–23, 127–28
covered interest parity, 62
CPI. *See* consumer price index
crawling peg, 135, 212, 258
credit default swap (CDS): common
    factor estimated for, 345, *348*, 349,
    350; data, 352*n*5; EMBI spread
    compared with, 337; operation of,
    336–37; sovereign risk measured by,
    334–39, *338*, 345, 349–51, *350*; as
    stationary variable, 338–39
credit growth: in Argentina, 136,
    142–44, 142–46, *146*; in Brazil, 136,
    142, *144*, 145, *146*
crises. *See* economic crises; financial
    crises
currency. *See* domestic currency; foreign
    currency
cyclical shocks: in balance-of-payments
    dominance, 212–13, 222, 224,
    225*n*2; capital account generating,
    213; external shocks and, 212–13,
    222, 224, 225*n*2

DC. *See* domestic currency
debt: external, 136, 138–42, *140–41*,
    156; indexed, 55; international, in
    economic development, 361; long-
    term, in economic development,
    365–69; payment capacity and,
    48–55, 366; rescheduling, 272, 276,
    280. *See also* foreign debt
debt defaults: of Brazil, 191; in financial
    crises, 276, 280; globalization and,
    276; risk of, 135. *See also* sovereign
    risk
decontextualization, 280
de-dollarization, of semidollarized
    economy, 104*n*33, 105*n*38
default risk. *See* sovereign risk
deficit, U.S., 315–16, 331*n*6

deleverage, 51
demand: aggregate, in Chile, *120*, 120–21; for foreign debt, 89–90, 143; IS curve and, 86; nominal exchange rate influencing, 86; production on, 27–28. *See also* price-elastic demand
democracy, in Chile, 113–14, 117
Democratic Coalition (*Concertación Democrática*), 113
deposit rates, 87–89
depreciated RER, 60, 230
deregulation: destabilizing, 278; efficient market hypothesis justifying, 285n8; elites pushing for, 280
devaluation: in absence of technical progress, 235–38, *237*, 244; balance of payments improved by, 93; contractionary effects of, 220; external debt and, 136; long-run effects of, 235–44, *237*, *240–41*; in presence of technical progress, 238–43, *240–41*; RER and, 232–33, 235–44, *237*, *240–41*; short-run effects of, 235–38, *240*
developing countries: balance-of-payments dominance in, 211–15, 217–19, 221–24; at Bretton Woods, 359; classic history of, 381; economic growth and RER in, 230–33, 250–57, 259–61, 263–64; emerging economies, 214, 225n5; external bottlenecks impeding, 368; financial crises in, 279, 333; self-insurance of, 215
development. *See* economic development
development channel, xxiv, 15, 229; globalization, 257–59, 261, 264–65; saving, 256–57, 259, 261; tradable-led growth, xxv, 259–65, 265n10
development economics, 357–58
dictatorship, in Chile, 113, 117
disequilibria: in Argentina, 134–39, 141, 143–44, 146–49, *147*, *149*; in Chile, 124–27, *125*; FDI and, 148;

149, 154, *154*; Frenkel on, 134–37, 156–57; liabilities of, 137; overview of, 134–38, 156–57; reasons behind, 146–49, *147*, *149*
disinflation policy, 9–10, 14, 101
disposable income, 317, *317*, 320, 331n7
dollar window, 276
domestic currency (DC): market of loans in, 103n15; monetary policy and, 84–85, 87, 104n25, 105n38; pass-through coefficients and, 102n7; reserve requirement ratios and, 83, 103n15; short-term interest rate in, 83; speculative attacks on, 134–35, 156
domestic market-led development, 377–78
domestic savings, growth with, 379
Dominican Republic, *337*, *341–42*, 344, *347*
dot-com bubble, 277
DSGE models. *See* stochastic dynamic general equilibrium models
dual exchange rates, 370–71
Dutch disease, 211; new developmentalism and, 377, 381–82, 383n6; RER and, 125–26, 260
dynamic economies of scale, 230, 239

East Asian financial crisis, 276
ECB. *See* European Central Bank
Economic Consequences of Peace, The (Keynes), 274
economic crises: in Argentina, 277; balance of payments and, 5–6, 83; comparison of, 8–9; economic science and, 280–83; in Ecuador, 276–77; EMEs and, 4–6, 8–9; in Europe, 4–5, 8–9, 225n12, 271; foreign debt, 380; macroeconomic and financial cycles leading to, 3–9; overview of, 271–77; policy lessons from, 8–9; types of, 272. *See also* financial crises

economic development: balance of
payments and, 360; Bretton Woods
and, xxvii, 358–61, 363, 371;
cognitive dissonance in, 360–62,
368; domestic market-led, 377–78;
exchange rate and, 369–71; export
expansion and, 369–71; external
resource scenarios, 363–65; foreign
savings and, 361–63, 379; IBRD
and, 359, 361, 366, 368; interest
rates in, 363–64; international debt
in, 361; international financial
stability and, 358–61; international
imbalances and, 358–61; long-term
debt sustainable scenarios, 365–69;
overview of, 357–58, 371; RER and,
xxiv, 14–17, 229; social development
and, 380; special theory for, 357–58;
UN and, 358–61; Washington
Consensus and, 357–58, 361. *See
also* development channel; new
developmentalism
economic growth: with domestic
savings, 379; employment growth
and, *237*, 237–41, 243–44; Kaldor
on, 230, 238–39, 247*n*6, 369–71;
Robinson on, 230, 238–39, 247*n*4;
tradable-led, xxv, 259–65, 265*n*10,
359, 361, 366, 368
economic growth, in Latin America:
of Brazil, xxiii–xxiv, 188–206,
189, 193, 195–97, 199–203, 205–6;
employment composition and,
160–69, *162–68*; income distribution
influenced by, 159; labor informality
and, 159–84, *162–68, 172–74, 176,
178–80*; labor market influenced by,
xxiii, 159; overview of, xxiii, 159–60,
181–82; wage gaps and, 160, 166,
169–81, *172–74, 178–79*, 183–84
economic growth, RER and:
asymmetries in, 254–55; across
countries and periods, 253–54;
in developing countries, 230–33,
250–57, 259–61, 263–64; empirical

findings on, 230–32, 250–56;
foreign exchange influencing, 260;
Frenkel on, 250; globalization
channel of, 257–59, 261, 264–65;
growth regressions and, 251–56;
mechanisms behind, 230–32, 250,
256–65; misalignment index and,
251–56, 261–65; overview of, xxv,
229–30, 243–44, 250, 264–65; real
wage and, 229–44, *234, 237, 240–41,
246*; saving channel of, 256–57, 259,
261; tradable-led growth channel of,
xxv, 259–65, 265*n*10; Washington
Consensus and, 256, 260–61
economic science: crises and, 280–83;
formalization in, 280
economic systems: conflict, cooperation
and, *289*, 289–91; defined, 290;
financial crises and, 288–92, *289*;
macroeconomy and, 288–92, *289*,
305–8; systemic dysfunction in, 288,
291–92, 305–8
economies of scale, 296
economists: financial crises and, 280–81,
284; master, xiii–xiv; as public
intellectuals, xix–xx
Ecuador: economic crisis in, 276–77;
employment composition in,
161, *162–68*, 164, 166; hourly
labor income in, *167–68*; income
segmentation in, *172–74*; labor
informality in, 161, *162–68*, 164,
166, *172–74, 176, 178–80*; sovereign
risk in, *337–38*, 340, *341–42*,
344–45, 346, 348, 349, 350, 351
efficiency wages theory, 170
efficient market hypothesis, 283,
285*nn*8–9
elite-dominated capitalism, 280, 284
El Salvador: employment composition
in, 161, *162–68*, 164, 166; hourly
labor income in, *167–68*, 169;
income segmentation in, *172–74*;
labor informality in, 161, *162–68*,
164, 166, 169, *172–74, 176, 176*,

178–80; sovereign risk in, *337, 341, 343, 346*

EMBI spread. *See* emerging markets bond index spread

emerging economies (EMEs): crises and, 4–6, 8–9; in developing countries, 214, 225*n*5; foreign exchange reserves of, 105*n*41; new macroeconomic problems in, 3; scale lacking in, 296

emerging markets bond index (EMBI) spread: CDS compared with, 337; common factor estimated for, 339–40, *340–43*, 344–45, *346*; defined, 334; sovereign risk measured by, *334*, 334–37, *337*, 339, *340–43*, 344–45, *346*, 349–51; U.S. interest rates influencing, 345, 352*n*4

EMEs. *See* emerging economies

employment: capital–labor ratio and, 238–39, 242, 244, 247*n*9; formal, 160; informal, 160 61; stability, 238, 242–43, 245. *See also* labor informality

employment composition: in Argentina, 161, *162–68*, 164, 166; in Bolivia, 161–62, *162–68*, 164, 166; in Brazil, 161, *162–68*, 164, 166; in Chile, 161, *162–68*, 164, 166; in Costa Rica, 161, *162–68*, 164, 166; economic growth in Latin America and, 160–69, *162–68*; in Ecuador, 161, *162–68*, 164, 166; in El Salvador, 161, *162–68*, 164, 166; in Mexico, 161, *162–68*, 166; in Paraguay, 161, *162–68*, 164, 166; in Peru, 161, *162–68*, 164, 166; in Uruguay, 161, *162–68*, 164, 166

employment growth: economic growth and, *237*, 237–41, 243–44; long-term dynamic adjustments of, *237*, 237–38; real wage and, *237*, 237–41, 243–45, 247; RER and, *237*, 237–41, 243–47

endowment effect, 174

equilibrium: in DSGE models, 282–83; external, 88–89; in general equilibrium approach, 57–58, 61, 64; in goods market equilibrium condition, 247*n*2; industrial, xxvii, 378–79, 381; market, 130*n*4; RER, 251–52, 255–56, 264–65; taxation influencing, 58. *See also* computable general equilibrium model

Europe: crisis in, 4–5, 8–9, 225*n*12, 271; instability in, 276

European Central Bank (ECB), 225*n*12

exchange rate: balance-of-payments dominance and, 216, 219–25; competitive, 378; crawling peg and, 135, 212, 258; defined, 252; dual, 370–71; economic development and, 369–71; expectations, xxii, 134–36; external shocks and, 84, 93–95, *94*, 212; Federal Reserve and, 226*n*14; financial crises and, 279; industrial equilibrium, xxvii, 378 79, 381; Keynes on, 360, 379; in monetary policy, 83–84, 86, 88, 91–101, *94*, 102*n*13, 103*n*17, 103*n*20, 104*n*24, 104*nn*28–30, 104*nn*32–34, 105*nn*36–37, 105*n*40; in new developmentalism, xxvii, 376, 378–81; predetermined rules, 135; protection, 378; risk, 136; wages influenced by, 220. *See also* fixed exchange rate; flexible exchange rate; nominal exchange rate; real exchange rate

exchange risk, 135, 138

expected costs, price volatility influencing, 28

export: expansion, 369–71; taxes, 71–76, *71–77*, 379

export-led development, 377–78

external balance: in Chile, 118–19, *119*; defined, 251

external bottleneck, 368

external credit lines, short-term, 103*n*16

external debt: devaluation and, 136; risk premia and, 136, 138–42, *140–41*, 156

external equilibrium, 88–89

external funding, volatility of, 105n38

external resource scenarios, 363–65

external shocks: in Brazil, 192; capital outflows and, 94–97, *96*; in Chile, 111–12, 118, 123; cyclical shocks and, 212–13, 222, 224, 225n2; effects of, 93, *94*, 103n22, 104n28; exchange rate and, 84, 93–95, *94*, 212; foreign exchange reserves for, 101–2, 104n26; FX market and, 83, 97–102; hybrid system for, 98; management of, 212; monetary policy and, 83–84, 91–102, *93–94*, *96*; Mundell–Fleming model and, 83, 91–92, 100, 102n13; overview of, 83–84, 101–2; in Peru, xxi–xxii, 83–84, 97–98, 100, 102, 102n6, 103n16, 103n21, 104n24, 104n32, 104n34, 105n36, 105n39; positive, in Latin America, 11; reserve requirement ratios and, 83, 90, 102n6, 103n15, 104n26, 105n38; in semidollarized economy, 83–84, 86–88, 97–100; of subprime mortgage crisis, 83

false prices, 298

FC. *See* foreign currency

FDI. *See* foreign direct investment

Federal Reserve System, U.S., 226n14, 277

Feldstein–Horioka test, 62, 80n3

financial assets, return on, 45n10

financial crises: anatomy of, 291–92; Bretton Woods system and, 274–75; capitalism and, xxvi, 271–84; central banks and, 279, 282–84; conflict in, *289*, 289–91, 300–301, 303–5; consequences of, 292; costs of, 271; debt defaults in, 276, 280; defined, 291; in developing countries, 279, 333; DSGE models and, 282–83; East Asian, 276; economic science and, 280–83; economic systems and, 288–92, *289*; economists and, 280–81, 284; efficient market hypothesis and, 283, 285nn8–10; exchange rate and, 279; financial dysfunctions and, 288, 291–92, 299–308; financial intermediation in, 292–99, *293*; financial normality distinguished from, 299–300; financial system and, 294–99, 301–5; free market theories influencing, 272; Frenkel interested in, 271; frequency of, 272–73, 276, 283; globalization and, 272–73, 275–79, 283; historical context of, 272–77, 279, 283; igniting factors of, 279; illegitimacy in, 284; IMF and, xxv, 272, 274–75, 281–82, 284; institutions and, xxvi, 287–302, *289*, *293*, 304–9; interpretation of, 277–80; in interwar years, 273–74; irrationality in, 272, 280–81, 283; macroeconomy and, xxvi, 287–92, *289*, 298–300, 303–9; in Mexico, 276, 284n4; monetary policies and, 279; neoliberal capitalism and, 272–73, 275–79; overview of, 271–77, 283–84; policy goals during, 306; political economy of, 280; property rights and, 287–88, 292, 300–306; quick resolution of, 304; regularities in, 279–80; research on, 307–8; safe assets and, 297–98, 301; sociopolitical context of, 278; spate of, 271–72, 278; transaction costs and, 295–302; types of, 272

financial crisis (2008–2009), 48, 51, 83, 105n41; causes of, 278; Chilean economy and, 111–12, 118–23, *119–20*, 130; complicated management of, 277; contagion effects of, 112; economists and, 284; as Great Recession, 333; IMF and, 272, 281; Lehman bankruptcy in, 214–15, 333, 335, 340, *342–43*, 344; policy responses to, 121–23; recovery from, 123–30, *125*; safe assets and, 297–98; sovereign risk influenced by, 333–34. *See also* subprime mortgage crisis

financial cycles: crisis in, 3–9; Frenkel describing, 4–7; MABP and, 7–8; Minsky's, 47, 51

financial dysfunctions, financial crises and, 288, 291–92, 299–308

financial fragility: financing structures and, 50–53; Frenkel on, 6–7, 47, 51; inflation and, xxi, 47–50, 52–55; investment financing and, 47, 51–55; loan system minimizing, 53–55; Minsky and, 4, 6, 47–53, 55, 285*n*12; in open economy, 6–8; price indexes and, 48–50, 52–55

financial integration: of Latin America, 2–3, 18; segmented, 214

financial intermediation: anatomy and functions of, *293*, 293–94; in Argentina, 143–44, *144*; in financial crises, 292–99, *293*; institutions and, 292–99, *293*; organizational dimension of, 293, *293*, 295–98; systemic dimension of, 298–99; user's dimension of, 294–95

financial normality, 299–300, 307–8

financial system: financial crises and, 294–99, 301–5; functionality of, 301–5; international stability of, 358–61; microeconomic efficiency condition of, 301; role of, 294–96; in systemic dimension of financial intermediation, 298–99; systemic efficiency condition of, 301–2; systemic stability condition of, 302–5; weak, 296–97

financial transaction costs. *See* transaction costs

financing structures: financial fragility and, 50–53; hedge, 50–52; Ponzi, 50–52, 361–63; speculative, 50–52

fiscal accountability, in new developmentalism, 376

fiscal dominance, 212

fiscal policy: balance-of-payments dominance and, 216–18; procyclical, 13

fixed exchange rate: external shocks and, 93–95, *94*; new developmentalism and, 379; shift from, 275–76; speculative attacks on, 97–98

flexible exchange rate: external shocks and, 93, *94*, 95; new developmentalism and, 379; shift to, 275–76

food basket, 121, 130*n*7

foreign countermint, 378–79

foreign currency (FC): deposits, 87–89; monetary policy and, 84–85, 87, 89–90, 94–95, 99–101, 102*n*6, 102*n*13, 104*n*25, 105*n*38, 105*n*41; reserve requirement ratios and, 83, 90, 102*n*6, 103*n*15; risks of, 48; sovereign spread and, 141, 146–47, 153

foreign debt, xvii, 8–9, 48; capital flows determined by, 89–91; crisis, 380; demand for, 89–90, 143

foreign direct investment (FDI): disequilibria and, 148, *149*, 154, *154*; volatility, 214

foreign exchange (FX) market: economic growth influenced by, 260; monetary policy, external shocks and, 83, 97–102; sterilized intervention in, 83, 98, 101, 102*n*13, 222–23; Taylor rules and, 98–101

foreign exchange reserves: active management of, 222; of Argentina, 141; of Brazil, 145; of emerging economies, 105*n*41; sufficient, 101–2, 104*n*26

foreign interest rate, in monetary policy, 84–85, 89–90, 103*n*16

foreign savings, economic development and, 361–63, 379
foreign structural constraint, 380
formal employment (IF), 160
formalization: in economic science, 280; labor, *180*, 180–81
formal sector (FS), 60, 160
free market theories, 272
free riding, 290
Frenkel, Roberto: in Argentina, xiv–xvi, 3; at Banco de la Provincia de Buenos Aires, xvi; biography of, xiv–xvi; in Chile, xv; comparative analysis by, xx, 3; contributions of, xiv, xvi–xx, 1–18; cycle described by, 4–7; on disequilibria, 134–37, 156–57; on economic growth and RER, 250; on exchange rate expectations, xxii, 134–36; financial crises and, 271; on financial fragility, 6–7, 47, 51; on microfoundations, xvii–xix; new developmentalism and, 373; on price decisions in high inflation, xviii, 23–24, 27, 44, 44*n*3; problem-oriented research of, xvi–xvii, 23; as public intellectual, xix–xx; on risk premia, xxiii, 134–38, 155–56; on structural and institutional parameters, 57–60, 80; in Venezuela, xiv–xv
FS. *See* formal sector
fundamentals-based equilibrium RER, 252, 255–56, 265
FX market. *See* foreign exchange market

GDP: Brazilian, 188, *189*, 190, 192–99, *193*, *201*, 201–6, *203*; capital growth related to, 192–94, *193*; Chilean, 111–20, *116*, *120*, 122–25, *125*, 128–29; RER and, 230–31, 252–53, 261; structural and institutional parameters and, 66, 69–78, *71–78*
general equilibrium approach, 57–58, 61, 64. *See also* computable general equilibrium model
GFCF. *See* gross fixed capital formation

Gini coefficient, 311
global capitalism, 273, 375
global common factors: for CDS, 345, *348*, 349, *350*; constant and, 352*n*2; for EMBI spread, 339–40, *340–43*, 344–45, *346*; identification of, 338–49, *340–43*, *346–48*; sovereign risk influenced by, 333–36, 338–51, *340–43*, *346–48*, *350*
global crisis. *See* 2008–2009 financial crisis
globalization: in boom and bust, 257–58; channel, 257–59, 261, 264–65; debt defaults and, 276; financial crises and, 272–73, 275–79, 283; first wave of, 273–74, 277, 279, 283; Latin American economics and, 2, 257–58; neoliberal, 275–77; second wave of, 254, 272, 276–77, 279
gold standard, 211, 220, 279, 359
goods market equilibrium condition, 247*n*2
Great Moderation, 278, 283, 300, 309
Great Recession, 333
Greenspan, Alan, 285*n*10
gross fixed capital formation (GFCF), 194–95, *195*, 198
growth regressions, RER in, 251–56
Guatemala, *337*, *341*, *343*, *346*

hardware, 300
Heckman's two-step estimator, 171, *172*, 184
hedge financing structure, 50–52
heterodox anti-inflationary plans, 10
high inflation: dealing with, 9–10, 14; long-term credit market challenged by, 55; uncertainties of, 23. *See also* price decisions, in high inflation
hourly labor income, inequality and, 166–69, *167–68*
housing loans: debtors' payment capacity for, 48–55; price index and, 49–50, 53–55
hybrid exchange policy, 98

IBRD. *See* International Bank for Reconstruction and Development
ideal type. *See* Weberian ideal type
IE. *See* informal employment
IF. *See* formal employment
illegitimacy crisis, 284
ILO. *See* International Labor Organization
IMF. *See* International Monetary Fund
imperfect capital mobility, 105n37
import substitution: industrialization and, 212; new developmentalism and, 377, 383n5
import taxes, 70, 72, 76, *76*
income: disposable, 317, *317*, 320, 331n7; hourly labor, 166–69, *167–68*; redistribution, in U.S., 311; sources, 315–19; uses, 318–19. *See also* size distribution, U.S.
income inequality: disposable income and, 317, *317*; hourly labor income and, 166–69, *167–68*; limitations in reducing, 311; in top 1 percent, *316–17*, 316–18, 320, *322*, 331n5; in U.S., xxvi, 311–14, *312–13*, 317, *317*, 320, 331n5
income segmentation: defined, 169; explanations for, 169–71; wage gaps and, 169–75, *172–74*
Independent Evaluation Office, IMF, 282, 285n12
indexation rule, 60–62
indexed pricing, 28
industrial equilibrium exchange rate, xxvii, 378–79, 381
industrialization, import-substitution, 212
inequality: labor informality and, 159–60, 165–82, *172–74*, *176*, *178–80*; labor market dynamics of, 175–81, *176*, *178–80*; neoliberalism leading to, 273; primary income distribution addressing, 182; reduction, 175–81, *176*, *178–80*. *See also* income inequality; wage gaps

inflation: anti-inflationary policies for, 9–10, 14, 101; in Argentina, xvii–xviii, 2, 10–14, 47, 144–45, 148; crisis, 272; financial fragility and, xxi, 47–50, 52–55; index, 49–50, 54; inertia of, 10–14; in new developmentalism, 378; in Peru's recessions, 105n39; RER and, 9–18; second-round effects contained in, 14; supply shocks accelerating, 9; targeting, 221, 224, 226n13; in Venezuela, 2, 11; wage, 235–36, 239–40, 245–46. *See also* high inflation
informal employment (IE), 160–61
informality. *See* labor informality
informal sector (IS), 160–61
input purchases: no advance cash constraints on, 29–30; unit costs and, 30–32. *See also* constrained input purchases
institutional investors, 297
institutions: approach to, 287–88; establishment of, 290; financial crises and, xxvi, 287–302, *289*, *293*, 304–9; financial intermediation and, 292–99, *293*; hierarchies of, 289, 295, 304–5; instability of, 302; legal and regulatory framework of, 299; macroeconomy and, 287–302, *289*, *293*, 304–9; political, 307; systemic dysfunction and, 288, 291–92, 305–8; transaction costs and, 295–99; undermining of, 291. *See also* structural and institutional parameters, uncertainty in
interest rates: banking system's, 84–85; deposit, 87–89; in economic development, 363–64; Federal Reserve and, 226n14, 277; foreign, 84–85, 89–90, 103n16; of loans, 84–88, 102n6; in new developmentalism, 376; pass-through coefficients and, 102n7; short-term, 83; in uncovered interest rate parity equation, 88, 102n13; U.S., EMBI spread influenced by, 345, 352n4

intermediary organizations, 295–96
intermediation. *See* financial
intermediation
International Bank for Reconstruction
and Development (IBRD), 359, 361,
366, 368
international capital mobility: degree
of, 62, 69–77, *71–77*, 79; structural
and institutional parameters and, 59,
62–65, 68–80, *71–77*, 80*n*3
international debt, in economic
development, 361
international financial stability,
economic development and, 358–61
international imbalances, economic
development and, 358–61
International Labor Organization (ILO),
160–61
International Monetary Fund (IMF):
capitalism and, 272, 274–75, 281–
82; economic development and, 359,
361; financial crises and, xxv, 272,
274–75, 281–82, 284; Independent
Evaluation Office, 282, 285*n*12;
RER and, 16; 2008–2009 financial
crisis and, 272, 281
interwar years, financial crises in,
273–74
inventories, accumulated, 44*n*4
inventory management: accumulated
inventories in, 44*n*4; constrained
input purchases and, 30–37, *33–34,
36*; general setup for, 29; literature
on, 44*n*1; minimum volume of
operation and, 37–43, *40, 42–43*;
no advance cash constraints on
input purchases, 29–30; numerical
simulations of, 32–33, *33–34, 36,
38, 40, 42–43*; price decisions in high
inflation and, xxi, 24, 28–43, *33–34,
36, 38, 40, 42–43*
investment: in Argentina, 148–56,
149–55; in Brazil, 190–94, 196, 198–
201, *199*, 204–5, 207*n*6; in Mexico,
152, *152*; relative price of, 198–200,

199–200; RER influencing, 231–32;
savings and, 153–56, *154–55. See also*
foreign direct investment
investment financing: financial fragility
and, 47, 51–55; financing structures
and, 50–53
irrationality, in financial crises, 272,
280–81, 283
IS. *See* informal sector
IS curve, 86–87, 95–96, 99, 102*n*12
IS-LM-BP textbook model, xxi–xxii, 83

Jamaica, *337*, 340, *341, 343, 347*

Kalman filter, 335, 338, 340, *342–43*,
344, 349
Keynes, John Maynard: on animal
spirits, 138, 281; counterrevolution
against, 358; *The Economic
Consequences of Peace*, 274; on
exchange rate, 360, 379; master-
economist defined by, xiii; *Treatise on
Money*, 101
Kirchner, Néstor, xx, 136

labor compensation, 315
labor formalization, distributional
impact of, *180*, 180–81
labor informality: in Argentina, 161,
162–68, 164, 166, 169, *172–74, 176*,
176–77, *178–80*, 179–81, 185*n*5; in
Bolivia, 161–62, *162–68*, 164, 166,
172–74, 176, *176*, *178–80*; in Brazil,
161, *162–68*, 164, 166, *172–74, 176*,
176–77, *178–80*, 179–81, 185*n*5;
in Chile, 161, *162–68*, 164, 166,
169, *172–74, 176*, 176–77, *178–80*,
179–80; in Costa Rica, 161, *162–68*,
164, 166–68, *172–74, 176*, 177,
178–80; decline in, 159, 175–81,
176, 178–80; economic growth in
Latin America and, 159–84, *162–68,
172–74, 176, 178–80*; in Ecuador,
161, *162–68*, 164, 166, *172–74, 176*,
178–80; efficiency wages theory and,

170; in El Salvador, 161, *162–68*, 164, 166, 169, *172–74*, 176, *176*, *178–80*; endowment effect and, 174; formalization impacting, *180*, 180–81; hourly labor income and, 166–69, *167–68*; impacts of, 159; importance of, 164; income segmentation and, 169–75, *172–74*; inequality and, 159–60, 165–82, *167–68*, *172–74*, *176*, *178–80*; labor market dynamics of, 175–81, *176*, *178–80*; legal approach to, 160–61, 169–70; in Mexico, 161, *162–68*, 166–68, *167–68*, *172–74*, 176, *176*, *178–80*, 179–81, 185*n*5; overview of, 160–65, *162–65*, 181–82; in Paraguay, 161, *162–68*, 164, 166, *167–68*, *172–74*, *176*, 177, *178–80*, 179–81; patterns, 165, *166*; penalty of, 171, 174, 177–78; in Peru, 161, *162–68*, 164, 166, *167–68*, *172–74*, *176*, *178–80*; precariousness of, 165; productive approach to, 160–61, 169; in Uruguay, 161, *162–68*, 164, 166, *172–74*, *176*, 177, *178–80*, 179–80, 185*n*5; wage gaps and, 160, 166, 169–81, *172–74*, *178–79*, 183–84

labor market: deficits in, 159; dynamics, of informality, 175–81, *176*, *178–80*; economic growth influencing, xxiii, 159

Latin American economics: Alliance for Progress and, 360; commodity boom in, 142–43, *143*, 146; evolution of, 2; financial integration of, 2–3, 18; Frenkel's contributions to, xiv, xvi–xx, 1–18; globalization and, 2, 257–58; innovations in, 1; positive external shock in, 11; sovereign risk in, 333–51, *340–43*, *346–48*, *350*; structural and institutional parameters in, 60. *See also* economic growth, in Latin America

legal and regulatory framework, of macroeconomy, 299

legal approach, to labor informality, 160–61, 169–70

Lehman bankruptcy: sovereign risk and, xxvi, 333, 335, 340, *342–43*, 344–45, *346–47*, *350*, 352*n*3; in 2008–2009 financial crisis, 214–15, 333, 335, 340, *342–43*, 344

liberal capitalism, 272

liberalization, capital account, 221–22

liquidity: gaps, 49–50; negative covariance between unit and total costs and, 35; price decisions in high inflation influenced by, 24, 29–32, 34–35, 44*n*1, 45*n*12

LM curve, 87–88

loans: in domestic currency, 103*n*15; financial fragility and, 53–55; interest rates of, 84–88, 102*n*6; price indexes and, 49–50, 53–55. *See also* housing loans

Long-Term Capital Management Fund, 276

long-term credit market, high inflation challenging, 55

long-term debt sustainable scenarios, 365–69

MABP. *See* monetary approach to the balance of payments

macroeconomy: cycles leading to crisis in, 3–9; economic systems and, 288–92, *289*, 305–8; financial crises and, xxvi, 287–92, *289*, 298–300, 303–9; financial dysfunctions in, 288, 291–92, 299–308; financial intermediation and, 292–99, *293*; imbalance, in Chile, 127–29; institutions and, 287–302, *289*, *293*, 304–9; legal and regulatory framework of, 299; mainstream approach to, 309; microfoundations of, xvii–xix, 1; new problems in, 3; policy goals of, 306; research agenda, 283–84; size distribution and, 311, *321*, 324, 327; transaction costs in, 295–99

macrofoundations, xviii
macroprudential policies, 216
Madoff affair, 51
mainstream approach, 309
market equilibrium exchange rate, 130n4
market failures, RER and, 260
market makers, 297
master-economist, xiii–xiv
matching estimator method, 174, *174*,
    184–85
maximum output constraint, 24, *38*
medium-term cycles, 215
Mexico, 215; employment composition
    in, 161, *162–68*, 166; financial
    crises in, 276, 284n4; hourly labor
    income in, 167–68, *167–68*; income
    segmentation in, *172–74*; investment
    in, 152, *152*; labor informality in,
    161, *162–68*, 166–68, *172–74*,
    176, *176*, *178–80*, 179–81, 185n5;
    minimum wage in, 180; sovereign
    risk in, *337–38*, *341*, *343*, 344,
    347–48, *350*, 351
microeconomic efficiency condition, 301
microfoundations, xvii–xix, 1
migrant workers, 225n4
minimum regret criteria, 78–79, 81n9
minimum-sales constraint, 24, 45n10
minimum volume of operation:
    conditional operation in *t* + 1 with
    finite cost of closing and constrained
    input purchases in *t*, 41–43, *43*;
    inventory management and, 37–43,
    40, *42–43*; unconditional operation in
    t + 1 and constrained production in *t*,
    40–41, *42*; unconditional operation in
    t + 1 and unconstrained production in
    t, 39, *40*; unit costs and, 37–38
minimum wage: in Argentina, 179,
    186n10; in Brazil, 179; in Chile, 179;
    increase in, 320, 324; in Mexico,
    180; in Uruguay, 179
Minsky, Hyman, 1, 8, 308; on financial
    cycles, 47, 51; financial fragility and,
    4, 6, 47–53, 55, 285n12; financing

structures and, 50–52; *Stabilizing an
    Unstable Economy*, 47–48; subprime
    mortgage crisis and, 48; "A Theory of
    Financial Fragility," 47
Minsky moment, 47
misaligned RER, 230–31, 251–56,
    261–65
misalignment index, 251–56, 261–65
monetary approach to the balance of
    payments (MABP), 7–8
monetary policy: balance of payments
    and, 83, 88–91, 93–98, 100–101,
    135, 216, 219–25; banking system's
    interest rates in, 84–85; consequences
    of, 100–101, 102n2; domestic
    currency and, 84–85, 87, 104n25,
    105n38; exchange rates in, 83–84,
    86, 88, 91–101, *94*, 102n13, 103n17,
    103n20, 104n24, 104nn28–30,
    104nn32–34, 105nn36–37, 105n40;
    external shocks and, 83–84, 91–102,
    93–94, *96*; financial crises and, 279;
    foreign currency and, 84–85, 87,
    89–90, 94–95, 99–101, 102n6,
    102n13, 104n25, 105n38, 105n41;
    FX market and, 83, 97–101;
    imperfect capital mobility and,
    105n37; overview of, 83–84, 101–2;
    RER and, 84; reserve requirement
    ratios in, 83, 90, 102n6, 103n15,
    104n26, 105n38; in semidollarized
    economy, 83–84, 86–88, 97–100
monetization, in Argentina, 144, 146
monoeconomics, 357
Mundell–Fleming model: BP curve and,
    88–91, 93, 95–96, 98–99; AS curve
    and, 91, 93, 95–96, 104n30; external
    shocks and, 83, 91–92, 100, 102n13;
    IS curve and, 86–87, 95–96, 99,
    102n12; LM curve and, 87–88

La Nación, xix–xx
National Coffee Fund, 216
national income and product accounts
    (NIPA), 311, 314, 316–17, 325

natural disaster shocks, 80*n*1

negative covariance, between unit and total costs, 35, 44

neoclassical economic theory, challenges to, 272, 280

neoliberal capitalism: in Chile, 117, 126; financial crises and, 272–73, 275–79; globalization and, 275–77; hegemony of, 381–82; igniting factors in, 279; inequality and, 273; new developmentalism and, 375–80

neostructuralism, new ideas of, 1–2, 18

night of the long batons, The (*La noche de los bastones largos*), xiv, xxviii*n*1

NIPA. *See* national income and product accounts

noche de los bastones largos, La (The night of the long batons), xiv, xxviii*n*1

nominal exchange rate: defined, 265*n*2, 265*n*5; demand influenced by, 86; fixation of, 5; stabilized, 16–17

nominal pricing, 28, 44*n*2

Oaxaca–Blinder decomposition, 171, 173, 184

OECD. *See* Organization for Economic Cooperation and Development

OLS. *See* ordinary least squares

open economy: financial fragility in, 6–8; RER and, 233–34; structural and institutional parameters in, 57

optimism criteria, 78–79

ordinary least squares (OLS), 171, 183–84, 345, 346

Organization for Economic Cooperation and Development (OECD), 358

organizations: conflict, cooperation and, 289, 289–91; financial intermediation by, 293, 293, 295–98; intermediary, 295–96; restructuring of, 304; safe assets issued by, 297–98

output capacity, of Chilean economy, 123–24

output–capital in-use ratio, 197–98, 198, 204–5, 207*n*10

overproduction, crisis of, 272

Palma ratio, 311, 313, 317, 320, 322

Panama, 337–38, 341, 343, 348, 350

Paraguay: employment composition in, 161, 162–68, 164, 166; hourly labor income in, 167–68; income segmentation in, 172–74; labor informality in, 161, 162–68, 164, 166, 172–74, 176, 177, 178–80, 179–81

pass-through coefficients, 102*n*7

Path to Prosperity, 324

payroll tax, 70, 77, 77, 83

perfect capital mobility, 62

Peru: employment composition in, 161, 162–68, 164, 166; external shocks in, xxi–xxii, 83–84, 97–98, 100, 102, 102*n*6, 103*n*16, 103*n*21, 104*n*24, 104*n*32, 104*n*34, 105*n*36, 105*n*39; hourly labor income in, 167–68; hybrid exchange policy in, 98; income segmentation in, 172–74; labor informality in, 161, 162–68, 164, 166, 172–74, 176, 178–80; recessions in, 105*n*39; sovereign risk in, 334, 337–38, 341, 343, 347–48, 350

pessimism criteria, 78–79

planning, in new developmentalism, 376

policy: anti-inflationary, 9–10, 14, 101; austerity, 217–18, 281, 284; fiscal, 13, 216–18; goals, 306; hybrid exchange, 98; lessons, from economic crises, 8–9; macroprudential, 216; mistakes, cost of, 57–58, 75–79; responses, to 2008–2009 crisis, 121–23; sovereign risk and, 351; U.S. size distribution and, 321–23. *See also* monetary policy

political economy, xxviii*n*3; approach, 288; of financial crises, 280

political institutions, 307

Pontifícia Universidade Católica of Ríode Janeiro (PUC-RJ), xv
Ponzi financing structure, 50–52, 361–63
portfolio model, of balance of payments, 7–8
positive external shocks, 11
PPP-based equilibrium RER, 251–52, 255–56, 264–65
predetermined exchange rate rules, 135
predetermined output, of production, 24–27
predetermined prices: predetermined output and, 24–27; price decisions in high inflation and, 24–28
price decisions, in high inflation: Frenkel on, xviii, 23–24, 27, 44, 44n3; high variability influencing, 45n7; indexed pricing, 28; inventory management and, 24, 28–43, 33–34, 36, 38, 40, 42–43; liquidity influencing, 24, 29–32, 34–35, 44n1, 45n12; literature on, 44n1; nominal pricing and, 28, 44n2; overview of, 23–24, 44; predetermined output and, 24–27; predetermined prices and, 24–28; price-elastic demand and, 24–25, 28, 30–31, 35, 37, 44, 44n3; pricing in real terms, 27; problem-oriented approach to, 23; production on demand and, 27–28
price-elastic demand: price decisions, in high inflation and, 24–25, 28, 30–31, 35, 37, 44, 44n3; unit costs and, 30, 44
price indexes: distortions in, 48, 54–55; financial fragility and, 48–50, 52–55; housing loans and, 49–50, 53–55. See also consumer price index
primary income distribution, 182
principal components methodology, 335, 338–39, 340–41, 344, 348
private banks, loans provided by, 50
problem-oriented research, xvi–xvii, 23

production: constrained, 40–41, 42; on demand, 27–28; in new developmentalism, 375; predetermined output of, 24–27; unconstrained, 39, 40
productive approach, to labor informality, 160–61, 169
productivity: gaps, in Chile, 130n2; RER and, 230, 233, 236, 238–44, 241; total factor, 198, 202–3, 202–3, 205–6
profitability, accumulation interacting with, 234, 234–35
profitability channel, xxiv, 232, 244. See also development channel
property rights: in Argentina, 153–56; financial crises and, 287–88, 292, 300–306; transaction costs and, 301
protection exchange rate, 378
public intellectual, economists as, xix–xx
public sector balance sheets, 213–15, 225n11
PUC-RJ. See Pontifícia Universidade Católica of Ríode Janeiro

Ramsey rule, 61
rational economic man, xxv, 272, 280–81
Reagan, Ronald, 275, 358
real exchange rate (RER): appreciation, xvii, 3, 5; in Argentina, 14–17; balance of payments influenced by, 229, 231–32; capital accumulation influenced by, 232, 234–44, 247n2, 247n4, 257; in Chilean economy, xxii, 111, 116–17, 124–27, 125, 129, 130n4, 131n16; competition and, 247n3; depreciated, 60, 230; devaluation and, 232–33, 235–44, 237, 240–41; development and, xxiv, 14–17, 229; Dutch disease and, 125–26, 260; employment growth and, 237, 237–41, 243–47; equilibrium, 251–52, 255–56, 264–65; fundamentals-based

equilibrium, 252, 255–56, 265; GDP and, 230–31, 252–53, 261; goods market equilibrium condition and, 247*n*2; in growth regressions, 251–56; IMF and, 16; industrial equilibrium exchange rate and, xxvii, 378–79, 381; inflation and, 9–18; investment growth influenced by, 231–32; Kaldor and, 230, 238–39, 247*n*6; management of, 256; market equilibrium, 130*n*4; market failures and, 260; misaligned, 230–31, 251–56, 261–65; monetary policy, external shocks and, 84; open economy and, 233–34; PPP-based equilibrium, 251–52, 255–56, 264–65; productivity and, 230, 233, 236, 238–44, *241*; real wage and, 229–30, 233–44, *237*; Robinson and, 230, 238–39, 247*n*4; savings and, 232, 256–57, 259, 261; stable and competitive, 12, 17; volatility, 127. *See also* economic growth, RER and

real interest parity, 62

real terms, pricing in, 27

real wage: economic growth, RER and, 229–44, *234*, *237*, *240–41*, *246*; employment growth and, *237*, 237–41, 243–45, 247; long-term dynamic adjustments of, *237*, 237–38; overview of, 229–30, 243–44; RER and, 229–30, 233–44, *237*; in small open-economy model, 233–34; stability, 245–46

recessions: long-lasting, 287; in Peru, 105*n*39. *See also* financial crisis (2008–2009)

reform: in Chile, 111–14, 117, 122, 129–30, 131*n*22; mainstream approach, 309

Regional Employment Program for Latin America and the Caribbean, 160

regulated capitalism, 272, 275

regulation: in Argentina, 153–56; capital account, 115, 223; control and, 223; framework, 299

relative price of investment, capital growth and, 198–200, *199–200*

RER. *See* real exchange rate

rescheduling, debt, 272, 276, 280

reserve requirement: countercyclical, in Chile, 114–15; increase in, 105*n*38

reserve requirement ratios: domestic currency and, 83, 103*n*15; external shocks and, 83, 90, 102*n*6, 103*n*15, 104*n*26, 105*n*38; foreign currency and, 83, 90, 102*n*6, 103*n*15; in monetary policy, 83, 90, 102*n*6, 103*n*15, 104*n*26, 105*n*38

resource allocation, in Chile, 132*n*23

restricted current output: constrained input purchases and, 32–35, *33–34*, 37, *38*; cost increase and, *34*; maximum output constraint and, 24, *38*

risk, sovereign. *See* sovereign risk

risk premia: in Argentina, xxiii, 134–36, 138–42, *140–41*, 146, 149, 153, 156, 157*n*5; external debt and, 136, 138–42, *140–41*, 156; FDI and, 148, *149*, 154, *154*; Frenkel on, xxiii, 134–38, 155–56; MABP and, 7–8; overview of, 134–38, 156–57; sources, 138, 153, 155

safe assets, 297–98, 301

salaried workers, wage gaps among, 169

SAM. *See* social accounting matrix

savings: in Argentina, 153–56, *154–55*; during booms, 218; in Brazil, 194–96, *195*, 206*n*4, 207*n*6; capital growth influenced by, 194–96, *195*; channel, 256–57, 259, 261; domestic, growth with, 379; foreign, economic development and, 361–63, 379; investment and, 153–56, *154–55*; in long-term debt sustainable scenarios, 366–67; RER and, 232, 256–57, 259, 261; U.S. size distribution and, 319; in Venezuela, 154 scarcity, 289

SCRER. *See* stable and competitive real exchange rate

self-insurance, 215, 222

semidollarized economy: de-dollarization of, 104*n*33, 105*n*38; monetary policy, external shocks and, 83–84, 86–88, 97–100

SFB. *See* structural fiscal balance

shared prosperity, 275

short-term external credit lines, 103*n*16

short-term interest rate, in domestic currency, 83

size distribution, U.S.: data sources, 325–26, *326*; income sources and, 315–19; macroeconomy and, 311, *321*, 324, 327; major social changes needed for, 324; model simulations, 319–24, *321–23*; model specification, 327–31; NIPA and, 311, 314, 316–17, 325; overview of, xxvi, 311–14, *312–13*, 324; Palma ratio and, 311, *313*, 317, 320, *322*; Path to Prosperity and, 324; policy shifts for, *321–23*; savings and, 319; social accounting matrix for, 311–14, *312–13*, 325, 327, 331*n*2; taxation and, 315, 319–20, 327–30; top 1 percent and, *316–17*, 316–18, 320, *322*, 331*n*5; U.S. economy as transfer union and, 314–16

social accounting matrix (SAM): CGE and, 65–66, *67*; for U.S. size distribution, 311–14, *312–13*, 325, 327, 331*n*2

social development, 380

social protection systems, 217

sociopolitical context, of financial crises, 278

software, 300

sovereign risk: in Argentina, 136–39, *141*, 146–49, *147*, *149*, *337–38*, 340, *341–42*, 344, *346*, *348*, 349, *350*, 351; in Brazil, 333, *334*, *337–38*, *341–42*, 344, *346*, *348*, *350*, 351;

CDS measuring, 334–39, *338*, 345, 349–51, *350*; in Chile, 333, *334*, *337–38*, *341–42*, 344, *346*, *348*, 349–50, *350*; in Colombia, *334*, *337–38*, *341–42*, 344, *347–48*, *350*, 351; in Costa Rica, *337*, *341–42*, *347*; data on, 336–37, *337–38*, 352*nn*5–6; in Dominican Republic, *337*, *341–42*, 344, *347*; in Ecuador, *337–38*, 340, *341–42*, 344–45, *346*, *348*, 349, *350*, 351; in El Salvador, *337*, *341*, *343*, *346*; EMBI spreads measuring, *334*, 334–37, *337*, 339, *340–43*, 344–45, *346*, 349–51; exchange risk and, 135, 138; global common factors influencing, 333–36, *338–51*, *340–43*, *346–48*, *350*; in Guatemala, *337*, *341*, *343*, *346*; in Jamaica, *337*, 340, *341*, *343*, *347*; Kalman filter and, 335, *338*, 340, *342–43*, 344, 349; in Latin America, 333–51, *340–43*, *346–48*, *350*; Lehman bankruptcy and, xxvi, 333, 335, 340, *342–43*, 344–45, *346–47*, *350*, 352*n*3; literature on, 335; in Mexico, *337–38*, *341*, *343*, 344, *347–48*, *350*, 351; ordinary least squares and, 345, *346*; overview of, xxvi, 333–36, *334*, 349–51; in Panama, *337–38*, *341*, *343*, *348*, *350*; in Peru, *334*, *337–38*, *341*, *343*, *347–48*, *350*; policy and, 351; principal components methodology and, 335, *338–39*, *340–41*, 344, *348*; reasons behind, 146–49, *147*, *149*; spread, 141, 146–47, 153, 334; TED spread and, 345, *346–47*; 2008–2009 financial crisis influencing, 333–34; in Uruguay, *337*, *341*, *343*, *346*; in Venezuela, *337–38*, 340, *341*, *343*, 344–45, *346*, *348*, 349, *350*, 351

speculative attacks: on currency, 134–35, 156; on fixed exchange rate, 97–98

speculative financing structure, 50–52

Stabilizing an Unstable Economy (Minsky), 47–48

stable and competitive real exchange rate (SCRER), 12, 17
state, in new developmentalism, 375–76, 382
state-owned banks, loans provided by, 50
states of nature, in structural and institutional parameters, 78, *78*
sterilized intervention: in FX market, 83, 98, 101, 102*n*13, 222–23; risks of, 222–23
stochastic dynamic general equilibrium (DSGE) models, 282–83
structural and institutional parameters, uncertainty in: CGE model for, xxi, 58, 62–68, *67*, 70, 74, 81*n*5; decisions with unknown probabilities and, 77–80, *78–79*; Frenkel and, 57–60, 80; GDP and, 66, 69–78, *71–78*; general equilibrium approach to, 57–58, 61, 64; institutional setting of, 62–65; international capital mobility and, 59, 62–65, 68–80, *71–77*, 80*n*3; in Latin America, 60; literature on, 59–62; in open economy, 57; overview of, xxi, 57–59, 79–80; policy mistakes and, 57–58, 75–79; states of nature in, 78, *78*; taxation and, 58–63, 65–80, *67, 69, 71–79*; unemployment and, 58, 60–62, 64, 70–72, *74–77, 75–77*; wage determination and, 60–64, 69–79, *71–77*, 81*n*6
structural fiscal balance (SFB), 128
subprime mortgage crisis: deleverage in, 51; external shock of, 83; Minsky and, 48
supply shocks: balance-of-payments dominance and, 212, 220–21, 225*n*3; inflation accelerated by, 9; management of, 212
systemic dimension, of financial intermediation, 298–99
systemic dysfunction, 288, 291–92, 305–8

systemic efficiency condition, 301–2
systemic stability condition, 302–5

taxation: ad valorem, 60, 63, 80; balance-of-payments dominance and, 217–18, 224; in Chile, 122, 128, 131*n*21; export, 71–76, *71–77*, 379; general equilibrium effects of, 58; import, 70, *72*, 76, *76*; income sources and, 315; payroll, 70, 77, *77*, 83; structural and institutional parameters and, 58–63, 65–80, *67, 69, 71–79*; unemployment and, 60–62; U.S. size distribution and, 315, 319–20, 327–30; VAT, 70, 72, *72, 75, 75*, 78, *78–79*, 217
Taylor rules, 98–101
technical progress: absence of, 235–38, *237*, 244; presence of, 238–44, *240–41*
TED spread, 345, *346–47*
"Ten Theses on New Developmentalism," 373–74
TFP. *See* total factor productivity
Thatcher, Margaret, 275, 358
Theil index decomposition, 175, *180*, 180–81, 185
"Theory of Financial Fragility, A" (Minsky), 47
top 1 percent, *316–17*, 316–18, 320, *322*, 331*n*5
total costs, negative covariance between unit costs and, 35, 44
total factor productivity (TFP), 198, 202–3, *202–3*, 205–6
tradable-led growth, xxv, 259–65, 265*n*10, 359, 361, 366, 368
traded goods sector, expansion of, 232
transaction costs: financial crises and, 295–302; institutions and, 295–99; property rights and, 301; volatility increasing, 297
transfer union, U.S. economy as, 314–16
Treatise on Money (Keynes), 101
Turkey, 277

UN. *See* United Nations
uncertainty, markups under. *See* price
decisions, in high inflation
unconditional operation in $t + 1$:
constrained production in t and,
40–41, *42*; unconstrained production
in t and, 39, *40*
unconstrained production in t, 39, *40*
uncovered interest parity, 62, 88,
102*n*13
unemployment: capital accumulation
influencing, 60; capital mobility
and, 61–62; disinflation and, 10;
insurance, 217; structural and
institutional parameters and, 58,
60–62, 64, 70–72, *74–77*, 75–77;
taxation and, 60–62
unit costs: input purchases and, 30–32;
minimum volume of operation and,
37–38; negative covariance between
total costs and, 35, 44; price-elastic
demand and, 30, 44
United Kingdom, 273, 359
United Nations (UN), 358–61
United States (U.S.): Bretton Woods
and, 359; deficit, 315–16, 331*n*6;
dot-com bubble in, 277; Federal
Reserve System, 226*n*14, 277;
income inequality in, xxvi,
311–14, *312–13*, 317, *317*, 320,
331*n*5; income redistribution in,
311; interest rates, EMBI spread
influenced by, 345, 352*n*4; as
transfer union, 314–16. *See also* size
distribution, U.S.
University of Buenos Aires, xiv–xvi
unregulated capitalism, 272
unrestricted current output, constrained
input purchases and, 31–32, 35–36,
36
Uruguay: crawling peg in, 258;
employment composition in,
161, *162–68*, 164, 166; hourly
labor income in, *167–68*; income
segmentation in, *172–74*; labor

informality in, 161, *162–68*, 164,
166, *172–74*, *176*, 177, *178–80*,
179–80, 185*n*5; minimum wage in,
179; sovereign risk in, *337*, *341*, *343*,
346
U.S. *See* United States
user's dimension, of financial
intermediation, 294–95

value-added tax (VAT): as automatic
spending stabilizer, 217; uncertainty
in structural and institutional
parameters and, 70, 72, *72*, 75, *75*,
78, *78–79*
Venezuela: Frenkel in, xiv–xv; inflation
in, 2, 11; savings in, 154; sovereign
risk in, *337–38*, 340, *341*, *343*,
344–45, *346*, *348*, *349*, *350*, 351
VIX index, 335
volatility: of external funding, 105*n*38;
FDI, 214; price, expected costs
influenced by, 28; RER, 127;
transaction costs increased by, 297
volume of operation. *See* minimum
volume of operation

wage gaps: economic growth in
Latin America and, 160, 166,
169–81, *172–74*, *178–79*, 183–84;
endowment effect influencing,
174; evolution of, 177–80, *178–79*;
income segmentation and, 169–75,
172–74; labor informality and,
160, 166, 169–81, *172–74*, *178–79*,
183–84; measurement methodology
for, 183–85; among salaried
workers, 169
wages: determination of, 60–64, 69–79,
71–77, 81*n*6; exchange rate and, 220;
factors influencing, 62; as income
source, 315; indexed, xxi, 49, 58, *69*,
70–73, *71–77*, 76, 79, 81*n*6, 191;
rate of inflation of, 235–36, 239–40,
245–46. *See also* minimum wage; real
wage